MAKING AND BREAKING THE YUGOSLAV WORKING CLASS

WORK AND LABOR
Transdisciplinary Studies
for the 21st Century

Central European University Press Book Series

Volume II.

Series Editors:

Eszter Bartha
Adrian Grama
Don Kalb
David Ost
Susan Zimmermann

Published in the Series:

Marsha Siefert, ed. Labor in State-Socialist Europe, 1945–1989: Contributions to a History of Work (2020)

Making and Breaking the Yugoslav Working Class

The Story of Two Self-Managed Factories

Goran Musić

CEU PRESS

Central European University Press
Budapest–New York

Published in 2021 by
Central European University Press

Nádor utca 11, H-1051 Budapest, Hungary
Tel: +36-1-327-3138 or 327-3000
E-mail: ceupress@press.ceu.edu
Website: www.ceupress.com

224 West 57th Street, New York NY 10019, USA

This work was supported by the Austrian Science Fund (FWF) under Grant P27008.

ISBN 978-963-386-339-8 (hardback)
ISBN 978-963-386-340-4 (ebook)
ISSN: 2732-1118

Library of Congress Cataloging-in-Publication Data

Names: Musić, Goran, 1981- author.
Title: Making and breaking the Yugoslav working class : the story of two
self-managed factories / Goran Musić.
Description: Budapest ; New York : Central European University Press, 2021.
| Series: Work and labor : transdisciplinary studies for the 21st
century, 2732-1118 ; volume II | Includes bibliographical references and index.
Identifiers: LCCN 2020053888 | ISBN 9789633863398 (hardback) |
ISBN 9789633863404 (adobe pdf)
Subjects: LCSH: Working class—Yugoslavia. | Labor movement--Yugoslavia. |
Factories—Social aspects—Yugoslavia. | Strikes and
lockouts—Yugoslavia. | Socialism—Yugoslavia. | Yugoslavia—Social
conditions. | Yugoslavia—Economic conditions—1945-1992. |
Yugoslavia—Politics and government—1980-1992.
Classification: LCC HD8633.5 .M87 2021 | DDC 338.6/90949709048—dc23
LC record available at https://lccn.loc.gov/2020053888

Printed in Hungary

To Emma, Anna and Katharina

Contents

Figures and Tables

Abbreviations

AVN: Analytical Evaluation of Work (*Analitičko vrednovanje zadataka za bolje poslovanje, bolju podelu rada i prikladnije nagrađivanje rada*)

BOAL: Basic Organization of Associated Labor (*Osnovna organizacija udruženog rada*, OOUR)

COAL: Complex Organization of Associated Labor (*Složena organizacija udruženog rada*, SOUR)

FAMOS: Fabrika motora Sarajevo (Sarajevo Motor Factory)

FAP: Fabrika automobila Priboj (Priboj Automobile Factory)

IMF: International Monetary Fund

IMR: Industrija motora Rakovica (Rakovica Motor Industry)

IMT: Industrija mašina i traktora (Machine and Tractor Industry)

KHD: Klöckner-Humboldt-Deutz AG

KPO: Collective Board of Directors (*Kolegijalni poslovodni organ*)

LC: League of Communists

LCY: League of Communists of Yugoslavia (*Savez komunista Jugoslavije*)

LSY: League of Socialist Youth (*Savez socijalističke omladine*)

LSYS: League of Socialist Youth of Slovenia

SIZ: Self-Managed Communities of Interest (*Samoupravne interesne zajednice*)

TAM: Tovarna avtomobilov Maribor (Maribor Automobile Industry)

Acknowledgments

This book would not have been possible without the support of a number of friends, colleagues, and institutions. The bulk of the material discussed on its pages stems from the doctoral research conducted at the European University Institute in Florence. It was thanks to my thesis supervisor Stephen Smith, his faith in my work and consideration for my family obligations, that I was able to complete the research. David Mayer inspired me to embark on this academic journey in the first place during my studies in Vienna. I thank him for his intellectual encouragement and introduction to the thrill of scholarly work. I am also greatly indebted to my fellow travelers, a group of like-minded scholars of socialism and Yugoslavia, Adrian Grama, Chiara Bonfiglioli, Vladan Vukliš, and Vladimir Unkovski-Korica, for the mutual exchange of ideas and solidarity extended along the way.

My post-doctoral research stays at the Centre for Southeast European Studies in Graz and the Central European University's Department of History in Budapest, where the doctoral dissertation was converted into a book, were made possible by the professional backing of Florian Bieber, Susan Zimmermann, and Marsha Siefert, as well as the funding provided by the Austrian Science Fund and the Central European University. Rory Archer, a fellow researcher and friend, deserves a special mention. He became my closest intellectual ally during this period, as we navigated through the precarious labyrinth of post-doctoral academic career.

During my fieldwork in Belgrade, Milić Radović from the Faculty of Organizational Sciences assisted me in accessing the archives in Industrija motora Rakovica. In Maribor, Cveta Matjašić and her husband greeted me as family and provided a unique tour of Tezno neighborhood. Branko Gerlič schooled me on the ins and outs of Tovarna avtomobilov Maribor and helped me in contact with the local libraries. Franci Pivec contributed greatly to my understanding of relations inside the Slovene party-state during socialism. Dino Demič and Borut Osonkar aided me in deciphering the self-management jargon in Slovene language and acquainted me with dolce vita in Ljubljana and Maribor. My deep gratitude goes to all former workers of IMR and TAM who took time to talk to me and reminisce on their life and work in socialist Yugoslavia. Any faults in the text and the transcription of their interviews remain my own.

In Florence, I would like to thank Dario, Marzia, Sandro, and the entire gang form Arci di Novoli for being my bridge to the city and its people beyond the walls of academia. In my hometown Belgrade, a motley crew of dear friends and comrades sparked ideas, assisted me with tips, materials, veze or simply hung out with me, helping me put my mind at ease. I am grateful to Boris Kanzleiter, Dalibor Vasković, Dimitrije Vojnov, Dragomir Olujić, Kosta Đorđević, Predrag Vukčević, Ratibor Trivunac, and Vladimir Marković. The late Pavluško Imširović welcomed me in his home in the early stage of my research and gave me access to press clippings on workers' strikes in Yugoslavia he meticulously collected over the years. In New York, I would like to give a shout out to Elizabeth Lariscy and William Hovland, thank you for teaching me the importance of camaraderie and showcasing optimism of the will through all these years.

The book benefited greatly from the language editing and overall suggestions provided by Michael Cragg and Jozsef Litkei from CEU Press.

Those closest to me deserve most credit for helping me endure through this project. To my partner Marina and our three girls, Emma, Anna, and Katharina, thank you for bringing tremendous joy and sense of proportion into my life. I love you. Finally, the acknowledgment goes to my parents, Ružica and Bećir Musić, my sister Ines, as well as my grandmothers, the late Baka and Ana, for their love, nurturing and all the stories they told me while growing up.

Introduction

Unfulfilled Expectations

Between the break with the Soviet Union in 1948 and the death of Josip Broz Tito in 1980, the Yugoslav communists proudly showcased their country as an example of the possibility of an autonomous modernization path in a world divided between two rival development paradigms. The claim echoed among both the local population and many sympathetic observers abroad, not least due to the impressive economic growth and rapid modernization of the traditional peasant Balkan society.[1] Yet, there was more to the success story of Yugoslav socialism than mere statistical indicators. The main feature, which set Yugoslavia apart from other socialist countries, was the existence of workers' self-management: a complex structure of self-management bodies embedded in the economic and state institutions with the aim of regulating and coordinating socialist society through popular participation.

The main protagonist of self-managed socialism was supposed to be the expanding working class. By the early 1980s, after more than three decades of persistent industrialization and urbanization, the share of the Yugoslav population living off the land dropped from 67.2 percent to 28.8 percent, a decline from roughly 11 million to 4.9 million people.[2] The number of industrial workers increased by almost nine times under socialist economic policies, from some 300,000 in 1939 to 2.6 million in 1990.[3] The League of Communists of Yugoslavia (LCY) recognized that an economically underdeveloped society embarking upon the path of socialist modernization would inevitably encounter different kinds of social conflicts. Yugoslavia was a patchwork of different ethnicities with divergent cultural and political heritage, inhabiting areas displaying great disparities in

1 Yugoslavia was among the countries with the fastest economic growth in the world during the 1950s and early 1960s. According to Rudolf Bićanić, the aggregate rate of gross national product growth in Yugoslavia between 1950 and 1960 was 8.9 percent, while Japan and Israel both achieved 10.8 percent growth. Oskar Kovač estimated that between 1950 and 1985 only Taiwan (6.64 percent), Japan (6.26 percent) and China (5.10 percent) achieved higher growth rates than Yugoslavia (4.46 percent). See Rudolf Bićanić, *Economic Policy in Socialist Yugoslavia* (Cambridge: Cambridge University Press, 1973), 122; and Oskar Kovač, "Foreign Economic Relations," in *Beyond Yugoslavia: Politics, Economics and Culture in a Shattered Community*, ed. Ljubiša S. Adamović and Sabrina P. Ramet (Boulder, CO: Westview Press, 1995), 282.

2 Gregor Tomc, "Classes, Party Elites and Ethnic Groups," in *Yugoslavia: A Fractured Federalism*, ed. Dennison Rusinow (Washington, DC: The Wilson Center Press, 1988), 61.

3 Ibrahim Latifić, *Jugoslavija 1945–1990: Razvoj privrede i društvenih delatnosti* (Belgrade: Društvo za istinu o antifašističkoj narodno oslobodilačkoj borbi u Jugoslaviji 1941–1945, 1997), 46.

their levels of economic development. Disagreements over common policies and grievances along regional, national, and class lines triggered periodic political crises and motivated constant restructuring of the Yugoslav state and its institutions. Large sections of the industrial workforce were of peasant origin with no experience in political activity and the LCY suspected many workers carried vestiges of "backward beliefs." Nonetheless, the economic progress and the existence of workers' self-management were supposed to facilitate the creation of an urban population with communist values, able to mediate and overcome all the challenges of socialist transformation.[4]

The debt crisis which hit the developing world in the 1980s affected Yugoslavia more than any other socialist country due to its great dependence on the world market. The increasing prices of raw materials, spare parts, and components, needed for the export-oriented industry, resulted in an increase in production costs and the loss of competitiveness. In addition, interest on the country's loans was rising steeply and, by 1981, the Yugoslav government discovered that the self-managed economy was highly indebted to foreign creditors.[5] The ruling party was forced to give up its policy of relative independence in international politics and enter into debt restructuring agreements with Western governments and economic reform programs under the banner of the International Monetary Fund (IMF). A series of "stabilization programs" was introduced with the aim of improving international competitiveness and stamping out galloping inflation. They consisted mainly of decreases in collective consumption and stricter market parameters for company performance. Self-management structures inside the factories were gradually starting to be seen as an obstacle to profitable economic operation. In the first three years of the decade, average incomes had fallen by 33 percent in real terms; by 1988, the standard of living for workers in the socialized sector was pushed back to levels not seen since the 1960s.[6]

Faced with an unprecedented economic crisis and diverging regional interests, the Yugoslav authorities were finding it increasingly hard to maintain social peace. The austerity policies provoked movements from below and stirrings at the top of society. In 1985, surveys showed that only 20 percent of citizens expressed satisfaction with the federal government. The LCY was rapidly losing its image as the leading institution capable of solving social problems. That same year it experienced a net loss of membership among blue-collar workers for the first time since the end of the war.[7] Tacitly accepted and positively perceived by the public, the workers' mobilizations were among the most prominent

---

4 For the envisioned political role of the working class and concerns about the lack of class consciousness, see the official program of the League of Communists of Yugoslavia: *Program Saveza komunista Jugoslavije: Usvojen na Sedmom kongresu Saveza komunista Jugoslavije 1958* (Belgrade: Izdavački centar Komunist, 1980), 139–42.

5 Jens Stilhoff Sörensen, *State Collapse and Reconstruction in the Periphery: Political Economy, Ethnicity and Development in Yugoslavia, Serbia and Kosovo* (New York: Berghahn Books, 2009), 136.

6 Carl-Ulrik Schierup, "Quasi-Proletarians and a Patriarchal Bureaucracy: Aspects of Yugoslavia's Re-peripherialization," *Soviet Studies* 44, no. 1 (1992): 86.

7 R.J. Crampton, *The Balkans Since the Second World War* (London: Longman, 2002), 139.

grassroots initiatives at the time. The number of strikes recorded nationwide increased from 247, with 13,507 workers involved, in 1980 to 1,851 strikes, involving 386,123 workers, in 1988.

Year	1980	1981	1982	1983	1984	1985	1986	1987	1988
Strikes	253	216	174	336	393	696	851	1,685	1,851
Participants	13,504	13,507	10,997	21,776	29,031	60,062	88,860	288,686	386,123

Table 1: Industrial action in Yugoslav industry during the 1980s[8]

These statistics place Yugoslavia among the countries with the highest strike activity in Europe at this time.[9] Unlike the strikes in previous decades—the efforts of which were focused mainly against the company management and which remained within the factory premises—workers were now eager to connect their demands to wider political issues and present their grievances to the authorities by staging marches, street demonstrations and gatherings in front of government buildings. Inspired by the Solidarity movement in Poland, many observers at that time predicted that the working class would play the role of ultimate arbiter in the resolution of the political and economic crisis that weighed down on Yugoslavia in the 1980s. There was hope that the system could be salvaged through an all-Yugoslav mobilization based on social issues and oriented toward a class identity, which would be able to democratize the country and keep it unified.[10]

However, the crisis was resolved in a radically different manner. The mounting popular discontent gradually spilled over into a shift in relations inside the ruling regional parties. Lower-rank officials and local state enterprise managers attempted to join forces with critical voices from below and various protest groups inside their republics. In 1986, the Slovene League of Communists elected a new leadership determined to safeguard Slovenia's autonomy within the federation and accelerate liberal reforms in local politics and the economy. One year later, the leadership of the Serbian party was taken over by the radical reformist faction, led by Slobodan Milošević, which stood for market-inspired modernization of workers' self-management coupled with the stronger political influence of Serbia and more centralized federal institutions of the party-state. The two leaderships were set on a collision course.

The watershed was reached in the autumn of 1988, when the Serbian branch of the LCY openly broke the federal government's unified line against the street protests and extended political support to certain hand-picked demonstrations.

8 Darko Marinković, *Štrajkovi i društvena kriza* (Belgrade: Institut za političke studije, 1995), 83.

9 Salih Fočo, *Štrajk između iluzije i zbilje* (Belgrade: Radnička štampa, 1989), 6.

10 Branka Magaš, *The Destruction of Yugoslavia: Tracing the Break-up 1980–92* (London: Verso, 1993), xxi.

Reinterpreting the hitherto dominant dichotomy between the "exploiter and exploited" along nationalist lines, the Serbian political elite organized a wave of rallies in Serbia and the surrounding republics which co-opted a labor movement previously based on class issues. These top-down nationalist mobilizations, which came to be known as the "anti-bureaucratic revolution," paved the way for the violent disintegration of the country.

Unlike the labor movement in socialist Poland, the Yugoslav working class never built a sustained political platform capable of defending its interests independently of the populist leaderships at the top of the party or the political bureaucracies in the republics. The dichotomy between the workers' formal position of power within Yugoslav society and the apparent ease with which they gave way to nationalist politicians and market reformers in the late 1980s opened doors for denunciations of labor as prone to supporting strong leaders and attracted to chauvinism. This book is an attempt to problematize such sweeping characterizations and to reassess the role of labor under workers' self-management by taking a long-term look at the evolution of political and economic institutions, the changing composition of the working class, and the different political and ideological discourses circulating among its ranks during the existence of Yugoslav socialism.

Mighty Elites and Subservient Workers

The break from Stalinism and the search for a "national road to socialism" turned Yugoslavia into an attractive topic for social scientists during the Cold War period. After the establishment of communist regimes in Eastern Europe and China in the wake of World War Two, the so-called totalitarian model, widely used in analysis of the Soviet Union, was increasingly becoming too narrow and simplistic to explain the growing complexities of world communism. As the first dissident state in the Soviet bloc, Yugoslavia certainly helped break the insistence on the ideology, coercion, and actions of the party leadership. The recognition of the popular base of the communist-led partisan movement during and after the war, the unique nature of workers' self-management, and the openness to Western influences all intrigued researchers. This was particularly the case with left-leaning scholars, eager to highlight the possibility of a more tolerant and broad-based socialist development model.

Ever since the early 1950s, Yugoslav social scientists were also keen to utilize the liberalized political atmosphere and tackle issues such as social inequality, the class structure of society, and the distribution of power within self-management. Nevertheless, despite the encouragement of intellectual debate in the party and society, the Yugoslav communists maintained a rather crude vision of labor politics and workers' relations with the party. The advance of working-class interests was officially proclaimed as the primary raison d'être of the socialist project. The teleological presentations of progress and the equating of class position and social consciousness implied that workers were inevitably realizing the historical tasks ascribed to them by the ruling ideology. The official historiography, dealing with the prewar Yugoslav workers' movement and workers' participation in the revolution, tended to focus on the politically most advanced layers of the proletariat who were painted as heroes, whereas sociologists preferred positivist methodological approaches when studying labor under socialism.[11]

The communists' protective stance toward industrial workers made it hard to conduct critical factory-level research.[12] Those scholars aiming to deal with social inequalities and class divisions relied mostly on quantitative data, with the interpretative frame strongly influenced by the party-endorsed assumptions about workers' self-management. Having restricted access to the factories and their archives, the research depended heavily on surveys, questionnaires, and official statistics.[13] Due to their limited knowledge of local languages, foreign researchers often relied on translated official government policy papers and conference declarations. The rich texture of social relations on the Yugoslav shop floors and the multifaceted experiences of workers' self-management were thus largely neglected, with themes such as nationalism, strikes, generational gaps, kinship, private business, and the role of informal networks remaining underexplored.[14]

The 1980s proved to be fruitful years for historians wishing to take a bottom-up approach to labor under state socialism. The reforms initiated by the communist regimes and the increased accessibility of state archives made it possible to investigate socialist societies beyond official institutions. The emergence of the Solidarność movement in Poland and the growth of civil society in Eastern Europe contributed to the totalitarian paradigms losing their appeal, as the power of ordinary people to influence and change government policies had finally been recognized. Practitioners of social history, and labor historians in particular, seized this moment to fill the gap by conducting studies of socialist societies without giving precedence to high politics.[15]

---

11 See Vladan Vukliš, "Writing Social History of Socialist Yugoslavia: the Archival Perspective," *Archival Science* 17, no. 1 (2016): 55–77; or Ulf Brunnbauer, "Compartmentalized Pasts: Workers' History in Socialist Yugoslavia" (conference paper, 2016 European Social Science History Conference, Valencia, March 30–April 2, 2016), https://ostblog.hypotheses.org/751 (accessed June 26, 2019).

12 John B. Allcock, *Explaining Yugoslavia* (New York: Columbia University Press, 2000), 170.

13 Rory Archer, Igor Duda, and Paul Stubbs, "Bringing Class Back In: An Introduction," in *Social Inequalities and Discontent in Yugoslav Socialism*, ed. Rory Archer, Igor Duda, and Paul Stubbs (Farnham: Ashgate, 2016), 15.

14 Conducting qualitative research inside the factories was difficult, but by no means an impossible task. A number of excellent ethnographic, sociological, and organizational studies written by Yugoslav and foreign researchers managed to shed light on diverse practices inside the industry not reflected in official party writings. This book relies greatly on such analytical insights, primarily: Cvetko Kostić, *Bor i okolina–sociološka ispitivanja* (Belgrade: Savremena škola, 1962), Ichak Adizes, *Industrial Democracy: Yugoslav Style; The Effects of Decentralization on Organizational Behavior* (New York: The Free Press, 1971), Ellen Turkish Comisso, *Workers' Control under Plan and Market: Implications of Yugoslav Self-Management* (New Haven, CT: Yale University Press, 1979) and Susan L. Woodward, *Socialist Unemployment: The Political Economy of Yugoslavia 1945–1990* (Princeton, NJ: Princeton University Press, 1995).

15 For instance, the history of the October Revolution and the role of organized labor within

In the case of Yugoslavia, the tendency to switch focus from the party-state to society was reflected in the multiauthor volume *Yugoslavia in the 1980s*, edited by Pedro Ramet in 1985.[16] Among other things, the volume dealt with critical discourses about self-management, the changing nature of popular media, political initiatives of the party base, and religion. In Yugoslav academia, historians seized the opportunity afforded by the end of the thirty-year archival access veto and embarked on an exploration of the incipient years of workers' self-management.[17] This newfound interest for the lived experience of the working classes largely disappeared with the fall of the communist regimes in Eastern Europe. As Mark Pittaway noted, the opening of the archives and lifting of censorship after 1989 brought great possibilities for new research.[18] Still, few historians were interested in looking at labor within the new political climate, which was either hostile to working-class traditions or saw workers' organization around class grievances as an obsolete phenomenon.[19]

In South-Eastern Europe, many of the former party historians switched from simplistic accounts of the proletariat's relentless march toward communism to stories of national resistance under totalitarian regimes and narratives of nation building.[20] In the case of Yugoslavia, a series of bloody civil wars in the 1990s paved the way for the return of political history and a focus on the elites. The public thirst for explanations of the "Wars of Yugoslav Secession" triggered the mass production of new titles on the history of the Balkans and the causes of Yugoslavia's disintegration. These early titles, labeled as "instant history" by the veteran historians of the region, fell into the trap of understanding the processes of the past in terms of their ultimate outcome.[21] To many writers,

---

it proved to be a particularly attractive topic for researchers in the West. The wave of new factory-based studies led Lewis Siegelbaum to refer to the trend as the "late romance of the Soviet worker in Western historiography." See Lewis Siegelbaum, "The Late Romance of the Soviet Worker in Western Historiography," *International Review of Social History* 51, no. 3 (2006): 463–81, quoted in Andrei Sokolov, "The Drama of the Russian Working Class and New Perspectives for Labour History in Russia," in *Global Labour History: A State of the Art*, ed. Jan Lucassen (Bern: Peter Lang AG, 2006), 414.

16 Pedro Ramet, ed., *Yugoslavia in the 1980s* (Boulder, CO: Westview Press, 1985).

17 See for instance: Olivera Milosavljević, "Država i samoupravljanje: 1949–1956" (Ph.D. diss., University of Belgrade, 1987) and Zdenko Radeljić, *Savez sindikata Jugoslavije i Hrvatske: Kronologija (1945–1985)* (Zagreb: Radničke novine, 1986).

18 Mark Pittaway, "Introduction: Workers and Socialist States in Postwar Central and Eastern Europe," *International Labor and Working-Class History* 68 (Fall 2005): 1–8.

19 For specificities of the usage of class language in post-socialist East Europe, see David Ost, "Class after Communism," special issue, *East European Politics and Societies and Cultures* 29, no. 3 (2015): 543–64. The neglect of labor should also be seen as part of a broader theoretical reorientation of social researchers from class to other identities beyond the East-West divide in the course of the 1980s and 1990s. See Lex Heerma van Voss and Marcel van der Linden, ed., *Class and Other Identities: Gender, Religion and Ethnicity in the Writing of European Labour History* (Oxford: Berghahn Books, 2002).

20 For an overview of the development of historiography in South-Eastern Europe in the post-socialist period, see Ulf Brunnbauer, ed., *(Re)Writing History: Historiography in Southeast Europe after Socialism* (Münster: Lit Verlag, 2004).

21 Gale Stokes, John Lampe, Dennison Rusinow, and Julie Mostov, "Instant History: Under-

the temptation of newly-acquired hindsight proved irresistible. The rise of nationalist mobilizations and the subsequent wars cast a long shadow over the previous decades, erasing all memory of social movements and initiatives not fitting into the projected stream of inevitable events leading to disintegration and war.

The scholars of Yugoslavia were under pressure to focus on ethnicity, religion, and clashes between the republican leaderships as the most obvious lines of differentiation, while class and social inequalities, or protest themes and social movements—topics which transcended the borders of single republics—had been largely forgotten. The logical outcomes of this approach are the prominent role of elites, the apparent power of ethnicity to mobilize, and skepticism toward any kind of sustained collective action of the masses.[22] In the case that traces of popular mobilizations were detected, they were quickly dismissed as orchestrated affairs. In one of the most elaborate studies of Yugoslav socialist politics to date, Dejan Jović explicitly argues that political elites were the sole relevant actors in the system, as the activism of the masses was "short-term, fairly unorganized and limited by the immediate intervention of the police and politicians."[23]

Workers' self-management and labor, certainly among the most important topics in observations of Yugoslavia during the Cold War years, have been steadily pushed into the background. The industrial strikes of the 1980s are usually mentioned incidentally in the context of the rise of Slobodan Milošević and the "anti-bureaucratic revolution" in the late 1980s, along with workers' alleged support for nationalist politics. Jasmina Udovički and Ivan Torov, for instance, have argued that the labor protests in the final decade of workers' self-management were "carefully masterminded by special groups."[24] Against this backdrop, writing about the labor movement in Serbia at the time, Mihail Arandarenko could confidently state that the local communist leadership "soon secured the support of virtually the entire nation . . . , nationalist euphoria spread equally to the intelligentsia, farmers, and white- and blue-collar workers . . . , no alternative conceptualizations were available for mobilization."[25]

---

standing the Wars of Yugoslav Succession," *Slavic Review* 55, no. 1 (1996): 136–60.

22 The final years of Yugoslav socialism in particular appear as a dark tunnel, at the end of which awaits an explosion. Chapter titles such as "The Gathering Storm," "Milošević's Irresistible Rise," and "Unstoppable Slide to War," reveal this fatalistic atmosphere. The first chapter title comes from Sabrina P. Ramet, *Balkan Babel: The Disintegration of Yugoslavia from the Death of Tito to the Fall of Milosevic* (Boulder: Westview Press, 2002). The following two can be found in Christopher Bennett, *Yugoslavia's Bloody Collapse: Causes, Course and Consequences* (New York: New York University Press, 1995).

23 Nevertheless, Jović's book remains a seminal work for anyone trying to understand the inner party debates in late Yugoslav socialism, and this study relies heavily on his insights. See Dejan Jović, *Jugoslavija—država koja je odumirala: Uspon, kriza i pad Četvrte Jugoslavije 1974–1990* (Zagreb: Prometej, 2003), 325.

24 Jasmina Udovički & Ivan Torov, "The Interlude 1980–1990," in *Burn This House: The Making and Unmaking of Yugoslavia*, ed. Jasmina Udovički and James Ridgeway (Durham, NC: Duke University Press, 2000), 88.

25 Mihail Arandarenko, "Waiting for the Workers: Explaining Labor Quiescence in Serbia," in *Workers after Workers' States: Labor and Politics in Postcommunist Eastern Europe*, ed. Stephen

The event most often used to illustrate the historiographical cliché of working-class backing of authoritarian politics and nationalist calls is the protest by blue-collar workers from the Belgrade industrial suburb of Rakovica, which occurred in front of the Federal Parliament in October 1988. The workers supposedly arrived in a militant mood, armed with economic grievances, but decided to return to work after hearing a speech delivered to them by the leader of the League of Communists of Serbia, Slobodan Milošević. At the time, journalist Jagoš Đuretić described the rally in the following words:

> When Milošević appeared the mass became calm as if hypnotized. They soaked up every word and greeted them all with approval. . . . He promised them a strong, united Serbia and the return of national dignity to the humiliated Serbian people." The workers forgot about all their troubles. They gained a higher goal: a powerful Serbia and national pride. *They came before the Parliament as workers and left as Serbs . . .* [26]

This last phrase illustrating the instant change of identities in the course of a single event has become iconic in the meantime, habitually used in both popular and academic discourses inside Serbia to describe the alleged ease with which the workers abandoned their long-term class interests for nationalist demagogy.[27] In the historiography dealing with the north-western parts of former Yugoslavia—most notably Slovenia—the topic of workers' mobilizations are often given more positive connotations by integrating them into the Central European narrative of burgeoning civil society, independent trade unions, and democratization. Despite the more favorable normative claims, the Slovene workers are still perceived as mere bit part actors in a broader transition toward the rule of law and liberal democracy, headed by the national intelligentsia and political leaders.[28] Much like the Serbian case, the dominant views on Slovene labor deny the workers an independent role and lack a more nuanced inspection of working-class protests at the time.[29]

Crowley and David Ost (Lanham, MD: Rowman and Littlefield, 2001), 161.

[26] Slavoljub Đukić, *Kako se dogodio vođa* (Belgrade: Filip Višnjić, 1992), 265–66, emphasis added.

[27] For instance: Momčilo Pavlović and Predrag J. Marković, *Od radničkog saveza do Saveza samostalnih sindikata Srbije* (Belgrade: Institut za savremenu istoriju, 2013); Nebojša Popov, *Radno mesto pod suncem: Radničke borbe u Srbiji* (Belgrade: Službeni glasnik, 2011); Zoran Paković, "Tri štrajka," *Politika (Kulturni dodatak)*, June 11, 2011.

[28] See for instance: John K. Cox, *Slovenia: Evolving Loyalties* (London: Routledge, 2005), 70; or Rudolf Martin Rizman, *Uncertain Path: Democratic Transition and Consolidation in Slovenia* (College Station: Texas A&M University Press, 2006), 38–49; and France Tomšič, Od stavke do stranke (Ljubljana: Nova obzorja, 2010).

[29] A notable exception is Tonči Kuzmanić's effort to reveal the impact of labor strikes on Slovene popular opinion inside Yugoslavia and to distinguish between the different political orientations of various different strikes. See Tonči Kuzmanić, "Strikes, Trade Unions, and Slovene Independence," in *Independent Slovenia: Origins, Movements, Prospects*, ed. Jill Benderly and Evan Kraft (New York: St. Martin's Press, 1994).

(Re)Discovering Labor

Since the late 1990s, a slow but notable turn away from elite actors has begun in historiography dealing with late Yugoslav socialism. Researchers have tackled consumption, everyday life, and social movements based on the issues of ecology, pacifism, feminism, religion, and counter-culture.[30] Lately, there has been a return of interest in labor as well. In 2014, Sabine Rutar's pioneering essay[31] set out to sketch different periods of modern forms of labor in Yugoslavia in the *longue durée* and attempted to connect the writing of regional labor history to the theoretical insights of Global Labor History, as developed by Marcel van der Linden and his associates at the International Institute of Social History.[32] The call was followed by a new generation of scholars motivated to grasp the Yugoslav socialist experience through the prism of the interaction between the party-state and labor.[33]

[30] For example: Melissa K. Bokovoy, Jill A. Irvine, and Carol S. Lilly, *State-Society Relations in Yugoslavia 1945–1992* (New York: St. Martin's Press, 1997); Igor Duda, *Pronađeno blagostanje: Svakodnevni život i potrošačka kultura u Hrvatskoj 1970-ih i 1980-ih* (Zagreb: Srednja Europa, 2010); Hannes Grandits and Karin Taylor, *Yugoslavia's Sunny Side: A History of Tourism in Socialism (1950s–1980s)* (Budapest–New York: Central European University Press, 2010); Breda Luthar and Maruša Pušnik, *Remembering Utopia: The Culture of Everyday Life in Socialist Yugoslavia* (Washington, DC: New Academia Publishing, 2010); Predrag Marković, *Trajnost i premena: Društvena istorija socijalističke i postsocijalističke svakodnevice* (Belgrade: Službeni glasnik, 2012).

[31] Sabine Rutar, "Towards a Southeast European History of Labour: Examples from Yugoslavia," in *Beyond the Balkans: Towards an Inclusive History of Southeastern Europe*, ed. Sabine Rutar (Berlin: Lit, 2014), 323–57.

[32] Global labor history attempts to revive labor history by turning away from methodological nationalism and traditional orientations toward male industrial workers, the idea of free wage work as the norm, as well as the spatial focus on the North-Atlantic. See Marcel van der Linden, "Introduction," in Marcel van der Linden, ed., *Workers of the World: Essays toward a Global Labor History* (Leiden: Brill, 2008), 1–17.

[33] See for instance: Rory Archer, "*Imaš kuću—vrati stan*. Housing Inequalities, Socialist Morality and Discontent in 1980s Yugoslavia," *Godišnjak za društvenu istoriju* 3 (2013): 119–39; Goran Musić, "'They Came as Workers and Returned as Serbs': The Role of Rakovica's Blue-Collar Workers in Serbian Social Mobilizations of the Late 1980s," in *Social Inequalities and Discontent in Yugoslav Socialism*, ed. Rory Archer, Igor Duda, and Paul Stubbs (Abingdon: Routledge, 2016), 132–54; Vladimir-Unkovski Korica, *The Economic Struggle for Power in Tito's Yugoslavia: From World War II to Non-alignment* (London: I.B. Tauris, 2016); Ulrike Schult, *Zwischen Stechuhr und Selbstverwaltung: Eine Mikrogeschichte sozialer Konflikte in der jugoslawischen Fahrzeugindustrie 1965–1985* (Münster: Lit Verlag, 2017); Anna Calori and Kathrin Jurkat, "'I'm Both a Worker and a Shareholder': Workers' Narratives and Property Transformations in Postsocialist Bosnia-Herzegovina and Serbia," *Südosteuropa: Journal of Politics and Society* 65, no. 4 (2018): 654–78; Chiara Bonfiglioli, *Women and Industry in the Balkans: The Rise and Fall of the Yugoslav Textile Sector* (London: I.B. Tauris, 2019); Rory Archer and Goran Musić, "When Workers' Self-Management met Neoliberalism: Positive Perceptions of Market Reforms among Blue-Collar Workers in late Yugoslav Socialism," in *Labor in State Socialist Europe after 1945: Contributions to a History of Work*, ed. Marsha Siefert (Budapest–New York: Central European University Press, 2019).

This research draws inspiration from this shift in the historiography of socialist Yugoslavia toward class, microhistory, and everyday history approaches, with a particular focus on the social layer which was central to communist understanding of historical change and progress: the industrial working class. The term "working class" remains loaded with ideological and political connotations, as it was widely used by the party-state to justify the existing sociopolitical order. The research therefore approaches the notion of class with great caution, recognizing that the working class as a social actor does not stem automatically from employment statistics, but needs to be viewed over time as a historical category.[34]

In his momentous study of the forging of the English working class, Edward P. Thompson saw class not "as a 'structure,' nor even as a 'category,' but as something which in fact happens (and can be shown to have happened) in human relationships."[35] This research relies on the theoretical tradition of "class formation," directly inspired by Thompson's work. It looks at the emergence of the Yugoslav, socialist working class as a protracted process extending between the end of World War Two and the dissolution of the country. The making of the Yugoslav working class was a contingent and open-ended development conditioned by state policies and the institutions of self-management, but also the inherited pre-industrial traditions, political and cultural influences outside of the workplace, and a variety of nonclass patterns of social division. Instead of starting from a ready-made definition of the working class, the research is thus more interested in the specificities of the creation of the self-managing working class on the ground, as well as the ways the workers perceived themselves in relation to other social groups at each critical juncture of Yugoslav socialism.

Yugoslav workers had an array of different, often contradictory, identities influencing the ways in which they interpreted their world. Some industrial workers were members of the party while others were not. Some were religious, some atheist. Workers were skilled and unskilled, women and men, semi-farmers and urban dwellers, migrants and natives, members of different ethnic groups, employees of rival enterprises, and members of local communities in highly differentiated regions. The Yugoslav communists inherited an uneven spatial spread of prewar industries with the northeastern part of the country, formerly ruled by Austria-Hungary, containing the majority of modern production facilities, while the Ottoman Southeast was still characterized mostly by small, craft production.

Socialist modernization proclaimed equal regional development as one of its main goals, but industrialization did not proceed in a linear fashion after World War Two either. Consequently, any research on the Yugoslav working class must pay attention to the different types of industries and demographic features in the respective regions. Like most socialist regimes, the Yugoslav state started its postwar economic growth by favoring heavy industry and metalwork, whereas lighter industries, such as textiles or food processing usually received fewer

[34] Michael P. Hanagan, *Nascent Proletarians: Class Formation in Post-Revolutionary France* (Oxford: Blackwell, 1989), 4.

[35] E. P. Thompson, *The Making of the English Working Class* (New York: Pantheon, 1964), 9.

investments and paid lower wages. The functioning of the market within self-managed socialism created its own hierarchies however, with those enterprises producing finished products in high demand and regions better connected to export networks attracting greater income and a better-educated workforce.

Next to class, the second most important source of political rights for the Yugoslav workers was certainly national identity. Following the revolutionary slogan of "brotherhood and unity," the Yugoslav socialist federation was supposed to foster the full equality of different nationalities and promote the cultural rights of minorities. However, the persistence of regional disparities opened the door for claims that certain nations enjoyed a favored position inside the federation. Blue-collar workers often settled into industrial centers from underdeveloped rural communities with a history of ethnic conflict, but the nationalist worldview could also be created and reproduced inside the urban industrial milieus. The self-managing enterprises were often placed in relations of market competition and rivalry. When faced with economic difficulties, the management of the work collectives could adopt nationalist-colored explanations for business failures and expect protection from their local political leaderships. Especially during periods when nationalist language would break into mainstream discourse, such as the late 1980s in Serbia, the industrial workers were tempted to embed their local grievances into larger explanatory patterns based on ethnicity and regional rights.

Approaching Class and Nation in a Yugoslav Factory

In order to capture the finesses of the life of industrial workers in socialist Yugoslavia, this research concentrates on two concrete case studies. The two factories and their wider communities, which give the research a micro-level focus, are Industrija motora Rakovica (Rakovica Motor Industry, IMR), located in the Belgrade suburb of Rakovica, and Tovarna avtomobilov Maribor (Maribor Automobile Industry, TAM), situated in the Slovene industrial center of Maribor. The two case studies are by no means representative of the overall experience of the Yugoslav working class; both enterprises were large factories situated in urban centers and employed a great number of skilled workers. Because of their size, location, and symbolic importance the party-state made sure they developed a rich internal political and cultural life. As such, the factories and their surrounding communities were bound to embody some of the main tendencies in the development of the Yugoslav working class and reflect the broader discussions taking place in their republics, but also were influential enough to impose their own concerns onto the public and the government.

The observed factories underwent an interconnected development throughout the existence of socialist Yugoslavia. In the initial postwar years, they competed head-on with each other as part of the government's "socialist competition" policies. In the following decades, they continued to be business partners in the expanding socialist market. In the late 1980s, the history of the relationship between the two factories entered popular discourses and political debates. The diverging development paths of the enterprises was picked up by the Serbian communist leadership to exemplify the allegedly unequal position of their republic inside the federation. As already noted, Rakovica workers played a prominent role in the Serbian social mobilizations of the late 1980s, ever since they staged a protest in front of the Yugoslav Federal Parliament in October 1988. Four months earlier, TAM workers had initiated a citywide general strike in Maribor, forcing Slovene government officials to address their grievances. In the summer of 1988, the Zagreb liberal weekly *Danas* used the strikes in Belgrade and Maribor to express concerns over a potential conservative backlash to the ongoing reforms:

> At times of crisis and tension, the historical socio-psychological matrix of our society always becomes visible. This is the time when society, whose roots lie in poverty and scarcity, comes back to its traditional values: egalitarian demands for social justice and authoritarianism. The protests in Belgrade and Maribor are proof that these values survive in the form of a latent consciousness. In Belgrade, the workers demanded the expropriation of the summer-houses of the bureaucracy. . . . In Maribor they called for the leveling of income with other producers in the metal industry, reduction of business trips, and removal of luxury cars parked in front of the factory. In tense and heated situations, we see that there are always cries for equality and justice and they are always greeted with applause and cheers.[36]

As the decade was ending, the liberal opinion makers, market-oriented enterprise managers, and reform-minded party functionaries increasingly viewed the working class not as an asset, but an obstacle to more rapid "catching up" with the West. Inspired by the sociologist Josip Županov's theory of the "egalitarian syndrome,"[37] the reformist-minded intellectuals in Serbia, Slovenia, and other republics insisted that Yugoslavia was lagging behind other industrialized countries due to patron-client relationships inside the factories, in which labor legitimized the dominant position of the communist elite in exchange for the bureaucratic redistribution of limited goods. According to such interpretations, egalitarian values were part of the primordial consciousness of the Balkan people standing in the way of successful modernization through the market.

There was fear among the liberal reformers that popular protests might connect with the hardliners in the party or embrace the politics of nationalist exclusion. As already noted, in hindsight, this reasoning became a dominant

[36] Milan Jajčinović, "Doći ćemo opet: Protiv koga se bune radnici u radničkoj državi," *Danas*, June 26, 1988, 18–19.

[37] Josip Županov was one of Yugoslavia's most influential sociologists and an ardent researcher of self-management. For a sample of his writings at the time, see Josip Županov, "Znanje, društveni sistem i 'klasni' interes," *Naše teme* 7, no. 8 (1983): 1048–54. For a critical account of Županov's "egalitarian syndrome" thesis and its impact on the Yugoslav sociological community, see Danijela Dolenec, "Preispitivanje 'egalitarnog sindroma' Josipa Županova," *Politička misao* 51, no. 4 (2014): 41–64.

interpretation of the working-class mobilizations of late socialism. Yet, careful observers at the time found it hard to put a definite label on the popular movements from below, often noticing conflicting tendencies and actors on the ground. There was a plurality of debate and seemingly opposing concepts existed and developed side by side.[38] Inherited notions of social equality, brotherhood and unity, and workers' participation interacted with "old/new" nationalism, demands for democratization, and market modernization.

This book revisits various watershed historical moments for Yugoslav labor by looking at the everyday routine of factory work, informal hierarchies on the shop floor, as well as workers' cultural life and leisure activities. At the same time, it does not hesitate to connect this "micro level" to official politics and broader questions about Yugoslav socialism. The study examines the changing nature of the connections between the workers in the two selected factories, their management, and the political leaderships. It does not approach workers as passive recipients of ideas and organizational forms from above. By describing the changing alliances between the political bureaucracy, the management, and workers, the book will try to shed light on the sheer complexity of Yugoslav labor relations, as well as the ability of workers to shape independent interpretations of the crisis, impose its grievances onto official discourses, and rally around autonomous initiatives.

In order to mobilize workers behind the reforms in all crucial periods of Yugoslav socialism, the political elites had to confront rival explanations on the shop floor, offer concessions, and strike deals with organized labor. The book will show how many themes adopted by the party leaderships in Belgrade and Ljubljana in the second half of the decade were successful partly because they acknowledged and addressed many concerns already discussed in the factories years beforehand. Apart from focusing on the inner factory debates developing over a longer period of time, the research will dedicate special attention to moments of industrial action, walkouts, and protests. These events offer good opportunities to observe different strands of oppositional discourse in action, as well as the process of the collective framing of particular grievances.

The idea is not to simply reverse the dominant lines of explanation by arguing that labor was somehow immune to nationalist and liberal ideology, nor to paint an idealized picture of industrial workers in full accordance with the virtues projected onto them by the ruling socialist ideology. Instead, the research presents the reader with a more nuanced view of working-class life, work, and political engagement in self-management. Keeping in mind the heterogeneity of the factory workforces, the book will shed light on the way the workers expressed their grievances and demands depending on their skill, age, gender or nationality. How did different occupational groups interpret the crisis and appropriate the official ideology from their particular position, and did they attempt to mobilize the work collective behind a common cause? Whom did the striking workers perceive as their main enemies and potential allies?

---

[38] Jasna Dragović-Soso, *"Spasioci nacije": Intelektualna opozicija Srbije i oživljavanje nacionalizma*, trans. Ljiljana Nikolić (Belgrade: Fabrika knjiga, 2004), 311–12.

Sources and Chapter Overview

Each Yugoslav enterprise was crisscrossed by a network of self-management bodies on all levels, holding regular meetings in which workers participated in the business of decision-making, but sometimes also discussed more general topics of concern for the communities they lived in or even for the country as a whole. Self-management bodies were therefore places where a unified company identity could be forged by contrasting the common interests of the entire workforce to that of other work organizations or the state. In other instances, these bodies could also serve as sites of contention between different occupational groups within the enterprise, each of which could seek alliances outside of the factory gates—along political, national or occupational lines—in other localities. The enterprise therefore presents us with a crucial level of analysis when trying to uncover the specific understandings and interpretations of macroeconomic processes and political slogans launched by the party apex.

Unfortunately, the majority of materials from IMR and TAM, especially the blue-collar departments, have not been archived. The research gets around this obstacle by focusing on the factory press. The spread of news and reports from various meetings among the workforce was seen as vital for reaching well-informed business decisions in self-management bodies. Both factories maintained a professional journalistic staff and issued a weekly newspaper. The factory papers were intended to unify the work collective behind common goals and project a favorable picture of the enterprise. They dedicated disproportionate space to the management, as well as the highly qualified and politically active workers who were supposed to set the tone for the rest of the factory. Nevertheless, these sources also routinely reflect on different problems inside the enterprises and their careful reading offers a good insight into the discussions taking place in the factory, including the reactions of shop floor workers.[39]

The openness of the factory press to grievances from below differs among various factories. The representativeness of debates reported in the IMR paper was proved by comparison with the minutes of Vehicle Workers' Assembly, a broad-based self-managing organ of an important blue-collar department. The archive of this department, itself a rare example of surviving documentation from within a factory, confirms the inclusive and pluralist nature of the paper. In the case of TAM, by the mid-1980s, the paper was increasingly coming under the control of the management and being shaped as propaganda directed toward the workforce and business associates. However, even here the articles and reports offer a sound overview of workers' grievances. In the case of TAM, a good additional source were the comics appearing in the factory press, which

[39] For a detailed description of the factory newspaper as a source in the study of Yugoslav self-managed industry, see Rory Archer and Goran Musić, "Approaching the Socialist Factory and its Workforce: Considerations from Fieldwork in (former) Yugoslavia," *Labor History* 57, no. 5 (2016): 44–66; and Sven Cvek, "Class and Culture in Yugoslav Factory Newspapers," in *The Cultural Life of Capitalism in Yugoslavia: (Post)Socialism and Its Other*, ed. Dijana Jelača, Maša Kovanović, and Danijela Lugarić (Cham: Palgrave Macmillan, 2017), 101–21.

are partly organized in separate appendixes. These comical drawings often reveal important issues otherwise not discussed in factory paper articles and official documents. In addition, the research is informed by interviews conducted with former workers and self-management activists from both factories, as well as municipal and city-level political functionaries.

The book chapters are structured in the following manner. The first chapter of the book offers an outline of the historical development of two factories through different periods of Yugoslav socialism. It displays different and often-opposing tendencies within the "Yugoslav road to socialism" as reflected in IMR and TAM, as well as the ways in which workers reacted to shifting official interpretations of self-management. Special attention is dedicated to the expanding influence of the market and the economic and political crisis of the late 1960s, which created conditions for workers' strikes and a revision of the dominant local understandings of what constituted a "self-managed work collective."

The second chapter starts by outlining the main aims and structures of the ambitious reform of workers' self-management initiated during the 1970s as a response to the growing influence of managers and market-induced inequalities in the previous decade. It shows how the 1970s reforms were implemented and adjusted to the specific management culture of each enterprise, while also describing the political culture inside the factories and workers' special connection to the populist rule of Josip Broz Tito. Finally, this part of the book looks at the everyday routines of work and leisure inside the two blue-collar communities at the height of the 1970s welfare state.

The third chapter focuses on social inequalities within the blue-collar communities and differentiates between different groups of factory workers based on their skill level, gender, and place of origin. A special emphasis is placed on the generation gap between the older workers, whose life expectations were shaped by the experience of World War Two, and the younger workers, who grew up in postwar prosperity. The chapter also exposes the problems of lax work discipline and workers' misuse of social property. The appendix presents many of the themes running through the chapter in the form of caricatures published in the factory papers.

The fourth chapter presents the devastating effect that the 1980s economic crisis had on the workers' standard of living. It goes on to explore the inability of the party to anchor its influence on the shop floor, and details how different occupational groups saw the crisis and fought to impose their own solutions. The core theme of this chapter is the party campaign of bottom-up discussions, conducted in 1984, with the aim of reviving faith in the party-state and gaining new momentum for reforms. It closely follows the main discussions and the results of the campaign in both localities. Finally, it shows how the management seized the opportunity of stalemate within the party-state to push for their own vision of market reforms.

The fifth chapter gives answers to the question of why workers abandoned the self-management concept implemented in the 1970s. The chapter demonstrates how workers broke their alliance with the factory's political activists and started (re)orienting to the top management. It also describes the entry of oppositional, nationalist discourses into the factories and explains their connection to local grievances. At the end of the chapter, the second appendix offers additional views of the main irrationalities of self-management practice as perceived by the participants with the help of caricatures.

The sixth chapter looks at the proliferation of workers' strikes and other social movements in the late 1980s and explains how this steady pressure from below finally brought political changes at the top of the Slovene and Serbian parties. The political liberalization and spread of nationalist themes encouraged a layer of the workforce to abandon the ideology of brotherhood and unity and form an internal alliance with the management in calls for faster market reforms and greater protectionism against rival producers.

Finally, the seventh chapter describes two momentous strikes organized by workers of the two factories in the summer and fall of 1988. It will demonstrate how different, often contradictory, understandings of the crisis and workers' demands were intertwined in public spaces. The chapter concludes by revealing the different ways in which the Serbian and Slovene officials addressed workers' grievances and set the tone for increasingly nationalist-charged official public language in the following years, leading to the ultimate breakup of the country.

CHAPTER ONE

Two Roads to Self-Managing Socialism

Two Blue-Collar Communities

The image of Rakovica as Belgrade's most blue-collar municipality was accepted as common knowledge in socialist Yugoslavia's capital. A glimpse at the distribution of the industrial workforce across Belgrade at the end of the 1980s does not seem to back up this widespread belief. The statistics show that Rakovica, with some 13,000 metal and rubber industry workers, lagged behind larger municipalities such as Zemun, home to over 30,000 industrial workers, or Palilula, which was located closer to the city center and still registered over 23,000 workers employed in industry.[1] Nevertheless, the blue-collar workers in the latter two municipalities were dispersed among numerous employees in the service sector and state administration. On the other hand, 70 percent of Rakovica's employed population worked in industrial enterprises.[2] The impression of a working-class municipality was therefore not based on absolute numbers, but on the high concentration of blue-collar workers in one smaller municipality.[3]

A closer look at the city topography might additionally explain what set Rakovica apart from other blue-collar localities. Zemun and Palilula are situated in the north of Belgrade, close to the Danube River, on the lower edge of the Pannonian Plain.[4] The broad spaces of the river plain allowed the factories to be set up with a significant distance between them, often separated by long stretches of roads and residential areas. In the south, the Rakovica industrial basin was a gateway to hilly Central Serbia, squeezed within the long and narrow valley along the small local river. The factories there were built in a straight line, one right after the other, with almost no clear-cut borders. In the morning, when the first shift workers would start arriving in the factories, the bottleneck at the entrance of the basin would resemble a big day at the football stadium.[5] Unlike most other municipalities hosting large factories, to which blue-collar workers commuted

1 *Statistički godišnjak Beograda* (Belgrade: Gradski zavod za statistiku i informatiku, 1989), 266.

2 In Palilula the share of industrial workers approached 30 percent of the total employed, while in Zemun this number went up to 50 percent.

3 In the 1981 population census Rakovica had 87,067 residents. See *Statistički godišnjak Beograda* (Beograd: Gradski zavod za statistiku i informatiku, 1989), 222.

4 Built on the confluence of the Danube and Sava rivers, Belgrade marks the southern end of the European Pannonian Plain and the beginning of the mountainous Balkan region.

5 Interview with Radoš Karaklajić, March 2011.

for work, Rakovica had the highest percentage of correspondence between workplace and residence.[6] This dense conglomeration of living and workspaces certainly contributed to a pronounced feeling of common predicament and shared identity. As one trade unionist from the time remembered, if there was a commotion in a single department of one factory, within one hour the news would spread through the grapevine and become the main topic of conversation in the entire municipality.[7]

The media, citizens, and politicians alike associated this part of the city and its residents with straightforward, working-class attitudes held essential for the maintenance of the self-management system.[8] Metalworkers formed the core of the basin's industrial workforce; the majority of them were employed by two motor factories. Industrija motora Rakovica (IMR) was the largest single factory in Rakovica, employing close to five thousand people at its height in the mid-1980s. It specialized in diesel engines and tractors. The second one was "21. maj," (May 21) oriented to more demanding automobile and airplane engines. Situated between the two centerpiece enterprises was the rubber and tire producer Rekord, the factory with the lowest wages, an unskilled workforce, and the toughest working conditions. The top position in the Rakovica inner economic hierarchy was reserved for the nearby Tehnogas, the extractor of natural gas. Its managerial board served as the springboard for many functionaries of the Serbian League of Communists, including the two main party figures in the second half of the 1980s: Ivan Stambolić and Slobodan Milošević.[9]

Along with the municipality's reputation for delegating outspoken representatives to political forums and its geographic closeness to the federal and republican institutions of power, the personal connection between Rakovica and the leadership of the Serbian League of Communists certainly contributed even further to its visibility and its political and economic prestige in the 1980s. Between 1980 and 1988, the IMR newspaper reported no less than five official visits made by Ivan Stambolić to the factory as the city and republic official. In that same period, four LCY Central Committee representatives, as well as the vice president and the president of the Federal State Presidency, also spoke at IMR. Foreign political leaders were often given a guided tour of the municipal plants as part of the protocol for state visits: among them were the president of Egypt, Hosni Mubarak, and the prime minister of India, Indira Gandhi.

---

6 Some 70 percent of Rakovica workers also resided in the municipality. This number ranged between 10 and 36 percent in industrial zones located closer to the city center. Dragan Petrović, *Istorija industrije: Razvoj i razmeštaj industrije Beograda u XIX i XX veku, II tom* (Belgrade: Srpsko geografsko društvo, 2006), 473–74.

7 Interview with Milan Kljajić, March 2011.

8 See, for instance, the way in which high LCY official Kiro Gligorov describes Rakovica as the place where "genuine workers' words always come to the fore" in D. Žujović, "Ostvariti Opredeljenja," *IMR*, November 22, 1983, 2.

9 Ivan Stambolić was briefly an apprentice on the IMR shop floor during his vocational education. Afterwards he went on to study law at the University of Belgrade. Before occupying key posts in the city and the republic in the late 1970s and 1980s, Stambolić was the executive manager of Tehnogas. Slobodan Milošević also worked as the general director of Tehnogas in the mid-1970s before pursuing a political career in the city party apparatus under Stambolić's tutorship.

One part of the components produced in Rakovica would certainly be sent to Maribor, another important site of Yugoslavia's automotive industry located close to the country's northwestern border with Austria. As Slovenia's second-largest city and a regional center, Maribor and its industrial basin Tezno were not sites of frequent high-profile political visits, as was the case with factories in Belgrade or Ljubljana. Indeed, the name of Tezno lacked familiarity outside of Maribor, but the local automotive industry, Tovarna avtomobilov Maribor (TAM), was a well-known and trusted trademark in Yugoslavia. TAM's trucks and buses were the transportation vehicles of choice for numerous companies and individuals throughout the country, while the factory was also a staple supplier of the Yugoslav People's Army. TAM's wider image was based on the quality of its manufacturing and marketing. It manufactured heavy-duty vehicles considered top-of-the-line on the domestic market. Maribor's geographical location seemed to predestine its high living standards and successful emulation of the most advanced production techniques. The media, political authorities, and workers from less developed regions were prone to see Maribor as Yugoslavia's most "Western" industrial center.

Upon returning from a visit to TAM in the mid-1980s, a group of transportation workers from Bosnia and Herzegovina wrote an article for their factory paper under the heading "The Giant of the Automobile Industry." Reporting on their trip to Maribor, the guests compared TAM's plants to a beehive. "One cannot witness this genuine laboring atmosphere and not feel a certain pride for being present in such an environment," the article exclaimed. The aspect that impressed them most was not the political work or social services offered by the factory, but the organization of the production process and work discipline, which, they were keen to observe, "did not take anything away from the friendliness and camaraderie of the hosts."[10]

The status of TAM was twofold. Observed from the perspective of the less-developed regions and judged by the inner criteria of the Yugoslav automotive industry, TAM was counted among the technologically most sophisticated and market-oriented enterprises. Yet, for many white-collar employees and students in Maribor itself, TAM had the image of a "political factory."[11] It employed a large number of low-skilled workers from Maribor's countryside, and a large part of its production program was dedicated to non-commercial, heavy transport vehicles. For over two decades, a single general director, Stojan Perhavc, stood at the head of the organization: a strong industrial cadre with partisan background, who managed to survive the managerial revolution of the 1960s. Perhaps the most defining feature which contributed to this image was TAM's

[10] By challenging the perceived dichotomy between work discipline and joyful social relations, the article obviously aimed to question the widespread image of Slovene workers as hard-working and cultured, but somewhat reserved people, standing closer to the traditions and ways of Central Europe than the Balkans. See "Radnici Zenicatatransa u Mariboru," *Skozi TAM* (Serbo-Croatian edition), November 1985, 6.

[11] One encounters this term quite often in the industrial and political milieus of socialist Yugoslavia. It had a clear pejorative connotation, describing a company unable to stand on its own in the market without government protection.

close relationship with the army. In 1987, the federal secretary for national defense honored the factory with the highest Plaque of the Armed Forces, to commemorate forty years of common work.[12]

The municipality of Tezno employed close to 11,000 industrial workers, only 3,000 fewer than the much larger municipality of Rakovica.[13] This implies that, in contrast to Rakovica, a large part of Tezno's workforce resided outside of Maribor and commuted to work. TAM's production made up 30 percent of the industrial output of Tezno and 16 percent of Maribor's total industrial production.[14] The factory was thus very important for the city but, at the same time, the local industry did not rely solely on automotive manufacturing. The second largest company located in Tezno was Metalna, a metal construction enterprise employing around 4,000 workers with renowned engineering and consulting departments, which managed to contract jobs throughout the developing world thanks to Yugoslavia's favorable geopolitical position, and could thus send its workforce abroad to gain much-needed hard currency. The third largest employer in Tezno was the railway vehicles and heating equipment workshop Tovarna vozil in toplotne tehnike (TVT) Boris Kidrič with 2,700 workers. One of the first industrial establishments in Maribor, the enterprise enjoyed the prestige of being named after Boris Kidrič, a Slovene partisan leader and one of the main theoreticians of workers' self-management.[15]

It is hard to tell the story of these two municipalities separately from the development of their two most distinguished factories. IMR was the only Rakovica enterprise with a prewar industrial tradition[16] and the first plant in a row of factories inside the basin. Over the years, the factory had built a small sports stadium, thanks to which it had become the focal point of social and political events in the area. It invested heavily in housing construction and other infrastructure for its employees and their families. TAM had a similar, perhaps even larger, significance for all aspects of life in Tezno and Maribor. The first thing a traveler arriving in Maribor by train would see was a giant factory logo on the main station's rooftop. It was the largest single factory in the city, with employment numbers surpassing 8,000 by the mid-1980s. The factory grounds contained an open-air swimming pool which would open to the public in summer and TAM sponsored numerous cultural and sporting activities in the community.

---

12 Danilo Vincetič, "Tamu velika plaketa JLA," *Skozi TAM*, January 1987, 7.

13 In 1981, Tezno started to catch up with Rakovica in terms of the total number of employed workers, even though the municipality had only 35,425 residents, almost two-thirds fewer than Rakovica. See *Statistički godišnjak Jugoslavije* 37, 1990 (Belgrade: Savezni zavod za statistiku, 1990), 631.

14 Lučka Lorber, "Functional Changes in Tezno, The Industrial Zone in Maribor," *Revija za geografijo* 2, no. 1 (2006): 95–108.

15 For more on the economic and political thought of Boris Kidrič, see Darko Suvin, "The Economico-Political Prospects of Boris Kidrič: A Betrayed Disalienation," May 20, 2015, accessed July 14, 2019, https://darkosuvin.com/2015/05/20/the-economico-political-prospects-of-boris-kidric-a-betrayed-disalienation.

16 The tire producer Rekord also existed in the prewar years, but in the form of a small workshop employing only a handful of workers.

Both factories witnessed their greatest expansion and influence in the second half of the 1970s, a decade of ambitious investment spending and heightened political sensitivity toward industrial workers. In the 1980s, IMR and TAM both underwent a prolonged crisis. By 1988, these two factories stood at the forefront of blue-collar protests in Belgrade and Maribor, which had an impact on broader political processes in Serbia and Slovenia at the time. The greater part of this book focuses on these last two decades of Yugoslav socialism. However, before continuing with the description of the Yugoslav welfare state's peak and the subsequent crisis in the two respective factories and their wider communities, this chapter will cover the formative two-and-a-half decades of socialist development. After a short account of the factories' origins and the early postwar years, it will cover the birth of workers' self-management and the economic growth of the 1950s. The final two sections in the chapter place special emphasis on the turbulent 1960s, since many of the social and political issues that arose in this period resurfaced and became magnified during the prolonged economic and political crisis of the 1980s.

Differing Origins

Despite efforts to modernize, Serbia remained an overwhelmingly agrarian country decades after its formal independence from the Ottoman Empire in 1878. Up until World War Two, the southeastern Yugoslav territories were the sites of slow and often futile efforts by a weak state to build up infrastructure and encourage manufacturing through attractive concessions to foreign capital and the connection of production to military needs. In the interwar period, Belgrade managed to attract finance capital and began its late industrialization as the capital of an enlarged state. In the late 1930s, the city had around 300 industrial enterprises employing over 30,000 workers. Nevertheless, the productivity of the local industry was low in comparison to the northwestern regions. More often than not, the industrial enterprises were small workshops, focusing on repairs instead of proper production, and operating with outdated technologies and an inadequately-skilled workforce.[17] According to Marie-Janine Calic, up to 60 percent of industrial workers in Yugoslavia in this period were agricultural laborers performing seasonal work in industrial facilities who did not cut their ties with the countryside.[18] In more developed areas, such as Belgrade, this number was certainly lower, but the fact remains that industrial workers were not a well-settled urban layer and stood far from Western European standards in terms of work discipline, education, and political activity.

The most modern industrial facilities, which employed a layer of skilled manual workers, were government-owned factories established to serve the most

[17] Dragan Petrović, *Istorija industrije: Razvoj i razmeštaj industrije Beograda u XIX i XX veku, I tom* (Belgrade: Srpsko geografsko društvo, 2006), 160–228.

[18] Marie-Janine Calic, *Socijalna istorija Srbije, 1815–1941: Usporeni napredak u industrijalizaciju*, trans. Ranka Gašić (Belgrade: Clio, 2004), 190–211.

pressing needs of the developing state and its military. IMR was founded in 1927 as an airplane motor factory by a consortium of domestic and French capital. In 1936, the Yugoslav state nationalized the plant to secure lower prices and a steady supply of aircraft parts. On the eve of World War Two, IMR obtained a license from the Czechoslovak automotive giant Českomoravská Kolben-Daněk and started to assemble Praga model trucks in a late effort to improve the overall motorization of the Yugoslav Royal Army.[19] A few years earlier, the communist party had managed to infiltrate the factory. The local cell was not particularly numerous, but it seems to have had significant influence among the wider workforce.[20] It managed to recruit at least three IMR workers for the International Brigades in Spain and organized a three-month long solidarity strike with the Belgrade aeronautical workers in 1940. During the war, the sway of the factory communists grew, as the surviving IMR cell became the center for organizing the antifascist resistance in the area. Between 1941 and 1945, some 300 workers from the factory joined the communist-led partisan movement.[21]

TAM was also established as an airplane parts manufacturer, but its origins were quite different from those of IMR. The German occupying army built the plant from scratch in the summer of 1941. Although the foundation of the future TAM factory was set up by Nazi Germany for war production, this should not lead one to the conclusion that industrial development in northwestern Slovenia was the result of a late state-led industrialization policy similar to that applied in Serbia during the 1930s. One of the main reasons that the occupying German army chose Maribor as the location for their plant was precisely the rich industrial tradition of the city. Unlike the parts of Yugoslavia formerly ruled by the Ottoman Empire, the erstwhile Habsburg territories—and Lower Styria in particular—were already sites of more spontaneous, market-led development and investments into modern manufacturing techniques in the nineteenth century.[22] The construction of the Südbahn railroad by the Austrian Empire in 1857 connected Slovenia with financial centers such as Vienna and Prague, making Maribor one of the cities with the longest industrial traditions in Yugoslavia.[23]

19 Bojan B. Dimitrijević, "Monopolističke ambicije i 'kašnjenje' u proizvodnji vazduhoplovne industrije u Kraljevini jugoslaviji," *Istorija 20. veka* 3 (2012), 19–38.

20 The cell numbered five members in 1940 and had grown to sixteen by the time the war started in April 1941.

21 Živojin Spasojević, ed., *Monografija 50 godina IMR-a* (Belgrade: Industrija motora Rakovica, 1977), 12–23.

22 Under the Habsburg Monarchy, northwestern Slovenia formed a southern cone of the Duchy of Styria. After the collapse of Austria-Hungary, some two-thirds of Styria remained in the Federal State of Austria, whereas the so-called Lower Styria, with Maribor as its capital, joined the newly-established State of Slovenes, Croatians and Serbs. In the interwar period, the Slovene part of Styria remained home to some 24,000 ethnic Germans, whose cultural, political, and economic influence remained strong, especially in urban settlements such as Maribor.

23 For the development of Maribor's industry before World War Two, see France Kresal, "Mariborska tekstilna industrija 1922–1992—vzpon in zaton," in *Mesto in gospodarstvo: Mariborsko gospodarstvo v 20. Stoletju*, ed. Željko Oset, Aleksandra Berberih Slana, and Žarko Lazarević (Maribor: Inštitut za novejšo zgodovino in Muzej narodne osvoboditve Maribor, 2010), 257–89.

With Lower Styria considered to be an integral part of the core German state by the Nazi authorities, they did not hesitate to set up a state-of-the-art factory which would serve as an important piece in the Wehrmacht war industry network. Combining the work of prisoners of war with technical expertise from Germany, the factory was constructed and began production in record-breaking time. Already by the summer of 1942, the Tezno suburb became a site of three production plants and their surrounding infrastructure (road, railway, workers' settlement, administrative building), which employed over 7,000 people. Some 14,000 pieces of brand-new machinery were producing to meet the needs of the Wehrmacht in three shifts while over 1,300 workers were sent to Germany for vocational training to operate them. Understandably, there was no organized communist cell or resistance activity inside a newly-erected factory of this type. Thanks to the hasty escape of the occupying forces in the spring of 1945 and the existence of underground bunkers, much of the installed machinery remained in place despite the Allied air bombardment and Berlin's explicit order to leave behind as little machinery as possible in case of retreat.[24] After the occupation, Maribor was thus left with the nucleus of the most up-to-date industrial infrastructure in Tezno—a unique situation in an economically underdeveloped and war-torn country.

After liberation, the partisan army leader, Josip Broz Tito, visited Czechoslovakia in the spring of 1946 as Yugoslavia's first postwar prime minister and minister of foreign affairs. Many Yugoslav companies, including the truck production enterprise in Rakovica and the local industry in Maribor, depended on technological imports from Czechoslovakia. While in Prague, Tito appealed for economic collaboration between the communist-dominated governments in the Soviet zone of influence. The Yugoslav communists believed that, with the assistance of the Soviet Union and other friendly countries in Eastern Europe, Yugoslavia could accomplish a grand modernization project in a relatively short time span. As Slovenia was the most economically developed part of the country, the leadership was convinced that the end of the first five-year plan could already mark the full industrialization of this republic.[25] The steady supply of heavy trucks was one of the major requirements for this ambitious task. Accordingly, the Federal Ministry of Heavy Industry decided to duplicate Rakovica's truck-producing technology in Tezno, placing the two factories into "socialist competition." Along with centrally-determined five-year plans, shock brigade work, and norm-breaking, the concept of socialist competition was copied from the Soviet propagandist brochures of the 1930s.[26] It implied a direct race in productivity among different manufacturers and the connection of these strained production efforts to the ultimate goal of achieving socialism.[27]

---

24 Slavica Tovšak, "Šest desetletij od začetkov Tovarne avtomobilov Maribor," in Slavica Tovšak, ed., *Tovarna avtomobilov Maribor: Sledovi mariborskega gospodarstva v arhivskem gradivu Pokrajinskega arhiva Maribor 60 let—spominski zbornik* (Maribor: Pokrajinski arhiv Maribor, 2007), 4.

25 Jože Prinčić, *Slovenska industrija v jugoslavenskem primežu, 1945–1956* (Novo Mesto: Tiskarna Novo Mesto, 1992), 30.

26 For the origins of socialist competition as an industrialization policy in post-revolutionary Russia and its evolution under Stalin's five-year plans, see Isaac Deutscher, "Socialist Competition," *Foreign Affairs* 30, no. 3 (April 1952): 376–90.

27 There are few studies of socialist competition in Yugoslavia. For its application in Croatia see

In Rakovica and Tezno, as in other industrial centers, the communist leadership therefore attempted to apply methods of mass political mobilization—successfully practiced during the struggle against fascism—as a tool of economic policy.[28] The forced resettlements and reprisals against the civilian population conducted by the Nazi occupiers as well as the conscriptions into the partisan army had scattered the old, skilled workforce in both localities, forcing the government to place greater emphasis on the work of volunteer brigades, communist youth, and the mobilized peasant youth. In IMR, there were no stable work hours and workers often found themselves staying inside the factory for days at a time departing from work only to catch a few hours of sleep. In TAM, the work revolved in two twelve-hour shifts six days a week, while on Sundays the volunteer brigades would take over the production efforts.[29] The mass mobilization into industry was carried out under the slogan of volunteer work, but records from the time show many freshly-recruited workers felt they had no choice but to follow the orders of the party-state.

Reports from the local governments and central economic planning bodies between 1945 and 1955 illustrate how factories often suffered from a lack of laborers and great turnover of their workforce, as peasants resisted recruitment or deserted their work posts due to dangerous working conditions, poor nutrition, and inadequate housing.[30] One should, however, distinguish between the attitudes of the forcefully-recruited peasantry and the politicized layer of workers and youth who joined the partisan movement during the war. The latter were accustomed to hardship and self-sacrifice and engaged in industrial reconstruction with great élan. As one IMR worker with prewar experience, Radomir Vuličević, recalled: "Nothing was too hard for us. We who knew the work conditions and life under capitalism [*kod privatnika*] felt our time had come."[31] Of course, one must take into account that this type of remembrance carried a great deal of romanticizing, since it was recorded at the height of prosperity in the late 1970s. Still, the general feeling of optimism spread by the victory over fascism and the promise of a better life under socialism should not be underestimated. The partisans were a popular mass movement and many uprooted peasant youth were eager to face the new challenges in peacetime despite the difficulties. The veteran TAM worker Ivan Mustafa described the early postwar years in Maribor in the following words:

Tomislav Anić, "Radništvo i propaganda: 'socijalističko takmičenje' u Hrvatskoj 1945–1952." (PhD diss., University of Zagreb, 2010).

28 For a better understanding of the reorientation of the Yugoslav communist leadership made during World War Two from alliances at the top, under Moscow-dictated popular front tactics, to broad mobilizations under the concept of the "popular front from below," see Vojislav G. Pavlović, "Stalinism without Stalin: The Soviet Origins of Tito's Yugoslavia 1937–1948," in *The Balkans in the Cold War: Balkan Federations, Cominform, Yugoslav-Soviet Conflict*, ed. Vojislav G. Pavlović (Belgrade: Institute for Balkan Studies, 2011), 11–42.

29 Simona Trčko, "Delovna zavest je bila povsem drugačna," *Skozi TAM*, April 1987, 11.

30 Ivana Dobrivojević, "'Svi u fabrike!' Instant industrijalizacija u Jugoslaviji, 1945–1955," *Istorija 20. veka* 2 (2009): 103–14.

31 Sl. A. "Tri decenije vernosti IMR-u," *IMR*, February 3, 1977, 8.

> From the beginning, we were forced to improvise. There were no organized meals, no protection gear, and no central heating. In spite of all of these problems, we did not complain or fall into desperation. We got down to work where necessary. We worked in shock brigades to rebuild the production facilities as soon as possible. These were volunteer brigades, but to us they seemed obligatory. We were aware that any gain had to be achieved through blisters. On Sundays, we helped with social work or assisted the farmers. We organized many solidarity actions. People appreciated our dedication and we were happy when the results of our work became visible.[32]

A guerilla leader turned statesman, Tito remained the central symbol of aspirations for a better life in peacetime. His visit to Maribor and the abandoned German factory in Tezno in June 1945 overlapped with the nationalization of the enterprise and the renewal of production.[33] In November of that year, with combat operations still taking place outside of the city, the celebrated war hero visited Rakovica and appealed for increased production for the battlefront. The remaining workforce in both factories saw these visits as a guarantee that production would be renewed and that the enterprises would play an important role in the new Yugoslavia. Tito was therefore treated as a sort of founder of the factories and the protector of industrial workers in general. The following recollection of a female worker, Jelena Reljić, reveals workers' excitement during the visit:

> The news suddenly spread throughout the factory. Comrade Tito is here! We ran outside the building and gathered spontaneously at the gate. All plans of protocol broke down amidst mass joy. It was the first time we saw the man we considered a legend. We were spellbound. Many of us were not sure if the man from the wanted posters really exists. The man for whose capture the Germans offered 100,000 gold marks! Until that day, we had only heard stories about him; fiction and reality were becoming mixed up in our heads.[34]

Another account of his exchange with the workers during this first visit to Rakovica shows how, very early on, Tito presented himself as a benevolent leader who understood the everyday difficulties of the people. An anecdote says that one worker responded to Tito's appeals for self-sacrifice in the face of tough working conditions and a lack of wages by exclaiming, "We do not need wages, we will work as much as we can." Tito allegedly answered, "A worker cannot work without a wage. If I came home without a wage, they would say 'if you are working, then where is your wage?' Comrades, this will soon be taken care of."[35]

---

32 Simona Trčko, "Delovna zavest je bila povsem drugačna," *Skozi TAM*, April 1987, 11.

33 Slavica Tovšak, ed., *Tovarna avtomobilov Maribor: Sledovi mariborskega gospodarstva v arhivskem gradivu Pokrajinskega arhiva Maribor 60 let—spominski zbornik* (Maribor: Pokrajinski arhiv Maribor, 2007), 5.

34 Ljubomir Vesković, "Tito je došao: sećanje Jelene Reljić na prvi susret radnika IMR-a sa Titom," *IMR*, October 14, 1977, 14.

35 Ibid.

Despite the popularity of the new regime and the widespread zeal for the reconstruction efforts, the policy of rapid industrialization did not generate the results expected. Self-sacrificing work could not make up for the lack of expertise and modern tools. Both enterprises were dependent on German specialists acquired through war reparations or taken as prisoners of war. TAM had great difficulty conquering the new technological process and fulfilling the five-year plan. In 1947, the planned output was 250 vehicles, but the factory managed to produce a mere 29 units on its own. In 1948, the plan envisioned 700 chassis, but the shop floor managed to assemble only 113. The year 1949 proved exceptionally hard as the political break with the Soviet Union triggered an economic blockade on the part of the Peoples' Democracies in Eastern Europe, while the production of trucks continued to depend on the import of parts from Czechoslovakia. The initial plan for that year was to produce 2,000 vehicles, but after a few months, this was cut to 1,250. By the end of the year, TAM fulfilled only 14.4 percent of the originally planned target.[36] The output in Rakovica during these years was only slightly higher, showing that IMR faced the same difficulties as its Slovene twin truck producer.

The idea behind having factories compete with each other was for each enterprise to show initiative by cutting costs and raising productivity on their own, while striving harmoniously together toward the common goal of socialism. Rakovica's engineers, however, were not enthusiastic about the duplication of their truck-manufacturing license in TAM. Their initial suggestion was to outsource production of certain components to Tezno and turn the Slovene factory into IMR's supplier. IMR's management eventually relented and handed all the blueprints to the Ministry of Heavy Industry.[37] TAM also exhibited selfish attitudes. In the course of the first five-year plan, the Central Directorate of the Federal Motor Industry sent three consecutive complaints to the local management, warning that the enterprise was exceeding its investments and spending beyond the general plan. TAM's management reportedly ignored all criticism coming from the federal bodies, seeking protection from the notable Slovene communists.[38]

The scarcity of raw materials, components, and qualified workforce forced companies to use all means available to acquire inputs, reach their quotas, and perform better than the competition. The industrialization drive was supposed to thrive on mass mobilization and integrate the most distinguished workers into political work, but the tendency on the ground seemed to go in the opposite direction. Factory management dominated the internal political life of the factories, neglected mobilizations from below, broke common plans, and

---

[36] Jure Maček, "Tovarna avtomobilov in motorjev Maribor v obdobju prve petletke," in *Tovarna avtomobilov Maribor: Sledovi mariborskega gospodarstva v arhivskem gradivu Pokrajinskega arhiva Maribor 60 let—spominski zbornik*, ed. Slavica Tovšak (Maribor: Pokrajinski arhiv Maribor, 2007), 48–77.

[37] "Sećanja Veterana (V) Nadmetanje sa TAM-om," *IMR*, October 30, 1984, 2.

[38] Marko Miljković, "Western Technology in a Socialist Factory: The Formative Phase of the Yugoslav Automobile Industry, 1955–1962" (master's thesis, Central European University, 2013), 76.

tried to secure favorable allocation of resources by lobbying the party-state at both local and federal level. The competition seemed to be losing its assumed socialistic content, instead turning into a scuffle for centrally-allocated resources and a search for political nepotism with negligible increases in productivity.

IMR was located in the federal capital and had a tradition of communist agitation among its workforce. This probably made it easier to place the factory under political control. On the other hand, in a newly-established, well-mechanized, provincial factory such as TAM, the party certainly faced a greater challenge to counter the pursuit of particular interests at the local level. As already noted, the plant was located in a prosperous northwestern corner of the country and had weak political structures. In its February 1947 report to the Yugoslav Central Committee, the Slovene party used the example of Maribor to illustrate the weakness of communists among the skilled labor in industrial centers. The report stated that among the 17,000 industrial workers in the city, barely 430 were party members. Out of the 1,200 employed at TAM, twenty-five workers were party members, but only one of them had been recruited from the factory itself, and this person was a white-collar worker.[39] A classified report in 1949 recognized that TAM was still operating under old organizational forms introduced by the German wartime management. The lag in the implementation of a "socialist organizational skeleton" inside the larger factories was justified by the potential disruptions of production which could accompany a hurried transition.[40]

As hastily as it was enacted, the socialist competition between IMR and TAM was suddenly brought to a halt in the second half of 1950. The government decided to continue with truck production solely in Maribor, whereas IMR was to reorient to the production of engines and agricultural vehicles. The exact reasons for this rearrangement of industrial sites remain unclear. However, it is indicative that the relocation roughly overlaps with two major political and economic shifts happening at the time. The first change in the country's industrial network locations was the result of geopolitical and military considerations. Fearing the advance of Soviet tanks from Hungary after the split with Moscow, in the first months of 1949 the government ordered the withdrawal of all army-related industries located in the northeastern flatland border regions, including Belgrade. These were moved into Bosnia and Herzegovina, the mountainous heartland of the partisan World War Two guerrilla resistance, and Slovenia.[41]

The second, economic change that might have influenced the decision to move truck production to Tezno was the break with the centralized command economy and a reorientation toward workers' self-management. The new system

39 Vladimir Unkovski-Korica, "Workers' Self-Management in the 'Yugoslav Road to Socialism': Market, Mobilisation and Political Conflict 1948–1962" (PhD diss., London School of Economics, 2011), 33.

40 Marko Miljković, "Western Technology in a Socialist Factory: The Formative Phase of the Yugoslav Automobile Industry, 1955–1962" (master's thesis, Central European University, 2013), 53.

41 Susan L. Woodward, *Socialist Unemployment: The Political Economy of Yugoslavia 1945–1990* (Princeton, NJ: Princeton University Press, 1995), 139.

implied workers' control over the production process, but equally important were the decentralization of economic decision-making and opening up to monetary incentives. The integral economic development, aiming at strictly-controlled, balanced industrialization through a central investment plan, was abandoned in favor of a more market-based system in which the most economically advanced regions served as the poles of development.

"Factories to the Workers"

As the previous section has shown, the Yugoslav communists faced what would become emblematic problems of all the command economies in Eastern Europe even before the end of their first five-year plan. Output lagged behind the planned targets, the quality of the produced goods was unsatisfactory, and there were clear limits to further industrialization through self-sacrifice of a population exhausted by occupation and war. The competition between the factories for limited production inputs and a qualified workforce resulted in an overall increase of wage levels beyond the set targets, consequent breaches of planned costs, lags in the rise of productivity, and the surfacing of narrow regional interests inside the party. Boris Kidrič, one of the main party theoreticians at the time, identified "bureaucratic centralism" and "economic particularism" as the two main tendencies causing such disruptions and hindering the further development of socialism in Yugoslavia. The first term alluded to the belief that the swelling apparatus of the central state and its legal acts could resolve all problems from above without connecting politics to the actual initiatives of individuals and their immediate environment. The latter referred to the existence of narrow thinking, allegedly widespread among enterprise managers, which "holds and defends one's own without any regard to the broader community, unless something can be gained from it." According to Kidrič, these two harmful tendencies could appear at once inside the party-state of the republics, which would start to act in a particularistic manner toward the central state and bureaucratically toward the workers below them.[42]

The introduction of workers' self-management in the summer of 1950 was an attempt to pierce through both of these undesirable tendencies by relying on grassroots initiatives inside the factories. The Basic Law on Management of State Economic Enterprises and Higher Economic Associations by the Workers' Collectives made a single enterprise a sovereign body, able to debate and vote upon fundamental factory matters through the workers' council, elected among its members. The law therefore established a de facto distinction between the "governing" (*upravljanje*) and "administrative" (*rukovođenje*) structures within the enterprise. The governing structure was the principal framework for the exercise of workers' self-management and rested upon the belief that workers had the political right to participate in the running of their enterprises. The workers' council was the basic governing body and functioned on the principles of popular vote and consensus-seeking. The administrative structure, on the other

[42] Boris Kidrič, *Sabrana dela V* (Belgrade: Komunist, 1985), 11–13.

hand, consisted of salaried personnel chosen on merit in compliance with market principles and the technological demands of production; namely the general directors, department directors, section chiefs, and supervisors. The professional management continued to function as a top-down hierarchical structure responsible to the workers' council, but also to the local state organs.[43]

The general director was responsible for the routine running of the enterprise, but strategic documents and decisions such as business plans, final accounts, and distribution of accumulation had to be authorized by workers' representatives inside the workers' council. The council members were reelected by secret ballot on a yearly basis and could stand for a maximum of two terms in that position. To prevent the alienation of the councils from the work collectives, three-quarters of this body had to consist of manual workers. The council members met once a month and elected a management board: a professional administration headed by an enterprise director. The party-state retained the right to appoint the enterprise director. The candidate was chosen for a four-year term, but the election had to be approved by the workers' council.[44]

The election of the first workers' council in IMR was organized in a ceremonial manner. The forty-five elected council members were norm-breakers (*udarnici*), innovators, trade unionists, party activists, and other distinguished workers and employees. Although the party celebrated the bill as the fulfillment of the prewar communist slogan "factories to the workers"—meaning workers running the enterprises—in practice, the legislation provided for the participation of the most skilled workers in the decision-making of the professional management. IMR's first council discussed ways to cut costs, approved balance sheets, and gave their opinions on investment priorities. According to the official factory history, self-management was received with great enthusiasm among the workforce and the first results were already obvious the following year when the factory recorded a 35 percent rise in productivity.[45]

Workers' councils proved able to boost performance on the shop floor. However, their actual power to influence factory income was limited, since the business results still largely depended on state economic policies, beyond the reach of a single enterprise. The factories remained heavily dependent on political intervention. During the first mandate of the IMR workers' council, the enterprise went through a brief crisis. The sales of finished vehicles came to a halt. The trucks started piling up in the factory circle and workers' wages were late. The meetings of the workers' council and the professional management went on until late into the night without result, until finally the workers' council came up with the idea of sending a factory delegation to Tito. In a matter of days, the stocks were cleared and the wages were paid on time.[46]

43 Adizes, *Industrial Democracy*, 32–46; Josip Županov, *Samoupravljanje i društvena moć* (Zagreb: Naše teme, 1969), 150–51.

44 Blagoje Bošković and David Dašić, ed., *Socialist Self-Management in Yugoslavia, 1950–1980: Documents* (Belgrade: Socialist Thought and Practice, 1980), 63–73.

45 Spasojević, *Monografija 50 godina IMR-a*, 45.

46 Slobodan Jovanović, "Tito među radnicima: susreti koji ne prolaze," *IMR*, June 28, 1983, 4.

During the early years of industrialization, visits to Tito became a sort of a ritual for IMR. Rakovica valley is located below Belgrade's Topčider hill, the élite neighborhood where many of the top-ranking communist functionaries resided. IMR workers would take advantage of the factory's proximity to the party apex and drive the newly-constructed vehicle models uphill to present them to Tito in the White Palace.[47] In Tezno, one can detect similar efforts to express allegiance to local communist strongmen and gain their patronage. As we have seen, the local railway workshop was named after the party theoretician Boris Kidrič. In 1952, one of the first prototype buses produced by TAM was named Luka, after the Slovene party official Franc Leskošek.[48]

The communist-led partisan movement took the form of a guerilla army, consisting mostly of the peasant youth operating far from the urban centers. In the postwar years, the party was therefore in need of a settled proletariat and cadres capable of spreading its influence in the industrial milieus. The introduction of workers' self-management helped the communists find a more stable anchor among the manual workers. The workers were encouraged to break from their dependency on the local managers and develop loyalty toward the top party leadership, the political force which guaranteed them inalienable rights within the enterprises. Workers' self-management internalized work discipline and the spirit of self-sacrifice among the broader layer of non-politicized workers, without direct ideological mobilizations from the top, while simultaneously serving as a check on the jurisdictions of the professional management. The apex of the socialist party-state played a crucial role in the maintenance and running of the self-management system. The organs of industrial democracy did not extend beyond the factories, and the working class was still reliant on the party for political representation. Economically, the self-managed factories also remained dependent on the party-state to coordinate production and channel investments. Central planning was abolished, but state control over the expanded reproduction was still ensured through heavy taxation, federally-imposed accounting regulations, and strictly-prescribed rules for distribution of net income between different funds.

Still, the overt dependency on the top communist leadership was a long way from the pattern the party hoped all factories would follow. As noted earlier, the official political theory considered bureaucratic centralism to be just as harmful as economic particularism. Even during the first years of its existence, in many localities workers' self-management had already evolved toward more commercial autonomy and stricter market criteria for enterprise performance. The government freed the enterprises from operating under strict production

---

47 The White Palace (*Beli Dvor*) was a royal court built as a residence for the Yugoslav royal family in the 1930s. After World War Two, the compound became one of Tito's dwellings and the setting for diplomatic processions. On a clear day, the palace complex positioned on the top of the hill could be seen from Rakovica's factories nestled in the valley.

48 Franc Leskošek (partisan nom de guerre "Luka"), a metalworker by vocation, was a staunch supporter of federal investments in Slovenia, managing to recruit trained personnel and direct resources for industrial projects in the republic, despite the scarcity of the early postwar period.

plans and encouraged them to maximize their income through competitive sales on the market.[49] A "socialist commodity production"—market exchange, grounded in the law of value, coupled with collective social ownership over the means of production—supposedly provided the only objective criterion for distribution.[50] In many cases, the introduction of workers' participation in the election of the management enabled company bosses to escape the direct control of the party-state and build a base of support among their workers. The directors, workers' councils, and the broader workforce could develop a group identity by contrasting their enterprise interests in the market with those of rival producers and the political authorities. In many factories it was the directors, more than the political functionaries, who became prominent figures to whom the workers addressed their grievances.

TAM was to become a good example of this trend. In 1953, Stojan Perhavc arrived at the head of the enterprise, and would play a decisive role in the factory's development over the next twenty-three years.[51] Perhavc governed TAM in a high-handed manner. On the shop floor, he enjoyed the image of a strict but righteous director. The doors of his office were allegedly always open for workers wanting to submit complaints. Nevertheless, it remained clear that—despite all the self-management bodies—he was the ultimate authority deciding on the validity of their claims. Perhavc secured his popularity by striking a clever balance between the blue-collar workers' demands for income redistribution and the white-collar workers' push for development investments. TAM based its business success on continuous innovation and a sound engineering department. However, when the shop floor showed signs of dissatisfaction, a strong character like Perhavc did not hesitate to round up the professional staff and put them in their place. One engineer remembered the general director was fond of telling TAM experts: "If you were worth anything, you would have been working someplace else a long time ago."[52]

Perhavc's political allegiance and authoritarian style of management did not stand in the way of a market-oriented business model. Quite the contrary: strong directors with good standing in the local party apparatuses often acted as bulwarks against the political pressure for radical organizational experiments and demands for the redistribution of profits. Workers' self-management enabled

49 Woodward, *Socialist Unemployment*, 169–73.

50 Boris Kidrič, *Izabrana dela I* (Belgrade: Izdavački centar Komunist, 1985), 66–69.

51 Stojan Perhavc was born in 1910 and completed his studies in mechanical engineering in the first Yugoslavia. He gained work experience in the north Italian industrial town of Monfalcone before joining the partisans in 1944. After liberation, Perhavc worked as a clerk for the metal and electrical industry at the Federal Planning Office and served as the chief of the metal industry sector in the Slovenian Ministry of Industry and Mining. Belonging to the same generation as the Slovene party leadership and having the advantage of being in the privileged group of prewar professionals who joined the partisans, Perhavc was well-positioned to represent TAM's interests in the higher forums of the new socialist state. He remained TAM's general director until his retirement in 1975.

52 Cited in the oral history project initiated by Maribor's Museum of National Liberation: Borivoj Breže, "Tovarne v Mariboru," http://www.muzejno-mb.si/spomini/home.html, last accessed February 2015.

the factories in Maribor to continue looking for pragmatic and self-centered solutions in business performance, relying on their inherited advantages, such as more up-to-date production facilities and the ability to adopt the newest trends from neighboring Western European markets. As early as 1951, Maribor's City Party Committee noted that local workers' councils were dedicating little attention to social issues such as labor safety and medical care for the workforce. Insufficient funds were devoted to collective consumption and public infrastructure. The self-management bodies tended to pass the decision-making initiative to professional management and became isolated from their blue-collar base. Moreover, Maribor communists complained that market incentives did not necessarily contribute to greater productivity by inspiring harder work and a cost-effective allocation of resources. The factories in their region were reportedly trying to boost total income by manipulating prices, competing among each other to establish parallel sales outlets, and hoarding assets in the most profitable products and services.[53]

The discussions that went on in the Maribor party in the early 1950s show that the revolutionary leadership was well informed about the harmful effects that market forces left on the overall economic solidarity and political unity of workers. Many places had obviously gone too far in the direction of enterprise autonomy and the market. Yet the communists chose to tolerate these tendencies amidst robust economic growth and the concomitant rise in living standards. Between 1953 and 1960, Yugoslavia's industrial production grew 13.8 percent annually, the highest rate in the world at the time. Self-management opened doors for cross-border exchange, but also provided stabilization of the core workforce at home. In 1952, the government canceled the state monopoly over foreign trade, aiming to encourage economic exchange with the West. Individual enterprises were now free to seek business partners abroad. The transfer of technological patents from highly industrialized economies and increased investment into the processing industry opened up possibilities for the growth of a manufacturing sector thriving on local consumption. The new organization of production required a smaller, settled, and well-trained workforce instead of constant mobilizations of laborers from the countryside and shock work. The party subsequently abandoned the policy of forced land collectivization, leaving the vast majority of food production to small family farming. Hundreds of thousands of workers mobilized into industry during the postwar industrialization drive returned to their villages, thus cementing the prewar social phenomenon of peasant workers.

The wave of economic liberalization, modernization of production, and rise in living standards reached Rakovica and Tezno in the second half of the 1950s. In 1954, IMR signed a long-term cooperation program with the renowned British engine manufacturer Perkins and obtained a license for its diesel motor. Perkins' diesel engines became the foundation of Yugoslav industrial motorization. IMR sold the majority of its motors to various truck, tractor, agricultural vehicle, and boat manufacturers at home, while a smaller part was exported to the UK under

[53] Jože Prinčič, "Mariborsko gospodarstvo," 198.

the licensing agreement with Perkins, bringing much-needed hard currency into the country. The cooperation with Perkins included IMR sending workers abroad to its partners' plants for training.[54] In the late 1950s, the factory workers' council decided to invest in a state-of-the-art foundry, which finally satisfied its demand for high-quality metal casts. The first assembly lines were introduced in 1960 and the enterprise evolved from a large workshop into a modern plant with serial production. The new technology made the work conditions inside the IMR plant less challenging, and the factory began to invest in social amenities. As one worker recalled, "we were facing fewer difficulties each day. Central heating was installed. New machines and better tools started to arrive. Everyday work demanded less physical strain. The enterprise started building and allocating apartments."[55]

In Tezno, the period between the mid-1950s and mid-1960s brought similar advances for the factory and its workforce. With the help of Perhavc's political contacts, TAM managed to obtain a licensing contract with the Cologne-based engine and vehicle producer KHD (Klöckner-Humboldt-Deutz AG). KHD's technology enabled TAM to manufacture light trucks named TAM 2000. In the course of the 1960s, this vehicle proved to be a big success, as it offered a solution for lighter cargo transport in a decade that saw a flourishing service sector and greater consumerism. The factory continued to produce heavy-duty vehicles for industrial and military use; however, this smaller commercial truck confirmed TAM's place as the leading transport vehicle manufacturer in the country. The workers' council used its influence to direct part of the income into improving the living conditions of the workforce. Much like in Rakovica, one of the main concerns in Tezno was housing. Between 1945 and 1965, TAM had built some 1,137 apartments in the municipality for its workers. Dozens of factory-based sports and hobby groups contributed to the spread of communal spirit and attachment to the factory. In the course of the 1950s, as part of the all-Yugoslavia trend, TAM's trade union also started organizing affordable collective summer holidays on the Adriatic Sea.[56]

The loosening of the centralized planned economy and the introduction of self-management reshuffled the broader industrial roles of the two factories and created distinct local identities in Rakovica and Tezno. IMR abandoned truck manufacturing and took over the production of agricultural vehicles. The mechanization of agriculture was an important goal of the revolution, and IMR took up the political and engineering challenge to develop Yugoslavia's first

[54] Visits to the Perkins plant also involved illicit means of acquiring modern technology, as IMR specialists would often secretly fill their pockets with various components, hoping to recreate them back home. It is interesting to note that older workers remembered British engineers choosing to turn a blind eye to these appropriations. Yugoslavia's image of a socialist country nurturing industrial democracy obviously awakened empathy and feelings of solidarity among the hosts. See Sećanja Veterana (III), "Odakle vam ta licenca?," *IMR*, September 11, 1984, 2.

[55] Sl. Avramović, "Naši veterani: Život se nastavlja na Zlatiboru," *IMR*, January 20, 1977, 8.

[56] Marta Rendla, "Mariborski gospodarski gigant TAM v skrbi za izboljšanje življenjske ravni zaposlenih," in *Mesto in gospodarstvo: Mariborsko gospodarstvo v 20. stoletju*, ed. Željko Oset, Aleksandra Berberih Slana, and Žarko Lazarević (Maribor: Inštitut za novejšo zgodovina, 2010), 553–77.

domestic tractor. The factory also became responsible for the development and diffusion of diesel engine technology through its partnership with Perkins. The existence of the state-of-the-art foundry encouraged the enterprise to specialize in heavy-duty motor parts, whereas technologies for smaller components were transferred to other factories. IMR showed no open signs of dissatisfaction with the fact that it had been moved down in the production chain. As the supplier of engines and the source of newly-developed technologies for other plants, IMR occupied an important position at the center of the Yugoslav automotive industry. This industrial arrangement, coupled with its geographical location in the suburb of the federal capital, brought the factory great political credentials and general recognition, contributing to a feeling of pride and entitlement among its workforce.

Situated far from the centers of institutional power, but at the same time in one of the most economically developed regions, the final producer TAM based its growth on marketing, application of the most up-to-date imported production technologies, and market specialization. The workforce developed a strong allegiance to the general director, under whose leadership the company flourished. TAM was among the first industrial producers to open sales outlets in the largest Yugoslav cities. The enterprise built its image through media campaigns, including rewards for truck drivers who covered the most mileage in its trucks and the inviting of potential customers to visit the production facilities. The factory began to create a network of domestic suppliers through vertical integration. This move allowed it to shift labor-intensive stages of production to its partners, releasing space for more income-generating products in its own plants.[57] By the late 1960s, the factory had established long-term subcontracting agreements with 158 companies all over Yugoslavia.[58] The Tezno plant maintained its own foundry, but it tended to channel investments into engineering innovations and outsource component production, thereby developing into a lean and mechanized assembler of contracted parts.

The two factories thus ended up at opposite ends of the Yugoslav automotive industry production network. Tezno's most successful product, the TAM 2000 light truck, was powered by the IMR-produced diesel engine. This made IMR one of TAM's chief business partners. During the years of rapid, extensive economic growth and high demand for their products, both factories seemed to benefit from the new division of work. IMR was prospering through sales of its unique diesel engines and had a niche for direct sales in the market through its tractor program. Higher up in the production chain, TAM enjoyed the position of the largest truck producer in the country, in contact with both commercial consumers and the army. It seemed that socialist competition had been replaced by cooperation on the market. Nevertheless, as the reforms deepened, newly-emerging producers and liberalized foreign trade saturated the Yugoslav market,

[57] "Najvažniji događaji u TAM u 35-godišnjoj historiji," *Skozi TAM* (Serbo-Croatian edition), March 1982, 9.

[58] Anton Vagner, "Kooperanti Tovarne avtomobilov Maribor," in *Tovarna avtomobilov Maribor: Sledovi mariborskega gospodarstva v arhivskem gradivu Pokrajinskega arhiva Maribor 60 let—spominski zbornik*, ed. Slavica Tovšak (Maribor: Pokrajinski arhiv Maribor, 2007), 43–48.

creating clashes between the companies and stirring debate over government policies, and the allocated roles in the automotive industry production chains.

Market Socialism

During the initial twenty years of industrialization, the main concern for Yugoslav producers was not how to sell their products, but how to catch up with demand. The country was passing through extensive economic growth from a very low level of industrialization. There was a great need for basic capital and consumer goods, causing the market to absorb entire factory outputs, regardless of their quality or price. Local authorities were opening factories and attracting foreign licenses with little concern for cost-effectiveness or duplication of industrial facilities. By the mid-1960s, the first signs of market saturation were already starting to appear. The federal industrial planners tried to overcome these structural challenges by integrating different producers, achieving economies of scale, and boosting exports. The year 1965 marks the watershed moment when implicit tendencies from the previous decade and a half were finally turned into an official party line, popularly known as "market socialism." The set of smaller reforms spilled over into a qualitatively new concept of the state as the leadership openly embraced liberal assumptions about economic development. Liberalization of foreign trade and more market-based reasoning inside the enterprises were the key components of the economic reform. The policymakers were hoping to enter a new stage of intensive economic growth with a modernized, well-connected industry, fully integrated into the world market.

In 1954, just a few kilometers away from IMR, a new tractor-producing plant named IMT (Industrija mašina i traktora) was constructed in the municipality of New Belgrade under a licensing agreement with the Canadian company Massey Ferguson. A fierce rivalry developed between the two factories. IMT took advantage of IMR's double duty to produce engines and agricultural vehicles. It specialized in finishing tractors and emerged as the largest and most technologically advanced agricultural machinery producer in Yugoslavia. IMR's skilled workers, engineers and management held IMT in low regard, despite its market success. They saw the city competitor as an inferior factory with no tradition in metalwork, assembling parts acquired from other producers.[59] In 1961, the local authorities decided to merge IMR with IMT, put an end to tractor production in Rakovica, and reorganize its oldest plant as an engine department of its New Belgrade rival. The decision infuriated both IMR's management and its workforce.

The directors invoked self-management rights to defend factory autonomy and reverse the integration process. In 1965, the company organized a referendum among its workers. Confronted with a popular vote in favor of an independent

59 IMR was proud of the fact that it produced its own engines, still keeping the foundry and a large part of component production inside its walls, whereas IMT was colloquially called a "screwdriver factory" (*šrafciger fabrika*): a fully-automated enterprise whose production process did not depend particularly on the skill levels of its workforce.

enterprise, the merger was annulled. The rhetoric used by the management to justify abandoning the merger was attuned to the political line of market socialism: IMR claimed IMT was refusing to pay the market price for its motors and that the fusion was creating a robust and costly central administration.[60] In 1968, the factory was pushed into yet another merger, as the party initiated an even more ambitious attempt to fuse the entire Belgrade metal industry into one giant enterprise.

Losing its share in the agriculture machinery market to more technologically advanced competitors, as well as the constant changes in its organizational form and legal status, took a toll on IMR's performance record. The steady rise in the output of IMR engines and tractors came to a halt in 1967, followed by a fall in total income.[61] As the local management struggled to stay competitive by introducing more automated and serial production, the employment level between 1963 and 1969 started to stagnate around 2,800 employees, only to record a sharp fall to less than 2,500 in 1970. IMR therefore found itself on the losing end of the market reform in its early stages. In 1968, the factory newspaper concluded the following:

> The economic reform placed the metal processing industry in a less favorable position in comparison to the previous period, causing a significant fall in enterprise income. Due to the lack of investments on the domestic market the demand for our products has fallen. On the other hand, our tractors are too expensive and do not reach the quality standards needed for export to industrially developed countries.[62]

For its part, TAM retained the status of the largest and most successful truck manufacturer in the country until the end of the 1960s, but its further development had also been challenged by the rise of other vehicle manufacturers and the inflow of foreign-produced trucks. In 1954, the start of the ambitious Fiat-licensed Zavodi Crvena Zastava (Red Flag Institutes) automotive industry in Central Serbia prevented TAM from expanding into the production of passenger cars. A year earlier, the Serbian government founded the truck producer FAP (Fabrika automobila Priboj) in Priboj, an underdeveloped mountainous municipality bordering the republics of Serbia, Montenegro, and Bosnia and Herzegovina, thus creating a direct challenger to TAM. In the beginning, TAM's management looked down upon FAP. The Slovene experts labeled it a "political factory," established in a locality with no industrial tradition and holding a license suitable only for craft fabrication, which did not meet the needs of a modern factory with serial production technology.[63] In 1969, however,

---

60 "Integracija je dobra ako je korisna," *IMR*, July 1965, 1.

61 Spasojević, *Monografija 50 godina IMR-a*, 73–80.

62 "Izveštaj o radu," *IMR*, April 1968, 4.

63 Martin Prašnički, "Oris glavnih razvojnih mejnikov in proizvodov Tovarne avtomobilov Maribor," in *Tovarna avtomobilov Maribor: Sledovi mariborskega gospodarstva v arhivskem gradivu Pokrajinskega arhiva Maribor 60 let—spominski zbornik*, ed. Slavica Tovšak (Maribor: Pokrajinski arhiv Maribor, 2007), 16–21.

FAP joined forces with the Sarajevo-based engine producer FAMOS and entered into a prestigious partnership with Mercedes-Benz, positioning itself as potentially the prime truck manufacturer in the country.

Instead of aiming for integration with FAP, TAM chose to match the challenge with its own forces. In 1969, the factory signed a ten-year extension of its cooperation agreement with the German company KHD, securing foreign credit for an increase of production capacities. In 1970, the Slovene party mediated a merger between the neighboring Tezno railway car workshop TVT Boris Kidrič and TAM, with the idea of specializing the former into a producer of truck engines. TAM also extended credit to—and integrated many of—its closest component suppliers in different parts of the country, forming its own industrial grouping.[64]

By extending customer and supplier credit, the factory managed to maintain sales and fulfill its production plans until the very end of the decade. Wages inside the enterprise were 17 percent higher than the average incomes in the Slovene metalworking industry. In comparison to the country as a whole, TAM workers enjoyed wages 39 percent higher than their other Yugoslav colleagues.[65] However, the management found it increasingly hard to maintain stable output due to the enterprise's suppliers, which were not able to follow TAM's pace of growth despite the extension of credit. The plant in Tezno faced scarcities in the supply of raw materials and components from the crisis-ridden basic industry.[66] It was not only the basic producers from less developed republics that found it hard to catch up with successful final producers like TAM. The preparations of the local communists for the Sixth Congress of the Slovene party in 1967 revealed that Maribor's foundries and textile spinning mills were also facing great difficulties operating in a liberalized economic environment.[67]

TAM began to face the fact that its further business growth was halted by the overall level of development of Yugoslav industry. Even the local infrastructure pointed toward the paradoxes of enterprise-centered and market-incentivized growth. In 1965, the usual number of housing units built by the enterprise for its workforce suddenly decreased by almost half (from 57 to 29). TAM had secured finances for its housing fund, but its individual success proved to be in vain, as Tezno's local government lacked the budgetary resources to connect the new living areas to the sewage system and asphalt the nearby roads.[68] As Alojz Rant, one of TAM's delegates to the 1967 party congress, commented, "we focused on the individual incomes, but neglected collective social standards."[69]

TAM's management, the trade union, and the party organization were generally supportive of the ongoing economic reforms, but even this prosperous enterprise expressed clear dissatisfaction with the further liberalization of foreign

64 Despite different arbitration attempts by the federal government, in the decades to come TAM and FAP remained competitors with different technologies dependent on foreign partners.

65 "Ocena poslovanja v letu 1968 je pozitivna," *Skozi TAM*, February 1969, 4.

66 "Sindikat ima vlogo pobudnika i organizatorja. Razprava," *Skozi TAM*, February 28, 1969, 2.

67 "Govorijo delgati za 6. Kongres ZKS," *Skozi TAM*, November 1968, 7.

68 Rendla, "Mariborski gospodarski gigant," 553–77.

69 "Govorijo delgati za 6. Kongres ZKS," *Skozi TAM*, November 1968, 7.

trade. The import of eight hundred foreign-made trucks to Yugoslavia in the winter of 1968 led TAM's management to send a protest letter to the Federal Secretariat of Foreign Trade, calling the government decision "unique in the world" and "discriminatory against domestic industry."[70] The final producer encouraged its suppliers to send letters of protest and put pressure on the central government. The management addressed the problem from the perspective of the entire Yugoslav automotive industry, yet this was not a genuine show of unity. When speaking to the local workforce, TAM's management and Slovene politicians were fond of casting Tezno's industry in the role of a neglected outsider in comparison to other plants.

Speaking in Tezno in 1970, the Slovene party leader Stane Kavčič claimed the Serbian Zastava factory was a thriving enterprise because the production of passenger cars remained protected from imports. Truck production, on the other hand, remained exposed to unfair competition, he noted regrettably.[71] Kavčič's speech reveals two symptomatic characteristics of launching criticism against official economic policies inside the self-managed industry. First, the enterprise elites rarely raised their voice directly against unwanted reforms, but instead chose to sabotage them by pointing to their inconsistent implementation in different places. Second, due to increasing political decentralization and the strengthening of bonds between managerial elites and the local party apparatuses, the uneven implementation of different reforms was often brought into connection with protectionism, regional power struggles between different republics, and consequently the national question.[72]

A sharp polarization was taking place between different factories, economic branches, and regions. The withdrawal of the state allowed successful final producers to have both intensive capital formation and high wages, while the component producers and basic industry were under pressure to catch up. It became received wisdom that one's place of work was what counted, rather than what one did. A semi-skilled worker in a reputable final goods producer could often earn a higher wage than the white-collar employees of a raw materials supplier. The management of less profitable work collectives was under pressure to allow wage rises for their workforce and they came to depend on local government, banks, or business partners for further investments. High-income final goods producers used the expansion of commercial credit to merge with financially troubled firms and integrate suppliers into conglomerates, restricting the sales of raw materials, shifting costs to their partners, and forbidding local firms to buy elsewhere.

---

70 Staša Marinković, "Obustavom rada protiv štrajka: Može li; sindikat organizator štrajka?" *Nedeljne novosti*, December 29, 1968, 7. For the open protest letter sent by the management to the Federal Secretariat for Foreign Trade, see "Uvoz kamionov ogorža naše proizvodne nacrte," *Skozi TAM*, December 14, 1968, 1.

71 "Stane Kavčič o združitvi TŽV i TAM," *Skozi TAM*, August 1970, 1–2.

72 The "Road affair," during which the central government decided to allocate an important World Bank development loan to Serbia while overlooking Slovenia's bid for the construction of the regional road network, is a good example of an economic dispute gaining nationalist overtones in the late 1960s. See Peter Štih, Vasko Simoniti, and Peter Vodopivec, *A Slovene History: Society, Politics, Culture* (Ljubljana: Inštitut za novejšo zgodovino, 2008), 486.

A favorable position in the production chain often overlapped with the geographical location of a factory. The decentralized, profit-driven, and export-oriented industrialization strategy created regional disparities through the overdevelopment of processing factories, concentrated in the northern republics, enjoying developed transportation and communication links with Western Europe, and the subordinated basic industries dependent on federal subsidies, located mostly in the southern republics.[73] The policy of closing the development gap between the regions with different levels of economic development ended in 1965, when the central government dismantled the General Investment Fund and established the Fund for the Accelerated Development of Less-Developed Republics and Kosovo. This act was a clear abandonment of government control over the extended reproduction and integrated development of the country as a whole. The profit logic prevailed, recognizing that the areas and enterprises offering higher returns on investments should be relied upon as the centers of economic growth, while the less developed regions should be compensated through the mechanism of solidarity transfers. Already by 1963, the federal government share in total investments had fallen to 22.5 percent, leaving the decision of investment proportions to the competitive capital market.[74]

The wave of pro-market reforms in the economy was preceded by the democratization and decentralization of the ruling party and the state apparatus. In 1952, the Communist Party of Yugoslavia changed its name to the League of Communists of Yugoslavia. The new name signified an altered societal role for the party. Internal debate was allowed more openly and communists were no longer instructed to lead by passing top-down directives. Instead, they were supposed to act as the most conscious elements within the self-management and state bodies.[75] Political democratization was tightly coupled with decentralization. The orientation toward federalization of the party-state was underlined at the Eighth Congress of the LCY in 1964 with the decision that in future, the congresses of the party branches in the republics should take place before the central congress.

The 1960s brought a new layer of liberally-oriented younger politicians, such as the above-mentioned Slovene leader Stane Kavčić, to the fore in the party apparatuses of most republics.[76] Immersed in the Western-influenced postwar modernization, these functionaries did not share the values of the older

---

[73] Woodward, *Socialist Unemployment*, 284.

[74] David A. Dyker, *Yugoslavia: Socialism, Development and Debt* (London: Routledge, 1990), 63.

[75] April Carter, *Democratic Reform in Yugoslavia: The Changing Role of the Party* (Princeton, NJ: Princeton University Press, 1982), 2.

[76] The rejuvenation of cadres was not limited to the highest party ranks, but also took place inside industry. The process was encouraged from the very top of the party-state, which was convinced that the older partisan cadres were undereducated and did not have the skills required to meet the challenges of modern society, new technologies, and an economic system open to the world market. In 1966, a party campaign inside the self-managing enterprises removed 1,369 general managers across the country, constituting 19 percent of all directors. See Jože Prinčić, "Direktorska funkcija v jugoslovanskem socialističnem gospodarskem sistemu," in *Biti director v času socijalizma: med idejami i praksami*, ed. Jurij Fikfak and Jože Prinčić (Ljubljana: Založba ZRC, 2008), 73.

generation of prewar communists and cadres recruited from the partisan army. They were eager to accelerate market reforms while pushing decision-making on economic, social, and cultural matters further away from the party forums. What distinguished them from the circle of older, top cadres was, among other things, their inclination to advocate for the wellbeing of their respective republics before the common federal objectives in a more determined manner.[77]

The economic elites in the self-managed industry contributed greatly to pushes for further liberalization. The liberal coalition, headed by the reform-minded politicians of the more developed regions, consisted of forces organized along production principles, such as the management of more successful companies, economic chambers, professional associations, and trade union officialdom.[78] The latest archival research shows that the Yugoslav trade union federation often acted as the maverick of market reforms during the first fifteen years of self-management.[79] Labor representatives connected the interests of their blue-collar base with the loosening of government control over economic flows and enterprise autonomy. The liberal coalition defined workers' self-management primarily as the freedom of workers in a single enterprise to exercise control over their income. More economic liberalization was thus presented as the victory of "workers' control" over "political forces," as well as the path toward higher wages and a greater standard of living for the working class.[80]

The maintenance of harmony between different occupation groups inside the two factories during the years of strong economic growth and liberalization in the 1950s and 1960s can partly be explained by the spread of the ideology of market socialism, coupled with staunch enterprise loyalty. As we have seen, the IMR management was using the collective self-management identity when opposing merger plans from above. Similarly, TAM was evoking the same sentiments when criticizing the import of foreign-produced trucks. Workers were prepared to support the reform, passing the initiative and responsibility for decision-making to the professional management and the specialists, as long as they felt that their measures were contributing positively to the company's total income.

However, as the next section will show, the liberal politicians, factory managers, workers' self-management bodies, and higher trade union officials were becoming increasingly out of touch with the grievances and critical language emerging inside those workers' collectives on the losing end of the market reforms and among the low-paid workers of more successful companies. As the economic crisis became more severe, the lingering frictions between different occupational groups started to take precedence over the structurally-favored cleavage between the self-managed collectives and the party-state. The widening differentiation between the blue-collar workers and white-collar employees led to the breakup

77 Sabrina P. Ramet, *The Three Yugoslavias: State-Building and Legitimation, 1918–2005* (Bloomington: Indiana University Press, 2006), 243–47.

78 Carter, *Democratic Reform in Yugoslavia*, 20.

79 Unkovski-Korica, *The Economic Struggle for Power in Tito's Yugoslavia*.

80 Dennison Rusinow, *The Yugoslav Experiment 1948–1974* (Berkeley: University of California Press, 1978), 115.

of the alliance between the self-management bodies, the trade unions, and professional management, inspiring shop floor workers to organize industrial action. It also motivated workers to reach beyond the factory gates and connect their dissatisfaction with critical political actors, who considered the existing social divisions and inequalities to be too great for a society presenting itself as socialist.

Losing Factory Unity

On the micro level, the biggest change in Yugoslav industry during the second half of the 1960s was certainly the further increase in enterprise autonomy. The government loosened its control over income allocation to different funds in each enterprise and gave up on heavy redistributive measures, thus allowing workers' councils to choose freely between investments and wage increases. The self-managed collective gained control over 70 percent of its income. The Constitutional Amendment enacted in 1968 gave the work collectives almost complete freedom to formulate their own self-management structures. Along with the ever-greater reliance on profitability criteria for industrialization and the loosening of the budgetary character of investments, the workers' councils were under pressure to allow the professional and managerial layer yet further influence inside the self-management structures. Many enterprises used this legal opening to abandon the compulsory membership quota of production workers inside the workers' councils and substitute them with specialists.[81]

In April 1968, TAM's party conference discussed the state of self-management inside the factory. In the early 1960s, workers' councils were introduced at the level of each work department, thus significantly increasing workers' participation. Communists expressed satisfaction over the fact that 1,450 workers—or 29 percent of the workforce—were active inside the self-management bodies. However, conference speakers were disappointed with the makeup of these bodies, especially the Central Workers' Council. Three quarters of the total factory workforce were direct producers engaged on the shop floor, yet manual workers occupied only 17 percent of posts in this body. The remaining membership consisted of engineers, economists, and other office staff (*režija*). Furthermore, party activists complained that there was only one female member on the Central Workers' Council even though women comprised almost one quarter of the employed workers. The conference revealed that some 20 percent of the workforce was under twenty-seven years of age, but not a single young worker was voted into TAM's highest council.[82]

There is no information about the makeup of IMR self-management bodies at the time. However, an incident which took place in August 1967 exposed the level of alienation from factory self-management activities on the shop floor. That summer an unprecedented event took place in Rakovica when metalworker

81 Cristopher Prout, *Market Socialism in Yugoslavia* (Oxford: Oxford University Press, 1985), 57.

82 "Naloge komunistov pred volitvami v organe samoupravljanja," *Skozi TAM*, April 1968, 5.

Milorad Karišik resigned from the IMR Central Workers' Council in an act of protest against the introduction of a new income distribution scheme favoring white-collar employees. Karišik claimed he was not prepared to be part of a body that reached decisions against the "socialist principle of reward according to work."[83] Interviews with workers on the shop floor showed that many disagreed with Karišik's resignation. This does not mean the workers were in favor of the new distribution agreement—most of the workers also perceived the favoring of specialists as an unfair measure—but they were of the opinion that their representative had the duty to remain inside the council and continue the fight for their interests. On the other hand, a number of manual workers applauded this act of defiance. Karišik's coworker Ljubiša Savić argued that there was no point in directing grievances to the workers' council, since it consisted of people who benefited from the new wage system and passed decisions in accordance with their own interests.[84]

The white-collar and highly skilled workers who dominated workers' councils in Tezno and Rakovica collaborated closely with the professional management in implementing the 1965 reform. The new measures required a sharp reduction in non-productive costs and the removal of previous income redistribution mechanisms at the factory level, such as bonuses for the manual workers and numerous non-wage payments. In the case of IMR, the rising wage disparities between the manual workers and the specialists created great anger on the shop floor and led many workers to stop perceiving the self-management bodies as defenders of the universal interest, but rather as places of contention between different occupational groups. Some workers went as far as abandoning the workers' councils altogether. In TAM, discussions inside the party show that the self-management bodies were just as alienated from the broader workforce. The minutes of trade union meetings at the time show that blue-collar workers were aware and very critical of the growing wage differences inside their factory.[85]

---

83 The slogan "distribution according to work" was one of the central criteria for the division of net income within the self-managed industrial enterprise. Both production workers and management used the saying equally to justify their positions. During her research time spent in one of the self-managed enterprises, American sociologist Ellen Turkish Comisso noticed just how differently the two main occupational groups interpreted the slogan. The blue-collar workers primarily saw direct *use value* in the objects they produced and estimated the result of work in relation to the quantity and quality of work actually performed on the shop floor. On the other hand, the management considered that, regardless of the production strain, the product had no value until it was confirmed by realization on the market. The second view thus focused more on the *exchange value* of the product as a commodity and the capability of the firm to attain a favorable position in competition with other producers. The meetings of workers' councils were therefore sites of endless competition over the "just" distribution of income. The end decision was usually based on a compromise expressed in the catchphrase "Distribution according to *work* and the *results of work*," with the first trope (work) meaning the actual physical and mental strain invested on the shop floor, and the latter (results of work) implying market evaluation of the end product. See Ellen Turkish Comisso, *Workers' Control under Plan and Market*, 159–71.

84 Ljuba Vesković, "Presedan u samoupravnoj praksi: Ostavka zbog socijalističkih principa," *Motor*, August–September 1967, 4.

85 "Občni zbor sindikalne organizacije," *Skozi TAM*, February 28, 1969, 1–3.

Still, there were no open acts of protest, as the management had a firm hold over the factory and the business results were satisfactory.

The blue-collar workers' connection to the party on the local level also seemed to wear thin. The factory branches succumbed to the professional management with little independent initiative or guidance from the communists, leading workers to lose interest in political work or to perceive the party as a place for the privileged. The people who were mobilized into the industrial workforce to construct a new society with the promise of workers' democracy felt that there was no longer any clear concept or direction behind the LCY's vague commitment to self-management. Once an organization whose ranks were filled by peasants and workers, the LCY became the representative of the middle classes and professionals. Between 1958 and 1970, the percentage of card-carrying LCY members who were low-skilled workers decreased from 8 to 5 percent. The number of skilled workers also decreased slightly from 18 to 16 percent. On the other hand, the percentage of highly technical staff that joined the party during the same period doubled from 22 to 44 percent.[86] In 1966, around half of the party membership consisted of people employed in administrative and white-collar positions, while 33.9 percent were manual workers of different skill levels.[87]

In TAM, the party members added up to 38 percent of the Central Workers' Council. As we have seen, the white-collar workers constituted a great majority in this body. In the workers' councils of the productive departments, where blue-collar workers had a stronger representation, the average share of communists went down to 15.8 percent, indicating that professional staff dominated the factory party.[88] A survey of party members in the city of Maribor, conducted mostly among industrial workers in 1969, disclosed that the local branches limited their work to the circulation of information, without any real political influence over business or social matters. Only 32 percent of the surveyed communists had the impression that their organization followed up on political conclusions with some type of concrete action. The survey stated that 22 percent of the members had a low knowledge of basic ideological concepts. Young workers in particular showed little interest in politics.[89]

The dissolution of a common enterprise identity and loosening of the party grip over the factories resulted in a disorderly atmosphere. TAM communists pointed out that the factory was losing skilled workers who used the regime of open borders to find employment in Western Europe.[90] Amidst the consumer

---

86 Jim Seroka and Radoš Smiljković, *Political Organizations in Socialist Yugoslavia* (Durham, NC: Duke University Press, 1986), 66.

87 The percentage of working-class membership was actually lower since many party members with vocational education, officially registered as workers, advanced to desk positions or were engaged in bureaucratic tasks. See Mirko Arsić and Dragan R. Marković, *68. Studentski bunt i društvo* (Belgrade: Prosvetni Pregled, 1984), 20.

88 "Naloge komunistov pred volitvami v organe samoupravljanja," *Skozi TAM*, April 1968, 5.

89 J.P., "Uspešnost organiziranosti komunistov v Mariboru," *Skozi TAM*, June 1969, 3.

90 TAM was suffering from a lack of qualified staff. In 1969, some 40 percent of its workforce were unskilled or semi-skilled workers. One quarter of TAM's workers had not finished the eight-year primary education.

frenzy of the 1960s, workers were looking for individual ways to earn more income and take part in the "good life" exemplified by the urban middle classes. Among the main problems identified by TAM's party branch was the spread of "illegal enrichment."[91] In 1969, TAM's wider image was tarnished when Slovene newspapers covered an incident involving a group of employees embezzling the factory holiday fund.[92] A year later, the factory paper wrote about the arrest of Vili Dominc, a twenty-five-year-old worker accused of systematically stealing expensive auto components from the factory circle. Accusations against this young worker carried a particularly political weight, as he allegedly came from a well-situated family and engaged in theft with the idea of collecting enough money to start his own private business.[93] The political tide inside the factory was slowly turning. The liberal reforms were no longer associated with raising the general living standard, but with the easy enrichment of unscrupulous individuals. The main usurper of the value created on the shop floor was no longer the abstract bureaucracy in the central government: it was now to be found much closer to home, inside the factory.

The process of the discrediting of factory communists and internal polarization can be observed in a much more rapid and clear-cut manner in Rakovica. By the second half of the 1960s, the reputation of IMR's party organization had been all but lost on the shop floor. There are no exact figures on the share of blue-collar workers and professionals in the organization. Among the twenty-five people sitting on the workers' council of one of the most blue-collar departments (Foundry), only two were members of the party, indicating that IMR's branches were also under the decisive influence of the white-collar workers and directors. The party members complained that communists were unpopular among the workers, who saw the functionaries as opportunists. The atmosphere in the party meetings did nothing to dispel such views. The proceedings often ended up in loud quarrels with different groups accusing each other of political maneuvering for personal financial gain. Competing functionaries would hold informal meetings with their supporters in the factory yard and local pubs in order to fix the elections and assign their own people to key positions. The factory press reported numerous disciplinary breaches among the ordinary party members, including a refusal to pay membership fees, verbal abuse of party functionaries, and skipping branch meetings in order to perform additional work in their villages and build privately-owned houses.[94]

Discipline in the workplaces was not much better. The most pressing concern for the factory management and the party organization was the migration of skilled workers to Western Europe.[95] The phenomenon of workers using the

91 "Govorijo delgati za 6. Kongres ZKS," *Skozi TAM*, November 1968, 7.

92 "Mešetarjenje z regresi," *Skozi TAM*, January 1969, 5.

93 F.K., "Prevejani zmikavt se je ujel," *Skozi TAM*, July 1970, 13.

94 Lj. Vesković, "Otvoreno i odgovorno o slabostima," *Motor*, September 1966, 2.

95 Unemployment appeared as one of the central problems of Yugoslav socialism during the 1960s. In 1965, the unemployment rate stood at 8.8 percent, or some 326,800 people unemployed in total. One of the ways to relieve the pressure the influx of rural population put on the cities was the encouragement of an immigration policy through bilateral agreements with Western European

open border policy to leave the factory seems to have been more widespread than in Tezno, despite TAM's proximity to Austria. The drainage of the workforce happened in a chaotic manner. Workers would use their vacations to travel abroad, where they found work and often never returned. The situation became critical when the distinguished party members started to abandon the factory. In the spring of 1968, the factory management discovered that the former president of the League of Socialist Youth and a functionary in the city youth organization, Mihajlo Milićević, had been employed in Switzerland for months even though officially he was still on the factory pay sheet. Milićević claimed he had to take leave in order to take care of his sick mother at home. Letters regularly arrived from his mother's address in his home village, asking for an extension of his leave, until the truth was revealed.[96] The incident led to a further loss of faith in the factory officials. What made the matter worse was that Milićević was one of the most outspoken critics of migration to the West.[97]

The professional management had little authority among the workforce. A rumor circulated on the shop floor that the general director joked about the wage differences between the specialists and blue-collar workers at a management board meeting, turning him into a hate figure. By the spring of 1968, wages started arriving with delays and workers did not hesitate to point the finger at the management. At the end of the year, the general director described the dominant mood inside the plant as a "psychosis of dissatisfaction."[98] The senior workers organized and regulated the work process on the shop floor with little control from above. In October 1968, the factory attempted to introduce a more exact work performance tracking system, whereby workers were supposed to fill in work cards daily, specifying their work operations and times. This triggered outrage among the more established manual workers, who called the measure "an insult."[99] IMR's shop floor obviously exercised substantial power in relation to the management and the sociopolitical bodies.

In 1969, the prolonged internal turmoil gave way to independent organizing by the blue-collar workers and a wave of work stoppages.[100] Between January and April, four small strikes had already taken place in IMR, leading the factory newspaper to conclude that "nowadays work stoppages have become

states in need of manual workers. For more on the history of labor migration from Yugoslavia to Western Europe and the eventual return wave, see Sara Bernard, *Deutsch Marks in the Head, Shovel in the Hands and Yugoslavia in the Heart: The Gastarbeiter Return to Yugoslavia (1965–1991)* (Wiesbaden: Harrassowitz Verlag, 2019).

96 "Milićević u inostranstvu?," *Motor*, May 1968, 7.

97 As already noted, labor migration toward Western Europe was an official policy, introduced in order to deal with rising unemployment. However, the idea of exporting workers from a self-managed society as a cheap workforce into Western capitalist economies was highly unpopular among the public and criticized in the media. The local party branches followed popular opinion and discouraged workers from leaving their workplaces, especially if they were skilled.

98 "Psihoza nezadovoljstva-otežavajuća okolnost," *Motor*, February–March 1969, 2.

99 "Pale teške ali neosnovane optužbe na rukovodioce," *Motor*, October 1968, 4–5.

100 Right up to the late 1980s, the officially-used name for the strike was "work stoppage," as the authorities refused to recognize the possibility of class conflict within self-management.

the fashion."[101] In May, a major work stoppage took place, with the tractor department being the most militant.[102] The month before, tractor workers recalled their trade union representative as he was not "active and energetic enough" when confronting the management.[103] It is remarkable that the workers had such expectations from their trade unionists, as the exact role of the unions had become somewhat vague after the introduction of self-management. The workers' councils were promoted as the main institutions of organized labor and the task of the trade unions was to take care of social standards and facilitate self-management activities.[104] With the workers' councils and the party coming under the control of the management, the trade union seems to have accommodated some of the shop floor frustrations.

Exposed to pressure from below, the trade unionists started taking a more active stance in broader forums and attaching their grievances to political issues. In the winter of 1968, IMR representatives in the city's Trade Union Council insisted that the Belgrade union organization should launch a demand for a decrease in Federal Parliament wages. They argued that the wages of metalworkers in Rakovica had been stagnating for two years in a row and asked why the political functionaries should be exempted from general efforts to cut costs. The media picked up this initiative, bringing recognition and popularity to Rakovica workers. At the Sixth Congress of the Yugoslav Federation of Trade Unions in 1968, the delegates from Rakovica built on the critical tone of Josip Broz Tito's opening speech, in which he attacked private businesses and earning money through rent.[105] IMR trade unionists demanded the radical redistribution of wealth and democratization of the party-state. "Is it not so that individuals got rich off our backs?" IMR foundry worker Miloš Kićević asked from the congress podium. "If this is the case, and it definitely is, then these assets should be taken away from them," he argued.[106]

Speakers from other republics supported the sharp criticism of Rakovica's delegate with demands for the introduction of a law enabling the confiscation of property acquired through corruption. Many conference delegates also condemned the practice of preselecting the groups of candidates included on the

[101] IMR was no exception. In the course of the 1960s, blue-collar workers started organizing spontaneous, wildcat strikes, independently from the trade unions and self-management bodies, in all corners of Yugoslavia. The pioneer researcher of industrial action in socialist Yugoslavia, Neca Jovanov, estimated that some 2,000 strikes took place between 1958 and 1969. Most of them were concentrated in basic industries and low-income manufacturing enterprises, where groups of workers were unsatisfied with their wages and the income distribution between direct production and the administration. See Neca Jovanov, *Radnički štrajkovi u Radnički štrajkovi u SFRJ od 1958. do 1969. godine* (Belgrade: Zapis, 1979).

[102] "Vreme u kome živimo," *Motor*, February–March 1969, 11; and Nikola Milinović, "Obustave rada," *Motor*, April 29, 1969, 6.

[103] "Smenili sindikalnog poverenika," *Motor*, April 29, 1969, 7.

[104] See Sharon Zukin, "The Representation of Working-Class Interest in Socialist Society: Yugoslav Labor Unions," *Politics & Society* 10, no. 3 (1981): 281–316.

[105] Pavlović and Marković, *Od radničkog saveza do Saveza samostalnih sindikata Srbije*, 271.

[106] For an overview of press reporting about the discussions taking place at the 1968 Trade Union Congress and critical interventions from the podium, see Carter, *Democratic Reform in Yugoslavia*, 159–68.

election lists, proposing open ballots and secret voting for the federal trade union's Central Council. A spontaneous initiative developed from the crowd for the outspoken Rakovica delegate Miloš Kićević to be included on the list of candidates for the highest Yugoslav trade union organ, since he "described in the best possible way our wishes and feelings."[107] The end decision on the voting procedure was a compromise. The vote was secret, but the lists remained closed with predetermined candidates. The grassroots candidates failed to enter the Central Council. Out of one thousand union delegates, some three hundred walked out of the conference in protest at the refusal to change the voting procedure, as well as the trade union's support for the toughening of pension requirements.[108]

Inside TAM, popular dissatisfaction was also channeled through the local trade union branches. Yet, in contrast to Rakovica, the enterprise and city union leadership was more responsive to the actions of the management than to the shop floor grievances. In the winter of 1968, for instance, Maribor's City Trade Union Council picked up TAM's campaign against the import of foreign trucks and launched an initiative for an officially authorized four-hour work stoppage across the entire city. The municipal trade union leader Ivan Kuzma defended work stoppages in principle, claiming that they could encourage "further development of self-management relations against the bureaucratic structures, including those inside the trade unions," and criticized the system for failing to connect workers beyond the enterprise level.[109] As TAM's trade union positioning during the stirrings inside the trade union on the federal level will show, this defense of work stoppages was offered more as a means to defend enterprise autonomy in relation to the party-state, rather than a show of political working class solidarity.

That summer, TAM's union delegate, Jože Planovšek, was present in Belgrade at the Sixth Congress of the Yugoslav Federation of Trade Unions. In a report written for the factory paper, he described being struck by the fiery speeches many delegates delivered. In the spirit of the Slovene leadership's liberal political orientation, Planovšek was in favor of open debate. However, he was also of the opinion that many of the most critical trade unionists from Serbia and other republics had missed the point. The rebellious delegates, he argued, acted as if the trade union stood outside of the self-management system. They called upon external political forces to intervene in the internal matters of the enterprises. According to Planovšek, it would have been more fruitful to channel the astonishing energy released at the congress toward the self-management bodies in each factory, as this would result in higher productivity and a better standard of living. The workers were allegedly in control of their factories and the trade union had the duty to act in a constructive way.[110]

107 Carter, *Democratic Reform in Yugoslavia*, 163.

108 For similar blue-collar workers' initiatives in 1968 inside the party as well, see Nebojša Popov, *Društveni Sukobi—Izazov Sociologiji: "Beogradski jun" 1968*, 2nd ed. (Belgrade: Službeni Glasnik, 2008), 226.

109 Staša Marinković, "Obustavom rada protiv štrajka. Može li: sindikat organizator štrajka?," *Nedeljne novosti*, December 29, 1968, 7.

110 Jože Planovšek, "Bilo je vroče kot malokdaj," *Skozi TAM*, July 1968, 3.

Right until the end of the decade, TAM's management therefore managed to keep its influence inside the factory sociopolitical bodies, cover up the growing internal polarization, and impose itself as the leadership capable of delivering sound business results in the middle of the economic crisis. While its suppliers' production was blocked by fierce occupational clashes, TAM continued to operate without signs of open industrial conflict. However, in the summer of 1970, the wider trend finally caught up with the truck manufacturer. That year, the wages inside the factory lost the race with inflation for the first time. Between May and August, a series of strikes broke out in various departments, with workers complaining about the low wages and unequal income distribution inside the enterprise. The striking employees used none of the existing factory bodies to organize their actions and even came into physical conflict with those staff who wanted to continue working.[111]

The dynamics taking place inside IMR and TAM during the late 1960s show how, under workers' self-management, labor grievances could have been framed differently, depending on the relationship of forces between occupational groups inside each factory and their position within the national economy. IMR's management structures were never particularly influential; moreover, they were further weakened through a series of attempted mergers. The workforce consisted of a high number of skilled workers who were in a position to exercise great control over the production process. The proximity of the federal institutions inspired workers to bypass the powerless factory elites and seek connections with the conservative factions inside the party, who were potentially willing to put a halt to the reforms. The trade union representatives discarded the ideology of harmonious self-managing units operating independently in the market and adopted the language of class distinction, workers' unity, and social equality promoted by the top federal communist leadership, embodied by Tito. Despite appealing to the party, Rakovica's trade unionists launched a rather independent campaign inside the higher trade union bodies, which identified the privileges of the managerial and lower-level political elites, the splintered nature of self-management, and the lack of working-class participation in official institutions as the root causes of the economic and political crisis.

Inside TAM, the situation was different. The enterprise was faring better in the market, it was headed by strong management, and it employed a great number of low-skilled workers. Internal polarization was present, though it developed at a slower pace. The management was able to prevent grassroots actions by encouraging a vision of common, enterprise-based interests stacked against the central state. It also undertook initiatives of its own to mobilize the workforce and shape understandings of the crisis locally. The workers' recollections reveal that as early as the mid-1950s, during the debates over the allocation of foreign licenses, TAM's management was using strikes as a threat in case the federal government did not connect the enterprise with a preferred business partner

[111] A.Ž., "Duhovi se pomirili po razgovoru," *Skozi TAM*, June 1970, 9; "Delavski svet o prekinitvi dela v MO 22," *Skozi TAM*, July 1970, 6.

abroad.[112] In 1968, the management and the city trade union leadership were able to channel workers' dissatisfaction toward demands for an industrial policy more sensitive to local needs. With the help of a management-friendly trade union and white-collar-controlled workers' councils, TAM's action was closer to an industrial lockout than a workers' strike.

As the decade was ending, IMR's trade unionists started looking beyond the factory-based self-management structures, seeking the empowerment of labor through political unity. They envisioned achieving this mainly by appealing for the support of the highest party leadership, through greater inclusion of working-class concerns in the existing organs of the party-state. On the other hand, Maribor's trade unionists cherished the concept of enterprise autonomy from political authority. When Tezno's municipal trade union talked about the expansion of self-management and the need to connect workers beyond the factory gates, they envisioned that this would occur through spontaneous market interaction and along functional, production principles—similar to the business relations TAM established with its suppliers through the production chain—not political class solidarity.

These were the dominant tendencies within each factory. Still, it is important to note that IMR and TAM were not consistent in articulating grievances along these two distinct lines. As we have seen, IMR's workforce was capable of uniting behind the management-organized internal referendum for independent status when faced with politically-steered merger plans. In the same vein, individual communists and workers inside TAM who raised their voices against "illegal enrichment" and the growing internal income gap were gaining popular support as the 1960s came to an end. During the summer of 1970, even in highly successful enterprises such as TAM, the prevailing liberal view of self-management was forced to give way to other explanations, when faced with open revolts on the shop floor. In the years to come, the top party leadership would connect to these rebellious voices, strike a blow against the managers, and revise the institutional setup of workers' self-management. This process was crowned with the passing of the Associated Labor Act—nicknamed the Workers' Constitution—in 1976. The next chapter will explain this peculiar phase of Yugoslav socialism, during which the working class gained unprecedented legal powers in industrial relations.

112 Danilo Vincetič, "Srečanja s Titom—najlepša doživetja," *Skozi TAM*, June 13, 1980, 23.

CHAPTER TWO

Factory Structures and Everyday Life under Associated Labor

Reviving Revolution through Normative Acts

The internal factory developments sketched in the previous chapter show that workers' self-management was a dynamic system with few fixed meanings. A person's understanding of the Yugoslav road to socialism largely depended on whether one perceived either "bureaucratic centralism" or "economic particularism" as the greater danger. Those who considered the alienated state as the largest potential threat to the revolution and welcomed the idea of "market socialism" tended to see workers' self-management primarily as the freedom of workers in a single enterprise to make their own collective business decisions and maximize incomes, regardless of the wider social implications of their activities. On the other hand, those who recognized growing regional and social polarization as the key problem inside Yugoslavia emphasized the class character of self-management. The second group recognized the existence of opposing interests inside the factories and wished to further the coalition between the blue-collar workers and the more conservative parts of the party, both pitted against the managerial layer. In this constellation, the factories and their products were seen as belonging to society as a whole and redistributive measures were encouraged.

The official interpretation at a particular moment in time and place was determined by alliances and conflicts building up between the three main social groups involved in the project—namely the party leadership, blue-collar workers, and the professional management—and their understandings of self-management. This mosaic was made even more complex by the fact that regional communist leaderships were becoming increasingly independent from central authorities and pursuing their own agendas. In the case of concrete enterprises, the practice of self-management was shaped through relations of power between the main factory institutions: the party, trade union, professional management board, and workers' council. To a certain degree, all of these bodies could fall under the influence of groups of workers with different skill levels, management and technical specialists, trade unionists, and the local party activists. The participants of the self-managing process could enter into conflict with one another over the exact nature of the system and its implementation, but they all recognized the same ultimate arbiter, the top revolutionary leadership.

The federal party apex, consisting of the veteran partisan cadres and personified in the figure of Josip Broz Tito, performed a crucial role in the functioning of the self-management system. The atomized economic and political landscape called for a cohesive ideology and a central institution that could provide a unified perspective and act as a mediator in social disputes. By carefully presenting himself as standing above factional squabbles and narrow entitlements, Tito assumed his role as undisputed mediator of political disputes and guarantor of all-national interest (*opštenarodni interes*). The ascent of every political tendency, whether inside or outside the party-state institutions, depended on its ability to gain the official sponsorship of Tito, as this support brought political legitimacy and safeguards from potential state repression.

During the first two decades of self-management, Tito tacitly supported the general trajectory of pro-market reforms. However, in parallel with liberal politicians gaining the upper hand inside most of the republics, the federal leadership ensured that the party forums remained open for opposing tendencies, which could act as a corrective force and put a check on the power of the radical reformers. Tito used every opportunity to draw a line between himself and the leaderships in single republics, issuing periodic warnings about the dangerous consequences political decentralization and market liberalization could have on Yugoslav unity and socialist egalitarian principles. For instance, in February 1958, the LCY Executive Committee sent out an open letter to the party rank and file, criticizing party functionaries for the lack of economic cooperation between municipalities, immoderate usage of social funds, and their luxurious lifestyles.[1] In 1962, Tito used a mass rally in the Croatian city of Split to deliver a speech that would be seen as a prophetic address in the years and decades to come. The speech warned of "localism and even signs of chauvinism" caused by "material reasons" and the "dormancy of communists," with "some party members forgetting about the broader interests of the entire community."[2]

Apart from regulating factional clashes inside the party-state, the veteran partisan leadership also accommodated grassroots grievances before they had the chance to evolve on their own and constitute a potential political opposition. As we have seen, the blue-collar workers were one of the central reference points for the top leadership. Next to equality among the Yugoslav nations and social justice, the historical mission of the working class to construct socialism was a central theme of Tito's political philosophy. Workers' self-management remained an enterprise-focused practice with few meaningful broader institutions that could facilitate the formation of an independent, all-inclusive workers' political platform. In this situation, the highest party leadership played the role of the guardian of the working class.

The party was the designer of the political identity and the common interests of the proletariat. Nonetheless, the symbolism and slogans used by the LCY apex to thwart autonomous organizing and crown itself as an indispensable social

1 Unkovski-Korica, *The Economic Struggle for Power in Tito's Yugoslavia*, 173.

2 Josip Broz Tito, "Treba preduzjeti mere koje će omogućiti normalniji razvoj naše zemlje (Govor u Splitu, 6. maja 1962)," in *Jugoslavenska revolucija i socijalizam*, ed. Josip B. Tito and Miloš Nikolić, vol. 2 (Zagreb: Globus, 1982), 112–24.

arbiter could also be appropriated by workers and used to assert their demands from below. Faith in the existence of direct, non-institutional communication between the shop floor and the party apex enabled the workers to have leverage over their directors and the local political authorities. The industrial workers believed they had an ally at the very top of the party-state and this conviction encouraged them to stand up and raise concerns more confidently. Tito's insistence on the centrality of manual labor in socialist society strengthened workers' faith in the system and gave blue-collar grievances much-needed public legitimacy.

The top institutions of the party-state were well aware of this political dynamic between Tito and the workers. The federal government's memo on industrial action, circulated among the highest leadership in 1963, noted how the first official strike organized by Slovene miners in 1958 was encouraged by the "favorable atmosphere" created after the publication of the LCY Central Committee open letter earlier that year, which had criticized wealthy functionaries. The memo also directly connected the upsurge in industrial action during 1962 with Tito's dramatic speech in Split, which condemned nationalism and easy enrichment. Later in the decade, the Rakovica delegate, Miloš Kićević, and other critical speakers at the Sixth Congress of the Yugoslav Federation of Trade Unions in 1968 also tended to position their contributions as follow-ups to the opening speech of the Congress given by Tito.[3]

The political liberalization of the 1960s encouraged the ascent of two distinct political currents, which escaped the control of the federal leadership. The first was the aforementioned amalgam of demands for further economic liberalization and political decentralization, personified by the younger party leaderships located mostly in the republics.[4] The second strand came from the left. Inspired by the ideas of the global New Left, the autonomous student movements in Belgrade, Zagreb, and Ljubljana were eager to articulate the popular dissatisfaction with social inequalities. Capitalizing on the ideas of the *Praxis* group of socialist-humanist intellectuals,[5] the students insisted that the emergence of privileged elites and the resurrection of nationalism were processes inseparable from the introduction of self-centered firms competing against each other in the market. Instead of associating self-management with decentralization, national rights, and opening up to the world economy, the student movement connected further modernization and democratization to the strengthening of the political power of the working class. One of the main

3 Neca Jovanov, *Radnički štrajkovi u SFRJ*, 101.

4 In Croatia, the party leaders who endorsed greater sovereignty for the republics and more market freedoms in the economic sphere found support among nationalists in local cultural institutions and universities. By 1971, a coalition of liberal politicians, nationalist intelligentsia, and student initiatives triggered a broader movement which spilled over onto the streets (*Maspok*). Demonstrations were also taking place inside Kosovo. In November 1968, inspired by the official federally-endorsed campaign of Albanian cultural revival and greater jurisdiction for Kosovo's authorities, students in Pristina took to the streets demanding that the autonomous province become a full republic.

5 For more on the history of *Praxis*, see Dragomir Olujić Oluja and Krunoslav Stojaković, *Praxis, Društvena kritika i humanistički socijalizam: Zbornik radova sa međunarodne konferencije o jugoslavenskoj ljevici; Praxis-Filozofija i Korčulanska ljetna škola (1963–1974)* (Belgrade: Rosa Luxemburg Stiftung, 2012).

slogans of the students in Belgrade, who managed to occupy the university building in June 1968, was "Down with the Red Bourgeoisie."[6]

Faced with political challengers left and right, the core LCY leadership felt the need to abolish political alternatives and reassert itself as the sole champion of national rights and guardian of social equality. The 1968 street demonstrations for more regional autonomy in Pristina were violently dispersed by the police.[7] In 1972, Tito used the excesses of the radical wing of the Croatian national movement as the pretext for a purge of nationalist and liberal elements in the state institutions and party apparatuses of the different republics. The 1968 student movement, on the other hand, was demobilized peacefully with the help of Tito's direct intervention. On the seventh day of the occupation of Belgrade University, Tito addressed the nation on television, declaring that the student protest was justified and that the party would take up their demands. With this act, Tito went over the heads of the student movement leadership, triggering the spontaneous lifting of the blockade and the jubilation of students on the street.

After the clampdown on institutional exponents of broader mobilizations, the federal leadership adopted the popular demands of the suppressed social movements and introduced them into the legislature as its own initiative. In the aftermath of the campaign against nationalism, the federal leadership drafted a new Constitution in 1974, which integrated many of the suppressed national movements' demands. The party apex continued to equate democratization with decentralization and the increasing rights of nationally-defined republics. The federation was left with regulating a handful of core state functions, such as the implementation of federal law, regulation of the economic system, and national defense; all other powers were transferred to the republics. The agreements between the republics were reached by consensus of the delegations voted into the federal bodies according to national quotas. Yugoslavia thus acquired the features of a confederation. Serbia itself was federalized, with increased competencies presented to its two autonomous republics: Vojvodina, in the north, and Kosovo, in the south.

Then once again, after accusing a number of left oppositional figures of representing an ideological deviation labeled "anarcho-liberalism,"[8] the party adopted an increasingly revolutionary posture in public. The earlier-mentioned Sixth Congress of the Yugoslav Federation of Trade Unions in Belgrade took place just days after the student rebellion. In his opening speech, Tito launched an attack on private profiteering and the alienated layer within the party and state institutions standing in opposition to workers' interests, but also made sure to characterize the left-wing dissidents at universities as political

6 Other slogans on banners hung from the walls of the occupied university building included "The Revolution is Still Not Finished," "Self-Management from the Bottom to the Top," "Bureaucracy: Hands off Workers," "Political Work: Free Work," "No to the Restoration of Capitalism," and so on. See: Popov, *Društveni Sukobi*, 97.

7 Mary Motes, *Kosova–Kosovo: Prelude to War, 1966–1999* (Homestead, FL: Redland Press, 1998), 103.

8 See Srđan Cvetković, "'Kradljivci tuđih leđa': Obračun sa anarholiberalističkim grupama u SFRJ posle 1968," *Istorija 20. veka* 3 (2011): 39–56.

opponents.[9] The efforts of the student movement to enter the factories, and the workers' responses to these attempts, remain poorly researched. In his account of the 1968 movement, former Praxis member Nebojša Popov suggests that the numerous letters published by the media at the time, in which the work collectives dismissed the student occupation, were drafted and sent by the factory party branches without the participation or knowledge of the workers. Popov cites several letters of support sent by individual workers irritated by public denunciations of students made by their branches.[10] On the other hand, a close reading of the speech delivered by the Rakovica delegate at the 1968 federal trade union congress, Miloš Kićević, indicates that the most radical trade unionists were ready to prove their loyalty to Tito and make their cause more appealing to the top leadership by criticizing the left opposition.[11]

In the following decade, the party apex went on to facilitate the expansion of workers' self-management under its tutorship, while campaigning against the professional enterprise elites. Summoned under the pejorative term *technocracy*, the business and technical experts were accused of misusing their influence inside self-management bodies to manipulate economic allocation. Allegedly, the introduction of self-management handed the decentralized social capital over to the working class, but the managers were in a position to place it under their control, spread the mentality of "group ownership" (*grupno-svojinski odnosi*) among the workforce, and gain powers similar to those enjoyed by private entrepreneurs in capitalism. The party claimed that company executives were joining forces with local state bureaucracies, causing the atomization of the Yugoslav market and harming common interests. This amalgam of local political leaders and managerial elites was labeled "techno-bureaucracy" and was presented as connected with rising nationalism, as well as the appearance of embezzlement and corrupt practices inside the enterprises. The political turn was thus used for the reelection of a great number of prominent directors in banks, trading companies, and the most successful manufacturers in all republics.[12]

The 1970s therefore brought a rediscovered importance of manual labor and the political rights of blue-collar workers. Along with the new Constitution, the Associated Labor Act passed in 1976 (also known colloquially as the Workers' Constitution) was supposed to lay down the legal blueprint for a society fast approaching the Marxist ideal of an association of free producers. The large, centralized enterprises were recognized as the epicenters of new forms of undemocratic social relations. Allegedly, workers could not exercise their self-management rights in big units, which require multiple representation levels and invite the creation of bureaucracy. All companies were thus broken down into units called Basic Organizations of Associated Labor, or BOALs

---

9 Pavlović and Marković, *Od radničkog saveza do Saveza samostalnih sindikata Srbije*, 271.

10 Popov, *Društveni Sukobi*, 86–88.

11 In his speech, Kićević criticized privileged groups living off the state budget who acted as "disseminators of 'progressive' ideas in the name of the working class," adding that the nationalist ideologists came from the same milieu. See "Ne uljuljkuje nas frazersko samoupravljanje," *Motor*, August–September 1968, 2.

12 Prinčić, "Direktorska funkcija v jugoslovanskem socialističnem gospodarskem sistemu," 84–88.

(*Osnovna organizacija udruženog rada*, OOUR), defined as the smallest part of the enterprise which constituted an economic-technological entity and whose financial performance could be assessed independently by market or other means.[13] Each of these smaller enterprise departments was equipped with its own set of self-management bodies and joined the larger collective voluntarily, based on a self-management contract and a delegation in the Central Workers' Council. The formerly unified enterprise was transformed into a "Work Organization": an association of BOALs enjoying full legal and political sovereignty.

Work Organizations were free to enter broader association agreements and form Complex Organizations of Associated Labor, or COALs (*Složena organizacija udruženog rada*, SOUR). The reforms therefore did not abandon the idea of improved efficiency through economies of scale and market incentives. Radical decentralization and the extended influence of the shop floor were to help stimulate a new wave of economic associations from below and unrestricted exchange of goods and services, while simultaneously preventing the emergence of alienated economic and political elites with the power to manipulate decisions in self-management bodies and bring about wasteful economic allocation.

Associated Labor was to free the market of monopolies and place it under the conscious control of direct producers. All horizontal economic relations between BOALs within a Work Organization, or between different enterprises along the supply chain, were to be discussed and passed into law by workers' delegates in the form of self-management agreements (*samoupravni sporazumi*), whereas the vertical relations between the industry and different levels of the state were regulated by a different type of delegate-approved contracts named social compacts (*društveni dogovori*). The term "contractual economy" (*dogovorna ekonomija*), often colloquially used to describe the new system, encapsulated this idea of a rich network of self-management institutions harmonizing industrial relations through elected delegations which remained in constant communication with their constituencies.[14]

The main task of the Associated Labor Act was nothing less than to finally promote direct producers to the position of chief regulators of the national economy, thus fulfilling the almost forgotten revolutionary promise of workers as the ruling class. This implied an expansion of the workers' self-management institutions and their prerogatives, starting with single enterprises. Once overtly influenced by the professional management, the Central Workers' Council was now made dependent on the agreement of delegates from the workers' councils of each BOAL, positioned closer to the shop floor. The democratization of the self-managing process was further ensured with the strengthening of more inclusive factory bodies and procedures. The freedom of workers' councils to reach autonomous business decisions was limited by Workers' Assemblies (*Radnički zbor*)—open meetings with a general vote, held as required in each BOAL—as well as Referendums, the plebiscitary voting of all workers in

13 Prout, *Market Socialism in Yugoslavia*, 65–70.

14 Henryk Flakierski, *The Economic System and Income Distribution in Yugoslavia* (New York: M.E. Sharpe, Inc., 1989), 11–12.

a Work Organization. All major choices concerning the Work Organization, such as income distribution agreements, large capital investments, collective consumption, and so forth, had to be discussed in workers' assemblies and ratified by the entire work collective through a referendum.

To make sure the workers were informed about the management process, Associated Labor gave special attention to enterprise communication channels, such as factory newspapers, bulletins, and internal radio systems. The spread of information was considered crucial for delivering broad participation in the decision-making process and ensuring rational common choices. Workers' Control (*Radnička kontrola*) was a unique impartial body empowered by the Workers' Constitution to prevent machinations and abuse of self-management by the factory elites. It monitored the work of the governing and administrative bodies and made sure they complied with the general Associated Labor laws and internal self-management agreements. Members of the workers' councils and professional bodies were excluded as candidates for posts in Workers' Control. Its membership was supposed to mirror the social makeup of the work collective.[15] Workers' Control was often the institution most willing to take up the causes of the more marginalized groups within the enterprise and advance the idea of workers' power in practice.

The Associated Labor Act also revised the importance of the factory sociopolitical bodies as the main supervisors of industrial relations. The three main sociopolitical organizations in Rakovica and Tezno were the League of Communists, the Trade Union Confederation, and the League of Socialist Youth. In an effort to win back control over its industrial branches, the top party leadership decentralized the enterprise-level party organizations. Single BOAL branches were turned into the center of communists' activities, while their coordination became limited to ad hoc Action Conferences whose decisions had no obligatory character. The Action Conferences and its elected Presidency remained dominated by the professionals, but BOAL-based blue-collar cadres were directed to communicate independently from local white-collar elites through higher forums (*Aktiv*) of communists from direct production established at the communal and city levels. Additionally, leading party figures from the republics and the federation would periodically invite secretaries from various notable industrial BOALs to discuss the implementation of Associated Labor, thus nurturing direct channels of communication with the shop floor communists.[16] Great efforts were invested to organize political schooling inside the factories and raise the quota of blue-collar members in the party.

As we have seen, the occupational clashes of the late 1960s unexpectedly found expression inside the formerly neglected local trade union branches. Within the concept of Associated Labor, the trade unions were awarded greater responsibilities and accordingly placed under more scrutiny. They were to participate in the drawing up of self-management agreements and suggest the candidates for self-management bodies. Apart from this, the trade unions also kept their

15 Tiosav Velimirović et al., *Zakon o udruženom radu* (Belgrade: Privredna štampa, 1976), 349–50.

16 For an illustration of this method of work among communists in Tezno and Rakovica, see

social welfare functions of organizing vacations, supplying basic foodstuffs, and providing other goods and services that social sector workers obtained outside of the market. Similar to the League of Communists, the trade union work was focused inside BOALs, but they kept a slightly more robust permanent apparatus at the factory level, which included a Presidency elected by the Conference. The youth organization was in charge of connecting young workers with the World War Two-era revolutionary heritage, recruiting people into the party and organizing spare time activities. It participated in the commemoration of all major public holidays, sent young workers to voluntary work brigades, and financed popular music concerts within the factory premises.[17]

Being the local branches of nationwide organizations, the duty of the socio-political organizations was to synchronize enterprise initiatives with wider social concerns. In effect, most of these organizations served as conveyor belts for official policies made by the political bodies outside the factories. Nevertheless, the new system also made sure the factories were able to voice their own concerns beyond the factory circle. The corporatist order inside the enterprises was now replicated inside the state lawmaking bodies. Workers were supposed to influence wider political decisions through elected delegations in the Chambers of Associated Labor (*Veća udruženog rada*), introduced at the communal level and within the republican parliaments.[18]

These legislative bodies allowed for workers' direct influence over the policy-making process. However, they were seen as a temporary solution, a bridge between the realm of self-management and the state, until self-management could expand and strengthen enough to dissolve state bureaucracy and take over the daily running of most tasks in society. The transfer of many state functions to alternative self-management institutions under the direct control of the workers was supposed to equip the working class to take over not only the running of their factories, but the totality of social reproduction. In due time, the Associated Labor Act would replace the Constitution and various self-managed bodies would assume responsibility for all tasks of the traditional state.[19]

The skeleton of the new institutional arrangement was already put in place. The foundation of communal self-management courts (*Samoupravni sudovi*) transferred parts of the judicial system outside of the state.[20] The national defense structures were set up in each Work Organization parallel to the official army bodies through Committees for People's Self-Defense (*Komiteti za opštenarodnu odbranu i društvenu samozaštitu*, ONO i DSZ). Another example of these parastate

---

Edvard Gabrič, "Uspešno delovanje aktiva radnika komunista," *Skozi TAM*, November 1980, 18; and M.M., "Jednoglasno za novo organizovanje," *IMR*, April 24, 1979, 4.

17 Apart from these three, each factory had numerous other sociopolitical organizations such as Women's Forums, Partisan veterans' organizations, etc.

18 It is important to note that the Federal Assembly did not contain the Chamber of Associated Labor.

19 Dejan Jović, *Yugoslavia: A State that Withered Away* (West Lafayette, IN: Purdue University Press, 2009), 142.

20 For a description of the self-managing courts and their practices, see Robert M. Hayden, *Social Courts in Theory and Practice: Yugoslav Workers' Courts in Comparative Perspective* (Philadelphia: University of Pennsylvania Press, 1990).

institutions were the Self-Managed Communities of Interest (*Samoupravne interesne zajednice*, SIZ), organs at the community and republic level consisting of delegates from different Work Organizations interested in joining funds and regulating a particular social function of common concern. By taking over many of the services usually offered by the state, such as healthcare, schooling, or public infrastructure, and placing them under the control of enterprise delegates, the SIZ network embodied the core idea of Associated Labor.

The new approach of the politically-steered contracting from below enabled the industry to alleviate much of the production strain caused by the laissez-faire socialist market of the 1960s. The new integration of final producers with suppliers and contractors based on self-management agreements and long-term planning enabled manufacturers to secure a steady inflow of raw materials and components. Inside the enterprise, tensions between different occupational groups were eased through more equal distribution of income enabled by "transfer prices," charged to allocate costs and benefits while keeping in mind the fact that the profitability of one BOAL was highly correlated with the contribution of another. The market pressure on the loss-making plants was alleviated. The state bodies were now in a better position to encourage less successful enterprises to integrate into profitable Work Organizations on favorable terms, thus fostering interregional cooperation whilst avoiding takeovers, bankruptcies, and unemployment. The promotion to the status of a BOAL or a Work Organization gave these plants a stronger say in collective decision-making and protected them from unequal exchange and monopoly pricing.

The robust intervention of the party-state into the "socialist market" paved the way for the most prosperous and peaceful decade of Yugoslav socialism. It was during the 1970s that the broadest layers of the population, including manual workers, experienced a substantial rise in their living standards and started to participate fully in the consumer culture. The expansion of the welfare state and the country's general prosperity made the economic crisis and political turmoil of the late 1960s seem like an accidental glitch on the straightforward path of socialist development. The factories in Rakovica and Tezno underwent radical transformation not only though altered legislation and organizational structures, but also new investments and an inflow of young workers. The growth of housing stock and social amenities turned Rakovica and Tezno into established communities where working people could feel at home and raise families. The final section in this chapter will describe the everyday life and factory routine during the peak of the Associated Labor reforms. Before this, however, it is necessary to pay attention to different ways in which the Associated Labor normative acts were practically implemented in both locations, and explain in more detail the efforts to strengthen the bonds between the top communist leadership and factory workers during the 1970s.

The More Things Change . . .

Associated Labor helped ease the pressure on the self-managed industry to modernize its capacities and produce highly competitive goods, putting the factories in a position to continue with their extensive growth. In Belgrade, the general encouragement of decentralization confirmed IMR's sovereignty in relation to more successful companies. Rakovica's industry benefited from the partial reorientation of Yugoslav exports from the demanding Western markets to the developing markets of the Global South and COMECON states in Eastern Europe. IMR was finally in a position to find an outlet for its tractors and secure the steady inflow of hard currency independently of income-sharing agreements with larger final goods producers and exporters. By 1981, almost 40 percent of IMR's output was exported through state-run import companies to Egypt and India, which now became its main trading partners.[21]

The years of crisis inside IMR were unquestionably left behind with the help of the ambitious new government investment cycle. A major renewal of machinery introduced the complete serial production of diesel motors and increased IMR's production capacity to 60,000 engine units per year. Unlike the late 1960s, this time modernization was not followed by slashing the work-force. In 1976, the number of employed persons stood at 4,600, marking over two thousand new employees in just six years. The factory had every reason to celebrate its fiftieth anniversary that year with great optimism for the future. The new five-year development plan envisioned IMR as a modern producer with 6,000 employees producing close to 100,000 motors and over 3,000 tractors per year. Most importantly, the early 1980s were seen as the years in which IMR would finally take decisive steps to reestablish itself as a final producer in the Yugoslav automotive industry through the development of light transportation vehicles.[22]

The new orientation also impacted TAM, making the company compensate the broader society for the gains achieved on the market by accommodating less successful work collectives and introducing stricter political control of internal income distribution. Still, the favorable economic juncture of the 1970s ensured the factory continued to thrive and retain its status as Yugoslavia's leading producer of trucks and engines. In 1976, the management decided to begin a renewal of its complete vehicle program. The stated intention was to undertake a slow transition toward more cost-effective final products for international markets, such as buses and specialized terrain vehicles. The more ambitious executives even talked about the need for additional foreign licenses and more exports to Western countries. However, the increased ideological alertness and negative image of technocracy silenced critical voices, which claimed the company should be developing more in line with global market trends. The main business orientation throughout the 1970s was geared toward extensive growth on the

[21] For statistical data on this period, see Spasojević, *Monografija 50 godina Industrije motora Rakovica*, 72–80.

[22] Ibid.

domestic market, exports to developing countries, and specialization through politically-steered agreements made with factories in other republics. In addition to this, TAM continued to be one of the main manufacturers for the Yugoslav People's Army.

In the second half of the 1970s, the factories invested great effort in trying to implement the ambitious new organizational design demanded by the Associated Labor Act. IMR began introducing Basic Organizations of Associated Labor in March 1975 and by 1980 finally managed to present an operative Work Organization, employing 6,000 workers and consisting of eight sovereign BOALs with independent self-management structures. Foundry stood at the lowest stage of the production process. This BOAL employed an unskilled workforce, and the neglect of investments over time turned it into a factory bottleneck. The department operated in three shifts and often failed to satisfy the demand of manufacturing BOALs due to its limited capacity and the variable quality of raw materials it received. Accordingly, it had very little power in collective decision-making. Motor was the largest department, employing 1,500 workers in 1980. This BOAL was responsible for the chief activity of the enterprise: the manufacture of vehicle engines. Its size and responsibility for the main productive task made it highly influential and placed it at the very center of the new structure. Vehicle dealt with the production of tractors. With 800 employees it was almost half the size of Motor; however, the presence of a skilled workforce and access to hard currency, through the export of tractors to foreign markets, gave this BOAL far greater influence than one would assume based on numbers alone. Taken together, these three BOALs constituted the technologically interconnected, industrial core of the factory.

Each of the above-described blue-collar BOALs had their own accounting, engineering, and planning staff, but there were also three autonomous organizational parts employing the shared factory administration.[23] Administrative Division was the bureaucratic center of the factory, which employed the general director and most office staff (350 people), published business results, and calculated wages. Engineering, with some 200 employees, was in charge of developing new products and introducing improved production technologies. Packed with highly-qualified staff, this was the BOAL from which many of the enterprise directors and specialists were traditionally recruited. BOAL Komerc employed around 300 people. The main task of this BOAL was to purchase production input materials for the factory and sell IMR's products on both domestic and foreign markets. Positioned somewhere between productive and administrative BOALs

---

[23] According to the Associated Labor Act, BOAL status was reserved for blue-collar departments, whereas the white-collar workers, servicing the Work Organization as a whole, were organized into Work Communities (*radne zajednice*). The Work Communities enjoyed slightly reduced self-management rights compared to productive departments, but contained all the formal structures of a BOAL. In practice, both institutions were usually treated equally. Accordingly, the text will not insist on a distinction between BOALs and Work Communities in order to avoid confusing the reader, since the general account of the 1970s reforms at the beginning of this chapter already introduced a multitude of different self-management bodies operating under novel, generic names.

were Maintenance, with 700 highly skilled workers responsible for the repair of the machines, and Social Standard, whose 200 employees worked in the kitchen and cleaning units. The latter BOAL employed mostly low-skilled female labor and had little influence inside the factory. The skilled workforce of Maintenance differentiated itself from the main body of production workers and tended to oscillate between the blue-collar and administrative groups of BOALs.

In the case of TAM, after the formal overturn of thirty years of centrally-steered growth, companies formerly sucked in through vertical market integration were now emerging as sovereign entities. The new organizational scheme was passed in a referendum in 1979, which granted nine plants the status of a Work Organization and grouped them back together in a Complex Organization of Associated Labor (COAL) based on a self-management agreement. Each of the nine Work Organizations was further divided into numerous BOALs scattered across Slovenia and other republics. The book focuses on developments inside two of the core manufacturing Work Organizations located in Maribor's industrial basin, Tezno. The first was TAM, the vehicle and engine producer, which continued to employ more than half of the COAL's total workforce (6,694 workers) and contributed the largest share of the total income. The second was a neighboring factory specializing in rail vehicles and heating systems, TVT Boris Kidrič.[24]

The Work Organization of TAM was divided into twenty-two BOALs. Eight of them formed the backbone of the production process, ranging from metal casting, to chassis and engine manufacture, to final cabin construction. This was the largest group of BOALs, employing close to 4,000 metalworkers of all skill levels. Next to these blue-collar departments, the factory hosted eight smaller BOALs consisting of 1,000 skilled workers servicing direct production with tool and machine repairs, energy supply, storage, and transport. The white-collar staff, comprised of accountants, economists, secretaries, and managers, was organized into four separate smaller departments, whereas engineers were concentrated in Research and Development. Unlike the other four white-collar departments, Research and Development was one of the largest sections of TAM, employing 750 people. As in IMR, the engineers not only played a crucial role in the development of the production process, they also occupied positions in the professional management chain.

TAM's strategy of functional vertical expansion down the supply chain was altered. The enterprise was now forced to grant its partners a stronger say in the common business plans and enter into politically-motivated horizontal integration schemes. TAM's relationship with Tovarna Jože Kerenčič Ormož

[24] In 1984, the COAL employed 12,760 people. In addition to the two plants already mentioned, it consisted of: *Avtotrgovina*, the former sales department with BOALs in Maribor, Zagreb, Sarajevo, and Belgrade (483 employees); *Avtoobnova*, a Maribor vehicle repair shop with 251 workers; *Karoserist*, a Maribor constructor of vehicle bodies (291 workers); *Autokaroserija*, a vehicle body constructor in Novi Sad (553 workers); *Remont i Servis*, a repair workshop in Novi Sad (267 workers); *BELT*, a foundry located in Črnomelj, southeastern Slovenia (929 workers); and finally, *Tovarna Jože Kerenčič Ormož*, a plastic and optical frames producer from Slovenia with one of its BOALs located in Croatia (550 workers).

is a case in point. In 1980, the COAL opened its doors to this plastic mass and optical frames producer, even though it had no immediate business interest for doing so. Tovarna Jože Kerenčič Ormož was founded in the greater Maribor area in 1960 as a pilot workshop for disabled workers and carried the name of a local partisan war hero. The factory also had a BOAL in Lika, an underdeveloped Croatian region. With the significant part of its workforce consisting of disabled workers and one of its plants located in a poorly-industrialized region, the company was a sensitive political issue. For years, it had been unsuccessfully integrated with different producers; finally, it was TAM's turn to accommodate this low-income enterprise and grant it full self-management rights. The neighboring TVT Boris Kidrič was another example. After restructuring, this loss-making plant, once envisioned to become TAM's motor department, evolved into an independent Work Organization with its own interests, making the management of TAM dependent on its votes in order to pass crucial strategic decisions at the COAL level.

It is important to note that this type of radical decentralization failed to generate significant enthusiasm among those whose interests the Associated Labor Act claimed to further, namely the industrial workers in productive BOALs. On the shop floors, the atomization of integrated technological processes was perceived as an irrational move, potentially hurting productivity, multiplying bureaucracy, and making the company product less competitive on the market.[25] In 1977, the IMR newspaper reported that workers in Motor protested against the plans to divide this largest company department into two separate BOALs, accusing the new organizational scheme designers of "dividing the workers."[26] Workers in Tezno seemed to share their skepticism. TAM's blue-collar workers believed that the administration was using the reform to assert its positions by promoting the already-existing white-collar departments into BOALs (*radne zajednice*) and creating numerous new desk jobs in the process.[27] In early 1978, the referendum on the conversion of TAM into a COAL had to be repeated since five departments rejected the plan.[28] In the spring of 1980, local party cadres had difficulty convincing TAM's workforce to crown the Associated Labor reform in Maribor with a vote in favor of splitting the unified city administration into six separate municipalities. Workers objected that atomization of the city government and the formation of six associated labor chambers on the municipal level would facilitate the flight of highly-skilled workers from production into offices and increase administrative costs.[29]

In the end, the reform proposals passed the popular vote in both factories. The majority of workers were ready to give Associated Labor a chance, despite the underlying cynicism toward grand political intrusion into self-management and fear of a mushrooming bureaucracy. Numerous factors had contributed

25 Interview with Mića Milanović, March 2011.

26 "Bez pogađanja," *IMR*, February 3, 1977, 2.

27 "Rezime i analiza samoupravnih odnosa u OOUR i ZS u RO TAM," *Skozi TAM* (Serbo-Croatian edition), September 5, 1976, 1–2.

28 "Ponovni referendum je uspeo," *Skozi TAM* (Serbo-Croatian edition), April 5, 1978, 1.

29 Zmago Gomzi, "Mišljenje o preoblišavajo opštine Maribor," *Skozi TAM*, April 1980, 9.

to this. Associated Labor was the brainchild of Edvard Kardelj, a member of the partisan old guard and Tito's closest ally. Its endorsement by the party apex certainly helped raise popular support for "boalization" (*ourizacija*), even though many workers were wary that the local factory elites might tailor the measures to their own advantage. Additionally, the rising standard of living throughout the decade contributed to a relaxation of the tense atmosphere witnessed inside the factories during the late 1960s. In Rakovica and Tezno, the 1970s essentially brought the work collectives back to their routine operations. New production orders started arriving and most workers were preoccupied with their daily work chores and personal advancement. This made the decision-making process less contested than it had been during the crisis years. Both general managements could regain initiative, rely on predictable business plans and, to a certain degree, restore inner cohesion.

One of the main intentions of Associated Labor policymakers was to weaken the top managers' capacity to forge an internal coalition with the workers. In IMR, the prerogatives of the general manager were dissolved into a Collective Board of Directors (*Kolegijalni poslovodni organ*, KPO), a forum of departmental directors with a powerless president at its head. Each productive BOAL consisted of sections, which were further divided into work groups. The shop floor foremen were at the heart of the system. They were in constant contact with workers in individual groups and reported on daily developments to the heads of the sections. The section heads oversaw the production process in groups and approved the assignment of individual workers to various work positions; they were directly responsible to the BOAL executives. The task of the general director was to oversee and coordinate the work of the BOAL executives. However, it is important to note that BOAL executives were not appointed by the general director, but instead proposed by the sociopolitical organizations and elected by the workers' councils of each BOAL. IMR's lower level directors were therefore quite powerful and independent figures, often defying the authority of the top management and placing the interests of their department before those of the company as a whole.

The BOAL executives showcased different management approaches. The director of Motor, for instance, followed the party line closely and regularly promoted foremen to heads of sections, thus strengthening the self-sufficient, blue-collar character of his department. On the other hand, Strahinja Kostić, the director of Vehicle, the second largest productive BOAL, surrounded himself with young engineers recruited from different parts of the company.[30] The former trade unionist Milan Kljajić describes how workers in Vehicle were hostile to the specialists the director brought to the department, as they believed that most technological improvements came from the shop floor and skilled manual workers, not university graduates. If the executives appointed as foreman a person whom the workers felt did not deserve the job, the group would protest loudly or even stop production until the decision had been reversed.[31]

[30] Interview with Mića Milanović, March 2011.

[31] Interview with Milan Kljajić, March 2011.

Nevertheless, Kostić was very popular among the workers.[32] His reliance on professionals was balanced with a special attention to manual workers and the shop floor. Each morning, he would take a walk through the production hall, making sure all the components were there. He paid special attention to the cleanliness of the machines. The BOAL director also made sure that all holidays were celebrated properly, with food and drinks on the shop floor.[33]

As already noted, IMR's decision-making power was largely concentrated at the level of powerful BOAL directors. However, the skilled manual workers and self-management organs maintained great influence over the production process and limited the executive prerogatives. In order to prevent delays in decision-making, the BOAL directors were therefore prone to developing client networks with workers who could influence the shop floor and help implement management decisions on the ground: namely the senior workers who advanced to the positions of group leaders, foremen, and section heads. The decentralized structure and strong production-oriented core of skilled workers placed limits on the power of specialists and the directors. In the landscape of Yugoslav self-managed enterprises, IMR's governing bodies and sociopolitical organizations were certainly among the more involved, and expectations of the blue-collar workers were high.

Almost all the interviewed former employees who held a position in the factory hierarchy remembered the constant stress they felt, as the BOAL assemblies and sociopolitical organizations were known for calling out professionals or political functionaries by name and accusing them of alleged wrongdoings. It was a common occurrence for workers to place executives under suspicion for embezzlement during periods of financial trouble. For instance, in March 1981, the Maintenance Workers' Assembly withdrew their director's rights to use the company car for commuting to work.[34] Similarly, in February 1986, after the Vehicle executive publicized the poor business results achieved in the previous year, a worker in the local Workers' Assembly loudly demanded that the factory paper publish the names of all employees who undertook business trips in that period, to conclude if they were justified or not.[35] The list was never published. Nevertheless, such instances clearly show the far reach of workers' criticism and their moral judgment made possible by the broad-based self-management structures, such as the workers' assemblies.

The hostile party line toward "technocratic managers" was aimed particularly at companies such as TAM, which relied on domineering directors for internal unity and business freedom in relation to the state. The obvious question posed among Maribor communists at the time was how TAM general director Stojan Perhavc's patriarchal style of management could be reconciled with the vision

---

[32] Strahinja Kostić belonged to the first postwar generation, which grew up in socialist Yugoslavia. He entered IMR directly after earning an engineering degree in the early 1960s and patiently climbed up the factory hierarchy, spending time in each responsible position, from shop floor constructor to top executive.

[33] Interview with Milan Kljajić, March 2011.

[34] "Direktor-pešice?," *IMR*, March 31, 1981, 7.

[35] Zapisnik sa Zbora radnika OOUR Vozilo, XI Zbor, februar 1986, tačka 2.

of a society made up of independent-minded, self-managing workers. The newfound ideological rigor demanded a change in TAM's managerial culture. For more than two decades Perhavc was able to weather many political storms, but in 1975, he was forced to retire due to old age. At a September 1975 common meeting of administrative, governing, and political functionaries of the factory, the main topic was the need to jettison the idea that directors were best equipped and always the most responsible for finding optimal business solutions, whereas the primary task of self-managing workers was to execute decisions.[36] The conservative wing of the party had finally broken into the TAM fortress. In the second half of the decade, the key seats in the company's Collective Board of Directors (KPO) became reserved for the "outsiders": senior politicians from the city party apparatus subservient to political dictates from above and less capable of defending TAM's business autonomy. Yet, the everyday running of the factory was still dependent on the executives and engineers who came of age under Perhavc.

The retirement of the iconic director and the subsequent decentralization of the enterprise must have partially weakened the shared identity and inner cohesion of the factory, but in comparison to IMR, the factory elites were still well capable of establishing common business goals. TAM's efficient, top-down managerial culture survived even under the new circumstances. The policies proposed by the professional staff were straightforward and different departments were held accountable for their realization. In 1976, the general management established a permanent committee responsible for the maintenance of good working relations. It performed weekly checks on the progress of production plans. BOALs and sections found responsible for slowdowns were called out in the factory paper. If the production problem was associated with a single worker, this person could fully expect to be named.[37] A repetition of the self-management voting procedure due to a veto from the governing bodies of a single BOAL was a rare occurrence.

The passing of five self-management agreements in January 1979, including the agreement over the internal distribution of income—a regular point of dispute in IMR—offers a good example of how well-oiled TAM's decision-making machinery was in practice. In late December 1978, the KPO issued a recommendation to the delegations inside the Central Workers' Council to discuss the proposed self-management agreements. The Central Workers' Council concurred and set January 15 as the date by which all BOALs had to go through the documents with their workers and send back comments and suggestions. By January 15, all the BOAL councils had responded, and the Central Workers' Council was able to present the final proposal of the five documents to be put to a vote at the workers' assemblies. To help prevent the rise of disagreements between different BOALs, the KPO formed an expert commission to mediate, study possible problems, and suggest solutions. Already

36 Tomislav Perlič, "Stručne službe nisu izvršile zadatke," *Skozi TAM* (Serbo-Croatian edition), September 1975, 1.

37 Liberat Budžon, "Ubuduće javno o krivcima za zastoje u montaži," *Skozi TAM* (Serbo-Croatian edition), March 1976, 4.

by January 20, the referendums in departmental workers' assemblies were conducted successfully and delegations in the Central Workers' Council got the green light to pass the final vote. In spite of the tortuous self-management procedure, all five of the agreements were pushed through in less than a month.[38]

Unlike IMR, where the Central Workers' Council acted as a mediation forum for lower-level councils and department directors, TAM's highest self-management body was doing just the opposite: it transmitted initiatives from the general management and experts down to the governing bodies. The main bridge between the administrative and governing structures was the Central Workers' Council Executive Board (*Izvršni odbor*), a body of up to a dozen elected veteran, highly-skilled workers and employees, well integrated into factory life. Another important feature enhancing TAM's efficiency was the outsourcing of business initiatives from the governing structures to expert bodies. Most strategic plans came from the economists and engineers concentrated in various expert commissions formed by the Central Workers' Council. Once the professional management, the experts, and the highest self-management body agreed on a policy and presented it as a measure, which would improve business performance and increase income, it was hard for groups of unsatisfied blue-collar workers to stand in opposition. The management presented all disagreements as obstruction of common decision-making, which damaged company unity, divided the work collective, and hindered future development.

The myriad of legislative acts and new institutions introduced by the Workers' Constitution therefore made few changes in the deep-rooted management cultures of the two enterprises. Associated Labor's ability to empower the shop floor and weaken the internal alliance between the workers and the managers was limited. One could say that IMR was the prime example of an enterprise in which the legislation disabled the central management from coopting the workforce. Nonetheless, in this case, the new organizational scheme simply codified the de facto long-standing self-sufficient and decentralized nature of the departments. Boalization loosened the authority of IMR's general management even further, but it is also important to note that it empowered lower-level executives and encouraged group identity at the level of a single BOAL.

In TAM, Associated Labor forced the management to comply with the new self-management procedures. This certainly slowed down the decision-making process, but the factory was still capable of rallying the workforce behind shared objectives and operated in a relatively efficient manner. The aforementioned grievances TAM's workers showcased during the implementation of the new structures offer us a potential explanation for the sturdiness of Perhavc's managing culture. Workers were of the opinion that the management was adapting the legislation to suit its own interests and finding ways to replicate—and even extend—its privileges under Associated Labor. Without grassroots control, it is conceivable that the reorganization was used to paper over the old relations of power.

---

38 D. Vincentič, "Sa sednice Radničkog saveta ZIV TAM," *Skozi TAM* (Serbo-Croatian edition), January 1979, 1.

The actual results of the Associated Labor legislative reform on the ground depended on the likelihood of the factory managements resisting external party pressure and implementing the new laws in a flexible way. In 1979, during the closing months of institutional restructuring, the professional elites of both factories took action to preserve the unified factory party organization under white-collar leadership and reinstate business-focused orientation. The opposite outcomes of their efforts demonstrate how a different distribution of power between the main occupational groups shaped the actual content of the Associated Labor reforms. In January of that year, IMR's League of Communists Secretariat issued a report written by the internal work group formed to address the company's business weaknesses. The work group was initiated by the communists from Engineering and enjoyed the support of general management. The report warned that, in order to stay on the development course envisioned in the mid-1970s, the enterprise would have to pay more attention to modernization and the recruitment of highly-qualified cadres.

The main obstacle in achieving these aims was allegedly the lack of discipline inside the large blue-collar BOALs to abide by the internal agreement on the distribution of wages. According to the white-collar-dominated Secretariat of the factory party, the piece-rate norms were set too low and there was an overall tendency for extreme income leveling (*uravnilovka*). Furthermore, the report criticized the BOAL executives for tending to isolate themselves from the enterprise as a whole.[39] The Engineering BOAL party branch followed up the Secretariat's initiative with even more alarming comments, rendering the factory's business achievements during the 1970s "illusory": allegedly achieved in a climate of extensive economic growth and ever-increasing market demand while the enterprise failed to build a stable foundation for future results. Engineers warned of the growing number of highly-educated employees leaving the enterprise.

The response of the party branches from direct production was ferocious. The blue-collar communists stood up in defense of their department executives. They denied the existence of *uravnilovka*, claiming that the overall system of income distribution was unfair to manual work from the outset. The factory party was accused of "chasing production quotas" and neglecting social relations. The Secretariat was deemed to be incompetent and alienated from its base (*forumski rad*). Most blue-collar branches called for the resignation of the Secretariat.[40] The following month, the factory party conference took place in the presence of the municipal party secretary. The conference voted down four members of the Secretariat and gave public warnings to the remaining eight.[41] By the end of 1979, the factory party Secretariat had been shut down altogether as a permanent body, in accordance with the Associated Labor reforms.

39 Sekretarijat SK IMR, "Odlučnom akcijom prevazilaziti slabosti," *IMR*, January 15, 1979, 4.

40 Lj.V. "Odgovornost Sekretarijata," *IMR*, January 30, 1979, 4; and D. Žujović, "Delovati brže i efikasnije," *IMR*, January 30, 1979, 5.

41 Dragan Žujović and Slobodan Avramović, "Energičnije protiv slabosti i teškoća," *IMR*, February 13, 1979, 1–5.

The dynamic was quite different inside TAM's party branches. Ten months after IMR's expert work group came out with its divisive report, a similar initiative took place in Tezno. In October 1979, the communists from Research and Development tried to salvage the unified party organization from the atomizing effects of Associated Labor by pointing to the fact that TAM communists had not convened at the enterprise level for more than a year. The white-collar members initiated a special conference, calling for the participation of all BOAL secretaries and general management. The conference discussed the ongoing business problems, effectively positioning the general management and the white-collar staff as the main points of reference for all the self-managing and sociopolitical bodies. The factory paper presented the gathering as a great success. One of its major conclusions was that this type of meeting should continue and that the communists should establish better connections inside the enterprise in the future.[42]

In October 1981, the reinvigorated general management launched an initiative to restructure the existing COAL. The idea was to introduce more discipline among the Work Organizations and their BOALs by relating all plants to the same final product, namely road vehicles. The proclaimed aim of the more vertically-centralized structure was to achieve faster decision-making, more efficient production, and greater income.[43] The TAM Workers' Control defended Associated Labor and came out against the suggestion. It warned that the broad interests of the workers were different from those claimed by the administrative bodies, and insisted that the new solution must take into account the voice of the wider layer of workers who had not participated in the discussions. The management responded, labeling the reaction of Workers' Control as "high-pitched and inappropriate." It claimed that the majority of workers were indeed supportive of the proposed changes.[44]

In March 1982, TAM's new, informal way of connecting the enterprise communists, as well as the issue of COAL reorganization, were the main topics at Tezno's LC (League of Communists) Municipal Conference. France Popit, the president of the Slovene LC Central Committee, a partisan cadre, and the prime representative of the hardline faction which insisted on the strict application of Associated Labor, attended the meeting. He criticized TAM's tendency to coordinate the factory's socioeconomic organizations under the guidance of the general management, arguing that this type of forum was beyond the influence of the blue-collar base. Nevertheless, Popit was reluctant to go all the way in condemning the factory and its leading white-collar communists. "I have nothing against TAM's model, but there are also other ways to link the work of the party branches," Popit diplomatically concluded. The president of the Central Committee stuck to narrow party matters and chose not to comment on the ongoing plans for the business reconstruction of the COAL. The initiatives

42 Danilo Vincetič, "Komunisti se raspituju," *Skozi TAM* (Serbo-Croatian edition), October 1979, 2.

43 "Dvostepeno preobraženje u jednoprogramsko usmeren SOUR," *Skozi TAM* (Serbo-Croatian edition), November 6, 1981, 1–2.

44 "Baza neka kaže kakav SOUR želi," *Skozi TAM* (Serbo-Croatian edition), November 1981, 3.

of the local leading white-collar communists for the recentralization of the enterprise passed unchallenged.[45]

The two incidents described above show how, in decentralized factories with weakened central management, the highest party leadership was able to enforce full implementation of the reforms by dissolving the factory party central bodies—which were usually dominated by the white-collar staff—and leaning on the blue-collar BOAL branches instead. In companies with a more durable central management, the political pressure could be resisted and the internal relations of power maintained through creative implementation of new laws and informal institutions. The reform wave of the 1970s therefore left mixed consequences on the industrial enterprises, depending on their previous shape. IMR's white-collar party leadership was discredited and the branches in the blue-collar BOAL served as the transmission belts for the city LC apparatus. TAM officially dismantled the permanent party Secretariat as well, but the regular action conferences continued to discipline the factory communists behind the local white-collar leadership. TAM's factory party thus remained a forum for the leading white-collar employees and the managers, in which they could crystalize their business vision, mobilize the workforce, and resist the higher party structures.

Claiming Tito

The successful implementation of Associated Labor was highly dependent on the existence of blue-collar communist cadres inside the factories. In the previous chapter, we have seen that the image of the party was tarnished among the industrial workers due to the lack of clear leadership and growing inequalities in the late 1960s. Throughout the 1970s, the LCY dedicated great effort to reversing the trend of manual workers leaving the party and to winning over more blue-collar workers into its ranks. Between 1973 and 1982, party membership peaked at a record high of 2,117,083 people in the country as a whole, or 9.5 percent of the population. Among the employed, party membership increased from 19 to 26 percent in the same period. In Serbia, 28 percent of employed citizens were party members in the early 1980s, whereas the share of communists among the total working population in Slovenia was around 13 percent at the same time. Participation was evidently much lower in Slovenia; nevertheless, the 13 percent figure constituted an all-time high. In Rakovica, the number of communists almost doubled from 2,800 to 5,000 between 1974 and 1978.[46] Considering the occupational structure inside the municipality, a significant part of these new members had to be manual workers. In TAM, the factory party conference in 1974 reported that 127 new members joined them during the previous year,

45 "Ne čudotvorni recepti več samoupravni put," *Skozi TAM* (Serbo-Croatian edition), March 12, 1982, 1.

46 "Povodom Dana oslobođenja Rakovice održana svečana akademija," *IMR*, October 17, 1978, 3.

mostly young workers from direct production.[47] In total, around 20 percent of the IMR workforce were members of the LC, whereas in TAM, the membership hovered at around 10 percent in the late 1970s.

On the surface, the party's expansion drive seemed to have countered the waning influence of communists inside Yugoslav industry. However, most of the above-mentioned growth was due to the new affiliation of highly-skilled workers and administrative staff. Out of 1.5 million members accepted between 1973 and 1982, less than one-quarter were industrial workers.[48] There are no exact data showing the participation of different occupational groups in the LC branches of our two case study factories, though professionals seemingly continued to dominate internal political life in both locations. As a rule, the white-collar BOALs had the highest party membership rates. Engineers in particular were the most active individuals in political life and held most of the top positions in both factory organizations. At the opposite end, BOALs with predominantly low-skilled workers, such as those in the foundries and social standard units, had the weakest party branches.[49]

The drives to win over blue-collar members might not have reversed the occupational structure of its industrial branches, but a closer look into both factories shows the party did indeed manage to produce a new layer of blue-collar cadres recruited from the shop floor. In 1972, the Slovene LC Central Committee established a cadre political school dedicated to industrial workers. On average, TAM sent three workers each year to this twelve-month intensive education course, during which the attendees were exempt from their work duties. In Rakovica, factories organized five-month-long political evening schools for their workers. Starting from the second half of the 1970s, IMR maintained two classes each semester, each with approximately twenty workers attending two seminars per week. The factory-based political schools had many dropouts, as manual workers found it hard to attend evening classes after the regular workday.[50] In 1976, both factories joined the daily newspaper *Borba*'s initiative to introduce distance political education for workers in Associated Labor. This type of education was less time-consuming, as workers would receive readings by post and send back weekly homework.[51]

The curriculum in the political schools consisted of basic Marxist theory and the history of the Yugoslav Revolution, but more importantly, there was also a practice-oriented introduction to the numerous institutions of Associated

---

47 A.Ž., "Ugodna ocena dela ZK v minulem letu," *Skozi TAM*, February 28, 1975, 1.

48 Seroka and Smiljković, *Political Organizations in Socialist Yugoslavia*, 64–65; and Štih et al, *A Slovene History*, 490.

49 For instance, out of 140 employees in TAM's Social Standard—a BOAL almost exclusively comprising low-skilled female workers—only ten were party members, and eight of them were managers.

50 In 1985, for instance, only seventeen out of forty IMR workers who appeared at the first session remained in the class. See S. Frajst, "Osipanje na početku," *IMR*, February 5, 1987, 7.

51 In Maribor, the reach of *Borba*'s distance education program was limited since the materials were published only in Serbo-Croatian. D. Vincetič, "Završi dopisnu školu Borbe," *Skozi TAM*, August 5, 1976, 7.

Labor and its decision-making procedures, as well as speechmaking skills and ways to conduct a meeting. The mastery of political jargon was a key prerequisite for engaging in discussions inside the factory. One had to know when to insist on "distribution according to work" and when to claim the existence of *uravnilovka*, depending on whether the party was aiming to close or increase the income gap. One also had to learn to differentiate and appropriately label different strains of "political deviations" from the party orthodoxy, such as the left ("anarcho-liberalism," "false solidarity"), right ("national-particularism," "chauvinism"), and proto-capitalist tendencies ("social relations of collective ownership," "technocratism").[52]

Those manual workers who managed to finish their political schooling and immerse themselves in the political culture of the sociopolitical organizations enjoyed a stellar reputation in the higher forums of the party-state. The addresses of blue-collar cadres carried particular weight as they were seen as conductors of the mood from the working-class "base," the social layer the communists still referred to as their main constituency, but with which they maintained little direct contact. One of the recognizable features of blue-collar cadres was that their speeches were less burdened by political and legal jargon. Workers in official bodies had to understand and navigate through the internal codes, but they were also encouraged to address issues head-on. This less opaque form of political speech was cherished as the original quality that the communists had lost with the creation of professional politicians and the bureaucratization of the party-state. The other political actors that were expected to use simple, everyday language in official communication were the top leadership, embodied in Tito.

Contrary to their image in higher political forums, workers who entered professional politics could expect little recognition from their peers. Ordinary workers usually perceived these individuals as careerists who were seeking a comfortable way of earning a living far away from the factory machine. Indeed, many workers who had the chance to leave the factory to obtain a political education tended to continue their careers in administration and political bodies. An example of this is provided in an interview with Anton Gačnik, a TAM metalworker and secretary of the BOAL branch. After a year-long Slovene Central Committee political school in 1975, Gačnik revealed that his plan was to use the school credentials to continue his education at the Law School or the Faculty of Organizational Sciences, typical entry points for a bureaucratic career within the state administration.[53] As TAM worker Adolf Kekec remembers: "Through schooling, workers would often end up with an office job. Some of them kept a sense of responsibility toward the shop floor. Most, however, became

52 IMR also sponsored a youth political school at the municipal level. The classes there were organized in collaboration with the Belgrade party's university organization and topics were geared to be more appealing for young workers. For instance, in the winter of 1984 Rakovica's political school for young workers discussed topics such as religion, drug abuse, sexuality, the students' movement of the 1960s, social protests in the province of Kosovo, and so forth. See "Omladinska politička škola," *IMR*, December 25, 1984, 5.

53 D. Vincetič, "Plansko osposobljavanje radnika," *Skozi TAM* (Serbo-Croatian edition), August 1975, 7.

indifferent."[54] In IMR, the fact that the political schools were organized within the factory did not prevent the spread of negative opinions about blue-collar workers with political functions. As one of IMR's workers commented in 1986, "We do not share the party or the homeland any longer. For the worker the homeland is his work suite, hard-working conditions, the public bus, etc.... For the official it is his cabinet and those who tap him on the shoulder ... so, are we the same party?"[55]

Recent research on industrial workers in Hungary and East Germany shows how an awareness of the privileges of the factory-level communist leaderships paved the way for the alienation of the working class from the party-state and the spread of cynicism toward the socialist system and its ideals.[56] The above-quoted worker, however, indicates a somewhat different dynamic at work in Yugoslavia. In the imaginary of the IMR worker, political functionaries did enjoy unjustified rewards, but this did not lead him to discard the party completely. Instead, he identified two different wings within the LCY, the working people and "the bureaucrats." Yugoslav manual workers tended to contrast the privileges of communist functionaries in their immediate surroundings to the idealized image of communists of the past or the virtues of the highest party leadership. The popular nature of the World War Two partisan movement, as well as the populist rule of Josip Broz Tito, gave credence to such views. The manual workers' allegiance was not to the party, but to Tito and the general values of the revolution.

Tito's cult of personality was widespread in working-class communities, and was preserved through a great number of official manifestations and rituals. The central state festivity honoring Tito's exceptional role in Yugoslav socialism was Youth Day, a manifestation dedicated to the celebration of socialist youth, which overlapped with his birthday. On this day, Tito would be presented with a baton previously carried by the youth in relay races through all the major cities in the country. In Rakovica, the welcoming of the baton was a major event attracting thousands of spectators each year. The honor of carrying the baton through the main streets of the neighborhood was usually given to Rakovica's best young workers, who were greeted by applause from crowds on the sidewalks and workers gathered in front of the factory gates. In Maribor, Youth Day was celebrated with a parade in the city center, where groups of workers from each enterprise would march next to their latest products.

In the blue-collar milieus, Tito's cult was also nurtured independently of the state and factory rituals. It was kept alive through numerous inside stories, firsthand accounts, personal reminiscences, and factory myths circulating on the shop floors. The top revolutionary leader was credited with assisting the factories whenever they experienced business troubles. The IMR factory catalogue from 1977 stated "Tito's hand is felt wherever help is needed and where the obstacles

54 *Umrli gigant: Tovarna avtomobilov in motorjev Maribor*, directed by Bojan Labović (Ljubljana: Studio Legen, 2002), DVD.

55 *Žulj*, directed by Mića Milošević (Centar Film: Belgrade, 1987), VHS.

56 Eszter Bartha, *Alienating Labour: Workers on the Road from Socialism to Capitalism in East Germany and Hungary* (New York: Berghahn Books, 2013).

are seemingly overpowering."[57] However, according to workers' stories, Tito could also be critical of the enterprises, especially of irresponsible managers. Many workers in IMR were convinced that after the great official rallies celebrating IMR's fifty years of existence in 1976, Tito phoned the general director personally and severely criticized him for using the anniversary as an excuse for lavish expenditures.[58] The older workers recalled how, during their visits to the White Palace in the early postwar years, Tito would take time to converse with ordinary laborers. The workers were honored that Tito engaged them in discussions on delicate political topics, usually reserved for members of the party-state's higher forums: "We talked for a long time, face to face about everything . . . about Stalin, the Soviet blockade . . . imagine that! All of these things interested us, but we did not ask him much. The questions were in our eyes, and he understood that well."[59]

Just as everyone else, the workers addressed the revolutionary leader simply as "comrade Tito," without official titles. The veteran communist workers were also in the habit of calling him "old man" (*stari*), Tito's inner party nickname and a term of endearment. Still, the last two sentences in the quotation above clearly indicate that the conversations were far from comradely exchanges. The personality cult was very much in place and the workers positioned themselves in the role of pupils standing before the all-knowing teacher, hesitant to ask questions.

Perhaps more interesting than these official encounters were stories of the surprise appearances Tito would supposedly make on the shop floor. These legends were commonly told in both IMR and TAM, with many versions circulating inside the factories. An old metalworker himself, Tito would allegedly leave the White Palace and use semi-secret visits to IMR production halls in the valley below to engage in open conversations with the workers, finding out how the new machines worked and witnessing the work conditions firsthand:

> One day, I don't remember exactly which year, the old man [Tito] was out hunting and then he came to the factory without an escort, so to say. He came to the shop floor and started talking to the workers. The word spread and we all gathered around him. Then the escort appeared and the visit was soon over.[60]

A chance to meet Tito in person brought workers prestige in their immediate surroundings. TAM foundry worker Emil Lesjak claimed to have had no less than four such encounters. The first one took place during a postwar reconstruction volunteer brigade in which he participated as a young man. Tito visited the worksite and stopped spontaneously in front of him, complementing him for being a shock worker (*udarnik*). Lesjak was unable to say much, but this was not necessary since, as he put it: "It was obvious that comrade Tito judged people by their deeds and not their words." The second time Lesjak saw Tito was during a holiday at Lake Bled where Tito had one of his summer residences. A TAM worker was curious to see the villa and somehow managed to enter the

57 Spasojević, *Monografija 50 godina Industrije motora Rakovica*, 2.

58 Interview with Mića Milanović, March 2011.

59 Slobodan Jovanović, "Tito među radnicima: susreti koji ne prolaze," *IMR*, June 28, 1983, 4.

60 Ibid.

estate without authorization. After some time, an army officer from Tito's escort spotted him and ordered him to leave immediately. However, before the officer was able to finish his command, a voice from the back interrupted: "Let the man go! If he is interested, let him see what it is like here." According to Lesjak the compassionate voice was that of Tito.

Tito led a high-profile and luxurious lifestyle. As we have seen, workers in Rakovica and Maribor were very critical of even the slightest perks enjoyed by their managers or political functionaries, but interestingly enough, this criticism was never applied to Tito. As this and other stories show, Tito's material wealth and physical separation from everyday society were seen as imposed upon him by ambitious and opportunistic personalities in the party-state. Whether using a spontaneous detour from hunting to enter a factory or making contact with a trespasser, the revolutionary leader was constantly seeking contact with the workers in defiance of official procedure. In the accounts Tito therefore comes across as a victim, a man of the people trapped in sterile surroundings, rather than a dignitary indulging in hedonism.

The next two occasions on which Lesjak saw Tito took place in more formal surroundings. In 1958, Tito scheduled an official visit to the factory. The entire welcoming committee, with Lesjak as one of its members, was nervous. In the months surrounding the visit, TAM had launched an open campaign within the federal bodies to bring a technology license from the German producer KHD to Maribor. A rumor was circulating that the factory was ready to press the authorities with the threat of a strike to obtain the desired foreign technology. According to Lesjak, the first words to come out of Tito's mouth upon entering the factory premises were "I hear there was talk about some kind of a strike among you." For a moment, there was silence. The welcoming committee feared the worst. Nevertheless, the anxiety soon disappeared as the honored guest continued to speak. "You did the right thing, otherwise you wouldn't accomplish anything!" Tito allegedly cheerfully exclaimed. The fourth occasion TAM's storyteller met Tito was in Belgrade in 1972. By that time, Lesjak had become a director of his department and took part in consultations on the federal industrial policy. What he remembered most from this meeting was the way Tito used every opportunity to steer away from the protocol and create a relaxed atmosphere. "With his approach he gave each one of us the courage to open up our hearts and souls and reveal what was bothering us," Lesjak concluded.[61]

The presence of a benevolent leader in the popular imagination prevented the buildup of anti-communist political opposition and focused workers' frustrations toward the reform of the existing system. Nonetheless, the idealized picture of Tito and the partisan movement could be used against managers and party functionaries once workers had suspected that these local elites departed from "Tito's path." In the same way that, in workers' accounts, Tito allegedly kept dodging his entourage and appearing on the shop floor, the popular image of Tito escaped sanctioned interpretations, continuing to have a subversive quality and presenting a point of reference in struggles for more social equality. The above-quoted account of Tito's visit to TAM around the time of the license

---

61 Danilo Vincetič, "Srečanja s Titom—najlepša doživetja," *Skozi TAM*, June 13, 1980, 23.

controversy in 1958 shows that blue-collar workers were confident Tito would support all actions aimed at improvement of the working-class' status, including strikes. All the way until the late 1980s, the party flag and Tito's picture were inescapable symbols present in the first row of workers' rallies whenever they were claiming their rights in public or confronting the authorities.

The amplified political confidence of industrial workers, along with the widespread faith that their grievances would eventually find an echo in the higher echelons of the party-state, stabilized the ruling party, but they also encouraged spontaneous independent action by blue-collar leaders inside the factories. In 1975, the TAM paper reported on the efforts of communists in the Repair and Service BOAL, located in the city of Novi Sad, to undermine the authority of unnamed individuals who "build positions under the mask of self-management rights and the struggle for the common good."[62] The article described how the factory party was trying to block these "professional discussants" from self-management meetings, thus enabling a "productive and democratic exchange of opinions which leads to proper conclusions." TAM's leading white-collar communists warned the workers that the true motivation behind this type of cry for the alleged common good was the personal interest of the rabble-rousers, who tried to divide the collective between the blue-collar workers and other employees. The party labelled this type of independent agitation for more egalitarianism as "false solidarity" (*lažna solidarnost*).

TAM's press did not offer personal details about the informal leaders. The accounts of IMR's internal life offer us a sketch of Đorđe Golubović, a blue-collar political activist who did not lose support on the shop floor despite holding official functions and being exposed to smear campaigns like the one described above. Golubović was a party member, a veteran worker who participated in the political turbulence of the late 1960s. During his rich political career, he served as a factory trade union president and even as IMR delegate in the republican Chamber of Associated Labor. In their recollections, the former IMR workers recognized Golubović as one of the rare delegates in the self-management structures who stood out from the crowd.[63] He was not the standard blue-collar political cadre who depended on the factory party apparatus for his position and formulation of ideas. A metalworker by vocation, Golubović used his free time to attend lectures at the Faculty of Law in downtown Belgrade, but he never abandoned the factory. One of his main gifts was the ability to read factory documents written in technocratic jargon and convey their meaning to the rest of the workers in simple terms.[64] Unlike most delegates, Golubović actually took time to study the documents before the meetings, knew how to level with the more educated delegates, and did not hesitate to enter into debates.[65]

The minutes of his BOAL Assembly meetings show that Golubović was a constant target of attacks by a group of fellow workers who were trying

62 "Nema uspeha bez aktivnog rada," *Skozi TAM* (Serbo-Croatian edition), September 1975, 3.

63 Interview with Milan Kljajić, March 2011.

64 "He spoke the 'workers' language,'" as Milan Kljajić explained to me in an interview.

65 Interview with Mića Milanović, March 2011.

to remove him from the trade union.[66] He was accused of strolling around the factory, attending various meetings during work hours, and receiving the wages of a skilled worker, even though he was officially only semi-skilled by vocation. The most serious claims against the renowned activist came in 1981, during the street protests by Albanians in Kosovo. Golubović allegedly threatened one of his long-standing critics that he would use his personal connections in the Serbian parliament to frame his opponent with involvement in the "counterrevolutionary activities in Kosovo."[67] Many workers and factory activists usually defended Golubović from such attacks. In 1986, he was finally removed from the trade union in the face of persistent defamation.[68]

The LCY drive to recruit blue-collar members brought some results in Rakovica and Tezno; it created a thin but important layer of politically active workers loyal to the party. The task of these blue-collar communists was to maintain a balance between different occupational groups. For most of the time they offered a voice to the marginalized manual workers. The communists were supposed to argue for a decrease in wage disparities once the managements were seen as gaining too much influence. Conversely, blue-collar cadres had to tone down incipient workerism and struggle against populist voices spilling beyond the party ranks. They were expected to justify favoring the specialists when the party gave the green light to more business-minded solutions. The factory communists found it hard to navigate between these two poles and often capitulated when confronted by either the professional management or shop floor pressure.

In TAM, the blue-collar political cadres seem to have oriented their activities toward the party-state, far away from the factory. There is no sign that the enterprise maintained a factory-based political school apart from the one organized within the Slovene LC Central Committee. The factory party was controlled by the white-collar employees, who fought ferociously against all local signs of independent, blue-collar leadership. By contrast, IMR was one of the rare enterprises that organized political education within the factory premises; the factory blue-collar communists thus kept a closer connection to the shop floor. The blue-collar branches had a strong say inside the enterprise party. Consequently, as the longevity of Đorđe Golubović's career shows, IMR communists behaved opportunistically toward workerism. Not only did the local party tolerate the rise of more organic working-class leaders, but it also allowed them to occupy crucial positions in sociopolitical organizations.

Some of the most outspoken workers might have been members of the party. Still, the voice of the communists carried more weight amidst the enterprise elites

---

66 Milan Kljajić claims that these were "party people" (*partijaši*) whose aim was to discredit Golubović.

67 These accusations were never proven. The fact that the accuser mentioned "counterrevolutionary activities" as the alleged threat Golubović directed against him, indicates the atmosphere of fear created by events in Kosovo. The last time this type of crass political denunciation had sounded plausible was probably in the early postwar years. For this and other accusations against Golubović, see Zapisnik sa Zbora radnika OOUR Vozilo, V Zbor, 7. maj, 1984, tačka 1.b and Zapisnik sa Zbora radnika OOUR Vozilo, 9. januar, 1986, tačka 7.

68 Zapisnik sa Zbora radnika OOUR Vozilo, XII Zbor, 22. maj, 1986, tačka 2.

than on the shop floor in both localities. The vast majority of workers in both IMR and TAM kept their distance from party matters and saw their enterprise primarily in economic, social, and even cultural terms, rather than political ones. As we have seen, the cherished figure of Tito was seen as standing above, or even against, the party-state and everyday politics. The idea of belonging to a broader Yugoslav community of industrial workers was always stressed by the official symbols, media, and political discourse. However, in practice, this was a vague notion and most workers connected themselves to the ruling socialist values primarily as members of a particular work collective. The factory was the most tangible socialist institution to which workers connected their well-being, rights, and obligations. In everyday communication TAM workers, for instance, often referred to themselves as *tamovci*, similar to supporters of different football clubs. In the next section, we will take a closer look at the self-managed factory as a social and cultural integrative institution, able to create a collectivist identity.

The Factory as a Collective

The 1970s proved to be the highpoint of the Yugoslav welfare state. Secure employment, rising incomes, and the extension of credit paved the way for a boom in house construction, the spread of affordable household appliances, and a significant increase in the number of automobiles and travel opportunities. Personal consumption increased more than 50 percent at the national level in the course of this decade. The number of Yugoslav households with refrigerators went from 25.1 percent in 1968 to 70.4 percent in 1978. The consumption of meat and fish jumped from 36 kg per capita in 1970 to 57.6 kg in 1980. The percentage of homes owning an automobile increased from 7.9 to 29.2 in the same period.

In Rakovica, the heavily subsidized rents in social housing and procurement of food through the factory enabled workers to use a bigger part of their wages to acquire durable goods. The documentary footage of IMR workers' dorms in the 1980s shows the rooms of working-class families living in factory dorms were often packed with washing machines, television sets, and functional modern furniture. The local motor club estimated in 1977 that up to one-third of the workers owed an automobile.[69] Between 1975 and 1978, the total retail space in the municipality of Rakovica increased by four times. In 1978, the second-largest retail store in Belgrade was built close to the industrial basin. The retailer boasted 200 parking places and 100,000 items on its shelves, including 145 types of wine and imported delicacies.[70]

Maribor developed into a traffic node and cultural hub, hosting numerous regional administrative institutions, service-oriented enterprises, trading companies, and tourism facilities. Following up on the strong tradition of vocational education and engineering schools, Maribor became the site of Slovenia's second university in 1975. One year later, the city was afforded a commercial airport

69 "Odjeci o našem jubileju," *IMR*, October 27, 1977, 11.

70 Živan Adamović, "Od igle do locomotive," *IMR*, June 9, 1978, 9.

hosting direct routes to Belgrade and the Croatian Adriatic coast. The parking lot in front of TAM's factory was becoming too small for the growing number of commuters who arrived at work in their own cars. The factory paper noted that workers who owned land were increasingly able to afford new agricultural vehicles. The pages of the factory newspapers were also filled with advertisements for tourist agencies. In 1975, close to 2,500 TAM workers decided to spend their winter or summer holidays traveling privately, alongside the subsidized vacations offered by the factory trade union.[71]

Both factories opened up to new recruits. In 1980, the IMR youth organization conference reported that some 1,500 workers, almost one-third of the workforce, were under 27 years of age.[72] In the first half of the 1980s, the economic crisis caused the overall national employment rate to drop again, but the intake of new employees at IMR continued under administrative measures. In order to combat youth unemployment, the city authorities prescribed a mandatory number of interns that each enterprise was supposed to admit every year. For instance, in 1982 IMR employed 402 new workers, 137 of whom were interns, ranging from people without primary education and no work skills to university graduates.[73] In Maribor, TAM also continued to employ young workers from vocational schools as well as the unskilled workforce from the countryside. A promotional brochure encouraged all those seeking employment to come to the enterprise directly without previous notice. "Our gates are wide open for you and the personnel unit will be glad to arrange an interview," the brochure stated.[74]

The recollections of workers who entered the factory during the prosperous 1970s suggest that the open-door policy was not just an advertising slogan. TAM was in constant need of skilled metalworkers and people without skills willing to undergo the basic training and earn a living through manual labor. As economist Božidar Ipavic recalls, being the largest employer in Maribor, TAM was also the target for many white-collar workers of all professions with no clear idea of how to advance their careers after graduation. According to Ipavic, the admissions procedure was brief. Upon arriving at the factory gate for the first time, he was offered an interview and sent to have a medical examination. The following day he was already employed.[75] The experience of less qualified workers further confirmed that getting a job in TAM was not particularly hard. Anton Brezljen, a metalworker, remembered that during his recruitment the company doctors diagnosed him with damaged lungs. He was given a job despite his chronic illness

[71] The growing number of individually-organized vacations could indicate that the enterprise did not offer enough places at the subsidized trade union hotels; however, the complaints about inadequate capacities were not numerous and the trend seemed rather to indicate a rising standard of living for a large percentage of TAM workers. See "Godišnji izveštaj Konferencije osnovnih organizacija sindikata RO TAM Maribor," *Skozi TAM* (Serbo-Croatian edition), April 1976, 6–8.

[72] Snežana Mitrović, "Protekao period stagnacije," *IMR*, November 24, 1980.

[73] The number of workers leaving IMR in that same year was 233, meaning that the factory management opened 169 additional work places. See Sl. A., "Prošlogodišnje zapošljavanje pripravnika: premašena sva iščekivanja," *IMR*, February 15, 1983, 6.

[74] *Radnice-Radnici, Pozivamo vas da saradjujemo*, TAM Maribor Marketing, JA/KT, 5000/78.

[75] Interview with Božidar Ipavic, April 2013.

and sent to have appropriate medical therapy. A foundry worker, Feliks Fekonja, recalled that the personnel unit was mainly interested in two things during the interview: if he knew how to cast metal and if he owned any land. He was self-taught in metal casting and the company offered to employ him and finance his further schooling. The second question was very important since many workers commuted to work from local villages where they held smaller plots of land.[76]

What attracted these peasant and—to a much lesser extent—urban youths to factories such as IMR or TAM? The factory was not considered an environment suitable for an ambitious professional career or a high salary, but it did provide a safe workplace, a steady income, and many smaller benefits usually attached to work within such large collectives. The TAM advertising brochure cited earlier mentioned some of the factory services the personnel unit thought would interest prospective job applicants. The publication listed "adequate" (*odgovarajuće*) wages, organized transport and nutrition, housing, paid vacations in company resorts, and the possibility of continuous education. As a factory with a highly-automated production process, TAM employed a large number of low-skilled workers, which lowered the enterprise wage average. In the post-Perhavc era, the company ceased to be a factory with outstanding wage levels: indeed, in the late 1970s and throughout the 1980s, personal incomes inside TAM usually stood below the Maribor and Slovene average. Yet, in the federal context, the average blue-collar wage in TAM was still well above the median Yugoslav wage. In the course of the 1970s, TAM became a magnet for many migrant workers from the Yugoslav south. A migrant worker in Maribor could earn an income two to three times higher than that received for the same type of work in the less-developed republics. IMR was not an income-generating company in the same rank as TAM, yet the money it directed to the wage fund habitually exceeded the planned proportions. The factory had an above-average concentration of skilled metalworkers and its wages usually topped the personal income of other industrial facilities in Belgrade, ranking among the highest in the Serbian automobile sector.[77]

The wage was certainly not the sole pull factor for the potential recruits. Employment in a social sector enterprise was the most direct way to access state-provided healthcare and pension insurance. In self-management, many social benefits were connected to the actual workplace and their quality depended on the financial standing of each enterprise. As a well-to-do company, by the late 1980s TAM had been able to amass 3,000 apartments for its workforce and build two dormitories with single rooms for apprentices and young workers. IMR financed the construction of nearly 1,500 modern apartments in Rakovica. Furthermore, it provided some 300 rooms for single workers in two dormitories and offered favorable credits for private house building.

The company possessions did not end with housing. TAM invested in two resorts on the Adriatic Sea and built a swimming pool within the factory

76 Feliks Fekonja's account was recorded in a television documentary, see Labović, *Umrli gigant*.

77 Komisija za društveno-ekonomske odnose, "Samoupravno organizovanje i ekonomski odnosi," *IMR*, January 29, 1980, 4.

complex, serving as one of the main attractions for the workers' families and the neighborhood youth in the summer months. IMR operated a sports stadium in Rakovica, which was used by many youth and workers' sports teams. The factory also maintained its own mountain resort, as well as regularly enabling workers to go to medical rehabilitation centers and take subsidized holidays at seaside hotels. In both enterprises, the canteen had an important place in the workers' daily routine. The factory restaurants guaranteed hot meals for each work shift and a special nutrition plan for people with chronic illnesses, all with heavily subsidized prices. TAM introduced breakfast delivery to the machines so that workers could dedicate more time to their production tasks in busy periods. The quality of meals was sometimes an object of criticism, but in general, organized nutrition was highly cherished, in particular by the commuters and single workers.[78]

Basic medical care was also organized inside the factory circle. IMR ran a dental care ambulance, while TAM offered general psychological support for its workforce and developed a highly successful program of support for its recovering alcoholics, involving family members and work colleagues. As many interviewees from both factories pointed out, the word "collective" used by the self-management bodies to describe the enterprises was more than empty rhetoric. If a colleague took sick leave, the workers were expected to take time to visit their coworker at home or in hospital, offering help and solidarity. Identification with the factory and a team spirit were also encouraged through an array of social practices and customs not directly related to material benefits. Both factories financed numerous hobby groups, sports teams, and leisure activities. TAM was known for its mountain-climbing society and photography club. IMR organized poetry clubs, amateur singing nights, and anniversary parties for retired workers, while its sports teams took part in regional leagues. The company contributed to the publication of two books of blue-collar workers' poetry. Its library had around 1,000 regular users and employed professional staff. The books in greatest demand were primary- and middle-school textbooks, indicating that many workers indeed used the opportunity for adult education.[79]

Employment in a self-managed factory therefore carried the privilege of access to a great number of services outside of the market, which in return increased workers' loyalty to the enterprise. Theoretically, the Yugoslav formula of "social ownership" implied that the entire working class, or society in general, was the possessor of the means of production. Nevertheless, as the solitary enterprise remained the microcosm of the workers' everyday activity, there was a strong tendency to interpret social ownership as a collective possession of the respective workforce. "I treated the factory as if a piece of that enterprise was mine," an unnamed TAM worker recalled.[80] The law prohibited companies from issuing

[78] For a detalied look into organized nutrition in Yugoslav self-managment, see Rory Archer and Goran Musić, "'Not all Canteens Are Created Equal': Food Provision for Yugoslav Blue-Collar Workers in Late Socialism," in *Brotherhood and Unity at the Kitchen Table: Food in Socialist Yugoslavia*, ed. Ruža Fotiadis, Vladimir Ivanović, and Radina Vučetić (Zagreb: Srednja Europa, 2020), 73–97.

[79] D. Jugović, "Nagrada najboljem čitaocu," *IMR*, February 10, 1982, 6.

[80] Labović, *Umrli gigant*.

shares and turning self-managers into private owners with inheritance rights. The workers' right to manage social capital came with employment and ended with retirement. Yet, there was an unwritten rule in both enterprises that the children of current workers were strongly favored among applicants for new work positions.[81] The children of employees received company stipends for vocational or university education and in the case of work-related disability or death, the self-management organs made sure the worker's family kept their steady source of income by employing another family member.

The factory-connected perks, participation in the decision-making process through self-management, and factory-centered social life internalized the overall vision of development set by the professional staff, making the workers willing to accept short-term sacrifices for the sake of higher incomes in the future. In the aftermath of the prolonged stagnation of the 1980s and the system's ultimate economic breakdown, workers' self-management in former Yugoslavia is today typically associated with low work motivation and wasteful production. Yet, the recollections of professional managers active at the time remind us that the system was often capable of rousing the collective behind a common goal and motivating workers to give their best. As an unnamed TAM executive recalled: "The collective responded well to campaigns. You could inspire people to work harder through certain messages. When things went well, there was no production goal we could not accomplish."[82]

The collective decision-making meant that the management and sociopolitical organizations had to dedicate great care to communicating with the workforce and mobilizing it behind the business goals. The introduction of new organizational forms or decisions to make a significant investment demanded months of preparatory work and campaigning inside the self-management bodies, the trade union, and at party meetings. At important turning points, the management would convene an open-air assembly of the entire factory in order to motivate the workers and secure the success of a referendum vote. Once the collective had embraced the business measure and recognized it as a goal from which everyone would prosper, the management could count on periods of unity and Stakhanovite-like work efforts.

Solidarity did not end at the factory gates. Both enterprises contributed part of their total income to the Federal Fund for Accelerated Development of Underdeveloped Republics and Kosovo. Moreover, workers regularly donated part of their personal income to various causes. These included: Tito's Fund, established to give educational grants to young workers; self-financing schemes to build local infrastructure; aid campaigns to Yugoslav regions affected by natural disasters; and solidarity spending for national liberation movements in the Global South. Voluntary labor was also common and ranged from Saturday work to youth labor brigades during the summer months. The labor brigade movement

---

81 For instance, in the summer of 1983 IMR's internal control warned that the departments were not sticking to prescribed rules when employing new workers and instead favored the children, wives, and relatives of the current employees. D. Žujović, "Prijem radnika bez privilegija," *IMR*, July 27, 1983, 2.

82 Labović, *Umrli gigant.*

lost its economic significance after the introduction of self-management. Still, the youth camps engaged in brigade work were kept as symbolic places where youth from various parts of the country and different social backgrounds could come together and socialize in the communist spirit of joint work and camaraderie.

The yearly work rhythm revolved around a series of state holidays commemorated inside the factories. Like the aforementioned Youth Day, most of the holidays were connected to the great events of the partisan struggle and the ruling ideology. The heroic endeavors of the partisan forces during World War Two were related to the willingness of new generations of workers to make sacrifices for the further modernization of industry. In 1971, the celebration of TAM's twenty-fifth anniversary emulated a military parade, with workers of different crafts and work units marching and saluting beneath a podium filled with party dignitaries and other honored guests. At the same time, the evening program was styled in the fashion of a television quiz show, with workers answering trivia questions about company history and winning prizes. This idiosyncratic mixture—a formal march of workers displaying their tools and symbols of socialism before the party functionaries in the morning, and a commercial spectacle with consumer goods offered as prizes in the evening—is paradigmatic for the eclectic nature of Yugoslav socialism. The actual content of celebrations, even when commemorating important ideological dates, was often carefree for the most part and oriented to socialization through having fun.

A self-managed factory was usually the sponsor of many cultural institutions in the wider community, such as theaters and dance groups, which in return held free events for the workers and their families. The Belgrade Film Festival organized special screenings of the latest Hollywood blockbusters and European cinema inside Rakovica's factories. TAM's celebration of International Women's Day (March 8) in 1988 is a good example of how socialist form was combined with commercial content and Western-influenced consumer and pop culture. The central celebration took place in one of the production halls, where machines were cleared to make room for a fashion runway. The event started with a talk about women's role in socialist society and the struggle for female emancipation, delivered by the president of the factory party organization. The program then continued with a fashion show featuring the latest designs of the Slovene textile and jewelry industry. The pinnacle of the evening was the tongue-in-cheek performance of a television star, Biljana Ristić. "A singer, imitator, entertainer and, above all, an extraordinary beauty," as the factory paper described her, she exited the television screen and entered the production hall, performing exclusively for TAM's female workers. Their wages may have lagged behind those of the downtown white-collar companies, but events such as these made the workers feel that they mattered and that society appreciated their hard work.[83]

The corporatist culture of Yugoslav industry was most potent in the periods of prolonged economic growth and political stability, when members of all occupational groups within the enterprise could connect their personal well-being

83 Danilo Vincetič, "Biljana in manekenke so ogreli srca in dlani," *Skozi TAM*, March 11, 1988, 3.

with the progress of the company. The 1970s were an exceptional decade in this regard, but even at the peak of general welfare, many industrial enterprises still had to appeal to self-sacrifice and deal with internal rifts. The picture of a united, social service-providing factory sketched in this section intentionally overlooked inconsistencies in order to point out the collectivizing power of workers' self-management. Descriptions of this type can be encountered in factory brochures of the time and nostalgic recollections of former employees today. In contrast, the following chapter will magnify the multifaceted cleavages present inside the observed factories. It will explain the ever-persisting friction between the white-collar office employees and the shop floor workers, as well as the complex divisions among the blue-collar workers based on skill, gender, generation, place of origin, and connection to the countryside.

CHAPTER THREE

Shades of Blue-Collar Workers

Proletariat in the Making

On paper, all members of a single work collective had equal access to social property and factory-based benefits. In practice, however, the distribution of company-provided goods and services was skewed in favor of workers with more qualifications, better earnings, and a higher position in the factory hierarchy. The allocation of social housing was a prime example of locally-generated inequalities. As with all other socially-owned property, the company apartments were supposed to be built and allocated based on need. Workers' assemblies approved the general plans for future investment in housing. Workers' councils elected housing commissions, which were in charge of maintaining the apartment waiting lists. The criteria for placing individual workers on the list included living conditions, work qualifications, seniority, health, family status, and so forth. However, the housing development budgets were chronically underfunded, and the construction plans rarely fulfilled. Moreover, one category of apartments was legally allowed to be allocated outside of the self-management procedures. These were the so-called "cadre apartments," used to attract skilled workers and professionals to the factory. As the industrial enterprises were constantly short of a qualified workforce, the distribution of cadre apartments became standard procedure and prolonged the waiting time for ordinary candidates.

In 1979, one third of IMR's workforce had an unresolved housing situation. The average waiting period for a socially-owned apartment in Belgrade was around fifteen years. Following the regular procedures, IMR workers could therefore expect to spend a good part of their working age on the waiting lists before having a chance to move into one of the modern high-rises.[1] The average waiting time for a socially-owned flat in Maribor was somewhat better: it ranged between five and ten years. During the 1970s, TAM bought some 100 flats per year on average. Still, the annual demand was three times higher.[2] Most of the senior workers had already managed to settle down over the years with the help of company-acquired apartments or individually-built houses. The waiting lists were typically filled with younger workers, but also long-time employees with lower qualifications and inadequate living conditions.

---

1 V. Andrejić, "Omladinci IMR-a o problemima stanovanja: nužni smeštaj kao san," *IMR*, January 15, 1979, 3.

2 "Srednjeročni plan ZDV u javnoj raspravi," *Skozi TAM* (Serbo-Croatian edition), October 1976, 6.

The great majority of young recruits arriving from other parts of the country had to rent a room on the free market. In 1979, the monthly rental price of a single room in Belgrade was around 2,000 dinars, while the average blue-collar wage in IMR amounted to 5,400 dinars. In other words, low paid workers without secured factory lodgings had to spend close to one-half of their monthly wages merely to live as subtenants in other people's apartments and houses. This type of accommodation was highly unpopular among younger workers. In addition to the high prices, they often complained about the bossy behavior of landlords and the fact that they were not able to have an intimate space or start a family.[3]

The alternative was to obtain a room in the company-owned dorms. This type of lodging was up to five times cheaper than renting rooms in private homes and was therefore in high demand. Still, the dorm tenants often complained about the unsatisfactory living conditions and the absence of house rules. In January 1979, TAM's youth organization organized a special conference dedicated to problems in company dorms. The speakers pointed out that the dorms had no space for collective activities, the heating and hygiene were poor, and people found ways to move in although they were not employed at the factory.[4] In IMR's dorms, many tenants continued to occupy rooms years after they had left the factory, and residents were notoriously late with rents.[5] The dorms were supposed to serve as short-term lodging for apprentices and young single workers until they found a more permanent solution. However, due to the scarcity of housing stock, many older workers with families lived in dorms as well. It was not uncommon for a working-class family to organize their daily chores in single rooms. On average there was one toilet serving thirty residents. Entire families slept, cooked, and spent their free time in the same nine-to-twelve square meter space.[6] What was supposedly a temporary solution would often turn out to be a long-term home in which the children grew up and their parents became pensioners.

Those IMR workers who decided to take the initiative and build their own houses usually lived in the "wild settlements" concentrated around the city. The more peripheral parts of Rakovica were sites of unplanned, semi-rural neighborhoods, which often lacked asphalt roads and a proper sewage system. These informal neighborhoods had rural features, and many residents supplemented their income with private farming. However, the agricultural work performed there was closer to garden cultivation and the possession of a few smaller domestic animals, rather than farming on proper plots of land or maintenance of animal barns. The peripheral settlements were not traditional villages, but improvised extensions of the city. Although built illegally, in practice the city authorities were forced to accept these settlements as parts of various

3 D. Kordulup, "Omladinske novine o mladima u IMR: Metla umesto struga," *IMR*, February 28, 1983, 4.

4 D. Vincetič, "Problemska konferencija o samačkim domovima," *Skozi TAM* (Serbo-Croatian edition), January 1979, 3.

5 D. Kordulup, "U samačkom hotelu: može i besplatno!," *IMR*, November 23, 1982, 2.

6 The organization of everyday life in dorms was presented especially well in the documentary film *Žulj*, shot in 1986, which focused on IMR workers.

Belgrade municipalities, and public transportation usually connected them with more centrally located neighborhoods.

A detailed description of the life of a migrant worker, published in the IMR factory newspaper, offers an insight into the living conditions of many blue-collar workers at the time. Milovan Čolaković arrived in Rakovica from Kosovo. After years of renting a room, he managed to build a house of his own in a village on the outskirts of Belgrade. The house was not complete and different parts were added each year. Milovan, his wife, and their two children occupied the first floor. The second floor was left for his mother and younger brother.[7] The family could not afford a car and depended on a place in the company-owned mountain resort for taking their holidays. Many foodstuffs for the household were obtained at subsidized prices through the trade union. Although the article does not mention it, Milovan, like many of his colleagues, probably also raised domestic animals and obtained vegetables from his own garden.

Workers who decided to build a private house frequently found themselves caught in a legal limbo, with reduced access to city- and factory-provided services. The residents of these "wild settlements" expected the city authorities to urbanize their communities further. Many workers who lived in inadequate conditions hoped the enterprise would enable them to escape their informal status and move into new, modern flats in other locations. A reader's letter published in the IMR factory paper described the case of Dragoljub Nešić, a low-skilled foundry worker with a work disability employed in the factory since the mid-1950s. Over the years, Nešić had built a house in a village near Rakovica where he resided with his wife and two children. He asked the company to grant him a housing credit in order to complete the house and connect his household to the public infrastructure, but the Foundry BOAL workers' council declined his request because the house had been built without proper authorization from the communal authorities. The petitioner then asked to be granted adequate housing in social property. With his seniority, work-related disability, and family status, Nešić was a strong candidate for a company apartment. Nevertheless, since he already had a house, the workers' council considered his case solved and his name was taken off the apartment waiting list.[8]

The border between Maribor and its countryside was less contested. TAM used the liberalization of the mid-1960s to complement investments into socially-owned apartments with credits for individual house construction. Unlike Belgrade, where a flat in a high-rise continued to be symbolic of a modern lifestyle and urban sophistication preferred to the surrounding rural existence, the villages around Slovene cities evolved into suburban settlements consisting of single-family houses whose residents commuted to nearby urban centers by car.[9] The pressure on the TAM housing stock was also eased by the presence of peasant workers. A large percentage of TAM's workers escaped the precariousness of the wild settlements and company dorms by never leaving their home villages.

---

7 "Ruke za dva takta," *IMR*, June 6, 1989, 6.

8 Toma Jeremić, "Imaš kuću-nemaš ništa," *IMR*, April 12, 1983, 7.

9 James Gow and Cathie Carmichael, *Slovenia and the Slovenes: A Small State and the New Europe* (London: Hurst & Company, 2000), 131.

Workers from the more distant villages were engaged in full-scale farming activities and undertook daily trips to Tezno without having to leave their family plot permanently.

TAM was the nearest large social-sector employer for the entire agricultural region of Međumurje, extending some fifty kilometers east and south of Maribor toward the borders with Hungary and Croatia. Thirty-nine factory buses and two hired train carriages supported the daily transport of the rural workforce to the factory. The larger villages had up to four buses departing for TAM in the morning, two in the afternoon, and one for the evening shift. In order to reach the factory, workers from smaller and more remote villages had to wake up in the middle of the night and walk for up to an hour to the nearest village that was visited by a factory-organized morning bus. These "semi-proletarians" would then travel up to two additional hours to work, collecting workers from other villages on the way to Tezno.[10]

Figure 1. A peasant worker with one foot in the factory and the other in the field, cartoon in *IMR,* April 15, 1980, 2

The examples above show how three decades after the introduction of workers' self-management, a significant proportion of the Yugoslav industrial workforce still did not constitute the settled urban proletariat that the ruling ideology saw as the ideal subject for constructing socialism. The larger industrial plants were usually located on the outskirts of the cities, bordering the nearby villages. This placement was symbolic. Ultimately, the factories failed to become the well-established locus of new urban social relations, but they did serve as a bridge between the surrounding countryside and the middle-class downtown communities. Associated Labor was supposed to return the working class and its

[10] The stories of these peasant workers were caught on camera in the documentary Labović, *Umrli gigant.*

institutions to the center of the political, social, and cultural development of Yugoslav society. Yet, for many workers the factory was a place where they could obtain a fixed income in addition to their land cultivation, or a mere stepping-stone for other, less physically demanding and better-valued jobs in the city. The low wage levels and scarcity of enterprise-provided services meant the industrial enterprises had few means to keep the arriving young migrant workers from the countryside fully attached to the factory.

The factory-derived income was often complemented with unregistered jobs in the city. It is hard to uncover the true scope of this practice, but oral interviews and records of disciplinary breaches give the impression that moonlighting was widespread. Informal work ranged from house repair services to smuggling scarce consumer goods from abroad. The factory was often used as a base for private business ventures, where individuals had access to work tools and a network of customers. Workers found numerous ways to smuggle materials into the factory and use the machines to perform work or conduct repairs for private purposes. In December 1981, the IMR self-management control told of groups of workers leaving their posts in order to participate in the official sales of redundant tools and machinery in the factory yard. The sale items were reportedly greatly underpriced and included brand new pieces not appropriate for sale.[11] In the production halls, parallel food and beverage services were flourishing. The Social Standard female workers prepared and sold coffee to production workers next to their machines. The paper reported that these informal coffee stalls also offered fried fish and snacks.[12] At the other end of the factory, the white-collar offices would often turn into showcase spaces where informal sellers offered books, foreign clothing, or foodstuffs from the countryside.

Worker turnover was another great problem for both factories. After repaying the company-sponsored stipend obtained during their vocational schooling, many workers left the factory altogether for other companies which offered higher wages. In the mid-1970s, the labor turnover rate in TAM as a whole was around 15 percent; in some BOALs, it reached the alarming rate of 30 percent.[13] The factory paper caricaturists joked that a rotating door at the front of the factory would serve the workers' needs much better than the entrance gate. The local party organization concluded that most workers were leaving because of tough work conditions, low wages, and bad coworker relations.[14] Between 1979 and 1982, the turnover rate in IMR ranged from seven to ten percent.[15] The turnover was certainly lower than in Tezno, where many peasant workers oscillated between Maribor and its countryside. Still, there was a worrying trend of skilled workers leaving the factory for companies with better standing in the city. In April 1981, Motor reported that 100 qualified workers had left the

11 D. Žujović, "O slučaju 'otpadnog materijala'," *IMR*, November 24, 1981, 5.

12 Momčilo Šćekić, "Pisma čitalaca: kafenisanje," *IMR*, February 16, 1978, 10.

13 "Srednjoročni plan ZDV (1976–1980) u javnoj razpravi," *Skozi TAM* (Serbo-Croatian edition), October 1976, 4.

14 Danilo Vincetič, "Jedinstvena sindikalna organizacija," *Skozi TAM* (Serbo-Croatian edition), May 1975, 3.

15 S. Avramović, "Smanjeni odlasci iz fabrike," *IMR*, April 26, 1983, 4.

BOAL, claiming that production might come to a standstill if an additional fifty skilled blue-collar workers decided to vacate their work places.[16]

For the factory management, those workers who stayed inside the factory but regarded it as a place to make additional income may have been more of a problem than those who left altogether, since these "semi-proletarians" contributed to undermine discipline on the shop floor. The "peasant workers" were certainly the largest group among them. This layer of blue-collar workers continued to reside in the villages and tended to neglect their shop floor responsibilities in favor of farmwork. One of the main ways to gain free time for farming on private plots was the liberal use of sick leave. In the course of the 1970s, TAM's management formed sick leave control units. Factory teams would pay random visits to the homes of allegedly sick workers, only to find them in the field instead of in bed. If the control unit discovered that the doctor's note had been forged, the perpetrator risked losing their right to a part of the sick leave money, but this did not significantly decrease sick leave figures.[17]

As already noted, the residents of the nearby villages spent up to two hours commuting and bus timetables always tightly matched the end of each shift. In 1975, TAM's factory paper complained that each day, a few hundred workers would gather in front of the factory gate trying to exit half an hour before the official end of their work hours and gain some time for personal affairs in the city before returning home. The wave of people would often push against the factory security and scream insults at the door attendants.[18] In Rakovica, in late 1981, the IMR management estimated that some 600 out of 4,800 workers were absent from work each day. Of this number, 495 people were on sick leave.[19] The rise in sick leave during certain months was closely related to the seasonal rhythm of work in the field.[20]

In an effort to introduce more discipline on the shop floor, TAM's management ordered that no one was allowed to exit the factory gate during work hours without written permission signed by the foreman. In spite of this, people always found ways to exit the enterprise premises and use their work hours to shop in the city or visit the nearby pubs.[21] Most of the time, therefore, the workday was cut short; but when there was enough processing material, and wages could be augmented through additional work, the management complained that workers stayed on single machines for too long. The foremen turned a blind eye on workers extending their shift hours in order to fulfill the individual output targets. The materials were applied in a wasteful manner, while machines were damaged by careless use and efforts to exceed the norms in the shortest possible time. The white-collar employees showed a similar lack of conscientious

16 L.V., "Proizvodnja sve manja," *IMR*, June 17, 1981, 5.

17 Interview with Branko Gerlič, April 2013.

18 Liberat Buždon, "Razrastanje nediscipline treba obuzdati," *Skozi TAM* (Serbo-Croatian edition), November 1975, 7.

19 D. Žujović, "Odvojiti rad od nerada," *IMR*, October 6, 1981, 3.

20 S. Frajst, "Umesto posla na njivu," *IMR*, June 12, 1984, 7.

21 Liberat Buždon, "Razrastanje nediscipline treba obuzdati," *Skozi TAM* (Serbo-Croatian edition), November 1975, 7.

work practices. In August 1976, the self-management control discovered the purchasing department had ordered a whole shipment of expensive tires that were incompatible with TAM's vehicles.[22] The misappropriation of factory property added significantly to the general feeling of neglect. In 1975, TAM's self-management control stated that toilets were often found with missing sanitation elements, while the canteen reported more than 3,000 eating utensils stolen in just one year.[23]

The disciplinary breaches at IMR were very similar to those already described at TAM. Workers would consume alcohol at work, jump over the factory fence to conduct personal business in the city, steal telephones, and so forth. Social Standard considered employing guards at the canteen entrance due to the widespread theft of kitchen utensils. The idea was abandoned, since the practice of workers being searched upon finishing their lunch would have been humiliating for the individual workers and the self-managed factory as a whole.[24] In 1979, the disciplinary commission handled 300 cases of breaches, most of them dealing with theft of factory property, brawls, alcoholism, refusal to obey the foremen, and leaving the workplace without permission. In total thirty-seven workers were fired, twenty-three were given financial penalties, and nineteen were issued public warnings. In other instances, the perpetrators faced no consequences.[25] The communists were supposed to set an example for other workers with their work efforts and conduct, but, in 1984, the trade union stated that 15 percent of the IMR communists were also implicated in disciplinary offenses.[26]

The careless attitude exhibited by parts of the workforce, and even members of the sociopolitical organizations, frustrated leading workers in the governing structures. This type of behavior went against the preconception of solidary social relations, which were supposed to flourish in a self-managed society. Many influential members of both enterprises believed that sanctions were not the best way to fight negligence and that the communists and leading self-managers should appeal to workers' awareness instead. "Where is the self-management consciousness?" was the question often posed in a desperate tone by the factory papers. Calls to treat social property with care constantly circled around the factories. The tone of the TAM newspaper reveals the level of frustration with the persistent devastation of factory tools: as one journalist asked, "Why such an attitude? Do we handle private property at our own house in the same way... do we use measuring instruments instead of sledgehammers, do we start cars with screwdrivers instead of keys... do we intentionally destroy what we created?"[27]

22 "Rad odbora samoupravne radničke kontrole," *Skozi TAM* (Serbo-Croatian edition), August 1976, 3.

23 Liberat Buždon, "Da li smo svesni šta je društvena imovina?," *Skozi TAM* (Serbo-Croatian edition), July 1975, 7.

24 Živan Adamović, "Čiju imovinu uništavamo," *IMR*, May 15, 1979, 5.

25 D. Žujović, "Kazne za nedisciplinovane," *IMR*, February 12, 1980, 3.

26 Lj. Vesković, "Rasprava o (ne)disciplini: autoritet rukovodilaca," *IMR*, March 13, 1984, 4.

27 Franc Lenhart, "Brižljiv rad sa društvenom svojinom doprinosi stabilizaciji," *Skozi TAM* (Serbo-Croatian edition), March 1984, 6.

In a similar article, after presenting a list of factory items found missing, TAM's distinguished self-manager functionary Liberat Buždon concluded: "We cannot be proud of ourselves, but we have all the preconditions to be different and to behave as *cultured people*. . . . We should be behaving quite differently in a self-managing society, considering the fact that social property is managed by all of us."[28] Buždon's words reveal the dominant understanding of factory relations among the management and the leading self-managers. The factory elites observed the enterprise in an idealized manner: as a collective of free producers with common interests, often choosing to ignore the disparities present among them. The dominant view was that malpractices were not the result of inequalities and deficiencies present in the systemic solutions, but a relic of old ways of thinking that the workers brought with them from the countryside, or the proletariat's lack of culture. Consequently, the role of the self-management organs and the party was to emancipate the workers further and transform them into "cultured people," who realized the full meaning and potential of self-managing socialism.

A few years later, when the economic crisis set in and disciplinary breaches expanded even further despite appeals from above, the leading cadres' eagerness to uplift the workers gave way to pessimistic conclusions about self-management as an allegedly idealistic system not yet fit for human beings. One of the reasons the appeals for conscientious work from above had limited effect was the widespread suspicion that manual workers nurtured toward the white-collar enterprise elites. The following section will shed more light on this persistent friction between the shop floor and office employees.

Who Creates Value?

The disparities in access to social property described in the previous section were based on deep-seated divisions inside the enterprises. The principal cleavage in both factories was certainly the one between the workers in direct production and the white-collar employees. In IMR, the ratio between the lowest and the highest wage bracket was 1:2 in 1979. There was always a number of low-skilled workers who slipped below the regionally-determined minimum wage, and a few exceptionally well-paid executives, but the personal income of the vast majority of workers and employees was within this range. The best-valued professions were engineers and highly-educated staff in the white-collar BOALs. However, the skilled manual workers did not lag too far behind, especially those in departments reliant on craftwork, such as Vehicle and Maintenance. Workers in the more mechanized BOALs, such as Motor, or low-skilled female service workers from Social Standard traditionally earned the lowest wages.[29] TAM upheld a similar wage differentiation policy during the climax of Associated Labor in the late

[28] Liberat Buždon, "Da li smo svesni šta je društvena imovina?," *Skozi TAM* (Serbo-Croatian edition), July 1975, 7, emphasis added.

[29] "Koliko smo zarađivali," *IMR*, October 16, 1979, 5.

1970s. As a final producer dependent on product promotion and customer relations, TAM's sales and marketing departments traditionally enjoyed the highest average salaries, whereas workers in fully-automated vehicle production departments and the factory canteen staff received below average wages.[30]

The wage spread was low by the standards of Western market economies. However, inside the Yugoslav industry, where the political culture cherished the manual worker as the prime producer of social wealth, assigning different levels of reward for shop floor and office work was seen as ideologically incoherent and often proved controversial. As Stojan Perhavc's successor at the head of TAM, Mirko Žlender, explained in his 1977 New Year statement, the discrepancy in salaries between the productive and non-productive BOALs were not justifiable, as personal incomes[31] were not only economical, but also a social and political issue.[32] The blue-collar resentment toward the white-collar employees did not grow so much out of wage differentiation as from different ways in which personal income was calculated. Being closely related to output norms, the wages of the manual workers could vary significantly. On the other hand, the white-collar workers' wages were fairly secure and calculated by the hour or job description.

The blue-collar workers were frustrated because they often had to work overtime and invest great effort to match and surpass the production targets so as to earn their expected wage, whereas the earnings of office workers seemed to be guaranteed, regardless of the actual physical output and overall success of the company. Direct production was highly dependent on the services and supplies offered by white-collar BOALs. If the marketing department failed to negotiate the necessary components, the production lines stood still. Likewise, if the sales department failed to find a buyer and organize the shipment, the products would overfill the storage capacities and start piling up in the production halls, thus preventing free movement on the shop floor. The fixed hourly wage of manual workers was counted with lower coefficients during waiting periods. The longer the waiting periods were, the less opportunity a production worker had to fill the monthly output norm and secure the variable part of their income. The shop floor felt the specialists carried great responsibility for occasional underperformance, but the production workers were the only ones bearing the consequences.

In order to back up their grievances, workers embraced the theoretical concept—introduced by the official Marxist economic theory and the accounting system—of rigorous separation between those economic branches that allegedly created new value, and those living off this value. According to this view, the basis of the socialist system lay in economic activities that injected surplus value into society. The sources of surplus value were located in the sphere

30 "Prosečni bruto lični dohotci u januaru 1977," *Skozi TAM* (Serbo-Croatian edition), April 5, 1977, 2.

31 The Associated Labor terminology abandoned the usage of the term "wage" as Yugoslav workers were allegedly not engaged in wage relations. They were collective managers of social property who deducted one part of the total income.

32 "Mirko Žlender, Novogodišnje poslanice," *Skozi TAM* (Serbo-Croatian edition), January 5, 1977, 1–2.

of material production (industry, building, transport, and so on). On the other hand, the typical non-productive economic sectors were healthcare, culture, or state administration. The division was largely inconclusive and contingent. The regimes in state socialist countries used the concept to justify high investments into heavy industry and keep a lid on the expansion of state bureaucracy and red tape. The workplaces in non-productive services were regarded as socially useful, but their spread had to be brought in line with the growth of the material base.

Yugoslav manual workers appropriated the concept of "productive and non-productive work" to promote their narrow interests inside the factories. The creation of common wealth was in the hands of the direct producers, and all other professions in industry were supposed to be rewarded strictly in accordance with their contribution to the smooth running of the production cycle. Ideally, the performance of an office worker was to be quantified and measured like norms on the shop floor. The official political economy textbooks classified the white-collar worker who also directly served material production as a producer of new value. Yet, the shop floors developed workerist attitudes, which regarded manual labor behind a machine as the sole "true work." The vulgar application of Marxist concepts such as the "labor theory of value" or "productive work" led to a questioning of the very usefulness of office staff. Workers often referred to white-collar employees as *režija*. This was an official bookkeeping term for non-productive job positions. However, when used by manual laborers, it usually gained additional pejorative connotations, implying a burden on production or the existence of a superfluous workforce.

In IMR, there was a strong feeling among direct producers that white-collar positions were increasing much faster than productive output. Official factory statistics claimed that the number of employees in *režija* was well below the Yugoslav industrial average, with almost 75 percent of the workforce stationed in production.[33] Nevertheless, the manual workers were convinced that *režija* accounted for 50 percent of total employment, if not more. The following two statements given by IMR blue-collar workers in a documentary film and to the press are exemplary of workers' attitudes toward employees:

> I hear from comrades that the numbers in *režija* climbed up to 3,000. This is the reason why, out of the whole tractor, we are left with a single switch. It is our own fault.[34]

> In my work group, we assigned one controller to each person standing behind the machine, not to mention those upstairs in the administration. In our society, there is too much bureaucracy and a worker has to work for himself plus three other people. That is the heart of the problem![35]

[33] Darko Marinković, "Štrajk u Industriji motora Rakovica," in *Obustave rada (štrajkovi) u Beogradu*, ed. Vukašin Pavlović, Ivan Radosavljević, and Zoran Stojiljković (Belgrade: Veće Saveza sindikata Beograda, 1987), 100.

[34] Milošević, *Žulj*.

[35] D. Kordulup, "Metla umesto struga," *IMR*, February 28, 1983, 4.

In Tezno, the suspicion nurtured by the shop floor toward the office employees was equally strong. The former TAM journalist Branko Gerlič remembers that most workers regarded everyone working behind the desk, from the interns all the way up to executives, as an overhead—a "pure cost," as he put it.[36] An anonymous TAM worker was recorded in front of the camera explaining the difference between productive and unproductive work in the following terms: "My job is to make money. Your job (*režija*) is to see how to spend it."[37] The factory had a clear policy of attracting professionals with high wages and company flats, yet blue-collar pressure and the broader political climate, which praised manual labor, forced the management to stage occasional balancing acts. In October 1980, for instance, the executive of TAM's Metal Cutting BOAL forced all desk workers to perform a day shift on the shop floor and engage in production work.[38] The factory's white-collar staff was the standard mocking victim of the comics in TAM's paper. The drawings presented the white-collar employees as lethargic personalities sitting at empty desks, passing the time with the help of coffee, cigarettes, and newspapers, constantly eyeing the shop floor, scared of workers' reactions.[39]

The management and white-collar workers nurtured their own prejudices and suspicion toward the manual workers. For managers, engineers, and economists, everyday efforts on the shop floor were futile without a proper long-term development strategy, marketing, and sales skills. The official ideology might have granted manual labor the special quality of being able to create surplus value. Yet, the managers knew that the Yugoslav market-oriented economy rewarded those producers who conducted business in a more efficient manner and managed to market their products. The workers were praised on the political posters and factory emblems, but the managers were the people who made crucial decisions and made the factories profitable. They had special expertise, making sure the factories obtained the necessary production materials, maintaining a good relationship with the banks, traveling abroad to make contacts with foreign partners, holding the highest positions in the local party branches, and enjoying direct access to important political authorities.

The white-collar elites in IMR and TAM were frustrated with the changes brought about by Associated Labor. The management in particular felt they had to answer to the higher government and party institutions for their business results, without having sufficient legal authority inside the enterprise. The strengthening of the governing, self-managing function and radical decentralization meant that the central administrative bodies had only consultative powers, whereas the real power was located in the BOAL councils. The managers felt that power had been handed over to the shop floor, yet the manual workers were not competent in making complex assessments and there was no concrete responsibility for collectively-reached unsound and harmful business decisions. The professional

36 Interview with Branko Gerlič, April 2013.

37 Labović, *Umrli gigant*.

38 Jože Gregoran, "Neproizvodni radnici radili u proizvodnji," *Skozi TAM* (Serbo-Croatian edition), November 1980, 6.

39 These comics are presented in the Appendix at the end of this chapter.

decision-makers asked for a clear separation of administrative and governing functions. In their view, professionals should be allowed the chance to bear greater responsibility for (and to guarantee) business results, but they should also be rewarded accordingly.

One of the main battle cries of market-oriented managers and professionals inside IMR and TAM was the struggle against income leveling (*uravnilovka*). *Uravnilovka* carried clearly negative connotations in the LCY jargon. It was associated with rigid communist regimes and underdeveloped economies, such as that of China, a clear antipode of self-managed socialism. As we will see, TAM's workers felt the need to deny any affinity to *uravnilovka* before they advocated for less income disparity in public. Wage leveling was allegedly unfair as it punished hard-working individuals while rewarding the lazy ones. Moreover, it stifled progress, since skillful workers and innovators were not motivated to strive further. In 1985, a newly-employed IMR engineer reflected the prevalent attitudes among the management and professionals in the following way:

> One of the biggest problems among the youth is the egalitarian life philosophy of equality in poverty. This is a dangerous ideology maintained by the politicians . . . if the consciousness that we are a poor country spreads, then people say let us at least all be equally poor. Social differentiations are justified, but only if they are based on distribution according to work and capabilities. The ones who are more capable among us should lead the way, not the noise-making demagogues who point their fingers and exploit social differences.[40]

In personal communication, the management and better-educated employees often looked down on workers as overprotected, ignorant, unschooled, unruly, infantile, and irrational. However, expressing an overtly critical stance toward the working class was not politically acceptable. The strategy often therefore used by the white-collar employees was to utilize the concept of "semi-proletarians" as an entry point for their allegations, insisting on a division between the pure proletariat—those immersed in the values of self-managing socialism—and the workers who still showcased a peasant, petty-bourgeois, or lumpen mentality. Many of these controversial views of the working class were expressed more freely through factory newspaper caricatures.[41]

Skill, Gender, and Place of Origin

The less obvious divisions were those between groups of blue-collar workers in direct production. The exposure of cleavages inside the production halls is crucial if one is to understand the success of the new elite-driven reforms of Associated Labor in the 1980s. The manual workers differentiated themselves as a bloc when confronted with the white-collar employees, but they were far from

40 "Drug predsednik bivši," *IMR*, December 9, 1985, 6.

41 See the Appendix at the end of this chapter.

a homogeneous group. The basic tenet of workers' self-management stated that those who work harder and achieve better results should be rewarded for their efforts. However, workers of a single work collective knew from experience that their wage levels depended less on their individual work efforts than their skill levels, job position on the shop floor, political engagement, and often-informal ranking within the enterprise hierarchy, which was connected to gender, place of origin, seniority, and fraternal relations with foremen and other leading workers.

IMR employed an exceptionally high number of skilled metalworkers. The unskilled and semi-skilled laborers made up 20 percent of the workforce, while in the automotive branch as a whole, the average share was 30 percent.[42] TAM's management could claim a roster of innovative engineers, but at the same time, close to 40 percent of the people it employed were low-skilled workers without a vocational education.[43] Workers with lower skill levels were usually assigned to assembly lines and other workplaces where they had little influence over the production process. On the other hand, those with more skills and seniority were operating single machines, consequently having more control over the organization of work and a better chance to exceed the production norms. This was especially the case if one was allowed to work on a more up-to-date machine. The foremen in both factories kept the output norms on certain work positions low. In this way, during months when production was in full swing, a skilled manual worker in a favorable work position could earn a higher wage than that received by most employees in white-collar departments.

The management of IMR's productive BOALs was hard-pressed to allow low-wage workers to catch up with their better-paid colleagues. The wages of low-skilled workers could have been augmented by allowing them to transfer to a norm-breaking position. An internal analysis conducted in 1983 showed that the practice of promoting workers to positions for which they lacked proper qualifications was widespread.[44] In TAM, the space for enhancing incomes in this way was limited due to the higher automation of the work process. In weeks when production was slow, the wages of low-skilled manual workers in both factories were often only just enough to cover the basic costs of living. Due to a high variable share in personal income, it was not unusual for the lowest wages to fall below the legal minimum. In such periods, the trade union would appeal for an amendment of the income distribution agreement and allow additional payments to groups of workers falling below the republican or municipal minimum wage requirements. In the summer of 1979, for instance, the IMR trade union warned that the salaries of 130 workers fell below the municipal minimum wage.[45] In Tezno, these numbers were somewhat higher; in 1980, TAM's paper reported that the wages of 588 workers (almost 10 percent of the workforce) fell below the legal minimum.[46]

---

42 Marinković, "Štrajk u Industriji motora Rakovica," 100.

43 Milena Iršič, ed., *Tovarna avtomobilov in motorjev Maribor 1947–1987* (Maribor: ČGP Večer, 1987).

44 Sl. Avramović, "Analiza stvarne i potrebne stručne spreme: Veliko šarenilo u raspoređivanju," *IMR*, May 31, 1983, 4.

45 L. Vesković, "Sa 'minimalcem' 130 radnika," *IMR*, June 12, 1979, 5.

46 "O minimalnim ličnim dohocima," *Skozi TAM* (Serbo-Croatian edition), November 1980.

The shop floor position to which a worker was allocated was also of great importance due to the differences in work conditions. TAM was praised for its modern production halls, but workers' recollections reveal that the work ambience was far from standardized. The spatial expansion through mergers with other plants brought about an unequal development of infrastructure, with smaller workshops still located in unheated wooden barracks and equipped with obsolete technologies. The lack of modern mechanization in these sites meant that workers often had to lift heavy parts with their hands. Even in fully-automated work positions, the norm-measured workers preferred to lift processed parts with their hands, as this made the operation faster.

The foundries were the places with the hardest work conditions in both factories. The work there was not only physically demanding, it was dangerous as well. In an interview for TAM's factory paper, the female foundry worker Amalija Miketič complained about the presence of toxic fumes and work in heavy draughts.[47] Up to 50 percent of male and 43 percent of female TAM workers who retired between 1970 and 1975 received an early disability pension.[48] In Rakovica, the temperature inside the foundry during winter months would regularly fall below freezing, and groups of workers in each shift were located outdoors, regardless of the weather conditions. The molds filled with molten metal were known to explode and the mechanic crane frequently jammed, threatening the lives of nearby operators.[49] In January 1982, the Serbian Chamber of Associated Labor discussed the inadequate state of foundries in the republic, pointing out that the average career of workers in this sector was only twenty years and a high percentage of them went into early retirement due to work-related disabilities.[50]

Gender also played an important role in the informal factory hierarchy. An article published in a youth magazine in 1983 featured an interview with Slavica Njegovan, a young female metalworker from IMR. She explained how as a skilled worker, she initially worked behind a machine, a place that matched her qualification. However, since there was not enough work, the foreman gave her a broom and made her clean the shop floor. After a while, she was transferred to a low-paid job in *režija*.[51] The shop floors in Rakovica were a masculine milieu, with ripped-out posters from sports and erotic magazines often hanging above the workstations. There was an unwritten rule that female manual workers should be moved to jobs beyond direct production if the opportunity arose, since work positions involving physical strain at machines were considered unsuitable for women. In 1979, there were 625 women in the enterprise (13.7 percent of the

47 Danilo Vincetič, "Naši razgovori povodom Dana žena," *Skozi ZIV TAM* (Serbo-Croatian edition), March 1981, 4.

48 Danilo Vincetič, "Jedinstvena sindikalna organizacija," *Skozi TAM* (Serbo-Croatian edition), May 1976, 3.

49 D. Žujović, "Plan proizvodnje u livnici: Teškoće na startu," *IMR*, January 15, 1979, 1 and D. Žujović, "Ne znaju za predah: Kako rade u kaluparnici nove livnice," *IMR*, April 27, 1982, 3.

50 "Kako pomoći livcima i livnicama," *IMR*, January 19, 1982, 5.

51 D. Kordulup, "Omladinske novine o mladima u IMR: Metla umesto struga," *IMR*, February 28, 1983, 4.

workforce) and only 89 of them were engaged in direct production. Women on the shop floor were either young workers just entering the factory or older women tied to a specific simple work task due to health disabilities, with slim chances of successful requalification. The majority of women held a desk job, although there were also departments consisting almost exclusively of low-skilled female workers serving workers stationed behind the machines. The Social Standard BOAL, responsible for cleaning and cooking, was a good example of this.

The share of female workers in TAM was somewhat higher. In 1986, they made up around 25 percent of the total workforce. The image of a woman standing behind a machine was present in the TAM factory press more often, but there are no data on how many women were actually working in direct production. A newspaper caricature depicting two lunch queues in the canteen, one consisting exclusively of men wearing work coats and the second of women, sexualized in dresses and high heels, suggests the majority of female workers in Tezno were also office employees (see Figure 2). The caricature shows one of the male workers pointing fingers at the women and commenting that their queue is buying lunches for the "bosses" (*šefovi*).[52] This detail suggests that, in a situation where women were a tiny minority on the shop floor and were consistently transferred to desk jobs, gender could be connected to class privilege.

Figure 2. Male and female lines in the factory canteen, cartoon in *Skozi TAM*, January 21, 1976 (caption: "They are buying snacks for bosses in that line!")

[52] This caricature is quite revealing on a number of levels. It implies that directors did not eat together with the ordinary workers in the canteen. In addition, the fact that the blue-collar workers in the caricature call the executives "bosses" is also telling, as the term evokes hierarchical relations supposedly limited to a capitalist enterprise. In formal speech, the professional manager was usually referred to as "comrade director" (*drug direktor*).

The women were presented as aligned with professional management, although not as the bosses' equals, but rather their subordinates, sent to pick up snacks for directors. The gender-specific factory work positions therefore replicated the division of labor found inside households and entrenched in patriarchal clichés. The low-skilled female manual workers were among the worst-paid members of the collectives responsible for catering and servicing the productive workforce. On the other hand, women with higher education, as well as those transferred from production halls to offices, were often viewed as little more than servants of the male directors or women of suspicious morals.

On every March 8, factory papers dedicated significant coverage to female manual workers behind the machines. When introducing single exemplary male workers, the articles usually focused on their vocation, work ethics, and political activity. In the case of women these aspects were also mentioned; however, their role as mothers and their responsibility for housework would usually receive equal if not more attention. The burden of performing house chores alongside a full-time factory job was well acknowledged. However, domestic work was usually presented as a kind of conscious sacrifice that proletarian women undertook for the common good, rather than a structural inequality. Many women pointed out that they would take a more active part in the political life of the factory, but family obligations did not allow them.[53] As a rule, institutionalized childcare remained within the jurisdiction of communal governments and there are no traces of demands for the factory to organize such services on its grounds. Factory life was therefore attuned to the needs of a politically active, skilled male worker acting as the sole breadwinner for his family.

In TAM, the same source, which offered an insight into the persistence of traditional gender roles, also reveals that patriarchal relations did not stay unchallenged under self-management. Caricatures in the TAM paper often featured satirical depictions of real-life situations in working-class families where men had to perform childcare and housework due to the political activity of their partners, as well as women taking an active part in military national defense training. The older generations of female workers often noted how the overall position of women was much more favorable than it had been in their youth. Women were underrepresented in the self-management organs and sociopolitical organizations of both factories. Nevertheless, in Tezno, they often formed semiformal circles on the level of work groups, organizing after-work activities and social events for women. IMR, on the other hand, maintained an active and highly visible organization of female workers (*Aktiv*), holding yearly conferences and reporting on the position of women inside the factory, despite their low overall number.

Apart from skill and gender, place of origin was also an important distinguishing feature among manual workers. Earning a living through manual labor in an industrial enterprise was a prospect with little appeal for most urban youth. Maribor's factories were dependent on attracting a large number of such workers

53 See, for instance, the interviews with female workers in Danilo Vincetič, "Naši razgovori povodom dana žena," *Skozi TAM* (Serbo-Croatian edition), March 6, 1981, 3–6.

from the countryside.[54] Apart from the daily work migrants, the local industry employed a significant number of workers from remote districts and other republics. TAM actively recruited apprentices from underdeveloped regions across the country, offering lodging and stipends for future factory workers. There are no exact figures on workers from other republics employed inside the factory, or the work structure according to nationality. In 1980, around 15 percent of the total working population of Maribor was non-Slovene.[55] As the region of Lower Styria had no significant national minorities after World War Two, the great majority of these workers must have been migrants from the southern republics. It is safe to assume that in a plant with many low-skilled work positions such as TAM, the share of migrant laborers was somewhat higher than the 15 percent city average.

Work migrants from the southern republics started arriving in Slovenia in larger numbers only in the second half of the 1970s, once the recession-hit Western European countries had closed their borders. For many migrant workers, the decision to move to Yugoslavia's most northwestern region brought challenges similar to the ones encountered when moving abroad. In Maribor, workers from other republics had to learn the Slovene language and find a way to cope with the settled customs of a self-reliant region bordering Austria.[56] Slovenia was the most ethnically homogeneous Yugoslav republic, and the local authorities and factory management customarily equated non-Slovenes with migrant workers. The chance of obtaining a socially-owned apartment and a higher standard of living was certainly greater in Slovenia than the underdeveloped regions from which the migrants arrived. Nevertheless, the migrant workers usually occupied the most difficult positions on the shop floor and there are indications that some of them fell prey to practices and levels of exploitation that the Yugoslav public usually associated with labor in capitalist economies. In February 1980, the Maribor LC City Committee warned that an intermediary company from the southern Serbian city of Vranje was employing workers and leasing them

54 Due to a lack of applicants, *Industrijska kovinarska šola—IKŠ*, the vocational school attached to the factory, extended educational grants and boarding to youth from the underdeveloped regions of the country.

55 Franjo Zorko, *Kronologija delavskega gibanja in družbenega razvoja Maribora in njegove okolice 1885–1983* (Maribor: Založba obzorja, 1989), 445.

56 Former TAM workers interviewed by the author recalled that relations between the Slovenes and workers from other republics were largely harmonious. Language was the single issue that the informants recognized as an obstacle to the integration of migrant workers in Tezno. In an interview that the Serbian-based weekly *NIN* conducted with a non-Slovene industrial worker from Maribor in 1988, language was also mentioned as a sensitive topic. This worker recalled how teachers in Tezno vocational school forbade the apprentices from speaking Serbo-Croatian with each other during breaks and complained that no matter how well integrated he was, for an average Slovene he remained "nothing more than a 'southerner.'" This source must be taken with caution, since the interview was published in the midst of a political clash between the Serbian and Slovene parties. See Svetislav Spasojević, "Maribor, dani posle," *NIN*, July 3, 1988, 21–23. Still, the social alienation of southern migrants in Slovene industrial communities was a recognized fact well described in the anthropological research conducted in the early 1980s, which unfortunately does not cover Maribor. See Silva Mežnarić, *Bosanci: A kuda idu Slovenci nedeljom?* (Belgrade: Filip Višnjić, 1986).

to various plants in Maribor on short-term contracts. The report stated there were 400 such workers who had no self-management rights inside the host enterprises.[57]

IMR also had a proactive employment policy in various underdeveloped regions of the country. Announcements for open work positions were regularly placed in the newspapers, as was required by law. Nevertheless, the personnel unit usually found it much easier to locate the desired profile of workers by relying on direct contact with employment agencies in rural areas and unofficial networks that IMR's migrant workers maintained with their home villages. As we will see, family and home village connections played a role in the formation of an allegiance between individual foremen or self-management functionaries and their groups of supporters on the shop floor. An interview with the former personnel unit staff revealed that IMR's recruitment network was especially well developed in Kosovo. By the early 1980s, Rakovica's factories employed around 1,000 migrant workers from Kosovo, while the greater municipality was home to an additional 3,000 Kosovars who were family members of the locally-employed migrant workers or who worked in other parts of Belgrade.

The share of migrant workers in Rakovica might have been greater than in Maribor.[58] The majority of migrants were Serbs from elsewhere in Serbia, or Serbian minorities from Kosovo and other republics, but other nationalities were also present. According to the 1981 census, the second largest national group in Rakovica were Yugoslavs, who constituted 10 percent of the municipal population. This data suggests that a number of migrants of various ethnicities, as well as part of the local population, were well integrated into the community and its official values, choosing to identify more readily with the ideology of integral socialist Yugoslavism than with the republics or provinces from which they arrived or their ethnic background.[59] In the federal capital, which underwent rapid economic and demographic expansion after the war, it seemed almost everyone was a newcomer, thus making it harder to cast the migrant workers as "others." However, the ethnic strife in Kosovo, which spread during the 1980s, had a great impact on the revival of Serbian national identity inside Belgrade. Rakovica, as a municipality hosting many migrant workers from this troubled region, would stand at the forefront of this change.

57 Zorko, *Kronologija delavskega gibanja*, 445.

58 In Rakovica, the percentage of non-Serbian residents stood at 20 percent, although it is much harder to equate Rakovica's non-Serb population with migrant workers than in the more ethnically homogeneous Slovenia. It is also important to keep in mind that the ethnic structures of the factory workforces did not necessarily mirror their surrounding communities. The factory management did not conduct nationality surveys among their workers. For the data on municipalities, see Dragana Grabeljšek et al., *National Structure of Population in SFR Yugoslavia, Vol 1: Data on Localities and Communes* (Belgrade: Savezni zavod za statistiku, 1991).

59 According to the 1981 census, the amount of Yugoslavs in Belgrade as a whole was 14 percent. In Maribor, this number was much lower (2.76 percent). Ibid.

Veterans and the Youth

The generation gap was perhaps the most important and obvious dividing line among manual workers. The youth occupied a sacred place inside Yugoslav socialism: the prewar communist party had its base in the universities, and the partisan battalions during World War Two were made up mostly of young peasants. The ruling ideology viewed the youth—like the working class—as an intrinsically progressive social force, with each generation carrying more advanced knowledge and ideas. Unlike women, for instance, the youth had their own sociopolitical organization at the national level. Inside the factories, all workers under twenty-seven years of age were encouraged to become members of their local League of Socialist Youth (LSY) branch.

By the mid-1980s, the youth organization at TAM had 3,500 members located in twenty factory branches and connected by a permanent Co-ordination Committee.[60] The great majority of the membership was not actively engaged in youth work. However, TAM's LSY was one of the more active sociopolitical organizations in the factory, attracting some of the most charismatic and talented young employees. In the early 1980s, the Slovene LSY became the epicenter of oppositional activism in the republic, adopting new political currents such as gay and lesbian rights, pacifism, and ecology. As we will see, this broader development had an influence on TAM's local branches, but the factory newspaper shows that the youth activists already had a voice of their own in the late 1970s. TAM's youth organization initiated problem-solving conferences about the living conditions inside the factory dorms and protected the interests of 600 young workers without a resolved housing status.[61]

In the early 1980s, the number of young workers in IMR climbed to 2,000. However, the factory LSY branches counted around 700 members and the leadership openly admitted that only seventy of them attended branch meetings.[62] It seems the organization failed to attract young white-collar workers in particular, who had many other outlets for social activism outside of the workplace. In the case of manual laborers, some of them arrived at the factory with some experience in political work. As the case of Momčilo Plećaš shows, the politically-active blue-collar IMR youth was more likely to go directly into the party and the trade union, rather than joining the LSY. Plećaš arrived in Rakovica in 1974, after completing a vocational education for metalworkers in the economically underdeveloped mountainous Croatian region of Lika. Plećaš had already become active in the party during his schooling. As the son of Lika highlanders, nurturing a folkish sense for social justice and not hesitating to express his opinions,

60 These figures indicate that TAM's LSY enrolled virtually all workers under the legal age limit in the organization, regardless of how active they were. In the words of Drago Gajzer, TAM's LSY activist, the youth leadership was very pragmatic and kept important cadres as members even when they exceeded the legal age limit.

61 Danilo Vincetič, "Pred omladinom je značajno i sadržajno bogato razdoblje," *Skozi TAM* (Serbo-Croatian edition), January 1979, 1–2.

62 D. Kordulup, "Više poverenja omladini," *IMR*, April 14, 1982, 2.

Plećaš was asked to join the IMR factory party and advanced to the position of BOAL secretary, without passing through the local LSY.[63]

Older workers did not always share the officially-endorsed optimism for the virtues of the young generations. The youth had a hard time expressing themselves and felt restrained by the strict patriarchal moral norms of factory life. In 1977, the IMR factory paper published an article which criticized the "uncultured conduct of many young workers." Behavior proscribed in the text included writing on the walls, playing football in the factory yard, and lying bare-chested in the sun.[64] Discussing disciplinary breaks, the IMR Trade Union Conference Executive Committee noted that many young workers arriving from the vocational school were not capable of adapting to work in an industrial enterprise. The apprentices allegedly came with "contra values" (*pogrešno usmereni*) and lacked proper manners.[65] The young workers were expected to become accommodated to the existing norms of behavior and prove themselves in the toughest work positions before advancing inside the informal shop floor hierarchy.

During TAM's Socialist Youth League conference, held in January 1984, there was talk about the lack of understanding shown by senior workers toward their younger colleagues and the inadequate political influence of the youth organization. According to the speakers, the lack of their own political voice resulted in the inadequate material rewarding of work positions usually occupied by youth.[66] A youth magazine published an article about the problems faced by young IMR workers; its coverage also gives more insight into the generational clash only hinted at in TAM's conference report. Among the main complaints mentioned by young workers in this article were unfair treatment in comparison to older colleagues, unrealistic production norms, as well as "dirty and hard work" reserved for younger workers. The supervisors were usually veteran workers, fostering circles of favored peers and supporters. The younger workers were often more educated than their older colleagues, but their advance to better-paid positions was blocked by the fraternal networks of seniors. As Radovan Jašić, one of the young IMR workers interviewed, stated:

> I started working when I was eighteen years old. There is injustice. When the older colleagues see that you are a threat, that you can earn more than them, then there is conflict. In this situation, the younger workers always lose because the foreman takes the side of the worker with more seniority since they are usually of the same generation.[67]

Even though the share of young workers rose significantly in the course of the 1970s and 1980s, the factory administrative and governing bodies were still under the control of those individuals who entered the industry in the early postwar years.

---

63 Interview with Momčilo Plećaš, May 2010.

64 D.Ž., "Nekulturno ponašanje," *IMR*, April 14, 1977, 4.

65 Lj. Vesković, "Rasprava o (ne)discilini: Autoritet rukovodilaca," *IMR*, March 1984, 4.

66 B. Kanižar, "Najobširnejše razprave o osebnem dohotku," *Skozi TAM*, January 12, 1984, 8.

67 D. Kordulup, "Omladinske novine o mladima u IMR: Metla umesto struga," *IMR*, February 28, 1983, 4.

The same could also be said about the cultural events and leisure-time activities. For the older generation of industrial workers, class pride, celebrations of the partisan war, and the language of solidarity between Yugoslav nationalities were much more than state rituals and officially-sponsored ideology. The partisan-led liberation movement, fascism, and the postwar reconstruction were events that marked their lives profoundly.

The biographies of veteran workers in IMR show that the majority of them arrived in Rakovica from different corners of the country as war orphans or uprooted peasant youth, who joined the partisan army to escape Nazi terror and ethnic cleansing campaigns conducted by different nationalist armies. For these men and women, the factory was a new home, in which they received boarding and schooling, and developed a collective identity through joint efforts to overcome poverty. The Slovene population of Lower Styria was exposed to a ruthless Nazi Germanization campaign during the war and many inhabitants were forced to find refuge in other parts of the country. Each year, many veteran TAM workers and their descendants would board the "Train of Brotherhood and Unity" at the Maribor Central Station and travel to Serbia in order to visit the host families that offered them shelter. TAM kept special fraternal relations with a railway vehicle factory in Kraljevo, the Serbian city where the majority of refugees from the Maribor area were evacuated during the war. Among the partisan generation, the hard years of war and reconstruction remained the benchmark for measuring the success of socialist modernization.

On the other hand, the generation that entered the factories during the 1970s and 1980s came of age in an era of unprecedented prosperity. Associated Labor did not put an end to domestic consumerism or the import of Western pop culture. Media projections of the "good life" and direct contact with more upscale neighborhoods in the city center shaped the life expectations of young workers. Over the years, the older workers were able to accumulate certain possessions, such as a socially-owned apartment, a house, or a car. They were settled inside the blue-collar communities and the factory remained the central focus of their life's activities. The youth, on the other hand, had little consumer power. They rented rooms in different parts of the city and looked for fun in downtown Belgrade and Maribor. Life in the big cities brought them into regular contact with their peers from other social strata. These experiences made them question their position in society and the values propagated inside the factories.

In order to understand the gulf between the official language, used to praise labor inside the factories, and the increasingly cynical views toward socialist symbols developing among the urban youth in broader society, one could give the example of "Maljčiki," a 1980 hit record by the Belgrade new wave band Idoli. The song was a parody of Stakhanovism, depicting a proletarian who wakes up to "fiery dawns and chimney smoke" and enthusiastically proceeds to work in a nearby factory. The lyrics contained nebulous Russian-sounding words, while the video showed stereotypical workers standing in monument-like heroic poses surrounded by lighthearted and cheeky band members with sarcastic facial expressions wearing three-piece suits.[68] In the middle-class milieus, the Associated

68 VIS Idoli, *Maljčiki*, Jugoton, 1980, vinyl.

Labor's revamped ideological insistence on the importance of manual work and celebration of the working class must have seemed artificial and outdated in the years of a booming service economy and the dawn of the computer era. To the well-educated—but chronically unemployed—big city youth of the 1980s, the industrial neighborhoods were foreign places and their inhabitants appeared caricature-like.

In downtown cafes of Belgrade and Maribor, the self-managers of Rakovica and Tezno could be paternalistically accepted as naïve and underprivileged, but nevertheless hard-working members of society. On the other hand, the manual workers could just as easily be regarded less favorably as pawns of the more conservative sections of the ruling party, remnants of the past blocking a chance to catch up more efficiently with affluent Western societies. The younger blue-collar workers seem to have felt the scorn of wider society toward manual labor more strongly than their older colleagues did. TAM's youth activist Drago Gajzer remembered how the youngsters from the LSY branches located closer to the city center often looked down upon Tezno youth as "country bumpkins."[69] As one IMR worker stated in an interview for a youth magazine, "when you step out of the factory, when you enter a somewhat more educated group of peers and tell them you are a worker, that you attended vocational school, they look at you with pity, as if you are somehow less worthy."[70]

One of the main tasks of youth organizations in all Yugoslav factories was to connect the youth with the revolutionary legacy by arranging a number of events celebrating the partisan movement and involving workers from different parts of Yugoslavia. In 1975, for instance, TAM's youth decided to mark the thirtieth anniversary of the victory over fascism and the twenty-fifth anniversary of the introduction of self-management by organizing a large festival with young workers from its partner factories in other republics.[71] In October that year, the factory paper summarized the impressions of local youth participants in a voluntary work brigade in Croatia in the following words: "We met many friends, . . . the blisters on our hands will disappear. Our arms, they grew stronger, just as the progressive socialist spirit inside of us did. We are proud that we were able to assist in the building of our country."[72]

The kitshy patriotic tone of such proclamations demonstrates just how divorced the factory elites' official language, intended to integrate their new recruits, was from the everyday reality young workers experienced. The LSY sections in both factories routinely praised the youth work camps, yet, in 1986, one female IMR worker remarked bitterly how middle-class parents did not send their children to the volunteer work brigades.[73] The differences in expected life paths, material status, and culture between working-class youth in vocational schools and factories, and their middle-class peers attending gymnasiums and

69 Interview with Drago Gajzer, April 2013.

70 D. Kordulup, "Omladinske novine o mladima u IMR: Metla umesto struga," *IMR*, February 28, 1983, 4.

71 "Susret mladih u Titovom Užicu," *Skozi TAM* (Serbo-Croatian edition), June 1975, 5.

72 M.P., "Opravdali smo poverenje," *Skozi TAM* (Serbo-Croatian edition), October 1975, 7.

73 Milošević, *Žulj*.

universities downtown, was something that young workers had to deal with. Faced with obvious inequalities, they could either identify more intensely with their immediate blue-collar surroundings or seek ways to move closer to the affluent and sophisticated inhabitants of more central neighborhoods. The hostile attitudes of the older workers, and the inability of the sociopolitical organizations to communicate with them in any meaningful way, made many young workers opt for the latter strategy.

A good part of the youth in Rakovica and Tezno was not willing to participate in the celebrations, which had little to do with their own experiences and cultural tastes. They were trying to win space for more contemporary ways of socializing, free from overt ideological markers. The principal focus of IMR's youth organization in the late 1970s and early 1980s was the construction of a municipal youth center, where the young workers could organize their own social and cultural life. Rakovica's already-existing cultural center tried to answer their demands by purchasing records of the "latest disco and rock hits," as well as installing a "state-of-the-art light show." In the 1980s, the TAM youth organization was also involved in the organization of rock concerts in the center of Maribor.[74]

In 1983, the youth organization in Slovenia started a campaign to ease the problem of youth unemployment by forcing older workers into retirement. The old notions of politically-favored, unskilled partisan cadres impeding the assimilation of new knowledge, heard during the liberal wave of the 1960s, were starting to reemerge. In TAM, the youth activists used this opening to strike a blow against the older workers and demand obligatory retirement at sixty years of age.[75] The LSY campaign also took root in Belgrade, but one finds no traces of it in IMR. As we will see, in the late 1980s the youth of both factories would be the section of workers most eager to break with the political status quo and the ideology of brotherhood and unity, accept radical reforms, and embrace nationalist ideologies.

The appendix at the end of this chapter, consisting of factory press caricatures, will present a more colloquial view on the aforementioned inequalities and tensions between different occupational groups in a self-managed factory. It marks the final section of the book dealing with the construction of Associated Labor and the welfare state of the 1970s. A careful description and elaboration of the main contradictions of workers' self-management—which persisted even during these prosperous years—is of the utmost importance, since it is impossible to understand the rapidly growing disharmony inside the factories and the political strife of the 1980s without this background. The remaining four chapters will focus on the final decade of socialist Yugoslavia in which all of the challenges that erupted in the late 1960s would return augmented, but in the changed social, political, and cultural landscape of late socialism.

74 D. Kordulup, "Kutak za mlade," *IMR*, April 12, 1983, 7; "Poročilo o delu konference osnovnih organizacij ZSMS DO TAM v letu 1989: Kaj smo naredili in česa nismo," *Skozi TAM*, May 26, 1989, 6–7.

75 Tomislav Perlič, "Zašto da još rade ostareli radnici?," *Skozi TAM* (Serbo-Croatian edition), March 1983, 7.

Appendix 1

Figure 3. Accountant ridiculing Karl Marx, cartoon in *Skozi TAM*, October 18, 1985

Figure 4. "Long live the Holiday of Work," cartoon in *Skozi TAM*, April 30, 1982

Figures 3 to 10 present the ways in which the blue-collar workers saw their white-collar colleagues, all of them taken from the TAM factory paper. In Figure 3, an accountant in dark glasses ridicules Karl Marx. White-collar workers and managers are often drawn with dark glasses, indicating cluelessness as well as shady intentions. The mocking accountant here symbolizes unjust income division in favor of non-productive work, despite the official primacy of manual labor and the communist norms of fair income distribution.

Figure 4 depicts a blue-collar worker and a group of white-collar employees celebrating May Day and holding a banner saying "Long live the Holiday of Work." The white-collar workers hold one side of the banner united in a group, whereas the manual worker is forced to carry it alone. Over the decades, the language of Yugoslav socialism gradually tended to substitute the term "working class" with "working people," a phrase which carried broader encompassing potential for occupations outside of direct production. As a result, the workers felt that their weight inside the self-management system was decreasing, together with the disappearance of traditional class interpretation. The white-collar workers in this drawing are portrayed as stowaways, profiting from the status of the working class (the May Day banner) while not investing the same amount of work as direct producers.

Figure 5. Worker carrying "culture" on his back, cartoon in *Skozi TAM*, May 29, 1981

Figure 6. "Oh, how I make my life hard without good reason!," cartoon in *Skozi TAM*, May 27, 1983

Figures 5 and 6 show the workerist interpretation of "productive work," according to which manual labor was the sole source of social wealth, while other professions lived off the value created by industry. In the latter picture, a worker is carrying a heavy rucksack labeled "administration" and complains "Oh, how I make my life hard

Figure 7. "Watch out for those out there doing nothing!," cartoon in *Skozi TAM*, October 1, 1986

Figure 8. "I just had a nightmare. I was back on the shop floor!," cartoon in *Skozi TAM*, September 5, 1984

without good reason." The drawing indicates that overbearing administration was not needed, yet the workers installed it voluntarily through the Associated Labor Act. The previous caricature displays the same scene, only this time the worker is carrying a huge box labelled "culture." The box clearly symbolizes numerous cultural institutions supported by the factories. It is interesting that the letter "L" on the culture box is drawn to resemble a learner driver's plate, indicating that much of the cultural production was substandard or considered unworthy of funding by the workers.

Figures 7 to 10 present white-collar workers in their workplaces. Their main occupations seem to be drinking coffee, playing the lottery, and passing time with idle chitchat. Figure 7 shows an anxious employee whose desk is covered with lottery tickets overhearing two workers on the shop floor complaining about the laziness of the white-collar workers. Figure 8 depicts a former manual worker transferred to administration waking up from a nap on his desk and exclaiming, "I just had a nightmare. I was back on the shop floor!"

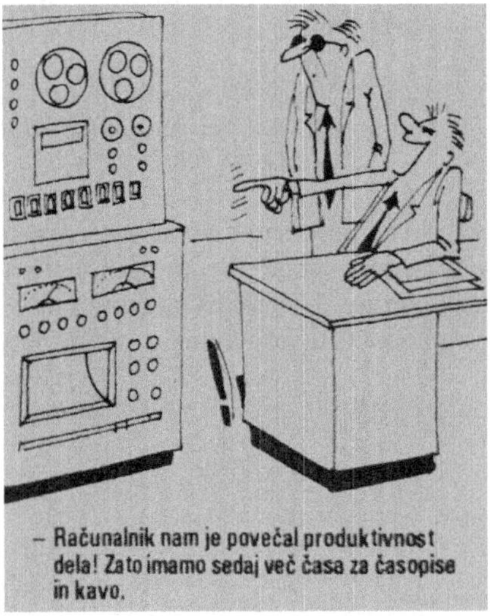

Figure 9. "The computer increased our work productivity," cartoon in *Skozi TAM*, May 10, 1985 (caption: "The computer increased our work productivity! Now we have more time for newspapers and coffee.")

Figure 10. "Intern!," cartoon in *Skozi TAM*, November 7, 1977

Figure 9 and 10 present different ways in which the white-collar workers allegedly avoided work. The first caricature shows a worker boasting to a colleague about their new computer, stating, "The computer increased our work productivity! Now we have more time for magazines and coffee." The second picture shows an employee with a cigarette and a coffee calling the intern to answer the phone for him.

Figure 11. "Comrades, I am not informed," cartoon in *Skozi TAM*, November 20, 1976

Figure 12. "Meeting enforcer," cartoon in *Skozi TAM*, July 15, 1983 (caption: "If there is no meeting, we will not work! If it does not take place in the morning, we do not want it in the afternoon.")

Figures 11 to 16 portray industrial workers in the eyes of the managers and white-collar employees. Figure 11 shows a worker surrounded by different communication channels spread by the Associated Labor Act so that the shop floor could make informed decisions (factory press, bulletins, noticeboard, public address system, and so on). In the face of all these efforts, the worker complains that he is still unaware of what is happening. "Comrades, I am not infoooooormed," he exclaims through tears. The worker is drawn as a spoiled, child-like individual, crying and refusing to take responsibility for his actions.

Figure 12 shows workers in a very different light. This time, a direct producer is presented as a stereotypical blue-collar worker: masculine and loud, pointing fingers and screaming ultimatums to the executive in front of him. He threatens a work stoppage if the management does not call for a meeting (presumably an assembly). However, the meeting has to be held during work hours and not in the afternoon. Either way, one thing is clear: the day will pass with little activity on the shop floor. This second caricature aimed to show two things: firstly, that the blue-collar workers had too much power; secondly, that the self-management meetings took precious time away from manufacturing.

Answering the supervisor's query as to why he is not working, the worker in Figure 13 states nonchalantly: "Sorry, according to the union, the minimum wage is guaranteed. Go bother someone else." Similarly, the following three pictures portray the workers as overprotected and indolent. Figure 14 makes fun of the concept of education at the workplace, showing a worker reading comic books next to a machine. Figure 15 shows a group of workers passing time around the machine. The title states "Iron work discipline," while the ironic subtext reads, "Our organs passed so many disciplinary measures that the pressure is simply unbearable." Finally, Figure 16 claims the workers were behaving like overpriced football stars. "Comrade Boss, if you do not grant me 30 more points, I am transferring to another BOAL," a worker threatens.

Figure 13. "How come you are not working?," cartoon in *Skozi TAM*, January 25, 1975 (foreman: "How come you are not working?" worker: "Sorry, according to the union, the minimum wage is guaranteed. Go bother someone else.")

Figure 14. "Education at work," cartoon in *Skozi TAM*, September 14, 1978

Figure 15. "Iron work discipline," cartoon in *Skozi TAM*, June 17, 1976 (caption: "Our organs passed so many disciplinary measures that the pressure is simply unbearable.")

Figure 16. "Workers imitating soccer stars," cartoon in *Skozi TAM*, September 5, 1978 (caption: "Comrade Boss, if you do not grant me 30 more points, I am transferring to another BOAL.")

CHAPTER FOUR

The Dragging Crisis, 1979–1986

The Sudden Breakdown

The death of Josip Broz Tito in May 1980 symbolically marked the end of prosperity based on hefty government investments and extensive economic growth. The rising price of oil on the world market during the 1970s and the resulting debt crisis confronted the self-managed industry with great challenges. After three decades of integration into the world trade system, the Yugoslav leadership had to accept that self-managed industry remained an exporter of technologically obsolete goods with relatively high manufacturing costs.[1] In addition, the interest on loans taken to maintain imports of necessary components and raw materials was rising steeply. In 1981, once the price of borrowing for a decade-long investment spree was finally calculated, the federal government discovered that the country was standing on the edge of bankruptcy, with over $20 billion in foreign debt.[2] Realizing the 1970s model of growth was no longer sustainable, the League of Communists rang the alarm in 1979, while Tito was still alive. The party declared much stricter criteria for state investments and announced a period of "economic stabilization." The new economic policy demanded that industry increase its competitiveness by bringing company performance more in line with market parameters and making the production process leaner. The stabilization also intended a stricter control over wage hikes and collective consumption.

This was certainly not the first time the Yugoslav industrial workers had heard such appeals from their political leaders. The self-management project was not immune to economic difficulties. The dependence of the local economy on imports and foreign credits made the authorities resort to periodic restrictions of consumption, cutting of production costs, and conservative fiscal policies in order to reduce the trade deficit and pay off foreign debts. The working class therefore experienced periods of consumption booms followed by cutbacks in living standards, a dynamic comparable to that of business cycles in capitalist economies.[3] Among the blue-collar workers, there was a culture of sacrifice for

1 Bruce McFarlane, *Yugoslavia: Politics, Economics and Society* (London: Printer Publishers, 1988), 92.
2 Stilhoff Sörensen, *State Collapse and Reconstruction in the Periphery*, 136.
3 For an analysis of Yugoslavia's specific economic cycles, see Branko Horvat, *Privredni ciklusi u Jugoslaviji* (Belgrade: Institut ekonomskih nauka, 1969).

higher goals. As we have seen, the ruling ideology often constructed continuities between current pushes for more efficient production and the previous participation of the working class in the revolution or postwar reconstruction. As a rule, the party-state would reward workers for restraint shown in periods of economic hardship with greater participation in the successive periods of prosperity.

If the occasional slowdowns during the three decades of relentless modernization could be compared to recessions in capitalist economies, the calamity of the 1980s could be deemed a full-scale depression. What proved to be the ultimate crisis of Yugoslav socialism differentiated itself from other strenuous periods through the longevity and intensity of the economic contraction. The government introduced the stabilization policies hoping that, just as in the previous decades, robust growth rates would return after a short setback. This never happened. Between 1971 and 1979, the economy recorded a yearly growth of 5.5 percent; this figure fell to 0.5 percent between 1981 and 1988.[4] What made things even worse was the fact that inflationary pressures followed the standstill in GDP growth. The inflation rate rose to 85 percent in 1985, only to reach triple digits in 1987.[5] The third distinguishing feature of the crisis decade was the party-state's steady loss of sovereignty over domestic economic policies. The federal government was forced to enter into debt restructuring agreements with Western governments as well as economic reform programs under the tutelage of the International Monetary Fund (IMF), making it much harder for the party to maintain its special relationship with industrial workers.

The prolonged halt in economic growth wreaked havoc in the self-managed industry. The hope that radical decentralization of economic units would force the work collectives to integrate from below beyond the entrenched monopolies, using the expanded self-management institutions to plan and coordinate their activities, evaporated into thin air as soon as the enterprises were pushed to compete more openly in the market. Instead of becoming the building blocks of the new economy based on solidarity, the BOALs turned into miniature models of the self-centered enterprises of the 1960s, absorbed in the struggle against other work collectives. Heavy industry was urged to export its products to convertible currency markets at all costs in order to accumulate the hard currency needed to service foreign debts. At the same time, the government introduced limits on imports. The manufacturers were thus thrown into a race for scarce raw materials. One of the main ways to catch up with inflation was by lobbying the authorities to allow a selective increase in prices.

In Tezno, TAM tried hard to contribute its fair share to the collective stabilization efforts. In February 1984, the factory paper declared:

---

4 Slavo Radošević, "The Collapse of Yugoslavia: Between Chance and Necessity," in *Yugoslavia and After: A Study in Fragmentation, Despair and Rebirth*, ed. David A. Dyker and Ivan Vejvoda (New York: Routledge, 1996), 65–80.

5 Jože Prinčić and Neven Borak, *Iz reforme v reformo: slovensko gospodarstvo 1970–1991* (Ljubljana: Fakulteta za družbene vede, 2006), 530.

> The objective of extreme saving has to enter our everyday thinking. We have to become aware that it is high time for this type of behavior. We will have to introduce limitations, above all in non-productive spending. It is true that these types of measures are not popular, but there is no other way out.[6]

The factory production plans had to be fulfilled by relying on "internal reserves," meaning intensification of work, elimination of wasteful practices, and cuts in collective consumption, without attempts to bypass the stabilization through additional credit, raising of prices, or greater imports. TAM was importing only 8 percent of its inputs, reorienting toward domestic suppliers instead.[7] However, as in the late 1960s, the factory management soon realized that Yugoslav industry as a whole was not fit enough to withstand such rigorous stabilization pressures. TAM's efforts were undermined through the lack of a unified approach. The producers of intermediary products and raw materials were constantly raising prices. Even when TAM agreed to the new pricing, the suppliers were rarely able to deliver the contracted quantities. The "waiting periods," during which the workers stood idle next to the machines, were increasing. Sometimes the paralysis of production would extend for days and the workers became more and more restless, knowing that their paycheck would be significantly lower at the end of the month. The rise in the prices of inputs on the domestic market and unplanned imports due to domestic scarcity led the enterprise to become increasingly dependent on those banks that were willing to extend short-term credit. By 1984, the factory had to appeal for new credit before each new production cycle just to acquire the needed inputs and pay the workforce.[8]

As the crisis dragged on, TAM's management protested ever more loudly against the "double standards" of the federal authorities, meaning the tolerance of low stabilization discipline among its subcontractors from other republics. What the directors in Tezno failed to realize—or conveniently ignored—was the fact that unlike TAM, which could still fall back on "internal reserves," most low-income basic producers simply had no more "fat to burn." IMR was fulfilling its production plans with constant production bottlenecks and pleas for sacrifices from its workforce even in times of economic boom. As we will see later in this chapter, the stabilization campaign was threatening to strain IMR's internal relations to the point where the enterprise was in danger of falling apart and triggering political protest. IMR's Central Workers' Council complained in 1981 that one never knew when the whole shift of workers would have to be sent home from the factory gate due to the irregular supply of work materials.[9] If workers in Tezno were kept on the waiting regime for days, in Rakovica certain assembly lines would stand still for weeks. Even when the inputs were finally obtained, their quality was so low that entire series of engines had to be discarded.

6 T. Perlič, "Isporuke ne smeju da stanu," *Skozi TAM* (Serbo-Croatian edition), February 1984, 2.

7 "Proizvodne mogućnosti ograničene skoro do kraja," *Skozi TAM* (Serbo-Croatian edition), November 1981, 4.

8 T. Perlič, "Isporuke ne smeju da stanu," *Skozi TAM* (Serbo-Croatian edition), February 1984, 2.

9 "Sve teže nabaviti materijal," *IMR*, February 24, 1981, 1.

Foreign markets were the only source for reliable components and raw materials, but IMR had decreasing access to convertible currency. In those years, excessive foreign debt was not a structural problem for the Yugoslav economy alone. In the face of rising trade deficits, other developing countries such as Egypt and India cut their demand for tractor imports, leaving IMR with only a fraction of its former hard currency earnings. In 1987, IMR's exports amounted to a mere 31 percent of those recorded in 1983.[10] As if this were not enough, IMT, the rival Belgrade tractor producer, also entered the Egyptian market, causing a price war. In order to acquire raw materials and realize its final products, IMR was again becoming ever more reliant on the business networks of larger final producers, such as IMT and TAM. In the first half of the 1980s, IMR's management perceived its city rival as its main opponent and an unfair competitor. The company claimed that the share of Rakovica-produced engines in IMT's tractors was steadily undervalued and their rival relied on dumping prices to enter foreign markets.

Apart from enhanced production efficiency, a crucial prerequisite for the success of the reform plan was the drastic reduction of individual and collective consumption. Workers' councils had to stop awarding wage increases above the general productivity trend. In 1983, despite being declared unconstitutional by the Constitutional Court, the government proceeded with the implementation of a decree that tied the growth of wages to the growth of net income in the enterprise. The new policy aimed to make the enterprises more disciplined in paying suppliers and returning bank credits.[11] In 1986, the stabilization measures were tightened even further, with laws explicitly forbidding the distribution of wages before the repaying of debts and bills owned to creditors. For the first time since World War Two, the federal government decided to start creating the legal preconditions for allowing company bankruptcies.[12] The austerity measures therefore placed the main burden of the reforms onto the shoulders of the industrial working class.

In Belgrade, the drop in living standards in industrial neighborhoods closely followed the national trend. Between 1980 and 1985, the living standards of its manual workers fell by 35 percent.[13] The continuing interruptions to the production process and fall in industrial output meant that low-skilled workers paid according to norms were the people most strongly affected by the crisis. In IMR, the trade union recognized that the earnings of entire sections of the workforce were falling below the minimum wage. The union tried to prevent pauperization by introducing individual social cards, which enabled them to recognize the most vulnerable workers and grant them occasional wage bonuses independent of work results. Agricultural work and moonlighting also served as an important cushion for many workers. The trade union was aware of this and denied social assistance to those who owned land or had a second job.

10 D. Žujović, "Gubici su, ipak, pokriveni," *IMR*, March 1, 1988, 1.
11 Magaš, *The Destruction of Yugoslavia*, 96.
12 McFarlane, *Yugoslavia: Politics, Economics and Society*, 138–43.
13 Lj. Vesković, "Život u oči," *IMR*, March 19, 1985, 4.

The factory was therefore forced to turn a blind eye to the disciplinary breaches and let many low-skilled workers dedicate more time to work on the fields and side jobs. At the same time, the limited funds were directed to uphold the wages of skilled workers vital for the maintenance of the production process. The policy of selective income redistribution produced results despite constant warnings about the dangers of *uravnilovka*. The absences of peasant workers and second-job holders could always be compensated by campaign work during crucial months. The overall average wage in IMR was falling, but, as we will see, the factory was able to reach record-breaking production results in the mid-1980s, while its lowest wages were up to one third higher than the minimum wage in Belgrade's industry.[14] The burden of austerity was additionally eased through internal provision of basic foodstuffs. Distribution of subsidized foodstuffs was a traditional activity of the trade union, but it became much more important during the crisis years.

The research failed to uncover statistical data revealing the relative impact of the crisis in Maribor in comparison to other parts of the country. Maribor was among the more affluent regions, but as already mentioned, by the early 1980s, TAM was among the lowest-paying large Work Organizations in the city. In 1980, 588 of TAM's workers, or close to 10 percent, received a salary which was below or barely above the minimum wage. In 1983, the individual factory trade union branches suggested an increase to the guaranteed wage inside the factory, but the trade union's standing Commission for Social Standards argued against the proposal, arguing that each worker should be enabled to earn a wage surpassing the legal minimum through work, with the help of a new evaluation of shop floor positions.[15] TAM's internal management culture and hostility to *uravnilovka* made the trade union leadership avoid direct, linear redistribution.

As in IMR, the personal incomes of an entire layer of low-skilled workers were losing the race with inflation. However, the more stable business results and larger share of proper peasant workers in comparison to IMR enabled the management to allow further polarization of income and continue to insist on the criteria of "distribution according to the results of work." Until the mid-1980s, it seems that the better-paid manual workers and professionals were still managing to preserve their standards of living without direct help from the trade union. Interviews on the eve of May Day holidays in 1983 show that workers were quite aware of the hardship around them, but the majority still managed to continue the lifestyle of the previous years and firmly believed the crisis would soon give way to another period of prosperity. As a result, they were ready to support the stabilization measures and even accept certain sacrifices. The words of a desk worker, Milica Gerič, reveal the prevailing mood:

> The free days are normally used for traveling. We decided to go to the seaside, despite the great fall in living standards. The economic situation is grave indeed

---

14 Ibid.

15 Danilo Vinetič, "Osebni dohodek naj bo rezultat dela!," *Skozi ZIV TAM*, April 22, 1983, 5.

> and it limits our purchasing power. I admit we were a bit spoiled during previous years and this sudden crisis caught us unprepared. The scarcity of items in the supermarket, higher prices, and similar stabilization measures had an effect on all of us. However, I am convinced that also this time around we will come out of the crisis by relying on our own capacities. . . . We should increase productivity and work discipline, shorten the time spent in meetings, cut back on personal and collective consumption.[16]

Even if they still had the means, workers were not always sure they could buy the items they had become accustomed to in the previous two decades. The citizens of Belgrade and Maribor found themselves lining up in queues to buy scarce imported products such as tropical fruits, coffee, and chocolate. Restrictions on car usage were already introduced during the first stabilization year, in 1979. In November 1982, the LC Slovenia Maribor City Committee discussed the lack of household goods, indicating that this could have "serious political consequences."[17] However, for a great number of low-paid blue-collar workers in Rakovica and Tezno, the austerity did not apply only to imported goods. The fall in real wages made it hard to purchase even basic foodstuffs and household items, such as meat and coal.

The introduction of social cards and rationing helped the most vulnerable layer of workers, but these were highly controversial measures. The ordinary party members found it hard to orient themselves toward the new circumstances and explain the official policies to fellow workers. The rationing of consumer articles and restrictions of personal incomes by the state went against the main principles of consumer-oriented, self-managing socialism. During the joint meeting of TAM's communists with the municipal and city leadership in February 1983, the party secretary of BOAL Metalworking, Milan Hojnik, appeared perplexed. He pointed out that political forums at all levels were nominally against the distribution of consumption coupons, yet this had become a widespread practice. "How should an average member understand this? Which line should we present in public?" Hojnik asked the functionaries.[18] In Rakovica, the party activists felt compelled to downplay the practice of introducing social cards. They upheld the popular conviction that socialism should enable a self-managing worker to earn enough money through a regular wage, claiming the social rationing was an exception and a short-term solution. "It is humiliating, isn't it?" the IMR paper wrote in late 1984. "The working class is the carrier of our system and now this ruling class is in need of social handouts."[19]

Both factories attempted to weather the storm in their own specific ways. Nevertheless, by the second half of the decade, as increased production was not bringing the expected financial return and the government seemed to be prolonging the austerity measures without an end in sight, the survival tactics

---

16 "Naši prvomajski razgovori," *Skozi ZIV TAM*, April 22, 1983, 8.

17 Zorko, *Kronologija delavskega gibanja*, 471.

18 Tomislav Perlič, "Poziv na javnu raspravu: Vanredna sednica sekretara OO SK RO TAM," *Skozi TAM* (Serbo-Croatian edition), February 1983, 6.

19 M. Petrić, "Solidarni a kartu nemaju," *IMR*, November 11, 1984, 6.

were beginning to strangle the enterprises. Their workforce was exhausted and started to disperse. In IMR, the wage augmentations were insufficient to maintain the standard of living in the midst of rampant inflation. Skilled workers started leaving the factory. The fear of the leading activists inside Associated Labor was that the industrial working class would dissolve under the burden of austerity. IMR worker and party activist Zdravko Petrović had the following to say during one of the sessions of the Serbian LC Central Committee in 1986:

> A large percentage of the working class has been living on the edge of poverty for quite some time now. The wage they receive at work does not enable them a decent living. They are unable to maintain their personal belongings and service their household appliances, not to mention buying new ones. Many are considering additional or alternative jobs. Our best craft workers are forced to work additional jobs in order to keep their families fed. If this process continues, there is a danger that these supplementary jobs might become the main ones and the factory work be reduced to a side activity.[20]

In Tezno, the tactic of relying on the countryside as a buffer and mobilizing the workforce through the expectation of higher incomes had reached its limits. In 1984, TAM's trade union concluded that the fall in living standards had ushered in an atmosphere of weariness in which the workers were no longer motivated to increase their work efforts.[21] In 1987, the factory trade union gave in and started proposing solidarity payouts to all workers whose wages were not enough to cover their basic living expenses, regardless of the work results.[22] By 1988, the factory paper estimated that up to 20 percent of Maribor's workers were living on the edge of poverty. In September 1988, the TAM factory paper interviewed some of its younger, female, unqualified, and peasant workers. Extracts from these interviews offer a closer look at the state of an entire section of industrial workers in the late 1980s.

> The constant price hikes make it hard for us to make ends meet. There are six of us in the household. I work in the afternoon as well. Fortunately, we live in a village, which allows us to produce a lot of food on our own. We buy only the most basic foodstuffs, shoes, and clothing. (Jože Belič)
>
> I am not married. I live with my parents. During my free time, I work on the black market. At home, I have a little bit of land and some cattle. I manage to get by with the help of my father's wage and the sale of cattle. Under these circumstances, I do not dare start a family. (Martin Kvar)

20 D.Ž. "Sa sednice CK SK Srbije: Opredeljenja sprovoditi u praksi," *IMR* October 15, 1986, 6.

21 B. Kanižar, "Tehtna vprašanja terjajo zadovoljive odgovore," *Skozi ZIV TAM*, January 13, 1984, 4.

22 Danilo Vincetič, "Kako pomagati delavcem z najnižjimi osobnimi dohodki," *Skozi TAM*, October 16, 1987, 2.

> My wage is not sufficient to cover the apartment rent and raise my child. We live modestly and buy cheap. Unfortunately, I cannot afford books or to go to the cinema. The food coupons help me to obtain basic foodstuffs. (Marta Demšić)
>
> Life is hard. In order to buy fruit for my child I had to give up drinking coffee, not to mention chocolate. A new pair of shoes will break our budget. (Andreja)
>
> I live day-to-day. I was recently transferred from the machine to a desk job in a phone connection unit due to my work-related disability. If it were not for the factory canteen, I would not taste meat for months. (Miroslav Vajs)[23]

The prolonged crisis pushed the stories of marginalized workers into the limelight. Formerly reserved for the bottom section of unskilled workers, such precarious conditions of existence were now threatening the entire shop floor, making it impossible to ignore them any longer. The realization that the hard times were not passing after years of sacrifice made the workers think more intensely about economic and political reforms. The following section will show how the party tried to discipline the state behind its vision of reform by mobilizing the blue-collar base during 1984. The campaign proved to be a failure for the federal party, as the leaderships from different republics did not join the efforts with similar dedication and workers felt betrayed by the lack of decisive changes.

The communists thus entered the second half of the 1980s with the loss of the feeble foothold they had established in industry during the previous decade. The professional management, on the other hand, used the weakening of the industrial party branches to roll back many limitations placed on its decision-making prerogatives during the 1970s and positon itself as the main reformist force inside the factories. The final two sections of this chapter depict the internal power struggles between the reformists and defenders of Associated Labor in both factories. They reveal how, during the course of the 1980s, the general management of TAM and IMR managed to regain company unity, helped by government austerity measures and the inactivity of sociopolitical organizations.

The Party at an Impasse

The differences in regional outlooks made it tremendously difficult to reach a consensus over the exact reform strategy inside the party and within the lawmaking bodies at the federal level. Six out of twelve meetings of the LCY Central Committee between 1982 and 1985 were devoted wholly to economic reforms, yet none of them managed to produce a workable unity.[24] During 1983,

---

23 "Kako živimo: Kriza je globoka zaskrbljujoča in že načenja živce," *Skozi TAM*, September 30, 1988, 6.

24 Magaš, *The Destruction of Yugoslavia*, 99.

the Federal Assembly passed only eight out of twenty-five major laws planned for that year, while the vote on another seventeen was postponed indefinitely.[25] The post-Tito political elite came across as cut off from society and resistant to new modernization impulses.[26] The recognition that the communist functionaries who were supposed to be at the vanguard of society had no clear ideas on how to exit the crisis amplified the general feeling of despair. However, this quiescence could not rule for long. The state was facing great pressures, both from beyond and from within its borders, to introduce more decisive reform measures.

From the outside, the lender nations and the International Monetary Fund made the restructuring of Yugoslavia's foreign debt conditional on the state's adherence to orthodox economic policies and greater exposure to the world market. The external stakeholders managed to find a reliable partner at the top of the party-state. As early as 1982, when Milka Planinc became the president of the Federal Executive Council (prime minister), the federal state and its teams of economic experts started collaborating closely with the IMF and became the main exponents of a liberal economic restructuring inside the country.[27] Nevertheless, the decisive move in the direction of reform was dependent on the agreement of the state and party leaderships of the six republics and two autonomous provinces, not the federal government, whose prerogatives had been stripped away in the course of previous pushes for decentralization.[28]

Internally, the intellectuals engaged in cultural organizations and economic institutes spread awareness about the scope of the crisis and the urgent need for widespread reform. The liberalized media radiated these critical discourses. The belief that the Yugoslav system represented a vanguard socioeconomic project in the world, superior to both capitalism in the West and state socialism in the East, had all but disappeared. As a keen follower of Yugoslav politics and society at the time, Pedro Ramet, observed:

[25] Pedro Ramet, "Apocalypse Culture and Social Change in Yugoslavia," in *Yugoslavia in the 1980s*, ed. Pedro Ramet (Boulder, CO: Westview Press, 1985), 9.

[26] For a thicker description of the uncharismatic party cadres that survived the purges of the early 1970s, see Nick Miller, *The Nonconformists: Culture, Politics, and Nationalism in a Serbian Intellectual Circle, 1944–1991* (Budapest–New York: Central European University Press, 2007), 241; and Dejan Jović, *Yugoslavia: A State that Withered Away*, 153.

[27] Dejan Jović, *Yugoslavia: A State that Withered Away*, 100.

[28] The position of Tito, as the lifelong President of the State, was passed on to the institution of the collective presidency, involving representatives of the six republics and two autonomous provinces, reaching decisions on the principle of unanimity. Similarly, inside the Federal Assembly, the most important legislative acts were introduced by consensus vote in the Chamber of Republics and Provinces, a body with delegations of equal size selected by assemblies of the republics and the two autonomous provinces. This left the League of Communists of Yugoslavia as the institution best equipped to bring life to new, all-embracing initiatives going beyond the political gridlock created by the disputing republics. Yet, ever since the early 1960s, the party itself was highly decentralized along territorial principles, with delegates inside the central bodies normally acting as representatives of the interests of their republican organizations.

> A subtle change has taken place in Yugoslav society over the past few years. The buoyancy, confidence, and self-congratulation of the 1970s are gone—casualties of the now-general realization that "self-managing socialism" has failed to live up to its promises. In their place, there are strains of pessimism, gloom, resignation, escapism of various kinds . . .[29]

The dissenting voices started connecting the ongoing crisis to the systemic solutions the party had introduced during the previous decade. There was a growing awareness in society, and in industry in particular, that consistent, pro-market economic reforms could not be conducted without challenging the very concept of Associated Labor. However, the solutions of the 1970s did not introduce consensus-seeking as the guiding principle just within industry; this approach was also upheld in political bodies and reflected in the institutional set-up of the federation. A decisive, open break with Associated Labor in the sphere of economics would inevitably open the question of reforming the Yugoslav political institutions, thus potentially jeopardizing the delicate status quo established between the republican elites under Tito's tutelage.

Throughout the first half of the 1980s, the Serbian and Slovene party leaderships therefore insisted that Associated Labor provided an adequate frame for the economic reforms. In order to be successful, the party claimed that the official stabilization policies should simply be applied more consistently and with communists' greater engagement inside the factories. However, it was one thing for the factory branches to mobilize industrial workers in campaigns for more social and national equality, or against the perceived privileges of other occupational groups. In these situations, the party would usually be following the dominant mood on the shop floors. Asking the blue-collar communists to inspire their coworkers into shouldering the brunt of the crisis was a completely different matter.

The manual workers believed that the white-collar staff and political elites were responsible for the disarray within industry and, consequently, they should pay the highest price for the stabilization drive. The party leadership of the 1980s was dependent on specialists in order to implement market reforms and hesitated to lead another blatant political campaign against the technocracy. The blue-collar workers expected clear answers, namely identification of the functionaries responsible for the crisis and a radical program of economic and political reforms. The party, on the other hand, continued to extend lukewarm appeals for unity and greater sacrifice under the existing organizational scheme. The inconclusiveness of the leadership made the factory party cadres stick to an ambivalent formulation while waiting for clearer signals from above.

On the shop floor, this use of woolly language and a hesitation to place the blame squarely on certain individuals and sections of the party-state became a detested practice often referred to as "hiding behind collective responsibility." In September 1980, a group of IMR party members from direct production gave a controversial interview to one of the most popular Serbian daily newspapers,

[29] Ramet, "Apocalypse Culture and Social Change in Yugoslavia," 7.

Večernje novosti. One of the interviewees, Petar Šikanić, characterized the factory communist functionaries as "professional talkers," people whose main talent was expressing verbal twists and turns depending on the changes in the official political line. Šikanić's fellow worker added: "The conclusions reaching us from above are full of empty phrases. To make matters worse, we often do not implement the decisions reached in the meetings." The text concluded that the decentralization of the factory party organization along the BOAL structure prevented it from adopting a unified line on internal business problems, as single party secretaries would side with the particular views of their department and its executives.[30]

These loud voices in the press were a reflection of accumulating dissatisfaction in Serbia's party leadership. Serbia was the first republic to sound the alarm in the federacy and demand a revision of the solution reached during the 1970s. The steady loss of political control over its two autonomous provinces, alongside the precarious state of its industry, made the Serbian LC stand up and demand a more resolute collective reform push. The Serbian proposals for change remained firmly anchored in the overall economic and political frame of the 1970s. Nevertheless, the Serbian party did launch calls for greater discipline inside the federal bodies of the party-state, and reduced powers for the autonomous provinces of Vojvodina and Kosovo. Furthermore, the LC of Serbia, and the Belgrade City Committee in particular, argued for an increase in the powers of Work Organizations in relation to their BOALs. The Slovene party came out staunchly against the Serbian initiatives. It feared that a coordinated economic reform at the federal level, and a more regulated relationship between Serbia and its autonomous regions, would inevitably raise the question of political recentralization and reduce the sovereignty of the republics.[31]

In 1984, the federal party leadership was finally forced to act under the joint pressure of the foreign lenders, the federal government, the Serbian LC, and the critical media. The LCY made an attempt to revitalize the reform by exposing the inert midlevel echelons of the party to political pressure from below. After the Thirteenth Session of the LCY Central Committee, held in the summer of that year, the party apex called for a countrywide campaign of extensive discussions within the party base. The conclusions reached during the Central Committee session would not be adopted without popular amendments. This was the first officially-structured broad debate of this type inside the party since it came to power after World War Two.

The LCY hoped that the campaign would awaken a new enthusiasm among its weary members and rally them behind the ongoing stabilization drive. A debate on the state of the party and society was initiated in roughly 70,000 branches.[32] Unsurprisingly, the draft document sent out to the party base was

30 Due to great interest, the factory paper reprinted this interview. See Đuro Bilbija, "Sposobni da savladamo teškoće," *IMR*, September 30, 1980, 4.

31 Wolfgang Höpken, "Party Monopoly and Political Change: The League of Communists Since Tito's Death," in *Yugoslavia in the 1980s*, ed. Pedro Ramet (Boulder, CO: Westview Press, 1985), 29–56.

32 Höpken, "Party Monopoly and Political Change," 37–38.

cryptic. It tried hard not to offend any republican leadership by extending an abstract call for unity and more resolute reforms. Commenting on the results of the campaign, one of the leading Yugoslav party historians of the time, Dušan Bilandžić, noticed "astonishing differences" in the level and sharpness of the debate between the critically-minded intellectuals and the regular party members. While the former engaged in debates "questioning the legitimacy of everything created and existing in the Yugoslav Revolution," the latter allegedly continued to repeat lethargic, ready-made, and outdated formulations.[33]

The investigation of events at the micro level in Rakovica and Tezno does not confirm Bilandžić's overall characterization. When observing the discussions taking place in IMR's party branches, one notices that fresh ideas and challenging interventions were not exclusive to the intellectual forums. Despite the dull character of the official document, the campaign managed to break the old routine and connect the local party organizations with the critical discourses circulating in the media and the party apex. Rakovica's communists conducted the campaign as thoroughly as possible, aiming to mobilize all potential forces still oriented toward the traditional institutions of the party-state. Some 6,000 communists participated in discussions. Non-party members were also encouraged to attend, and a guarantee was given that no sanctions would be applied to those who spoke out in a critical tone.

After its first open meeting, IMR's Motor BOAL party branch concluded that so many contributions and topics had emerged that it was necessary to stretch the discussion over three weeks and divide it into three thematic parts. The first week was reserved for internal factory matters. The second week was dedicated to the state of IMR's party structures, and the third to reflections on the general situation in society.[34] During those three weeks, the factory meeting rooms transformed into vibrant places where workers stood up and spoke passionately about all the problems they thought deserved to be tackled.

Addressing broader society and politics, the speakers focused mostly on the lack of respect for manual labor and social differentiations, which were unacceptable for their understanding of socialism. When it came to the situation inside the factory, workers spoke out against *režija*, which allegedly stood closer to the financial flows and molded the basic income distribution agreements to their own advantage. There were critical references to the peasant workers as people occupying jobs that should have been reserved for the unemployed and continuing objections about the unfair distribution of factory apartments. These were all customary complaints. Many speakers, however, also openly criticized what they referred to as boalization,[35] or the isolation of single departments and the difficulty this caused in maintaining production and reaching common decisions. The workers' political instinct was to strive toward the unity of the

33 Dušan Bilandžić, *Historija Socijalističke Federativne Republike Jugoslavije: glavni procesi* (Zagreb: Školska knjiga, 1985), 534.

34 D. Žujović, "Kritički i samokritički," *IMR*, September 11, 1984, 1.

35 The term BOAL obviously gained a negative connotation through the usage of the verb *ourizacija*. Previously seen as a way to introduce workers' democracy and enhance business performance, the process was now connected with particularistic interests and the blocking of decision-making.

working class; but as Momčilo Plećaš, one of the most distinguished blue-collar party activists of the younger generation, noted, "the political solutions are splitting labor much more than they are bringing us together."[36] Discussing the work of local communists, workers complained that the people in leading positions were constantly taking up discussion time during the meetings, whereas ordinary members did not feel free to speak about the management due to possible repercussions. One worker stated that the factory functionaries were threatening his coworkers with sanctions and even police action if they publicly complained about wages.

The threat of force was strongly condemned when directed against the workers. However, state repression in general was not necessarily perceived as a negative measure, especially if used against the privileged social layers. For many speakers it was time for the party to close ranks, denounce vague proclamations, and introduce greater discipline. The combination of calls for stricter control from above and more equality in society can be clearly detected in the speech a party member from Engineering, Petar Hinić, made in the course of the campaign:

> There is a lot of crime, billions have been plundered, and yet the sanctions are mild. As far as I know, since the end of the war no one in this country has been placed in front of the firing squad for embezzlement. . . . Is our society not ripe for another nationalization of surplus goods? We would gain from such measures, as our internal and external debt would decrease. This act would also lower social differentiations and *increase unity among the people.*[37]

The desire for greater "unity among the people" exposed another burning issue. There was eagerness to lift the taboo from discussing the national question and political relations between the republics. As Života Životić, a Foundry worker, commented: "I cannot talk about production quotas and waste in my BOAL if I don't know what the comrades are doing inside the Central Committee, if we do not discuss the issue of nationalism and problems in the delegation system."[38] The workers regarded further federalization of the party-state and the obstinate, uncooperative protectionism of individual republics as harmful tendencies. Again, the Engineering communist Petar Hinić, whose speech was transcribed in full by the factory paper, was among the most direct speakers, openly calling for repression of the "nationalists":

> How many people were taken to court for the events in Croatia and Kosovo? We see that clericalism is raising its head again, many religious movements are blossoming, and nationalism has made its way back into many parts of the country. The party has to clear these things up. Otherwise, the political underground will start taking over, and this is certainly something we do not want to see.[39]

---

36 D. Žujović, "Bez mudrovanja i uvijanja," *IMR*, October 16, 1984, 1–4.

37 D. Žujović, "Ugled na proveri," *IMR*, October 30, 1984, 4, emphasis added.

38 D. Žujović, "Najpre disciplina i odgovornost," *IMR*, October 16, 1981, 4.

39 D. Žujović, "Ugled na proveri," *IMR*, October 30, 1984, 4. When talking about the "the events in Croatia and Kosovo," the speaker referred to the aforementioned "Maspok" movement in Croatia

The discussions did not stop at the factory level. In January 1985, the IMR delegate Veljko Vranješ spoke at the Central Committee of the Serbian LC, repeating some of the main motifs heard inside the factories during the fall and winter:

> Workers are occupied with bare survival while one layer of rich people lives comfortably. Under these conditions all other theoretical discussions, programs, and consensus-seeking are futile, . . . certain comrades complained about the speakers who were harsher and more concrete in their presentations, . . . this shows that the Central Committee forgot the meaning of criticism, while self-criticism has been erased from the party vocabulary altogether. In our factories, we address each other differently. . . . It is high time that we start naming those individuals and forums which are slowing down the stabilization programs. The workers expect this from you, . . . anyone who has followed the media in the last period knows we would have many things to tell each other in a direct communist way. Who will be the first to start?[40]

The more radical voices from the party industrial base were trying to find allies at the top.[41] Yet, for the time being, there was nobody in the Serbian leadership ready to respond to the expressed grievances. By the spring of 1985, this type of discussion was no longer encouraged inside of the factory branches. After a short period of relative opening-up at its base, the Serbian party continued to pursue careful elite politics behind closed doors, where each move against the status quo had to be agreed upon in the federal bodies. As a result, there was great disappointment with the results of the campaign among Rakovica's workers. The spirited debates raised expectations, and yet, in the workers' eyes, the entire effort was once again devalued with "empty talk" when it was handed over to the higher levels of the party-state. The themes of social and national inequality, as well as hopes for a more combative attitude from the top leadership, remained ignored.

in the early 1970s. With regard to Kosovo, the speaker was probably referring to the protests which took place in 1981. In March 1981, a protest over living conditions held at the University of Pristina evolved into street demonstrations by Kosovo's Albanian population, and its youth in particular. The protesters raised concerns about exploitation of the local economy by Serbia and demanded that the autonomous province be given the status of a republic. The intervention of federal police forces resulted in at least nine deaths and thousands of arrests, followed by the instatement of martial law inside the province. See Faton Raçi, *Demonstrations in Kosovo in 1981: The Short History that Preceded Demonstrations, The Reasons Behind, Media Coverage and Possible Organizers* (Pristina: Kosovo Institute of Journalism and Communication, 2009); and Atdhe Hetemi, *Student Movements for the Republic of Kosovo: 1968, 1981 and 1997* (London: Palgrave Macmillan, 2020), 171–99.

40 "Ko će prvi da počne?," *IMR*, January 22, 1985, 2.

41 In 1984, Ivan Stambolić and Slobodan Milošević, younger politicians and former managers in Rakovica, who were more in touch with the party base and its industrial branches, entered top leadership positions in the Serbian LC Central Committee and the Belgrade LC City Committee. It seems plausible that the blue-collar activists registered the sharpened tones of the new reform-oriented faction inside the leadership and tried to reach out to them. The factory press recorded that Slobodan Milošević was present in at least one of the IMR branch discussions (BOAL Foundry) during the campaign.

The letdown was great. In the years to come, the workers would often return to those few months of open debates, referring to them as probably the last time they had hope that things would get better.[42] The official party paper, *Komunist*, could usually be seen lying unpacked in heaps under the mailboxes in the workers' halls. The critical discourse present in the media, and increasingly inside the factories, continued to go well beyond the official political proclamations. The disappointment paved the way for another wave of apathy and cynicism among Rakovica blue-collar workers in the second half of the decade. When asked by the factory press how the party could better involve new members in its work, a young female worker from IMR's Foundry complained in 1987 that an explanation of current issues and events was missing from the party meetings. She found the materials sent to her branch meetings from the City Committee to be "outdated," since workers had already informed themselves on all the issues from the newspapers weeks beforehand.[43]

During the months leading up to the Thirteenth Session of the LCY Central Committee, one also notices increased restlessness in Tezno. In January 1983, the president of the Central Workers' Council, Stane Letonja, identified the three most pressing issues from the point of view of TAM's blue-collar workers. The first was the scarcity of production inputs and the waiting times this caused. The second was the weakness of working-class voices in the municipality and the federation. Finally, Letonja complained about ever-increasing business crime, or the theft of social property, calling for more resolute actions by the state to hinder such acts.[44] The latter two issues went beyond the factory circle, aiming to show that TAM's internal problems were connected to broader discussions in society; however, the floor comments at the meetings of sociopolitical bodies reveal that production standstills were indeed the first and foremost concern on the shop floor. Once they had a chance to be recorded in the factory paper, almost all the workers from direct production complained about waiting times.

The management routinely blamed the suppliers and their irregular shipment of satisfactory parts for the stoppages on the shop floor. The workers, however, tended to locate the responsible parties closer to home. Letonja called for greater accountability of the individuals in the professional commissions attached to the Central Workers' Council. In April of that year, the open discussion at the end of the factory trade union conference was used by the workers to sharply criticize the experts, claiming that they spent time working on side jobs while neglecting their main professional duties.[45] A few days later, the trade union's Commission for Social Standards blamed the Research and Development BOAL for artificially enlarging its wage fund through overtime work.[46] In January 1984, TAM's youth

[42] See, for instance, D. Žujović, "Najpre menjati ponašanje," *IMR*, April 8, 1986, 2.

[43] D. Dikić, "Izgubljeno poverenje i strpljenje," *IMR*, April 14, 1987.

[44] Stane Letonja, "Ujedinimo snage za još bolje povezivanje," *Skozi TAM* (Serbo-Croatian edition), January 1983, 3.

[45] Danilo Vincetič, "Pažnja posvećena humanizaciji rada i nagrađivanju," *Skozi TAM* (Serbo-Croatian edition), April 1, 1983, 5.

[46] Danilo Vincetič, "Lični dohodak mora biti rezultat rada!," *Skozi TAM* (Serbo-Croatian edition), April 22, 1983, 6.

organization quarreled with their higher forums at the municipal and city level over wage disparities. The higher forums accused TAM's youth organization of supporting *uravnilovka*, while its delegates claimed they simply wished to reduce the widening gaps in personal incomes.[47] Interviews with workers from the assembly lines conducted in February 1986 present us with a good insight into workers' reasoning:

> I am convinced that the directors who do not know how to organize work are the main guilty parties. Therefore, we must intensify personal responsibility.
>
> The guilty ones for these deeds always escape responsibility. At the same time, if a worker makes the smallest mistake, he is instantly put in the front of the disciplinary commission.[48]

The professionals were allegedly overpaid and often proved to be incompetent. But who, from the workers' perspective, was in a position to hold them accountable for their errors? Stane Letonja's latter two points of concern hint at an answer. First of all, the workers saw the expansion of workers' self-management and blue-collar political influence in society as the key step toward more efficient production. This reasoning followed the logic of ever-expanding workers' democracy underlined in Associated Labor. However, working-class rule was still not a reality. In April 1983, one of the first questions posed to TAM's newly-elected factory trade union leadership at an inauguration meeting was why blue-collar delegates had so little influence over policymaking, even in the city of Maribor.[49] As workers were still not empowered enough to exercise the political influence they desired, the party-state was expected to act on their behalf. Letonja's call for stricter measures against economic crime displays this logic, which resembled the calls for greater involvement of the repressive state apparatus heard in Rakovica.

The Thirteenth Session of the LCY Central Committee was a chance for TAM's blue-collar workers to seek support among the higher echelons of the party, in the same way as the IMR workers had. However, the campaign in Tezno failed to replicate the grassroots participation documented in Rakovica. Already at the beginning of 1983, the party functionaries from Maribor's City Committee held a meeting with TAM's branch secretaries in an attempt to lay the groundwork for the coming discussions. The city leadership urged the factory secretaries to fight against the "petty-bourgeois attitudes" inhibiting open debate. They insisted communists should not allow themselves to be easily offended and the branches should provide space for critical voices. The secretaries were advised to change their old habits in conducting political work. Instead of simple transmission of policies from above, the party line should be popularized through broad discussions from below.

47 B. Kanižar, "Najobširnejše razprave o osebnem dohodku," *Skozi TAM*, March 1984, 9.

48 Danilo Vincetič, "Do kada neujednačena proizvodnja?," *Skozi TAM* (Serbo-Croatian edition), February 1986, 6.

49 Tomislav Perlič, "Sindikalisti o pitanjima o kojima se (ne)rado razgovara," *Skozi TAM* (Serbo-Croatian edition), April 1983, 2.

The city officials assured TAM's secretaries that this new method of work would unite the rank and file behind the reforms and spread the appeal of the party. However, their suggestions were greeted with resistance and skepticism. The secretary of Research and Development, the branch that had successfully united the factory party behind the management's leadership in the previous years, claimed that they did start discussing the political themes tackled by the Slovene LC Central Committee, but there was little interest among the membership. "The comrades have still not understood that we have a new way of doing things," the secretary concluded. Other secretaries did not show any more enthusiasm; they allegedly had no base to motivate. The factory management insisted the political meetings had to take place after work hours and many workers were not prepared to attend them at this time. The younger workers had little interest in the party and the older members who lived through the purges of the 1970s hesitated to speak up, fearing the potential consequences.[50]

In August 1984, the factory received yet another visit from the higher party echelons. This time, TAM's guest was a member of the Slovene Central Committee, Štefan Korošec, who presented the conclusions of the Thirteenth Session of the LCY Central Committee. The high-ranking functionary invited the party base to "lay their cards on the table," probably expecting to connect the latest conclusions of the party apex with grassroots industrial grievances. However, the well-organized factory officials seem to have prevented any meaningful contact with the regular blue-collar members by presenting their guest with a list of grievances from the management's point of view, along with a unified company strategy for enhanced business performance. The factory management felt it had no need for government advice. On the contrary, it was about to offer a concrete example of reform solutions and expected the Slovene party to follow its model. As the article in the factory paper stated, after the interventions of the leading factory communists the party secretaries from blue-collar departments had no more questions for Korošec.[51]

This is not to suggest that the campaign raised no controversial issues, nor that TAM workers stood unified behind their general management. Looking at the discussions on the level of the BOAL branches, for instance, it becomes clear that communists from the white-collar departments and their counterparts from the shop floor did not have the same outlook on the crisis or on business priorities. The white-collar BOALs, such as Research and Development or Engineering, insisted on the necessity of supporting "creative work," the introduction of a computerized database, and a closer relationship with their German business partner KHD. On the other hand, TAM's blue-collar workers were suspicious of their management and detested efforts to increase the wage differentiation. Workers in Motor mentioned "unjustified investments" and the losses made by trying to export at all costs.[52]

50 Tomislav Perlič, "Poziv na javnu raspravu: Vanredna sednica sekretara OO SK RO TAM," *Skozi TAM* (Serbo-Croatian edition), February 1983, 6.

51 Tomislav Perlič, "Široka razprava in konkretna akcija," *Skozi TAM*, August 24, 1984, 1–3.

52 D. Vincetič, "Komunisti ocenili stanje," *Skozi TAM* (Serbo-Croatian edition), October 1984, 3.

Unlike the white-collar workers, who kept their discussions firmly related to business matters, the voices from direct production were prepared to talk about wider social issues. The Motor workers complained about the rising prices in stores and overcrowding in hospitals. Still, workers in Maribor were not prone to backing up their grievances with overtly political demands. There was no explicit criticism of Associated Labor, even though the local workers were highly skeptical toward the atomization it had already introduced by the late 1970s.[53] In contrast to Rakovica, the workers did not tackle the national issue or relations inside the federation. In Serbia, the ethnically-charged social clashes in one of its autonomous regions brought the national question into the media limelight. Many of Rakovica's migrant workers also had personal connections to the events in Kosovo. The everyday problems in Tezno seemed significantly detached from the type of tensions present in the south of the country.

TAM's shop floors were burdened by the same occupational cleavages and popular perceptions of inequality present in IMR. Nonetheless, during the campaign these divisions did not emerge in front of the party officials or the work collective as a whole. In its summing-up of the discussions conducted inside the branches, the first thing TAM's party Action Conference mentioned was that personal income policy should not be based on the guaranteed wage, nor allow *post-festum* increases of the lowest incomes, as this would allegedly lead to *uravnilovka* and discourage technical innovations. None of the complaints raised by the Motor BOAL entered this last round of discussions.

When it came to common federal political issues, the factory party leadership largely ignored them. They characterized the conclusions reached at the Thirteenth Session of the LCY Central Committee as too general and abstract to be commented upon. TAM's leading communists cynically stated that they were wary of attempting to tackle the latest political conclusions, since numerous prior "historical sessions" were not followed up with any concrete measures. "The same people who pushed the country into economic crisis are still occupying the top positions inside the federal bodies without even having the decency to apologize for their faults," declared the Action Committee.[54] The existence of a strong and unified enterprise management ensured that the factory party could not act as an intermediary between the communist elite and its local blue-collar constituency.

TAM's factory party apparatus entered the second half of the decade utterly uninterested in motivating the wider workforce. Branch meetings suffered from low attendance. The BOAL branches had little internal impetus and usually lagged behind the discussions taking place in self-management bodies and the professional management boards. In May 1986, TAM party member Anton Harb complained that workers were "leaving the party" and added that, among those who stayed, most were active only on paper. The party members

53 This can be explained by the fact that TAM's management had already picked up this issue and put pressure on the political authorities to allow for the reform of Associated Labor. As we will see in the following section of this chapter, by the time the federal party launched its campaign, TAM's top management had already made great strides in altering its organizational structure.

54 D. Vincetič, "Nekateri so le člani ZK, ne pa tudi komunisti," *Skozi TAM*, October 19, 1984, 7.

were "feeling powerless" and becoming "disinterested in political work," Harb concluded.[55] The factory branches received political materials from their city committees and tried to explain them to the membership. Nevertheless, these documents did not correlate with the factory reality and failed to address the burning issues.

The campaign conducted around the Thirteenth Session of the LCY Central Committee failed to establish a stable link between blue-collar grievances and the ongoing efforts to introduce top-down, politically-controlled economic reforms. In Serbia and Slovenia, the party leaderships were losing their positions as independent arbiters in society. If the top party cadres appeared to the public as clueless about how to handle the economic stalemate, a group of intellectuals and politicians shared the popular sense of urgency and claimed to have the answers. The economic liberals, pushed to the margins of political life after the abandonment of market socialism in the early 1970s, returned invigorated in the mid-1980s. The following two sections will describe how the professional management gradually reclaimed their powers in the course of the 1980s, spurred by this change of political climate and economic orthodoxy.

TAM's Pushback of Associated Labor

The liberal economic experts weathered the years of purges inside the economic chambers, universities, and economic journals.[56] They maintained good relations with the enterprise elites and, as the decade advanced, regained lost positions in the party and the state apparatus in particular. Their ideas now seemed to be in tune with the modern global trends in economic thought. According to liberal interpretations, the party allegedly capitulated in the face of social demagogy and left posturing in the late 1960s. The chance for creating economies of scale, forming a competitive industry, and catching up with developed Western societies through market reforms had been wasted, and society was paying the price for it. The renewed faith in market economics rehabilitated the professional business management. Throughout the 1980s, the pejorative term "technocracy" was scarcely heard inside the party forums and the media. The enterprise management emerged as the only force with enough presence and influence inside the factories to rally workers behind the reforms and initiate changes from below. The proposals of enterprise directors were presented as in the interests of Associated Labor as a whole, directed against the incompetent state.

This trend is best observed in the case of TAM. In 1980, five years after Stojan Perhavc's retirement, TAM gained yet another authoritative personality

---

55 "Težko je dobiti ljudi ki bi delali z voljo," *Skozi TAM*, January 31, 1986, 5.

56 For an account of the Yugoslav business magazine *Ekonomska politika* and its influence on the liberal-oriented management and political elite, see Mijat Lakićević, ed., *Ispred vremena, 1963–1973, sudbonosna decenija, uspon i pad srpskih liberala, uzroci i posledice od tada do naših dana, kroz prizmu Ekonomske politike, novine kakvih više nema* (Belgrade: Fond za otvoreno društvo, 2011).

at its head. Under the leadership of Vitja Rode, TAM's general management accelerated efforts to reduce political control over the enterprise.[57] The KPO board was rejuvenated with young engineers and experts from the white-collar BOALs. Being a senior politician and experienced manager, it seems that Rode had little faith in the capability of the party-state to navigate the reforms. Under his leadership, instead of waiting longer for decisive government measures, TAM's management intended to launch its own initiatives for restructuring the enterprise, but it also tried to alter broader relations in the automotive industry. Encouraged by the successful recapture of the factory party apparatus between 1979 and 1982, the management began to voice open dissatisfaction with the overall state of Associated Labor. In September 1982, a member of the KPO, Mihael Gole, addressed the factory Central Workers' Council with the following words:

> Associated Labor is badly organized. Individual producers have been broken up and remain disconnected in manufacturing and sales. For years, this type of fragmented organization of the industry was supported by an economic policy which adjusts itself to less productive and less successful producers. . . . The policy of extensive growth must be substituted with a new orientation which would respect economic laws and reward the more productive and more successful enterprises.[58]

With regard to TAM's internal organization, the main grievance of the new management was the redistribution of the total income according to non-market criteria. TAM's management complained that the existence of a multi-product COAL with vague common interests opened the door to payment extortion and manipulative internal pricing. With the help of politically-steered self-management agreements, the common income—accumulated mainly through the sales of engines and trucks—was allegedly redistributed in favor of servicing departments and plants with low productivity, such as the railway coach producer TVT Boris Kidrič and parts of the plastic frame manufacturer Jože Kerenčić. This left the TAM Work Organization with insufficient funds to finance its own innovative projects and vertical integration in the auto industry. The practice was often pejoratively called the "solidary cover of losses" and allegedly threatened to pull the entire COAL into insolvency.[59]

In the course of 1983, ideas about the reorganization of the COAL structure along more vertical, supply chain lines gave way to outright abandonment of the form. TAM's KPO openly declared that it intended to dissolve the COAL and continue to function as a "Business Community": a larger and looser

---

57 A former partisan and a high-ranking functionary with longstanding experience in the industry, Vitja Rode had the standing and contacts to steer TAM independently of the local party prerogatives. For more on Rode's career, see Bela Sever, "Rode Vitja," *Enciklopedija Slovenije*, vol. 10 (Ljubljana: Mladinska knjiga, 1996), 250.

58 Danilo Vincetič, "Kraći rok za reorganizaciju SOUR ZIV TAM," *Skozi TAM* (Serbo-Croatian edition), October 1982, 1.

59 "Dvostepeno preobraženje u jednoprogramsko usmereni SOUR," *Skozi TAM* (Serbo-Croatian edition), November 6, 1981, 1.

association of enterprises, recognized by the Associated Labor Act, envisioned for technologically sophisticated producers that aimed to unite forces in the research and development of specific products and achieve their joint realization on domestic and foreign markets.[60] The new structure did not mean an outright rejection of Associated Labor. TAM remained divided into BOALs, and the Business Community was supposed to be governed by a common body consisting of worker delegates. In practice, however, the new organizational structure snubbed the spirit of workers' control over the management. By elevating important decision-making far above the BOAL level, the KPO gained greater freedom to pursue its own business visions. The Business Community was supposed to be coordinated by a white-collar BOAL (*radna zajednica*) dominated by TAM's executives, lacking the complex political structures found in a COAL. A successful reorganization along these lines would have enabled TAM to connect more closely with its numerous suppliers based on market principles and regulate income-sharing schemes on its own terms.

The potential formation of a new business association integrated along a vehicle production chain meant that non-compatible plants would soon be left to their own devices. At the beginning of 1983, TVT Boris Kidrič announced it was ready to leave the COAL, pointing out that TAM never fulfilled its investment promises inside the plant. In March that year, the management of TAM COAL reached a decision to release the Croatian-based Likaplast BOAL from the Jože Kerenčić Work Organization. The high price of imported plastic materials pushed the disabled workers' eyewear manufacturer into bankruptcy. The broader Work Organization was instructed to focus on the production of intermediate parts for TAM's trucks, whereas the financial consolidation of Likaplast was left to the local Croatian municipality.

Around this time, media in other republics started reporting on the Slovene enterprises abandoning Associated Labor and enabling the return of the old monopolies. The news had particular resonance in the Serbian media, which accused Slovenia of abandoning collective reform efforts.[61] Once again, the resistance to unfavorable economic policies through exposure of inconsistent regional application was in full effect. Just as TAM's management was trying to loosen the grip of stabilization by pointing out the price increases allowed to southern suppliers, Serbian industry was now asking for more flexibility by complaining about the organizational restructuring in the north. In January 1983, the Maribor-based daily *Delo* tried to counter the negative press by publishing interviews with Vitja Rode, the general manager, and Tezno municipal functionaries. The interviewed officials argued that TAM was not engaging in a disintegrative process, but rather trying to establish closer cooperation with even more producers based on common economic interests.[62]

In October that year the secretary of Tezno's municipal party organization, Alojz Vindiš-Dunda, used similar arguments to justify the new vision to TAM's

---

60 Velimirović et al., *Zakon o udruženom radu*, 262.

61 "OOUR ukidaju, zar ne," *RAD*, March 2, 1984, 10.

62 The interviews were reprinted in *Skozi TAM*: Miran Koren, Danilo Utenkar and Ivan Vidic, "Rad složene organizacije će biti bolji," *Skozi TAM*, January 1983, 2.

communists. He presented TAM's efforts to associate based on market principles as the very essence of the stabilization measures. A factory secretary asked Vindiš-Dunda to clarify why the COAL was suddenly being dismissed as a bad idea when the party had spent years convincing the workers of Associated Labor's economic validity. Vindiš-Dunda's cynical answer to party cadres from the base, still clinging to the 1970s Tito legacy, was quite revealing of the ideological weariness and defeatism inside the Slovene party:

> Time goes on, and with it our general development. Nothing is static and nothing is regulated so well that it cannot be further improved. The Business Community opens up space for better connections with different partners from the automotive branch. After all, comrades, let us not rehash [*podgrejavati*] the past.[63]

With the green light from the local party-state, the TAM COAL organized a referendum in January 1984, asking its constituent BOALs to decide on the transformation into a Business Community. The referendum was successful: as the factory press reported, a "considerable majority" inside the TAM Work Organization voted in favor of the suggestion. With the sway the management enjoyed inside the factory self-management bodies, such a result was hardly surprising. However, the same article also noted that a "significant minority" declared itself against the reorganization; the share of negative votes stood at 22.3 percent in the enterprise as a whole. Inside the blue-collar BOALs, such as Foundry, Metalworking, Engine Production, and Machine Maintenance, the negative vote climbed to around 30 percent, indicating that a passive opposition to the management was mounting. The factory paper, by then under the control of the top management, recognized this opposition, but insisted the workers who did not vote in favor were "in agreement with the proclaimed goals, just unconvinced about the road chosen to reach them."[64]

In May 1984, the TAM Business Community was officially established. It numbered thirty-two Work Organizations, mostly TAM's traditional component suppliers, but also other producers seeking stable sales of their products. The Business Community employed close to 25,000 workers nationwide. TAM immediately used its newly-acquired market weight to avoid procuring components through long-term self-management agreements and to try and influence government stabilization measures. It singled out the partner factories whose sales on the foreign market were realized primarily via TAM, extended them credit, and made the distribution of common income dependent on steady pricing and regular shipment of intermediary products.[65] At the same time, the factory launched a lobbying campaign through its representatives inside the Slovene and

63 Tomislav Perlič, "Sekretari SK podprli predlog obrazovanja Poslovne zajednice TAM," *Skozi TAM* (Serbo-Croatian edition), October 7, 1983, 1–2.

64 "O uspelom referendum za Poslovnu Zajednicu TAM," *Skozi TAM* (Serbo-Croatian edition), January 1984, 1.

65 B. Gerlič, "Zajednički rad mora da je usmeren na tržište!," *Skozi TAM* (Serbo-Croatian edition), November 1984, 3.

federal political institutions. In February that year, TAM's KPO instructed its delegates inside the Slovene Chamber of Associated Labor to pose the question of why Serbian truck producers were allowed to raise their prices while Slovene manufacturers were allegedly still kept under tight administrative control.[66]

The reorganization also left its mark on internal factory life. KPO introduced a new informal management body, which transgressed the strict separation between the governing and administrative functions. The so-called extended KPO meeting would regularly summon the BOAL executives, functionaries of the self-management bodies, and leadership of the sociopolitical organizations into one room under the guidance of the top management.[67] In February 1984, the TAM paper stated that "drawn out self-management meetings are a thing of the past." The article reminded readers that marathon sessions in search of consensus had been a standard procedure for years, but people became tired in such meetings and consequently there was little possibility of conclusions being reached at them. "Today we all start looking at the clock as soon as the meeting lasts over an hour," the article concluded.[68] In September 1985, the Workers' Control raised the issue of numerous trips abroad that the enterprise experts were making. The Central Workers' Council Control Commission concluded that every single business trip was justified, adding that the collective had to understand there was no such thing as an unfounded trip abroad if the enterprise really wanted to reach its export targets.[69] The days when the management was ready to extend symbolic concessions to the blue-collar workers were over. At the end of 1986, in his New Year message to the work collective, the KPO President Vitja Rode stated:

> In the coming years, we will have to respect the economic laws much more than was the case previously, . . . simply put, let those who work better also live better, let them receive a bigger proportion of what they created. In our society, these norms are still not accepted in the way that they should be.[70]

The battle to increase income differentiation was in full swing. During 1985, the main topic of all the business meetings inside the factory was the introduction of a new wage accounting method, Analytical Evaluation of Work (AVN).[71] The main idea behind the introduction of AVN was to introduce clear limits to informal wage augmentation practices on the shop floor. The new rules provided meticulous award indexing for each worker in line with official qualifications and allocated blue-collar laborers to fixed work positions. The measure was promoted

66 Tomislav Perlič, "Iz rada KPO RO TAM (ovog puta proširenog), Razmatranje sadašnjih pitanja privređivanja," *Skozi TAM* (Serbo-Croatian edition), February 1984, 4.

67 Ibid.

68 "Razmatranja sadašnjih pitanja privređivanja," *Skozi TAM* (Serbo-Croatian edition), February 1984, 1.

69 M.P., "Neopravdanih putovanja u inistranstvo nema," *Skozi TAM* (Serbo-Croatian edition), October 1985, 3.

70 Vitja Rode, "Veliki korak napred," *Skozi TAM* (Serbo-Croatian edition), January 1986, 2.

71 The full name of the calculation system was *Analitičko vrednovanje zadataka za bolje poslovanje, bolju podelu rada i prikladnije nagrađivanje rada* (AVN).

as the solution for "true reward according to work," but the workers were unconvinced. The storage worker Oskar Šturm and the metal worker Franc Leskovac commented:

> If everything was as they claim, we would be more than happy with the suggestion. Still, after twenty-two years of experience with different organizations and reorganizations, I can tell you that the promises are always huge, but never fulfilled. I doubt it will be any different this time around.

> Personally, I am satisfied with the new reward system. However, I noticed that the atmosphere around me is not the best. The majority opinion, and I agree with it, is that certain work places are not rewarded adequately. This leads to polarization on the shop floor. My comrades and me, we do not want *uravnilovka*, we simply judge based on our experience and knowledge of concrete situations. The divergence will be greater and the wage gap is not always justified.[72]

In contrast to IMR, TAM workers were choosing their words carefully and constructing justifications when opposing their management. As the second statement shows, the workers did not want to be identified and singled out as rabble-rousers ("personally, I am satisfied") or accused of supporting proscribed income levelling ("we do not want *uravnilovka*"). Still, there were clear signs that the manual workers were unhappy, and that the management had taken their version of reform a step too far. The referendum on introducing AVN, organized in early 1986, failed. Five productive BOALs, and even two white-collar departments, came out against the new rewarding method. The management tried to minimize the significance of this oppositional stand, claiming that workers used the referendum to express their overall dissatisfaction with the situation in the country and the high levels of inflation. A few months later, the referendum was repeated, and this time AVN won the popular vote. In 1987, the Slovene Economic Chamber recognized TAM's entrepreneurial achievements by awarding Vitja Rode Manager of the Year.

The workers were increasingly critical of the top management, but there were no signs of them standing up to defend Associated Labor structures. The failed referendum over the new remuneration system showed how decentralizing the decision-making process enabled the workers to score occasional jabs against the management. Yet, it seems that the perception of the self-management institutions as stable instruments in the fight for better living conditions was not present on TAM's shop floor. The most the referendum defeat in 1986 had achieved was to postpone the unpopular measure: the workers had no power to put it *ad acta*. After a few more weeks of stronger pressure inside the self-management bodies, the management was able to force through the new wage accounting scheme. To the workers, their experience with self-management in a factory like TAM made them see these bodies as fundamentally alienated from the shop floor, with the sole function of spreading and underscoring the

72 Branko Gerlič, "Več ko je informacij, bolj so zadeve jasne," *Skozi TAM*, January 1, 1986, 2.

management's decisions. If there was one measure on which the workers from direct production seemed to agree with the top management, it was that the party-state should invest more effort in dismantling Associated Labor.

The management's proactive stance and critical language in relation to the state positioned it as the locus which could best represent all voices inside the factory. The reform initiatives around the Thirteenth Session of the LCY Central Committee had a hard time motivating the workforce, as they paled in comparison to the activities of Vitja Rode and his associates. TAM's deep-rooted culture of alliance between the shop floor and the top management potentially explains how the enterprise was able to advance its list of pro-market reforms between 1980 and 1986. However, in a top-down managed factory like TAM, the significance of the unsuccessful referendum could not be overstated. The management's rhetoric of blaming the state and other enterprises for production difficulties was wearing thin. The dissatisfaction with managements' neglect of workers' grievances and the growing income polarization was brewing, and the manual workers were searching for novel ways to express their anger. The failed referendum set a precedent and the work collective, which appeared calm on the outside throughout the crisis, would enter a turbulent period by the end of the decade.

IMR Tries to Catch Up

IMR's management and white-collar employees had great difficulty implementing their own plans for the reform of Associated Labor during the first half of the decade. The reform-oriented professionals had had their fingers burned in 1979, when they attempted to influence the factory party and initiate reforms. The outcome of this failed initiative was the removal of the leading white-collar communist functionaries and the disbanding of the united IMR party secretariat. However, the economic conditions were deteriorating fast, and the white-collar staff felt it necessary to take risks and act further in order to salvage the enterprise. The Engineering department used what was left of the common party structure on the factory level—namely the ad hoc Action Conference—to relaunch attacks on IMR's overall development strategy.

In February 1981, Engineering claimed that in the previous year, the collective pressure of other BOALs forced it to accept and vote for the new five-year plan. The engineers now demanded a revision of this strategic document. They claimed that the goal of returning to vehicle production, lost some three decades ago to TAM, became an "obsession" of the blue-collar departments, stemming from the "sentimental orientation of the older colleagues."[73] The department noted that even the most distinguished truck manufacturers in Western Europe were in crisis, and consequently IMR should find a more realistic goal of specializing in component parts and entering the larger cooperation

[73] Lj. Vesković, "Kako do istine," *IMR*, February 24, 1981, 5.

schemes that were inevitably about to emerge in Yugoslav industry. According to Engineering, instead of a "subjective estimation" of product development, practiced up to that point, what the factory needed were investments in new professional cadres, able to systematically research and follow the real demands of the market.

By springtime, the debate had spilled over into the pages of the factory paper. Vehicle's director Strahinja Kostić, a senior engineer well respected among the blue-collar workers, answered a series of critical articles and letters written by the Engineering employees. In his reply, Kostić firmly defended the general orientation of productive BOALs toward the production of motor vehicles. Whipping up enterprise pride, he declared IMR was determined to grow further independently. The crisis might bring about a change in tactics, but the strategy had to remain the same.[74] According to Kostić, IMR would not enter any new broader cooperation agreements on detrimental terms. Instead, the enterprise was set on reconquering the production of more sophisticated products on its own. The discussion in the pages of the factory press heated up to the point where the general management had to intervene with a statement, accusing the paper of stirring up controversy and becoming the voice of individuals, instead of affirming common policies and work results.[75]

The centralizing white-collar initiatives did not cease. Following Engineering's line of reasoning, a proposition was pushed through in the Central Workers' Council to form a new white-collar BOAL integrating the planning, finance, and accounting sections, which were duplicated in each department. In a similar vein, an attempt was made to make the factory more sensitive to market signals by strengthening its marketing section and setting up an internal bank. The blue-collar BOALs successfully blocked all of these actions. For them, such suggestions were unacceptable, as the factory was already intolerably burdened by *režija*.

The tug-of-war soon became focused on the question of factory reorganization. Between late 1983 and 1986, the factory organs were sucked into a prolonged debate on the organizational alternatives possible under the existing Associated Labor legislation. Two new factory schemes crystallized over time, both of which aimed at more effective decision-making. The first option was favored by the productive BOALs. It envisioned an enterprise consisting of four core BOALs, engaged in direct production, and an additional Work Community, which would group all administrative functions together. The second solution, supported by the white-collar BOALs, suggested getting rid of BOALs altogether. The factory staff argued for a coherent Work Organization with a single workers' council, a unified management, and eight well-defined sectors. Both solutions aspired to a leaner model of organization, but the model advocated by the blue-collar departments kept the BOALs as the basic organizing unit, as this guaranteed them autonomy and a stronger say within the Central Workers' Council and the Board of Directors (KPO, the general management).

---

[74] Strahinja Kostić, "Naše zlate jabuke," *IMR*, March 31, 1981, 6.

[75] Lj. V., "Oštro kritikovan list," *IMR*, April 14, 1981, 6.

The restructuring of the Work Organization was central to any internal reform attempt since the existing BOAL structure prevented a clear turn in any direction. As already noted, the Associated Labor Act demanded that all major decisions affecting the enterprise as a whole had to pass through a complex voting procedure inside the self-management organs. A draft document would first be discussed inside the top organs of the administrative and governing structures, the Board of Directors and the Central Workers' Council respectively, before being distributed to the lower level workers' councils of each BOAL. The local councils would then present the proposals to the workers' assemblies of each BOAL, which had the right to discuss and add their remarks. The draft document would then be returned to the Central Workers' Council, which issued the final version to be voted on in the assembly referendums. Any strategic document thus had to be passed by a consensus decision of all BOAL assemblies. IMR's almost symmetrical divide between the BOALs composed of opposing occupational groups meant that this process rarely functioned smoothly. It often took months to persuade the BOAL delegations in the Central Workers' Council to adopt a business decision, and even then the workers' assemblies, as the primary legislative bodies, could still overturn a measure initially supported by their BOAL leading organs.[76] A well-organized group of workers and managers in a single BOAL could therefore block the entire process and that is exactly what Vehicle and Motor did with white-collar reform pushes.

Much like in TAM, the blue-collar workers' reaction to the crisis in IMR was to raise demands for stricter control of the administration and its costs. In contrast to Maribor, IMR's industrial BOALs had the organizational and political power to pursue some of these measures. Already in 1979, the IMR Trade Union Conference discussed the legal possibilities for tying the income of non-productive BOALs to the final product.[77] The director of Motor stated that his department was not ready to tolerate a situation in which large numbers of IMR employees received their wages regardless of the trends in engine sales. That same year, the Motor Workers' Council demanded insight into the contracts signed by the sales BOAL Komerc with IMR's main business partners, in light of suspected irregularities.

The Vehicle BOAL Assembly meeting, held in December 1981, reveals the level of dissatisfaction and agitation among the blue-collar workers at the time. As explained, production bottlenecks were causing long waiting times on the shop floor. The workers reacted to wage reductions by demanding that group foremen and section chiefs—both of whom were paid based on effective time spent in the production hall, regardless of the production rate—undergo similar pay cuts. The proceedings from Vehicle Workers' Assembly meetings show that some workers went as far as demanding the abolition of the mid-level executive positions within the department and a 50 percent cut of IMR's total employees in *režija*.[78]

---

76 D.J., "Svi ili većina," *IMR*, December 25, 1984, 6.

77 "Ozbiljan prilaz rešavanu slabosti," *IMR*, March 27, 1979, 3.

78 Zapisnik sa Zbora radnika OOUR Vozilo, IX Zbor, 14. januar 1982, tačka 2.

Faced with this type of pressure from below, the blue-collar BOAL executives had to take a firmer stand within IMR's central administrative bodies. The shop floor thus exercised its muscle by vetoing the decision-making process in the self-management structures, but it also made sure its interests were protected inside the professional management by forming alliances with lower-level executives. This alliance between skilled manual workers and their foremen and executives made sure that factory surplus funds were used to maintain production targets at all costs, despite the irregular supplies, as the wages on the shop floor were highly dependent on physical output. Nevertheless, this tactic brought diminishing results in the crisis environment.

The increasing costs of inputs and the rise in interest rates, coupled with high government taxation, caused the net enterprise income to shrink despite the increase in production and gross revenues. Ultimately there was barely any money left on the factory accounts for wages, not to mention investment into equipment modernization or the new factory apartments. The money left over for the investment fund decreased each year, giving way to the wage fund, until finally, in 1986, all the enterprise net income was spent on wages. Indeed, during the first half of the decade, IMR workers managed to avoid the severe drop in income that was taking place in many industrial enterprises around them, but their wages were also losing the race with inflation. In 1984, for instance, the inflation rate stood at 66 percent while IMR's wage increases amounted to 44 percent, resulting in a 22 percent drop in workers' real wages.[79] By the mid-1980s, it became clear that workers' reliance on production department executives had brought disappointing results for the work collective. Thanks to the appeasement of the blue-collar workers, the year 1984 marked a historical record in the number of engines produced, but due to rising costs and the closing of the Egyptian market, financial results were still poor. The specialists and highly-qualified personnel started leaving the enterprise. For the general management, these were clear signs to start reconsidering the overall business strategy and leaning more toward the initiatives proposed by the Engineering specialists. The emphasis in income distribution was supposed to switch from manual to innovative work.

In late 1984, the Executive Board of the Central Workers' Council issued a recommendation to Motor and Vehicle to accept an increase in income stimulation in the Engineering department. The engineers engaged in special development projects were supposed to be granted wage increases beyond the general income distribution agreement. The directors of productive BOALs initially accepted the decision in the central management bodies, but then changed their minds once they faced reactions in their own BOALs. Looking at the commotion this initiative provoked among the workers in the Vehicle Assembly, it is not hard to understand why the directors decided to reconsider their position:

> If it turns out that Engineering receives three wages and we and *our engineers* only one, I do not accept this. I understand that somebody works more and

[79] "Život u oči," *IMR*, March 19, 1985, 4.

receives one-and-a-half wages, but three wages more! This I cannot understand, . . . this cannot be earned by work.

If we continue down this road, I am not sure where it will take us. The only thing I know is that this type of suggestion creates great dissatisfaction among the workers. It is unacceptable that someone can earn twelve to fifteen million dinars and the others cannot. We don't need these types of projects.[80]

The blue-collar BOALs started blocking initiatives for the income stimulation of professionals engaged in urgent development projects. If the pressure from their own blue-collar executives became too strong, the workers would simply boycott the referendum or leave their BOAL assembly meetings without a quorum. However, this exercise of power inside the enterprise did not amount to much. After years of internal conflict, all occupational groups were exhausted, and nobody emerged as the winner. The only general conclusion was that the organizational structure, set up in the 1970s, had to be changed as the clashes facilitated by it threatened to tear the factory apart. The question was: who was about to take the lead and present the most consistent critique of Associated Labor?

The political liberalization during 1984 presented an opportunity not only for the workers, but also for professional management to express their grievances. Once news about the restructuring of Associated Labor in Slovenia reached Belgrade in 1984, the management of the local factories decided to put their differences aside and try to lobby the Serbian LC, which appeared increasingly responsive to outside influence. In April, a joint statement by the general directors of key metal factories in the city, including IMR and IMT, called for special legislation, which would ensure that the government taxation burden and bank credit interest did not endanger the reproductive capability of the industry. The directors complained that even though their factories fulfilled the planned output targets, they still did not make profits, as the industry was overburdened with different financial obligations to the state and various Associated Labor institutions. Out of the total income, the industrial enterprises had to make the necessary transfers to funds for common social needs and the running of self-management structures, separate obligatory funds for the less developed regions, pay the government taxes, and return credit with interest to the banks. The total incomes were increasing, but these gains were annulled by heavy state interference and high interest rates.[81]

The joint statement made no concrete proposals on how to return Belgrade's factories to profitability. However, the fact that the obligatory Fund for Common Social Needs—the source of financing for the structures of Associated Labor—had been singled out as the main problem hinted at the direction of the reforms desired by the management. At the presentation of the document, IMR executives openly complained about the rising costs of maintaining the sociopolitical

80 Zapisnik sa Zbora radnika OOUR Vozilo, V Zbor, 12. april 1985, tačka 4, emphasis added.

81 D. Žujović, "Šta traže metalci," *IMR*, April 24, 1984, 3.

and self-management institutions. According to IMR, in the first six months of 1984, the total sum set aside for the common social needs fund came close to the net gain of the enterprise. The Self-Managed Communities of Interest (SIZ), introduced to coordinate and organize social care and local infrastructure outside of the state, were of particular concern. The IMR factory paper estimated that across the country, these bodies employed up to 45,000 people, whose income was constantly rising with the help of self-serving administrative acts. According to the factory managers, the solution was to halt the wage hikes of this lower-level political bureaucracy or, better yet, dismantle many such organs altogether. The report claimed that the Slovene party was already considering freezing wages in non-productive sectors. IMR's top executives were presenting the Slovene party and its measures as a good role model for the Serbian politicians.[82]

In reality, the managers were presenting the situation in a selective way. By targeting the self-management bureaucracy as the prime burden, the criticism avoided tackling the banks and credit-extending final producers. In the first nine months of 1985, the sum put aside by Yugoslav industry for repaying bank debts became equal to its total accumulation. Just three years before, credit costs had amounted to 20 percent of total accumulation.[83] The freedom of the financial market to set "realistic" interest rates was the cornerstone of Yugoslavia's monetary reform efforts. The money spent paying down interest on credit was suffocating the factory just as much as, if not more than, the government taxation. However, IMR's dependence on Belgrade-based banks was so great that confrontation with the financial sector was unimaginable for the management.

Encouraged by the lack of hostile political reaction from the city and the republican political apparatus, IMR's management continued to hone its reform ideas and present them in a bolder manner. In 1986, the key positions in the Serbian party were conquered by a new generation of politicians more closely attuned to the problems of industry, such as Ivan Stambolić and his protégé Slobodan Milošević. IMR delegates in higher forums of the party and Associated Labor structures launched another campaign for retaining a larger part of income within the factories. Speaking in a session of the Belgrade LC City Committee, the Vehicle BOAL executive, Siniša Anđelić suggested concrete measures. He called for a reform of the labor legislation, which would give professional management more powers and make work discipline tighter under the threat of material sanctions and loss of employment. Playing on the existing generational divisions inside the factories, Anđelić mentioned these measures would "free up space for young and unemployed workers eager to prove themselves."[84] Cuts in taxation, lowering of institutional prerogatives for blue-collar workers, freedom to introduce more discipline on the shop floor, as well as a reduction in labor costs were some of the main proposed lines of action. The reform of the Associated Labor Act was a necessary step in this direction. Furthermore, Anđelić suggested that companies should take control over their

82 R.G., "Putevi rasterećenja privrede," *IMR*, June 12, 1984, 7.

83 Sl. A., "Visok rast kamata," *IMR*, March 19, 1986, 2.

84 D.Ž., "Nije vreme za kitnjaste reči," *IMR*, June 3, 1986, 4.

funds for underdeveloped regions from the state and invest these resources on a for-profit basis in the targeted areas.

Unlike in 1984, when the Serbian party greeted the grievances stemming from Associated Labor with approval but backed away from initiating concrete reforms, in 1986 the Serbian parliament initiated a procedure to implement a series of changes in the self-management legislature. The initiative launched by the parliamentarians called for increasing the rights of the central workers' councils and decreasing the powers of BOAL workers' assemblies, which were supposed to vote only on a limited number of issues considered crucial for the enterprise. Clearly, the political tide inside Serbia was turning. After unsuccessful attempts to conduct a common, all-Yugoslav, politically-controlled reform, the Serbian party was about to retreat to its own republic and emulate the Slovene line of handing more initiatives to the managers. The Serbian leadership's focus on the reform within its own borders implied it had to become even more attentive to the specific needs of local industries. IMR's powerful blue-collar BOAL executives, such as Vehicle's Siniša Anđelić or Strahinja Kostić, used the opportunity to put forward their ideas. With the political backing of the new republican leadership, IMR could possibly avoid the pressure to enter one of the emerging monopolies as a mere contractor and fulfill the business objectives set in the late 1970s.

In 1986, Strahinja Kostić was coopted into the enterprise general management. He was placed at the head of a working group in charge of evaluating alternative suggestions for the reconstruction of the enterprise. The waning influence of factory communist cadres and renewed political acclamation of the professional management paved the way for realignments inside IMR. After a seven-year-long tug-of-war, IMR's central governing and administrative bodies agreed to adopt the white-collar reorganizational plan of a unified enterprise without BOALs as the single proposal in a new factory referendum. The assembly protocols show that BOAL Vehicle, the bulwark of former resistance to white-collar reorganizational plans, spent surprisingly little time discussing the approaching referendum. The Vehicle workers noticed that the option supported by their BOAL had suddenly been left out. They reminded the functionaries that the alternative scheme, which envisioned keeping four productive BOALs and one work community (*radna zajednica*), was their preference, but did not insist on the issue.

Strahinja Kostić presided over the last Vehicle Assembly meeting prior to the reorganizational referendum vote, and strongly advocated for the offered solution. Kostić claimed it would enhance the functionality of the enterprise and organize internal responsibilities in a much clearer way. The "rabble-rouser" Đorđe Golubović was a lone voice arguing against the proposed solution until the very end. Four months earlier, he had been removed from the factory trade union officialdom amidst persistent accusations, but there are no signs that this purge was in any way connected to the pending change in course. The assembly transcript unfortunately gives only a brief mention of Golubović's speech, but he was clearly arguing that the new enterprise structure would be detrimental to workers' self-managing rights.[85] Surprisingly, the blue-collar workers backed the

[85] Zbor radnika OOUR Vozilo, XII Zbor, 22. maj, 1986, tačka 2.

management initiative. Out of 5,330 workers on the voting register, some 4,284 participated in the referendum. The suggestion was accepted in all BOALs, with the vast majority of workers voting in favor of the reorganization.[86] The referendum was an unprecedented success and a convincing display of enterprise unity.

Around the same time that TAM was facing its first open signs of internal division with the failed referendum on internal remuneration, its business partner in Rakovica experienced a reawakened sense of unity. Why did IMR's rebellious workers, who only two years before had furiously rejected all white-collar suggestions as a matter of principle, suddenly decide to back down? Ultimately, they found themselves in a desperate situation with no alternative. As we have seen, the peak of political activity in the winter of 1984 did not create steady links with the party leadership. The communists offered no persuasive program of their own for overcoming the economic crisis, while the years of resistance inside the self-management bodies failed to protect against the steady fall in living standards. The factory was facing bankruptcy, in which case the internal debates over the income distribution agreements would prove futile as the company would automatically come under the government restrictions for wage increases. Threatened by the government's strict anti-inflationary policies, closing ranks within the factory was emerging as a priority. The professionals and executives were the key figures, with contacts in politics and the banks, capable of salvaging the factory from the restraining government measures. However, professionals were leaving the factory en masse. In the first months of 1987, some 366 employees had left IMR, most of them specialists.[87] The acceptance of restructuring and a new income-sharing agreement favorable to the white-collar workers could perhaps keep the last nucleus of specialists loyal to the factory.

The approval of the white-collar reorganization scheme was thus in many ways a capitulation, after years of stubborn opposition had led the workers up a blind alley. Yet, this insight fails to explain the massive turnout at the referendum. The manual workers did not merely give the proposal a free pass; they made sure it advanced through the legislative process with an overwhelming number of yes votes across all BOALs. The feeling of helplessness was obviously being offset with traces of new hope. The management's increasingly combative stance in relation to the government and its more confident criticism of Associated Labor certainly contributed to the forging of this new enterprise-based unity and vision of a better tomorrow. In the early 1980s, the reform measures proposed by the white-collar BOALs were modest plans demanding primarily internal enterprise changes. They were presented as a genuine application of the market reform under the existing macro structures. More importantly, their outlook was defeatist. The work collective was supposed to make peace with the role of a minor player on the Yugoslav market, shut down its upgrading plans, and dissolve itself into larger conglomerates.

86 D.J., "Dokazati opredeljenja," *IMR*, November 25, 1986, 1.
87 "Kriza i dalje traje," *IMR*, November 3, 1987, 1.

The newfound language did criticize internal affairs, but also connected the enterprise problems to wider obstacles in industry and politics. The rhetoric picked up by the section of IMR's management between 1984 and 1986 targeted the lower-level bureaucracy and political solutions reached under Associated Labor. This new discourse managed to reawaken the anti-statist instincts of the blue-collar workers and make them put the interests of their work collective first. It also tapped into the widespread feeling of dissatisfaction with the ruling party and its politics. As Siniša Anđelić's plea for the interests of the youth and the unemployed during the 1986 Belgrade LC City Committee meeting reveals, the management aimed to mobilize those layers of workers who felt marginalized by the self-managing elites. Furthermore, the messages directed toward the work collective became much more optimistic and motivational. In January 1987, the former Vehicle executive Strahinja Kostić became the general director. During his inaugural speech, Kostić spoke of his ambition to transform TAM into a "factory of a European caliber" (*fabrika evropskog ranga*).[88]

Blue-collar executives like Anđelić and Kostić played a decisive role in the forging of a new alliance between the workers, the enterprise administration, and the new generation of politicians inside Serbia. As a rule, the workers were suspicious of specialists. Yet, as the trade unionist Milan Kljajić explained in an interview, those white-collar workers positioned closer to the shop floor and seen as being in a direct relation to production were looked upon more favorably. As already noted, one of Strahinja Kostić's main talents was his ability to attract young engineers to his BOAL and make them gain workers' trust through concrete improvements in the production process. The Vehicle workers' aforementioned reference to "our engineers" during the intervention against the wage stimulation of Engineering in 1984 exposes this sentiment. The Engineering employees were in charge of development projects, too abstract and detached from everyday problems on the shop floor. The engineers stationed inside the blue-collar BOALs, on the other hand, were perceived as loyal professionals responsible to the shop floor. Their standing assured the workers that reforms would be implemented in the common interest. Moreover, Kostić encouraged the incipient emphasis on national identity by presenting Serbian industry as lagging behind Slovenia in reforms and bringing into question the political allocation of solidarity funds for the underdeveloped regions.

As we will see in the next chapter, upon coming to the head of the enterprise, Strahinja Kostić introduced a new official discourse which placed the factory in the position of a continuous victim of high politics, one that was nevertheless determined to break with its unequal treatment and finally seek justice. Rhetoric of this type followed in the footsteps of more openly nationalist language in the media and dissident circles in Serbia and Slovenia. Engaged in an increasingly heated fight for the rights of their own respective republics within the federacy, the Serbian and Slovene communists were less prepared to sanction public expressions of nationalism, making it easier for the most engaged activist layer inside the factories to connect industrial grievances to new oppositional themes.

[88] Sl. Avramović, "Možemo postati evropska fabrika," *IMR*, March 17, 1987, 1.

CHAPTER FIVE

Breaking the Pact: Workers, Liberals, and Nationalists against the Status Quo

Cutting out the Middlemen

The 1970s weakened the power of technocracy in industry by inserting a wedge between the lower-paid workers and the management. Under the new institutional constellation, the shop floor could break free from its dependence on the top management. Instead, it could push for higher wages and better work conditions by relying on political representation from an added layer of blue-collar self-management and sociopolitical activists. The previous chapter has shown how, faced with harsh austerity measures and the refusal of the LCY to articulate popular grievances, many workers tended to abandon this Associated Labor alliance, reestablish links with the professional management, and recognize the state and political bureaucracy as the main obstacle to improved business results and higher wages.

The animosity toward heavily-negotiated and decentralized industrial relations developed parallel to critical discourse spread by the dissident intelligentsia and the media, tackling the inefficient state, lack of democracy, and deadlock in the federacy's political decision-making. Before the chapter proceeds to explicate these broader anti-statist and nationalist understandings of the crisis and their echoes inside the factories, the present section will dwell on the more prosaic grievances against Associated Labor from the shop floor perspective. It looks at the criticisms on the micro level which grew spontaneously from workers' everyday experiences of various flaws in self-management. It was the persistence of these mundane problems that made the workers more attentive to wider political discourses circulating throughout society in the second half of the 1980s.

After investing great energy to reorganize industrial relations along the contractual economy blueprints in the 1970s, and spending the first half of the following decade trying to find ways to overcome the crisis though the maze of new self-management institutions, industrial workers were growing increasingly weary of the political grip over the economy. The following statements made by workers from direct production, recorded both in IMR's factory paper and on camera, reveal the level of disappointment with Associated Labor which ushered in the second half of the 1980s:

> In the early 1970s, I was a young worker and I remember we welcomed the Associated Labor Act as a door to the Promised Land. We thought the new laws were the solution for all the problems we had experienced until then. The working class is a defeated winner, . . . we won the revolution, but in the meantime, we went through a defeat.[1]

> I am reflecting deeply upon why I did not leave Yugoslavia in the 1970s so I could then have come back, fifteen years later, as a gentleman, with a nice car and a house. Instead, I decided to stay here and build a socialist society based on self-managed, democratic foundations.[2]

> We call ourselves a socialist country, but if we look at the social relations inside of it, there is no socialism here, just a pure bureaucratic system, . . . the Yugoslav workers are the most exploited workers in Europe.[3]

What frustrated the workers to such an extent that they started becoming hostile toward the very concept which gave them unprecedented legal and political rights? One of the main problems was certainly its bulkiness. Associated Labor's formula of workers' democracy demanded self-management activity from a great number of people within a factory. For instance, the central, truck-producing plant of TAM COAL, the Tezno-based TAM Work Organization, had twenty-two workers' councils with 338 members. Each of these councils had numerous operating commissions attached to them (disciplinary, housing, and so forth). Moreover, the factory contributed worker delegations to self-management institutions outside of the enterprise, such as the municipal and republican legislative bodies (Chamber of Associated Labor) and various other inter-enterprise organs responsible for drafting and implementing common infrastructural projects, social policies, and so on (Self-Managed Communities of Interest, or SIZ). In the late 1970s, TAM COAL maintained 264 delegations numbering 1,781 workers in two chambers of associated labor and numerous SIZ.[4]

In total, 2,200 workers from the TAM Work Organization, or more than one-quarter of the enterprise, participated in various self-management organs. The plebiscite-type activities, such as voting in the Workers' Assembly, required the presence of a minimum of half of the people employed in a BOAL, whereas a referendum envisioned the participation of the entire Work Organization. Most meetings of smaller bodies, such as workers' councils, various commissions, as well as the sociopolitical organizations, were usually held outside of the regular eight-hour work day. The larger meetings, however, had to take place during the main work shifts in order to reach the quorum. As mentioned earlier, the protocols of factory meetings could stretch out for hours. A great amount of

1 Mića Milošević, "Radnici neće žedni preko vode," *IMR*, July 29, 1986, 6.
2 Milošević, *Žulj*.
3 "Da se čuje radnička reč," *IMR*, December 6, 1988, 2.
4 Liberat Buždon, "Delegatski sistem u ZIV TAM," *Skozi ZIV TAM* (Serbo-Croatian edition), September 5, 1978, 4.

enterprise resources and energies were thus dedicated to the running of workers' self-management.

On the shop floors, the maintenance of such a huge apparatus was often seen as a burden and a distraction from the main task of the work collective, namely production. In February 1984, communists from a blue-collar BOAL inside Tezno's TVT Boris Kidrič concluded that self-managing bodies demanded too many cadres from them and wondered who would stay behind to work. Highlighting the absurdity of a system in which everyone decides on everything, the workers mentioned that their BOAL was forced to send a crane operator to the commission for market research, as the few economists they had were already selected for various delegate responsibilities.[5] In October that same year, the conference of TAM's communists complained that political functionaries were not returning to their workplaces after the end of their mandates, thus weakening the enterprise.[6] Already having a hard time hiring and retaining educated staff and skilled workers, the factories were now forced to let these cadres spend a good portion of time in higher-level self-managing bodies, instead of using their talents to help their work collective directly.

Another important grievance was that manual workers were unable to engage meaningfully in self-management activities without cutting ties with the shop floor. The majority of enthusiastic participants in meetings without a standing self-management function were well-positioned professionals from white-collar departments. IMR engineer Nikola Uzelac, for instance, regarded sociopolitical activism as an "honorable deed" and despised careerism. Uzelac portrayed himself as "a bit of an idealist." He identified strongly with self-management as an idea and spent years in Third World countries with various Yugoslav enterprises working on local infrastructural projects as a part of cooperation agreements related to the Non-Alignment Movement.[7] In TAM, people such as the aforementioned Liberat Buždon, a member of the white-collar staff, invested great energy in writing open letters to the factory press, in which he appealed for the respect of social property and stressed the importance of the new social relations enabled by socialism.

For the manual workers, especially the lower-paid ones, who had to work long overtime hours in order to surpass the norms and lived far away from the factory, active participation in self-management bodies proved to be a difficult task. Most of them observed the factory primarily as an employer to whom they sacrificed time and energy in order to earn a wage, not an institution of sociopolitical emancipation. Their "no-nonsense" attitude and belief in hard work as the central component of life made them exceptionally distrustful of people who earned money by debating in meetings. For the most part, the workers viewed proceedings inside the self-management organs and sociopolitical organizations as "empty talk," or yet another irrational bureaucratic obstacle they were forced to live with.

5 Zmago Gomzi, "Sindikat mora oblvadati politične razmere," *Skozi TAM*, February 1984, 11.
6 M.Č., "Zveza komunistov usmerja vse oblike SLO in DS," *Skozi TAM*, October 1984, 7.
7 Lj. Vesković, "Inženjer Nikola Uzelac: 'Ne volim improvizacije,'" *IMR*, June 12, 1984, 4.

In April 1983, IMR Central Workers' Control received a letter from an angry worker who demanded to know how much time the workers with self-management functions spent on the factory floor and how they managed to earn the same wages as highly-qualified workers, since nominally they were paid according to production norms.[8] This complaint struck at the chief contradiction of Associated Labor. The reforms of the 1970s tried to combat the influence of "techno-bureaucracy" inside the enterprises by transferring the majority of important decision-making to delegate workers who sat in elected self-management factory organs for a limited mandate without a full-time functionary wage. Nevertheless, the idea of worker-delegates, who participated in the governing structures in parallel with their daily jobs, was never accomplished in practice. The increasingly complicated and demanding self-management factory structures required that the highest delegates spent most of their workday debating and voting on self-managing compacts and agreements, with little opportunity to perform their basic work duties. In most of the firms the white-collar employees, whose desk-job workload was less demanding, filled the time-consuming delegate duties. However, in the representative metalworking plants such as IMR and TAM, the political imperative was for the production workers to engage in self-managing and sociopolitical activities.

At the height of Associated Labor in 1980, the conference of TAM's trade unionists concluded that an ever-increasing number of workers were refusing to participate in governing bodies and sociopolitical organizations, as doing so took time away from their work chores and leisure activities. The instruction given to them by the trade union functionaries from Tezno municipality was clear: those individuals willing to sacrifice and participate in the self-managing functions should be financially rewarded.[9] In practice, this meant that politically-active workers were promoted to better-paying positions on the shop floor even though they could rarely be seen behind their machines. In other words, they continued to receive the full wage of a highly-skilled worker, despite their frequent absences. The ordinary workers who received their wage based on strict norm measurement tended to be distrustful of their politically-active colleagues, viewing them as careerists, people who betrayed the craft and sided with the white-collar staff:

> Many lazy workers enter the party just to have a shield behind which they can hide . . . the only working-class thing about them is their blue work suit . . . these are not real workers . . . they should be kicked out of the party.[10]

> Comrades with self-management functions in BOAL Motor forgot about their working-class background, . . . they no longer think as workers.[11]

---

8 D. Žujović, "U suženom krugu," *IMR*, April 26, 1983, 2.
9 "Prva sednica konferencije OO SS," *Skozi TAM* (Serbo-Croatian edition), November 1980, 18.
10 "Opori optimizam," *IMR*, February 5, 1985, 6.
11 "Bez uvijanja," *IMR*, January 21, 1986, 6.

Indeed, the delegate function came to be one of the main channels for social mobility and a transfer from direct production into administration. Aside from receiving the wage of a norm-breaking manual worker for an office job, the self-management and political functionaries enjoyed numerous other advantages. Functionaries who entered different Associated Labor bodies beyond the factory, financed from the state budget, could bring their wages in line with inflation much more easily than manual workers pressed by income-sharing self-management agreements and stabilization measures. As we have seen in the case of party cadres who attended political schools, many workers involved with self-management functions never returned to production. Others would be promoted to the position of supervisor or other leading positions in the professional management chain after the end of their delegate function. Of course, delegates could count on such rewards only if, during the time spent in sociopolitical organizations and self-management bodies, they showed an understanding for the demands of the party and the management. As one of the rare IMR workers who returned to the shop floor after his delegate mandate said: "For a functionary career you have to be a hypocrite, obedient, and willing to openly defend things you normally would not. . . . Here in the production hall, the atmosphere among the people is somehow different . . . [there is] some kind of camaraderie, honesty not found on the other side."[12]

It would be wrong to think the self-management apparatus had no base on the shop floor. However, the nature of this support was far from one between the democratically-elected delegates and their base. The reports of IMR's Central Disciplinary Commission show that elected self-management organs evolved into a network of cronyism. In 1985, the commission warned once again of growing disciplinary breaches and the illegal appropriation of social property, disclosing that the main reason for the low number of sanctioned workers was that the lower-level workers' councils often revoked the decisions of the Central Disciplinary Commission, thus abolishing members of their own work collective.[13] The report hinted that this was the result of a patron-client system, which extended between the executives, supervisors, and self-management functionaries on the one hand, and groups of favored workers on the other.

In 1988, IMR's white-collar worker Vasilj Cvijanović wrote a letter to the factory press complaining about the unhealthy atmosphere of suspicion caused by "cliquish behavior" (*grupaško ponašanje*). The letter claimed that most workers were spending time bad-mouthing other colleagues, speculating on "[w]ho was employed with the help of connections, who has an uncle in a leading position, and who extracted individual profit from metal disposal," instead of thinking strategically about the business future of the company.[14] Two years earlier, IMR manual worker Mihalj Đurčik noted that self-managing and sociopolitical functionaries were trading work positions behind the machines for desk positions and used their powers to employ "wives, children, all their cousins."[15] Manual

---

12 Mića Milošević, "Radnici neće žedni preko vode," *IMR*, July 29, 1986, 6.

13 Sl. Avramović, "Radnički saveti—za nered," *IMR*, December 24, 1985, 2.

14 Vasil Cvijanović, "Sami sebi cilj," *IMR*, January 26, 1988, 7.

15 D. Ž., "Dosta je bilo price," *IMR*, March 19, 1986, 4.

worker Berzad Krasnić accused the supervisors of assisting peasant workers to leave work during work hours and rewarding them with wage stimulations during their absence.[16] This accusation indicates that some functionaries were buying shop floor acceptance of their attending meetings during work hours by extending paid leave to favored workers.

Many productive workers started relying on the support of blue-collar functionaries to obtain small perks, such as transfer to a new machine, employment of a family member, or periodical absence used for fieldwork or parallel jobs. These client networks often overlapped with traditional kinship ties or factory circles connected by place of origin. As already described, the recruitment of new workers depended on established migrant workers who attracted family members and other laborers from their home villages.[17] The apartment commissions were the epicenter of shady practices. The IMR paper reported "ugly and illegal behavior" on behalf of individuals trying to move in to company apartments. The candidates were providing the apartment commission with faked medical reports, entered into arranged marriages, and registered extended family as members of the household solely to advance on the waiting lists.[18] In return for favors, the informal networks extended political support to leading BOAL cadres whenever their functionaries were confronted with the higher sociopolitical forums or the central management.

The groups of manual workers connected by the production process developed a group loyalty to the local leadership, even when family or village ties did not connect them. Single BOALs and work groups tended to see the prosecution of their members as an attack on the entire immediate collective. The blue-collar BOALs in particular seem to have held the opinion that disciplinary measures were directed disproportionately against the manual laborers, whereas the wrongdoings of the white-collar workers and the top management passed by undetected. For these reasons, they tended to turn a blind eye to offenses in their workplaces and developed an allegiance to their department and mid-layer functionaries, who could offer them protection from top management and disciplinary bodies. In IMR, the defensive stance of the manual workers and an alertness to what they perceived as double standards were expressed very openly:

> The one who stole should be named appropriately: a thief. A worker gets punished if he steals a few screws; a director brings the company to the edge of bankruptcy and nobody is held responsible.[19]

16 D.Ž., "Zna se ko radi," *IMR*, October 30, 1984, 4.

17 For instance, the *IMR* paper carried a story about the Malinović brothers. The oldest brother belonged to the first postwar generation of workers and, over time, he helped employ two of his younger brothers in the factory. All the brothers were active sociopolitical workers and equated the factory with their home. The article mentioned that the Malinović family was by no means an isolated case, stressing that many families had multiple members in the same factory. See Sl. Avramović, "Fabrika nas odgajila," *IMR*, April 12, 1978, 8.

18 D. Žujović, "Na ispitu savesti," *IMR*, October 14, 1980, 3.

19 Milica Lučić-Čavić, "Paraliza a ne kriza," *IMR*, July 28, 1987, 6.

> A worker's wage is lowered as soon as he breaks a screwdriver, or he is fired if he steals a component. On the other hand, we have machines which were imported and then lay unused for years, . . . responsibility is already lowered for a foreman, not to mention the directors.[20]

By the mid-1980s, however, the patron-client relationship was proving to be of declining worth for the manual workers. The political climate was changing in both republics, and the managements were given the green light to introduce stricter discipline inside the enterprises. The cuts in non-productive spending severely limited the power of the mid-level bureaucracy to offer favors. Most importantly, the prolonged economic crises contributed to the increasing polarization of blue-collar workers. The cleavage between the minority of workers who could reap small benefits from patron-client networks and the majority of workers, who were excluded from these schemes, became more visible. The former were typically senior workers, sociopolitical cadres, or individuals who enjoyed additional sources of income in the form of land or side jobs. The latter group included younger workers, women, and low-qualified individuals dependent solely on the factory wage. The focus of workers' criticism was slowly switching from top executives to the better-standing layer of manual workers present on the shop floor.

Franci Pivec, a former Slovene functionary and leader of the Maribor party in the late 1980s, revealed in an interview that if there was one section of the industrial elite the workers despised more than the top executives, it had to be the blue-collar workers who used Associated Labor channels to advance to different functions and gain material benefits.[21] Workers with high incomes, those whose seniority or political position enabled them to acquire spacious company apartments and who then used their improved purchasing power to build weekend retreats and summerhouses, became symbols of inequality. As already noted, rent in the private market could add up to one-half of a blue-collar worker's income and those workers whose housing situation had been resolved automatically had a greater part of their wages at their disposal. This made them rich in the eyes of their less fortunate colleagues. The antagonism grew even stronger when the well-paid and established workers appeared in the role of rent-seekers to their less privileged colleagues. IMR youth organization activist Radoš Karaklajić effectively expressed the anger against the privileged blue-collar workers in front of the camera in 1986:

> Let us be fair and admit there are rich workers among us. The systemic solutions allowed them to become rich. We are not all in the same economic predicament in this factory. There are very rich workers, who are not more hardworking than my colleague here or than me, but during the 1960s, they were able to access credits, apartments, and houses and now they are exploiting the person next to them.[22]

---

20 Milošević, *Žulj*.

21 Interview with Franci Pivec, April 2013.

22 Milošević, *Žulj*.

In order to understand the indolent attitude of workers toward management offensives against Associated Labor, or even their outright support for it, it is also important to realize that the workers' councils were never envisioned as organs of representation for the interests of various personnel categories, but rather as a managerial body where people contributed individually to achieving the best possible business strategy.[23] During the stabilization period, technological innovations and marketing strategies once again took precedence over production, and the blue-collar workers felt they had little to contribute to the meetings. The office employees, better educated and more skilled with words, could argue their positions much more effectively than the blue-collar delegates. As blue-collar workers active in these structures remember, the lack of arguments in meetings to confront the well-informed professionals was their main frustration, often leading to feelings of inferiority.[24] Workers lacked well thought-out and organized representation in workers' council meetings. The only guidance was the party, but once the communists chose to orient their politics toward the professionals, there was no preparation beforehand, nor any common blue-collar platform.

An interview with worker-delegates in TAM's press reveals how the blue-collar delegates in self-management organs often felt like embellishment in a process run by the party and the white-collar factory elite. The delegates complained that they received preparation materials only shortly before the sessions, thus they had no time to prepare. The documents were long and written in a complicated language full of legal, economic, and political jargon, so many workers did not bother to read them. In the legislative bodies outside of the factories, the paper complained that workers were unacquainted with the procedures and "posed questions incorrectly [*sic*]." The delegates were allegedly not capable of reporting to the factory councils on the decisions made inside the municipal bodies, as they did not understand the discussions in the proceedings.[25]

The IMR Vehicle BOAL Assembly was one of the more contested self-management forums where blue-collar workers were present in large numbers. The inspection of minutes from this assembly shows that even when pressure from below was applied, it came spontaneously, with one dissenting voice built upon by the next until a critical mass was reached. This means the workers' oppositional sentiment could rise in one meeting and die out by the next, with few continuities or remaining traces of alternative suggestions. For many workers there was no point in raising issues, since all battles were seen as lost even before they began. In the end, the prepared, organized, and articulate administration always emerged as the winner. As one IMR worker complained in 1986:

> I look at the comrades coming out of these meetings, their heads bowed down, in a bad mood, full of shame, . . . you have the feeling that somebody is constantly deciding in your name and they need a cover, . . . the feeling of manipulation, powerlessness and shame has accumulated. The workers do not

---

23 Comisso, *Workers' Control under Plan and Market*, 60.

24 Interview with Momčilo Plećaš, March 2011.

25 B.M. "Da li zaista odlučujemo?," *Skozi TAM* (Serbo-Croatian edition), January 1979, 9.

> want to participate in these meetings, and then they say we are not interested. When you decide to show up and say something, it's as if there is nobody on the other side, as if you are talking to a wall. People don't even bother to go to assemblies any longer, . . . they are tired of playing the role of extras in this film, while on the other side they keep telling us we are the main protagonists of society and history.[26]

In October 1986, an IMR delegate reported about the state of self-management in his factory to the Serbian LC Central Committee:

> Under the present circumstances, the motivation for work on the job and in the self-management organs is fading. This is reflected in the fact that we have not been able to organize a union conference in years. Out of 1,500 members in one BOAL, some forty people show up for the trade union meeting. In the assemblies, it is not much better. If we did not pull people in by their sleeves and escort them into the meeting hall, only ten to twenty percent of workers would appear.[27]

Finally, the key concern that brought the manual workers and the top management closer together was their frustration with unaccountability. The shop floor workers were used to the strict daily monitoring of their performance behind the machines and responsibility to the foreman. In order to leave their workplace they had to receive permission from the supervisor, or escape from work under the risk of sanctions. On the other hand, the politically-active workers had the freedom to walk from one part of the factory to the other and attend meetings in the municipality and city center. In IMR the activists, but also the technicians and maintenance specialists, were pejoratively called "wanderers" on the shop floor, as the ordinary workers were envious of their freedom of movement. As one TAM worker describes:

> It is great to walk in the park with friends during work hours . . . some do it every day. It is different on the shop floor. The production norm haunts a worker and he must achieve it otherwise his wage will suffer. Behind him, there is the man in the coat [foreman] who grades him, moves him to different machines, punishes and holds responsible . . .[28]

The lack of clear tasks and liability of blue-collar sociopolitical activists, along with their distance from the shop floor, motivated the workers to stop distinguishing between them and white-collar, non-productive employees. As we have seen, manual workers wildly overestimated the number of desk workers in their factories. They believed that politically-active workers were inflating this figure even further by employing new people through their connections.

---

26 Mića Milošević, "Radnici neće žedni preko vode," *IMR*, July 29, 1986, 6.
27 D.Ž., "Opredeljenje sprovoditi u praksi," *IMR*, October 15, 1986, 6.
28 Franc Pajtler, "Sem storil prav?," *Skozi TAM*, July 1988, 3.

The crony networks allegedly filled the key posts in the offices and the shop floor with mediocre, incompetent cadres, encouraging general sloppiness and contributing to poor business results. The absence of clear responsibility inside the self-management structures was allegedly mirrored inside the production halls among the ordinary workers through the reckless use of tools, wastage, and misappropriation of social property. It seemed nobody was able to hold to account the countless middlemen positioned between the shop floor and the top managers and political authorities. The executives and apparatchiks introduced by Associated Labor were hiding their ineptitude behind the collective decision-making of the working class, while the enterprises were sinking into anarchy.

The top professional management seemed best positioned to discipline this dispersed crowd of favored workers, crooked supervisors, opportunistic delegates, underperforming specialists, and ambitious lower-level executives. Despite the underlying tension with the management, the blue-collar workers seemed ready to identify with the enterprise as a whole and stand behind the directors and specialists in their calls for more enterprise autonomy, greater accountability, and the setting of clear business objectives whenever the general management gathered strength. The factory political bureaucracy was seen as a pricey superstructure, hampering decisive strategic business decisions which could increase the factory profitability. The entire self-management edifice was deemed superfluous without an income whose division the workers could discuss. IMR's young party activist Momčilo Plećaš put it bluntly in 1987 when he addressed the higher party forums with the words: "Give us back our income and we will hand you back self-management."[29]

Instead of the usual appeals to raise participatory and collective consciousness, in the second half of the decade TAM's newspaper opinion pieces started openly disputing the virtues of workers' self-management. In 1986, the TAM professional Jože Čuješ wrote a series of articles arguing that the industry had to free itself from "tutorship and intermediaries." According to him, workers needed "true democracy" instead of "small circles, which base their authority on positions of power."[30] This call for an industry free of middlemen and the supervision allegedly exercised by tiny groups without democratic legitimacy was a clear blow against the self-management and sociopolitical apparatus of the factory, as well as a recollection of a time when the workers and the general management enjoyed more direct communication. That same year, in an interview for the IMR paper, a skilled worker from Maintenance summed up the workers' hostile attitude against self-management and their readiness to extend support to their professional management:

> It is about time we make a distinction between self-management and proper management. When I say this, I refer to people who act as if they possess unlimited authority once elected to governing or sociopolitical positions. Apart from this, I am tired of the constant bickering between the self-management structures

[29] D.J., "Kakav nam treba Savez komunista," *IMR*, March 3, 1987, 2.

[30] Jože Čuješ, "Ni mogoče taktizirati s samoupravljanjem in hkrati ohraniti oblast," *Skozi TAM*, March 1986, 12.

and various sociopolitical organizations. They act as if we are not all in the same boat. I support granting greater powers to professional management, but this should be followed by greater accountability.[31]

A decisive change to the factory decision-making edifice was becoming a popular demand. Moreover, a good number of workers, especially in Serbia, were of the opinion that the reforms should not be limited only to the realm of industry. In 1986 IMR's paper started revealing statements in which workers openly compared the economic inefficiency of atomized work collectives with the political obstructions and economic protectionism of the republics within the highest Yugoslav political bodies: "We greeted the Associated Labor Act with open arms, however, it soon transpired that it creates a *mini federation*, separate bank accounts, autonomy of basic organizations. The BOALs became an excuse for all kinds of isolationism and misbehavior. . . . The workers have no benefit from this."[32]

The conflict-ridden factory therefore became a symbol for the country as a whole. The internal efforts against Associated Labor were related to broader struggles against the state bureaucracy and status quo in the relations between the republics. The following two sections will describe the rise of nationalist sentiments in Serbia and Slovenia respectively, as well as the various ways in which these previously abstract national disputes were connected to workers' daily concerns. At the end of the chapter, the second appendix once again underlines the absurdities of factory life under Associated Labor through the witty factory cartoons.

The Stolen Golden Apples

The economic liberals were not the sole challengers to the mainstream political understandings inherited from the 1970s. The inability of the communists to step forward with an unambiguous message and set the trend within society provoked intellectuals of all shades to start searching for answers, independently of the indecisive and weakened party-state. Inside Serbia, the formation of what was to become known as the "nationalist intelligentsia"[33] started in the early 1980s, with a wave of cultural production that questioned the official narrative of historical events. In 1984, the Croatian LC Central Committee published a lengthy document listing and describing various theatrical plays, novels, films, and aphorisms containing "politically unacceptable messages." The vast majority of this production, which aimed to find answers to existing social tensions through a critical reassessment of the past, took place in Serbia and Slovenia.[34]

31 D. Žujović, "Najpre menjati ponašanje," *IMR*, April 8, 1986, 2.

32 "Bez uvijanja," *IMR*, January 21, 1986, 1, emphasis added.

33 Jasna Dragović-Soso, *Saviours of the Nation: Serbia's Intellectual Opposition and the Revival of Nationalism* (Montreal: McGill-Queen's University Press, 2002).

34 Kosta Nikolić, Srđan Cvetković and Đoko Tripković, *Bela knjiga—1984: Obračun sa "kulturnom kontrarevolucijom" u SFRJ* (Belgrade: Službeni glasnik, 2010).

One of the most widely-read writers in Serbia, Dobrica Ćosić, perfected the imagery of the Serbs as a victimized nation. In his novels, the Serbs had to bear the brunt of the socialist project and received the least in return. The Serbian nation entered the revolution and adopted communist ideology in massive numbers, naively believing that Yugoslav identity would spread beyond the existing Balkan ethnicities. At the same time, other nations were allegedly using socialist Yugoslavia as a cover for their selfish aims of nation-building. The condition of the decentralized and dysfunctional Yugoslav state, where each republic protected its own specific set of interests, could be relied on to support this thesis. Consistent with Ćosić's understanding, the Serbian people had to free themselves from Titoist dogmas, rediscover their cultural essence, and create a new modernizing program in touch with the times.

This task was adopted by numerous artists, journalists, and other intellectuals who sparked the collective imagination of Serbian citizens by taking fresh approaches to old historical topics finally available for discussion outside of privileged party circles. One of the main themes was the painful legacy of ethnic cleansing by rival nationalist militias during World War Two, but also the previously taboo accounts of factional squabbles, dissidence, and suppression within the ruling party, often exposing different republican leaderships standing in rivalry rather than the proclaimed "brotherhood and unity." The idea of the nation as the principal subject of history was slowly replacing the notion of class in public discourse. These controversial themes appeared to be of utmost importance in the atmosphere of heightened ethnic tensions in Kosovo amid claims that the Serbian population was being forced out of the province under pressure from Albanian separatists. The autonomous region had been under the spotlight of the Serbian media ever since the 1981 street protests by local Albanians and the subsequent state of emergency.[35]

The political articulation of the abundant oppositional themes produced by the dissidence of the early to mid-1980s was made possible through a document drafted by the Serbian Academy of Sciences and Arts, popularly known as the Memorandum. The document was leaked to the press before it was finished, in September 1986, and instantly gained notoriety as the political platform of Serbian nationalism. The Serbian party banned its further publication and started a campaign in the local branches to condemn its content. The historiography usually focuses on the second part of this lengthy document, entitled *The Status of Serbia and the Serbian Nation*. This section dealt with the Serbian national question under the 1974 Constitution, bringing together some of the

[35] Kosovo was an autonomous province inside Serbia with a majority Albanian population. The region was the most economically underdeveloped part of Yugoslavia and a place where social tensions were often expressed along ethnic lines. The multiethnic partisan movement in Kosovo never took strong root during the German occupation. After World War Two, Kosovo was overseen by a strong police presence, while Serbs dominated the regional party-state. During the decentralization and liberal policies of the 1960s and 1970s, Kosovo began the cultural and political emancipation of Albanians, and local non-Serb elites were increasingly occupying places in local institutions. The economic slowdown of the 1980s increased ethnic tensions and accelerated migration out of the region.

main pillars of the nationalist mythology created in cultural circles during the previous years, and arranged them into a coherent narrative. However, it was the economic and social analysis found in the first part of the document, entitled *The Crisis in the Yugoslav Economy and Society*, which managed to connect these transcendental themes of historical victimization to the concrete grievances of people in their homes and workplaces.

The Memorandum insisted that the 1974 Constitution betrayed the original concepts of the united Yugoslavia set up during the partisan-led struggle against fascism. Granting unprecedented constitutional prerogatives to six republics and two autonomous provinces created eight separate markets, which was at odds with the demands of rational economic behavior. This tendency toward decentralization was matched inside the enterprise with the implementation of the Associated Labor Act. Economic efficiency and workers' democracy were allegedly subordinated to the interests of political bureaucracies, which held a monopoly on power in the republics, provinces, municipalities, and single enterprises. This overstaffed apparatus suffocated economic incentives and made Yugoslavia fall behind in the technological race with the economically highly-developed nations. The country's twisted institutional set-up and illusions about a "contractual economy" left no room for the market or the planning function of the central state. The answer was a modern, unified state, where the rules of the game were simple and constant: a new, centralized Yugoslavia, where state officials, rather than being selfish elites hiding behind national interests, would be elected based on competence, and decisions made in accordance with calculated costs and gains.[36]

The Memorandum was a mixture of different ideological strains that had been circulating among the Serbian intelligentsia in the previous decades. The document reflected the clear influence of liberal economic experts in its demands for a greater market role and a smaller, more efficient state apparatus based on meritocratic principles. On the other hand, it also carried smaller vestiges of the left-wing opposition from the 1960s, proposing, for example, to extend the power of workers' councils through the introduction of the Chamber of Associated Labor into the Federal Assembly. The third and most dominant ideological streak was that of Serbian nationalism. Unlike the economic liberals, the nationalists felt that the question of development strategy, a choice between the market and the planned economy, was secondary to constitutional reforms and the centralization of the state. Serbia was allegedly suffering the most under the existing federal setup, since it was the only republic inside of which two additional autonomous regions had been created. It was now incumbent upon the Serbian people, as the most numerous and—allegedly—the most humiliated nation in Yugoslavia, to regain a sense of political direction and lead the country toward necessary reform. In contrast to the main oppositional direction of the 1960s and 1970s, when reforms were connected with the greater role of the working class, the democratization of the country and its economic progress were now put into the context of national homogenization.

36 The full text of the Serbian Academy of Sciences and Arts' *Memorandum* can be found in Slaviša Lekić and Zoran Pavić, *VIII Sednica CK SK Srbije: nulta tačka "narodnog pokreta"* (Belgrade: Službeni glasnik, 2007).

In March 1987, the president of Rakovica's Municipal League of Communists boasted in front of the City Central Committee that, "unlike downtown," in his municipality, "there are no influences of the bourgeois right, religion, or nationalism."[37] Yet, there is plenty of evidence showing that the blue-collar neighborhoods did not lag behind the city center when it came to the spread of oppositional themes. Already in the mid-1970s, the IMR paper warned its readers about the spread of religious influence in the municipality. The articles stressed the increased activity of the Serbian Orthodox Church as well as smaller religious groupings, such as the Adventists and Scientology.[38] Interestingly, religion did not have a prominent place in the Serbian oppositional discourse of the 1980s and Rakovica's workers showed no public signs of a greater connection to the church. On the other hand, discussions around the Thirteenth Session of the LCY Central Committee showed that controversial political and economic questions, such as the position of the Serbian minority in Kosovo, national divisions inside the party-state, social inequalities, illegal appropriations of social property, and the atomizing nature of Associated Labor were stirring much emotion inside the factories.

The Memorandum polemic did not bypass Rakovica. An interview in the Serbian trade union paper *Rad* with a group of Belgrade shipbuilding workers recorded the following when discussing the Memorandum: "The banned or condemned books are the ones read the most. In our enterprise, this is also the case. Everybody knows who has the book, how much time one can keep it, and to whom it goes next."[39] It is hard to imagine that the same practice was not taking place in Rakovica. The City Central Committee had sent out cadres to explain the nationalist essence of the document in the local party branches, but IMR party members found it hard to work out exactly which part of the document they should condemn. The ideas put forward in the Memorandum were the same ones that had been circulating for years in the press, through both oppositional and official discourses. Throughout the decade, parts of the Serbian party integrated elements of the nationalist and liberal opposition agendas into their own body of ideas. By this time, for many, the Memorandum was simply common knowledge put on paper. The fact that the document was banned only increased workers' curiosity to read it. The IMR party Action Conference asked the city party to distribute the document, so that they could see for themselves what they were voting against.[40] The IMR LC Action Conference finally passed the resolution condemning the Serbian Academy of Sciences and Arts, but instead of creating a consensus against the nationalist ideology inside the factory, the whole initiative ended with another hollow resolution passed against the will of the workers.

The Memorandum saw various strains of public criticism and firsthand experiences with the system summarized in a common explanatory narrative for the first time. A conviction spread across the social layers inside Serbia that

[37] Slobodan Avramović, "Šta traže radnici," *IMR*, March 31, 1987, 4.

[38] Ž. Adamović, "Dušebrižnici," *IMR*, October 1, 1975, 5.

[39] "Izdeli pa vladaj," *Rad*, October 31, 1986.

[40] D.Ž., "Brže rešavati probleme na Kosovu," *IMR*, November 25, 1986, 2.

disintegrative processes had gone too far and were threatening to obliterate Yugoslavia. All grievances could now be integrated into this general frame. The impasse created by BOAL structures inside the factories was likened to the decentralized nature of the state as a whole. Numerous workers started describing their enterprises as a "mini federation."[41] As the former Rakovica youth activist Radoš Karaklajić remembers: "either secretly or openly, upon reading the fragments of the Memorandum, workers immediately recognized 'this is it!'"[42] The most engaged factory activists could finally break the cryptic code of party proclamations, put their finger on something concrete, and locate the guilty parties.

The breakthrough of dissident themes into the media and the party certainly made it easier for workers to raise sensitive issues openly and form a more coherent political line, but it would be wrong to think that oppositional language was entering the factory primarily from the outside. The metaphor of a Work Organization made up of BOALs as a "mini federation" or the idea of introducing the Chamber of Associated Labor into the Federal Parliament had been in circulation in Rakovica for months, if not years, before the publication of the Memorandum. The presence of migrant workers from Kosovo in Rakovica's factories ensured that local forums were engaged specifically in debates around Kosovo well before the province and its Serbian population became an obsession for the Serbian press and nationalist-minded intellectuals.

In the summer of 1982, a joint team of Albanian and Serbian communist functionaries, led by Kosovo's LC president, Sinan Hasani, and the president of Belgrade City Committee, Ivan Stambolić, visited IMR to discuss the economic ties between Rakovica and Kosovo-based enterprises, as well as the street clashes in the southern Autonomous Province from the previous year. The meeting was organized primarily for the local party officials and the factory management. However, the workers showed great interest in the event and joined the discussions. For them, it was an opportunity to push for popular demands, summed up by the factory press as "the protection of the Serbian minority in the province and full disclosure of the protest instigators." The Kosovo migrant workers of Serb origin contributed to the disquieting tone of the proceedings with firsthand accounts of the difficulties their families were facing back home. One worker demanded that the authorities prevent further immigration of Serbs from the region and warned "patience has limits." The trade union representative said that the workers were "revolted with both Albanian and Serbian chauvinism and especially with instances of people becoming rich overnight."[43]

The rejection of nationalism on both sides and the switching of the focus to the class divide, as the primary cleavage inside Kosovo, was more than just a forced attempt by trade union officials to channel the discussion toward officially-accepted tropes. As the discussion in the meeting evolved, contributions from

---

41 See, for instance, excerpts from the speech presented at the Yugoslav Trade Union Federation Congress by the IMR delegate, published in S. A., "Konsenzus kao smetnja," *IMR*, April 28, 1986, 2.

42 Interview with Radoš Karaklajić, March 2011.

43 "Neophodna je pomoć svih," *IMR*, June 22, 1982, 2.

the floor also seemed to move from ethnic relations toward the issue of "easy enrichment." According to these views, the Albanian and Serbian working classes had the same interests and understood each other's everyday concerns well, but were temporarily separated from each other by the nationally-colored and corrupt techno-bureaucracy. Two interviews conducted with IMR workers by the Serbian weekly *NIN* and the factory paper, in 1985 and 1986 respectively, show similar reasoning:

> I am afraid that much of the funding that went toward the faster development of Kosovo ended up being used for some other purposes. Many of my colleagues are of the same opinion. I am also convinced that many federal functionaries, as well as those in the province, knew what was coming and yet they kept quiet. We put misled kids in court. . . . The counterrevolution is gaining ground thanks to Yugoslav disunity. I mean the disunity of the leadership, not the people. . . . I met some Albanians during the time I served in the army and I remember them as honest, very dear people. In my building hallway, over there in Rakovica where I live, there is a person named Nebih [presumably an Albanian] and his family. A great man, a father, a husband, a neighbor . . . I do not see as many nationalists and as much nationalism as it is portrayed. Sometimes I end up thinking that the source of the matter is exactly those people who push these stories—they are the ones trying to be camouflaged behind them.[44]

> People talk a lot about Kosovo and you see that they are hurt inside and revolted by the fact that it came to this . . . especially by the fact that those most responsible for the situation are escaping without punishment. Nationalism is the result of the fact that we have a bunch of demigods who play the role of protectors of their people from the neighbors. They make their population content by initiating conflicts with other nations.[45]

The quotations above show how the workers still stuck to traditional concepts of national equality and class solidarity. The weakening of "brotherhood and unity" and the waning influence of the working class and the party-state were seen as the chief factors contributing to national divisions. For most workers, the main problem was not the dwindling of Serbian national rights, which presumably came together with the 1974 Constitution and political decentralization, but the conditions this new institutional setup had created for the buildup of bureaucracy and the looser control that the authorities had over illegal, private appropriations of social property. There was thus a clear tendency inside the factory to view nationalism as the secondary product of a political alliance between local managerial elites and lower-level party bureaucracies, both trying to protect their self-serving interests.

---

44 The interview was reprinted in full on the pages of the factory paper; see Svetislav Spasojević, "Opori optimizam," *IMR*, February 5, 1985, 6.

45 Mića Milošević, "Radnici neće žedni preko vode," *IMR*, July 29, 1986, 6.

The political imaginary inside the factories therefore differentiated itself in many ways from the oppositional discourse of the nationalist intelligentsia. Workers shared the general concern about the Serbian minority in Kosovo and appeared appalled by what was officially considered a "counterrevolution" carried out by Albanian irredentists. However, unlike the intelligentsia, they saw the strengthening of the party and a return to the ideology of brotherhood and unity as the solution. The antidote to Albanian nationalism was not seen in the greater unity of the Serbian nation, but in insistence on the classic Titoist formula of more integral Yugoslavism and the strengthening of class consciousness. In the sphere of economics, instead of more market and meritocratic principles, the workers focused on the fight against the misappropriation of social property and the reduction of social inequalities. The key to resolving the crisis was the unity of the people (*narod*) beyond national borders, achieved through the unanimity of the federal communist leadership. Finally, the grand political narratives were seen as important, but they were rather abstractly connected to the everyday problems in the factory.

A decisive shift in the way political problems were discussed inside IMR came in the course of 1986 and 1987, when the management started more confidently connecting the enterprise's business problems with broader political issues, and nationalist discourse penetrated the factory's sociopolitical organizations. The up-and-coming managers of the blue-collar BOALs and the younger party activists were the main transmitters of this new language. The first public sign of an attempt to connect IMR's business problems to the allegedly subordinated position of Serbia inside Yugoslavia can be traced back to 1981, with the aforementioned exchange of opinion letters in the factory press between the white-collar departments and Vehicle executive Strahinja Kostić. The dilemma faced by the factory at that time was choosing between an orientation toward larger market conglomerates, initiated by final producers such as TAM, or continuing with the development of its own final products. In order to back up the latter choice, Kostić described a long list of favors that IMR had allegedly given over the years to the state and other factories, sacrificing its own interests in the process. His open letter referred to them as "our golden apples," namely technological transfers and economically-unsound agreements that IMR made, pressured by higher political decisions.[46]

With Kostić's ascent to IMR's general management in 1986 and his inauguration as the general director in 1987, this type of self-victimizing language became pervasive. In March 1987, the distinguished daily paper *Politika* ran an interview with Kostić in which he summarized IMR's historical path from a factory with airplane-manufacturing technology, to a truck and tractor producer, to an underfunded intermediate manufacturer of engines for other final producers. He listed various unfavorable deals that the factory had concluded with other enterprises, but the original sin, the first and most important of the alleged harmful political decisions against IMR, was clearly the transfer of truck technology to Slovenia in 1950. "We are not insisting on borders, but people,

46 Strahinja Kostić, "Naše zlate jabuke," *IMR*, March 31, 1981, 6.

knowledge, and money exited our factory too easily," Kostić concluded.[47] The local executives therefore started projecting their own microhistorical account of the factory and its alleged ill-treatment by the centers of political power into the broader narrative of Serbia's neglect within Yugoslavia.

The discourse on Kosovo and the federal leadership was also changing. In the winter of 1986, the IMR LC Action Conference expressed the bold opinion that the top party-state leadership was incapable of resolving the Kosovo problem. However, the meeting's conclusions pointed out that this criticism did not apply to the Serbian LC. According to IMR communists, what Serbia needed above all was internal unity. The Conference also mentioned reform of the Yugoslav Constitution as the chief condition for the further development of self-management, and provocatively invited the City Committee to inform the communists about the content of the Memorandum.[48] IMR communists were obviously exerting pressure on their own republican leadership, trying to see how far it was willing to go in appropriating oppositional discourse. The insistence on the common Yugoslav transformation platform and working-class solidarity had been traded for the support of one's own republic inside the federal arena and the unity of all pro-reform forces inside of Serbia. The modernization of self-management would not come from the strengthening of blue-collar interests inside the industry, but rather the constitutional changes reshaping the balance of forces between the republics.

As we have seen, IMR's management connected the issue of Kosovo more closely to the debates about factory profitability and market orientation by demanding autonomous control over the enterprise fund for the underdeveloped regions. In March 1987, IMR's delegate in the Serbian Chamber of Associated Labor, Milorad Despotović, showcased how the factory elite combined the nationalist agenda and demands for market reform. He claimed the Serbian proposal for greater control over the funds it dedicated to Kosovo via the federation was rejected by the Yugoslav Parliament because, in contrast to the Kosovar delegation, its representatives were not speaking with a united voice. Despotović claimed that the Kosovo aid funds were not used for productive investments but ended up in the villas of Albanian politicians. He also raised the issue of the Albanian population's high birth rates. "Why don't we locate the funds to those regions and parts of the industry that are prosperous, from those that can push us upward, instead of constantly tying weights around our legs and sinking deeper," he concluded in his address.[49]

The women's organization also took part in promoting the new nationalist consciousness. The paintings of Mića Popović, one of the leading figures within the Serbian oppositionally-minded intelligentsia, were exhibited inside the factory in 1987, as part of a larger exhibition of popular Serbian painters organized by the women's Aktiv.[50] That same year, the women's organization issued an emotionally-charged proclamation after the killing of five soldiers in

---

47 "Drugi o nama: Kako do evropske akumulacije," *IMR*, March 31, 1987, 6.

48 D.Ž., "Brže rešavati probleme na Kosovu," *IMR*, November 25, 1986, 2.

49 D.J., "Kako se koristi pomoć," *IMR*, March 3, 1987, 2.

50 Mića Popović's pictures often depicted political themes from the perspective of the Serbian nation

the Yugoslav Peoples' Army barracks in Southern Serbia by an Albanian recruit.[51] The protest letter was not written from the position of the female workers, but that of mothers standing up for their sons. It stated, "Today, just as during World War Two, we will not allow the enemy to kill our youth."[52]

The examples above show that the language of the factory elites was changing. However, what about the understandings of the ordinary workers? Did they follow the trend at the same pace and with the same intensity as their representatives? As we will see in the next chapter, many workers, especially the older ones, had a hard time adjusting to these new lines of reasoning and continued to speak of the old tropes, such as class unity. Yet, for a great number of others the shift in emphasis from class to nation opened up new possibilities to frame dissatisfaction from the perspective of kinship, motherhood, or the generation gap. Popular historical memory was also expanded backward beyond the partisan war, and with it the possibilities for claiming different lineages, discovering new sources of legitimacy, and drawing fresh parallels. Workers who came from families or areas not aligned with the communist movement during World War Two, or younger workers who simply could not identify with the ruling ideology, certainly found this discontinuity inspiring and liberating.

Strahinja Kostić resigned from the position of general director in the summer of 1988, at a time of increasing pressure from the factory party.[53] A couple of months later, 500 workers organized a visit by the former director to the factory on their own initiative. On this occasion, they presented him with a gift: a large portrait of Karađorđe, the leader of the First Serbian Uprising against the Ottoman Empire.[54] The choice of the painting went against the tradition of identifying blue-collar workers' cause as an extension of the World War Two partisan struggle. Instead, it chose to connect the shop floor combativeness with the fight for the national liberation of the Serbian nation in the nineteenth century.

The Diligent Ones

Being ethnically the most homogeneous republic, in the first three decades after World War Two Slovenia showed few signs of broader political mobilizations based on national identity. If the government in Ljubljana did launch campaigns

---

and its alleged humiliation by the Titoist regime. In 1989, the factory paper recommended to its readers that they visit the new retrospective exhibition of Popović's latest phase, praising it as "socially engaged painting of a new type." See M. Nikolić, "Izložba Miće Popovića," *IMR*, February 7, 1989, 7.

51 It was never concluded if the rampage was in any way motivated by ethnic hatred. The murdered recruits came from different parts of Yugoslavia, but many papers inside Serbia presented this incident as a terrorist attack by Albanian separatists directed against the Serbs.

52 "Oštar protest radnica IMR-a," *IMR*, September 15, 1987, 7.

53 The exact reasons for his resignation remain unclear. Party meetings show that the local communists were unsatisfied with the pace of his enterprise restructuring, but there could also be other factors in play, such as Kostić's tone in the media.

54 "Strahinja među svojima," *IMR*, November 11, 1988, 6.

with demands for national rights, it was mostly in relation to Slavic minorities in Austria and Italy, not the position of Slovenes in the Yugoslav federation. However, a Radio Free Europe research piece, based on a six-month survey of the Yugoslav press during 1983, reported on a growing trend of national homogenization inside the most prosperous republic. It stated that "this small nationality's cultural and economic achievements, which have been shaped by sober and rational attitudes toward life and work that are typically Central Europe and not Balkan, have spawned a sense of common purpose coupled with a *covert* yet strong feeling of nationalism."[55]

The fact that Slovene nationalism came across as "covert" was probably due to its entanglement with criticism of political centralization and state interference in the economy. These ideas had been the mainstay of Yugoslav socialist ideology since at least the early 1960s, and were therefore a legitimate public grievance. Unlike the Serbian wave of national revival, Slovene nationalism did not draw inspiration from the alleged harm done to its people in the past, but from the higher productivity of its economy and calls for democratization along the lines of liberal democracy. Unofficially, however, economic success and democratic potential were also increasingly being related to culture, mentality, and national heritage.

As noted by the editor of *Mladina* magazine, Miha Kovač, the Yugoslav political edifice encouraged particularistic and "nationalized" interpretations of universal demands for democratization. The nationally-defined republics were the main political subjects licensed to introduce changes into the system. The idea of progress and democracy was increasingly related to Western European cultural traditions—those to which Slovenes had allegedly been most thoroughly exposed through history—in comparison to the other Yugoslav nations which were geographically located more to the East. According to such views, the Serbs belonged to the traditions of Byzantium and "Oriental despotism," the influence of which was slowing down Slovenia's further modernization.[56] The inability to communicate directly with the federal legislature, the threat of Serbian centralizing nationalism, and a relatively privileged economic position amidst a full-blown crisis in the southern regions: all of these factors created fertile ground among the Slovene workers for the spread of conservative, isolationist sentiments and orientalist prejudices against the inhabitants of the less-developed republics.

Since ethnic nationalism was disqualified as a valid political language, defenders of regional interests were forced to connect their national grievances to officially-recognized themes in the ruling ideology. In Belgrade, nationalists referred to the protection of Kosovo Serbs' minority rights in the face of the allegedly estranged local bureaucracy. In Ljubljana, Maribor, and other Slovene industrial centers the economic and political elites drew attention to the disregard for the principle of "distribution according to the results of work" by the central

55 Steve Reiquam, "Is Slovenian Nationalism on the Rise?," HU OSA 300-8-3-12140, Radio Free Europe Research, RAD Background Report, no. 190 (Yugoslavia), August 9, 1983; emphasis added.

56 "The Slovene Spring: Interview with Miha Kovač," *New Left Review* I, no. 171 (September–October 1988): 119.

state. The operating law of value was an accepted mechanism of allocation in the "socialist market," supposed to reward those who worked better and incited economic growth. By projecting national interests through issues such as the defense of the decentralized state architecture, more political freedoms, and the market, Slovene functionaries and intellectuals could place themselves in the roles of modernizers, in touch with the most industrious traditions of Yugoslav socialism, without the risk of easily being dismissed as nationalists.

The main target of public criticism inside Slovenia was the long-standing and most visible institutionalized mechanism for wealth redistribution in the country: the Federal Fund for Accelerated Development of Underdeveloped Republics and Kosovo. In the aftermath of the 1981 street protests by Kosovo's Albanians, the high-ranking Slovene functionary Matija Ribičić condemned the use of force by the federal state, but he was also quick to connect the "excess" of Albanian national aspirations with economic development based on the mechanism of aid for less developed republics. The budgetary financing was allegedly creating an unhealthy social atmosphere of entitlement and unrealistic expectations. He used the crisis in Kosovo as a starting point for general criticism of the economic system as a whole, stating that many people "work poorly and earn a great deal, while others work well and earn little." Ribičić concluded that Slovene workers were unsatisfied with seeing the results of their work used to cover the poor work of others.[57]

Six years later, the idea of productive, and therefore self-sustaining, nations on the one hand, and indolent, assisted nations on the other, was used by the philosopher Ivan Urbančič to draw more far-reaching conclusions in the fifty-seventh issue of the journal *Nova revija*. For Urbančič, the Yugoslav socialist state was kept alive by a harmful symbiotic relationship between the LCY and the "new nations": ethnic groups whose national identity flourished after World War Two, but which were allegedly still not confident enough to survive on their own, without the system of wealth redistributions.[58] The communist authorities sustained permanent underdevelopment since this created the need for their patronage. The only exit from the impasse, therefore, was the advancement of "positive nationalism," which would free different Yugoslav ethnicities from the tutelage of the transnational communist elite and enable them to transform into full-fledged nations, with independent nation-states and full democratic rights—as well as responsibilities—for their citizens.[59]

Nova revija was established by a group of dissident intellectuals in 1982, aiming to provide Slovenia's critically-minded writers with a new platform after the relative passivity and intellectual conformism of the 1970s. The first issues

57 Slobodan Stanković, "Slovenian leader against draconian prison sentences in Kosovo," HU OSA 300-8-3-11922, Radio Free Europe Research, RAD Background Report, no. 278 (Yugoslavia), September 28, 1981.

58 The term "new nations" here refers to those ethnic groups whose process of national identity formation lagged behind the three "old" nationalities in the region (Serbian, Croatian, and Slovene) and whose national rights were not fully recognized in the first Yugoslavia; for instance Albanians in Kosovo, Macedonians in Macedonia, or Muslims in Bosnia and Herzegovina.

59 Dejan Jović, *Yugoslavia: A State that Withered Away*, 318–22.

focused on literary themes and the defense of artistic freedoms, but by 1985, the authors associated with the journal began to perceive themselves as champions of Slovenia's national interests and cultural heritage. The fifty-seventh issue, suggestively entitled *Contributions to the Slovene National Program*, was published in 1987 as a direct response to the Serbian Memorandum. Allegedly, the Serbian cultural elites had already defined their national goals and it was only right that the Slovene nation did the same. According to the nationalist intelligentsia, Slovenia had to resolve its identity dilemmas at the crossroads of a new cybernetic and information era. There were apparently three ways forward. Slovenes could become a minority inside a unitary Yugoslavia, or they could keep their status as a sovereign state inside of a modernized federation. However, the third option, previously taboo, was now also placed on the table: the republic could declare independence and separate from Yugoslavia. The first scenario was unacceptable. The middle solution seemed the least realistic one. Most authors openly leaned toward the third option.[60]

It would be wrong to assume that the ideas put forward on the pages of *Nova revija* were able to motivate the public beyond the relatively small circle of people who followed the debates inside cultural institutions and critical intellectual journals. In its 1987 report, the Council for the Protection of Constitutional Order, a security organ of the Presidency of the Socialist Republic of Slovenia, confidently concluded that the group gathered around the journal was not spreading. On the contrary, the document argued that it was going through a process of "internal differentiation."[61] In other words, the nationalist intelligentsia was still isolated from the broader layers of society and lacked internal coherence and political clarity. Accordingly, when it comes to workers in Tezno, the main transmission belt of nationalist ideas must be looked for inside the factories.

Unlike the layer of Kosovar workers in Rakovica, the blue-collar citizens of Tezno, born after World War Two, had no firsthand experience of open nationalist disputes and ethnically-motivated social unrest. In their immediate surroundings, the issue of interethnic relations was related to the non-Slovene speaking, migrant workforce inside of Maribor's factories. In 1983, Silva Mežnarić, a researcher within the Slovenian Confederation of Trade Unions, noticed how "uncontrolled immigration" in Slovenia caused many "personal and social conflicts," adding that "[t]he share of those who say that there is a threat to the Slovenian language and way of life has been rising drastically in the last few years."[62] Any public expression of ideas which contradicted the official motto of the brotherhood and unity of Yugoslav nations was bound to be met with at least strong moral condemnation, if not legal consequences. It is thus hard to track sentiments on the ground directed against the "southerners," as the migrant workers were colloquially called inside Slovenia. This is even harder to do inside the factories, where revolutionary values of working-class solidarity were propagated with added fervor. However, one can spot instances of more

---

60 Ibid., 315–17.

61 Božo Repe, *Slovenci v osemdesetih leti*, Zbirka zgodovinskega časopisa 23 (Ljubljana: Zveza zgodovinskih društev Slovenije, 2001), 36.

62 Quoted in Reiquam, "Is Slovenian Nationalism on the Rise?," 2–3.

open nationalist attitudes in the factory milieus, which may be indicative of the various ways in which general nationalist themes could have been integrated into workers' everyday complaints.

As already shown, climbing up the enterprise job hierarchy with the help of political positions was one of the most despised practices on the shop floor. In his autobiography, France Tomšič, a trade union leader at Ljubljana-based heavy machinery manufacturer Litostroj, recalls that one of his main complaints in the mid-1980s was that the top positions in the enterprise party branch, as well as those in the self-management organs, were disproportionately occupied by the "southerners." There is no data indicating if migrant workers were more active inside TAM's sociopolitical organizations than their Slovene colleagues were. Keeping in mind that party membership quotas were higher in the southern republics, it is possible that migrant workers brought this political culture along with them. Furthermore, it is conceivable that migrant workers saw political engagement as a way to establish themselves in their new surroundings, and that this could have been interpreted as unfair advancement through home-based connections or political favor by their Slovene colleagues.

The allegedly slow adoption of the Slovene language by migrant workers who continued speaking Serbo-Croatian years after they settled in Yugoslavia's most northern republic was the main point of contention, and a symbol of difference between "us" and "them." For instance, the aforementioned party educational material in *Borba*'s federal campaign to include blue-collar workers in political work was not available in the Slovene language, thus limiting its spread among TAM's workers. Ever since 1975, TAM's factory paper had been published in a Serbo-Croatian edition in order to reach workers in BOALs outside of Slovenia. The trade unionist and youth activist Drago Gajzer recalled an instance of a worker complaining in the self-management meeting about the decision to dedicate extra resources for translating the newspaper. The worker argued that Slovenes learn Serbo-Croatian in school and asked why workers in other republics did not bother to learn some Slovene.[63]

These were all, however, minor everyday antagonisms between workers of different backgrounds, which lacked the potential to produce a widespread embrace of exclusionary politics. If one seeks more nationalist-oriented sentiments with the potential to mobilize the enterprise as a whole, the public statements of the factory's higher forums would be a more suitable place to look. TAM's executives, and even its sociopolitical functionaries, were reluctant to discuss controversial political issues. In Tezno, nationalism was invoked to rally the local workforce behind the management and the interests of their own republic when it came to concrete internal business issues, but was rarely raised in relation to high politics. As noted, two of the most pressing issues for TAM's blue-collar workers were production disruptions due to the insufficient supply of work materials and increasing wage differentiation. In order to put themselves beyond criticism and restore enterprise unity, factory officials often

[63] Interview with Drago Gajzer, April 2013. Gajzer also claimed that the police questioned the worker after he had raised this issue inside the factory. No written sources were found to confirm this incident.

connected these grievances to the dysfunctional nature of the Yugoslav economy, redistributive macroeconomic policies, and TAM's allegedly discriminated position in relation to other companies.

The management did not hesitate to criticize TAM's suppliers from other republics in the pages of the factory press whenever shipments were late or of unsatisfactory quality. The business partners were, therefore, receiving the brunt of the blame for production line waiting times. As one of the largest partners and a supplier of engines, IMR was a particular target of criticism.[64] In February 1983, KPO member Maksimilijan Senica described the factory subcontractors as "extortionists" due to constant price hikes and demands to increase their share in the hard currency earned through export. The negotiated economy and political influence allegedly allowed companies positioned at lower ends of the supply chain to exploit TAM:

> How long will we live under political solutions where some continuously extort, while others only give? In this mess, nobody respects self-management agreements and similar documents any longer. For how long will we continue to look for loopholes in the law and abuse it, meaning to ignore it and compete over who lives better without work, while others pick up the bill? Due to its size, status, as well as well-defined goals, TAM is one of the Work Organizations exploited by many who live well on its account.[65]

The factory trade union was particularly active in propagating local interests and calling for protectionist policies. As early as April 1983, the annual conference of TAM's unionists asked their delegate in the Slovene Trade Union Confederation Council to issue louder criticism of the federal government and its taxation of Slovene industry. The contributions from the floor were consistently based around the defense of national interests. Slovenia was presented as too small and politically weak to resist the harmful policies of the federal administration. The union officials fought energetically against all administrative reductions in wage ranges, arguing this would reward workers in less developed regions and punish the more productive Slovene enterprises. The other republics were allegedly raising wages regardless of their failure to reach the planned business results. The loss-making factories were seen as the main wrongdoers. Wage rises in other republics were directly connected with growing poverty and hardship inside Slovenia. The Conference delegates agreed that Slovenia was lagging behind other republics and concluded that, if this dynamic continued, the republic might find itself among the underdeveloped regions of Yugoslavia.[66]

The strategy of TAM's management and the trade union were thus very similar to those previously described in Rakovica. However, there are important

64 See, for instance, B.M. "Je li kraj neizvesnosti?," *Skozi TAM* (Serbo-Croatian edition), October 1979, 1; and M.P., "IMR Rakovica nas koči," *Skozi TAM* (Serbo-Croatian edition), October 1984, 7.

65 Danilo Vincetič, "Iz rada KPO," *Skozi TAM* (Serbo-Croatian edition), February 1983, 4.

66 Tomislav Perlič, "Obezbediti socijalni položaj radnika," *Skozi TAM* (Serbo-Croatian edition),

differences. First, IMR's forums started with public self-victimization and accusations against business partners from other republics in the second half of the decade, once the first ideological cracks started to appear in the Serbian LC. In Tezno, the strong language directed against suppliers was already in use by the early 1980s. Open complaints about federal policies date back to the Perhavc era and came into play again during the 1980s, once the Slovene communist leadership lost its power to censor the industry professionals. In IMR, the factory party first dared to question the federal party-state over its ability to resolve the Kosovo tensions in late 1986. As already described, in the case of TAM, the local communists openly expressed cynicism toward the federal party leadership and already refused to participate in common political campaigns during the Thirteenth Session campaign in 1984.

The early voicing of oppositional tones and the proactive stance of TAM's factory elites enabled the enterprise to rally the workforce behind a common cause and make important reformist strides during the first half of the 1980s. Nevertheless, by the second half of the decade this mechanism started to wear thin. Despite the management's efforts to portray the component manufacturers as the main cause of the production slowdown, the majority of workers were unconvinced by the official explanations and chose to blame their own specialists for this problem:

> Sometimes the lines stand still for days. When we ask why the motor parts are missing, they answer that the machines, which are making them, are out of order. Personally, I do not believe this. A few days ago, we were put on the waiting regime for hours because the screws were missing. The screws were in the warehouse, but the administration was not aware of it. Someone must be held accountable for this type of work, namely the wrong orders and bad record-keeping.[67]

As the next chapter will show, these fiery discussions, once contained to the factory meetings and oppositional circles, would burst out into mainstream discourse between 1986 and 1988 due to the spread of social mobilizations and changes of leadership in the Serbian and Slovene parties. In Rakovica, a layer of the most active workers would appropriate the radical slogans of national dignity, economic protectionism, and entrepreneurial freedoms, sparking wider interest in political discussions and encouraging strike action. In Tezno, the relative quiescence would last all the way until the summer of 1988. In Rakovica, the language of nationalism and radical reforms in the official institutions was something fresh and provocative, and therefore had the power to attract. By contrast, in Tezno, where the management utilized these themes for years in the face of persistent income polarization, the workers had started becoming increasingly skeptical and unresponsive to such messages. However, as we will see, in other parts of Slovenia workers were indeed becoming politicized and even made attempts to form independent alliances with the anticommunist opposition.

April 1983, 4.

67 Danilo Vincetič, "Izguba je presenečenje, čeprav smo jo pričakovali," *Skozi TAM*, September 1987, 6.

Appendix 2

Figure 17. "In front of someone else's doorstep," cartoon in *Skozi TAM*, March 30, 1984

Figure 18. "Who was steering?!," cartoon in *IMR*, July 26, 1988

Figure 19. "I think someone should prepare a report about the new situation!," cartoon in *Skozi TAM*, September 8, 1983

Figure 20. "Even score," cartoon in *Skozi TAM*, September 18, 1976 (caption: "Comrade, I claim that your department is responsible for the piling inventories and the unfulfilled plan!", "Comrade, this is not true, I say it is exactly the other way around!")

The cartoons above portray the desperate feeling of lacking responsibility in the factories. Figure 17 shows the factory as a baby orphan left in front of a stranger's door, while Figure 18 paints the factory as a vehicle crashing into a tree. The workers/passengers look confused as the police officer asks who was sitting behind the wheel: the obvious answer is everybody and nobody. Figure 19 depicts three white-collar workers on a sinking ship. The situation clearly requires urgent action, yet the employee with dark glasses proposes that one of them drafts a report about the situation instead. Figure 20 shows two executives confronting each other at a self-management meeting. "Comrade, I claim that your department is responsible for the piling inventories and the unfulfilled plan!" the first one screams. "Comrade... it is exactly the other way around," the second responds. Another meeting participant is pictured hiding under the desk. The enterprise has sunk into chaos due to its indecisiveness in implementing changes and internal deadlock between conflicting self-governing departments.

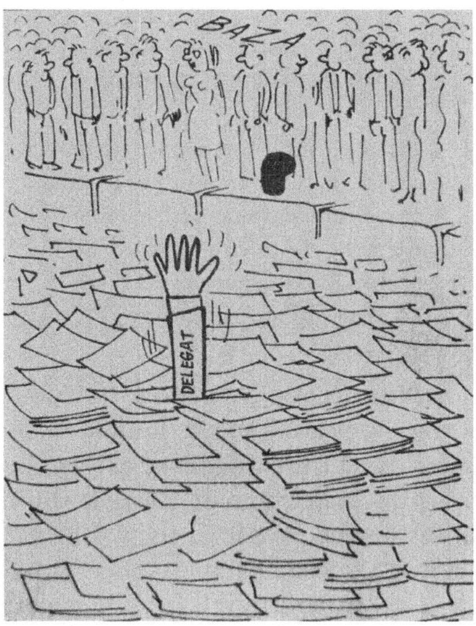

Figure 21. "Delegate drowning," cartoon in *Skozi TAM*, July 30, 1977

Figure 22. Cart drivers delivering paperwork for self-management meetings, cartoon in *Skozi TAM*, October 20, 1976 (caption: "I am delivering materials for assembly discussions", "Well, I am transporting BOAL objections to previous materials...")

Figures 21 to 24 depict how the enterprises viewed Associated Labor as a bureaucratic quagmire and a burden. Figure 21 shows a delegate drowning in a sea of documents while the workforce (the base) stand at the dock minding their own business. Figure 22 depicts two cart drivers bypassing each other while carrying paperwork for the BOAL assemblies. One cart is full of materials waiting to be voted upon, while the other carries objections to the already-discussed set of documents. The message is clear: the factory has been transformed into

Figure 23. "Hey Mica, open up! I am bringing you the referendum voting ballot!," cartoon in *Skozi TAM*, March 5, 1978

Figure 24. "At the psychiatrist," cartoon in *Skozi TAM*, October 14, 1986 (caption: "Comrade, I asked you to tell me about your problems. However, until now you have described to me over twenty self-management agreements")

a political body occupied with constant discussions and paperwork instead of productive activity. Figure 23 shows a worker appearing in the middle of the night at the window of his female colleague, Mica. The situation describes how the worker found an original excuse to visit his female comrade, but also shows the constant burden of meetings and ballots on the psyche of the workforce. A similar message is conveyed through Figure 24, which depicts an employee during his visit to a therapist. "Comrade, I asked you to tell me about your problems. However, until now you have described to me over twenty self-management agreements," the doctor says.

Finally, Figures 25 and 26 reveal the absurd nature of self-management meetings and workers' lack of interest in the proceedings. The first cartoon shows a few hands raised for each of the three voting options (for, against, abstained), while the majority of workers remain indifferent. The second shows the assembly disbanding after passing no fewer than eight self-management agreements. However, an activist is depicted rushing toward the crowd screaming: "Comrades, do not disperse; the management has just informed me that they are sending us thirteen more agreements."

Figure 25. "How do we vote," cartoon in *Skozi TAM*, April 10, 1976 (caption: 1. "Who is in favor?," 2. "Who is against?," 3. "Abstentions?")

Figure 26. "After agreeing on eight self-management agreements," cartoon in *Skozi TAM*, February 16, 1976 (caption: "Comrades, do not disperse; the management has just informed me that they are sending us thirteen more agreements.")

CHAPTER SIX

Mobilizations at the Bottom—Realignments at the Top, 1986–1988

Reaching Beyond the Factory Gates

In late 1986, amidst persistent sluggish economic growth and high inflation, the federal government decided to apply its reform measures more vigorously. In December that year, the Federal Assembly passed a number of legislative acts enforcing greater fiscal discipline onto enterprises.[1] Additionally, between the summer of 1986 and the spring of 1988, the Federal Executive Council made two attempts to implement a general wage freeze and establish a closer connection between the rise in personal incomes and the changes in productivity.[2] These measures triggered a surge of industrial action, as well as broader social mobilizations across the country.

The question of workers' right to organize a "work stoppage" became a key media topic in the course of 1986. By 1987, the word "strike" ceased to be taboo and many workers started talking about strikes as justified methods for achieving their interests. A sociological survey conducted by the Belgrade Trade Union Confederation Chamber in the summer of 1987 revealed that only 17.1 percent of workers in the city held the opinion that strikes have no place inside the system of self-management.[3] In late 1987, the Slovene trade union leadership took concrete steps and launched an initiative for the legal regulation of strikes in their republic.[4]

The altered attitudes toward industrial action were prompted by increased labor activity on the ground. There are no signs of larger strikes in Tezno until 1988. Yet, in Slovenia as a whole, the number of strikes climbed from 163, recorded at the end of 1986, to 227 instances the following year.[5] In Belgrade, the absolute numbers were lower due to a smaller number of industrial facilities,

---

1 McFarlane, *Yugoslavia: Politics, Economics and Society*, 143–44.

2 Prinčič and Borak, *Iz reforme v reformo*, 544.

3 Pavlović, Radosavljević, and Stojiljković, *Obustave rada (štrajkovi) u Beogradu*, 70.

4 S. Lalović, "Korak dalje od ZUR-a: tragom slovenačkog predloga o regulisanju štrajkova," *Rad*, January 29, 1988.

5 Miroslav Stanojević, "Workers' Power in Transition Economies: The Cases of Serbia and Slovenia," *European Journal of Industrial Relations* 9, no. 3 (2003): 283–301.

but the proportional increase in strikes during 1987 is similar (see table below).[6] Faced with such fierce resistance from below, the new head of the Federal Executive Council, Branko Mikulić, was forced to capitulate and give up both attempts at wage freezes, first in March 1987 and then in May 1988.

Year	Number of strikes	Number of participants
1983	10	1,300
1984	18	1,300
1985	45	7,000
1986	71	7,000
1987	105	19,219

Table 2: Labor strikes in Belgrade, 1983–1987[7]

While Tezno remained calm, the strike wave did not bypass Rakovica. Between the winter of 1986 and the fall of 1987, IMR was the site of two strikes. The changing discourse of striking workers and the organizational form of these two events reveal the closing of the gap between workers and management. On March 11, 1986, the second shift of IMR's engine assembly line workers in Motor downed their tools and declared a strike. This was not the first work stoppage inside IMR. Periodically during the crisis years, a group of workers dissatisfied with the internal income distribution agreement or working conditions would go on strike. However, this time around, the work stoppage rapidly spread across the shop floor and work shifts, involving some 500 workers from the Motor BOAL and an additional fifty workers from the Vehicle BOAL. That same afternoon, the assembly line was stopped across town in Belgrade's second tractor producer IMT, but the two strikes were in no way a consciously-coordinated action.[8]

6 For a closer look at the Belgrade industrial workforce during these crisis years, see Rory Archer and Goran Musić, "The Belgrade Working Class between Tito and Milošević: New Geographies of Poverty and Evolving Expressions of Grievances in an Era of Crisis, 1979–1986," *Revue d'études comparatives Est-Ouest* 50, no. 5 (2019): 53–79.

7 Pavlović, Radosavljević, and Stojiljković, *Obustave rada (štrajkovi) u Beogradu*, 70.

8 The overlap was a coincidence; workers in both factories were unaware of their colleagues' actions. In the years covered by this research, both IMR and IMT were the sites of several strikes and street protests. Nevertheless, there are no records of direct communication between the workers of the two rival tractor factories during the course of these events, apart from regular business contacts between the managements. This fact reveals the persistent rivalry between the two factories, but also the inability of self-management to establish meaningful communication channels for workers beyond single factories.

The immediate causes for the strike in IMR were the unexpectedly low figures on the paychecks for the previous month.[9] After the initial commotion on the shop floor, the striking workers moved into the canteen where they engaged in discussions with various delegates of the sociopolitical organizations, self-management organs, and the administration. The strike came out with a single demand for higher wages.[10] The targets of the criticism were vague, ranging from rising prices in the stores to the problem of high taxation and the interest rates imposed upon industry. Still, the enterprise management was clearly the main object of dissatisfaction. Workers demanded to know why they had more than doubled the output of engines while their salary remained the same. The management's argument that one cannot distribute income not earned in the market was incomprehensible on the shop floor. As IMR communist Dušan Ćatović had stated four months earlier at one of the meetings of the Serbian LC Central Committee dedicated to the question of income distribution:

> We always believed in the just nature of distribution according to work and the results of work . . . we were looking for practical solutions for the application of this type of distribution and could not always participate in highly theoretical discussions on this topic on an equal footing . . . to put it in simple words, we feel that our work effort on the machines . . . is not producing the expected results; it is as though it depends less and less on us and our work.[11]

Increased reliance on the market as the main evaluator of factory output in the second half of the 1980s obviously frustrated the workers, once the results they achieved clashed with their subjective feelings of the effort invested in the increase of production. It was as if somebody was stealing the value created by them once the goods left the production hall. The manual workers found it incomprehensible and absurd that someone was denying them the income they had already "earned" on the shop floor. However, the main causes or persons responsible for this "theft" remained unclear. Judging from the general grievances leading up to the strike, the workers still located the main culprits inside the factory. In other words, their criticism broadly followed the intellectual frame set in the 1970s and focused on the issue of enterprise techno-bureaucracy.[12]

---

9 As explained earlier, a large percentage of the blue-collar workers' wage was variable. In self-management, the blue-collar workers were not considered "wage workers," but managers of social property. The exact wage thus depended greatly on the previous period's business results. Strikes usually erupted on the days the "personal income" (wage) was announced and the value of the paychecks failed to match the workers' subjective feeling of invested work effort.

10 D.J., "Zahtev za veće zarade," *IMR*, March 19, 1986, 3.

11 "Konkretno bez uopštavanja," *IMR*, December 9, 1985, 4.

12 Discussion of a document entitled "The Critical Analysis of the Functioning of the Political System of Socialist Self-Management" (*Kritička analiza funkcionisanja političkog sistema socijalističkog samoupravljanja*) in factory sociopolitical organizations in early 1986 reveals that the lower-level party cadres had become more articulate in their criticism of boalization. However, among the ordinary workers, especially the older ones, the inherited themes from the 1970s remained dominant. The workers envisioned the amalgam of economic and political bureaucracy without clear national allegiance as the main opponent of the united Yugoslav working class.

The two sides remained entrenched in their positions. After fifty-eight hours on strike, the workers went back to the production lines with no clear gain. The administration and the sociopolitical organizations stuck behind their political obligation to discourage strikes as legitimate forms of protest. The strike was condemned as an inappropriate method for advancing working-class interests inside the self-managing enterprise. Instead of industrial action, the governing and administrative functionaries argued that the workers should channel their grievances through the official delegations in Associated Labor. The factory elites therefore took a firm federal reformist stand during the debates. In line with the slogan of "distribution according to the results of work," the executives insisted the factory could not distribute what it did not earn and pointed out that, despite all the difficulties, IMR's average salary was still above the republic and city averages of the metalworking branch.

The administration agreed to outline a new system modifying the remuneration of productive work and waiting times on the assembly lines, which would be more favorable to manual labor. At the same time, however, it instructed the factory organs to introduce more discipline on the shop floor and ensure that factory property was well protected in the future. In addition, the fact that journalists appeared at the factory gates shortly after the strike outbreak, as well as the timing of the work stoppage, which took place in the middle of elections for self-management delegate posts, were all taken as indicators that there were hidden interests involved.[13] What these shadow forces might exactly have been was never disclosed. The whole insinuation was likely just a tactical move on the part of the factory management, constructing potential excuses for more severe repression in case the strikes persisted.

The strike did not, therefore, achieve much for the blue-collar workers. If anything, it revealed just how unfit for collective action Rakovica's shop floor workers had become during decades of self-management and labor's political reliance on strong protectors inside the party. Of the myriad organizations the workers nominally had at their disposal, none could be used to further the strike. Moreover, the existence of two parallel strikes in the same industrial sector that were completely oblivious to each other—even though the factories were separated by only a few tram stops—showed the level of workers' atomization in Associated Labor. As one disappointed worker noted in a documentary filmed that year, "the strikes are badly organized . . . nobody knows who leads, what the demands are, other groups of workers are not informed . . . it is easy for the bureaucracy to break us, we end up being laughed at."[14]

On September 8, 1987, a bigger strike ensued inside IMR, mobilizing some 750 workers of all the productive BOALs from the two main shifts. This second

IMR's amended version of the document, sent out by the federal party leadership in order to initiate changes in the political system, reflected this by stating: "A critical analysis must offer guidelines for fighting against the established rich men-capitalist layer in our society, which represents a danger for the development of self-management and social property." See "Kako izaći iz krize," *IMR*, March 19, 1986, 4.

13 "Zadaci i obaveze," *IMR*, April 8, 1986, 3.

14 Milošević, *Žulj*.

strike marked a clear shift in the behavior of both striking workers and the management. Unlike the previous strike, which took place mostly inside the factory canteen, the workers now marched to the municipal assembly building. Allegedly, the walkout was inspired by a rumor that the president of the LC Municipal Committee had forbidden the factories to pay out wage bonuses. The striking workers now directed their anger at the Associated Labor bureaucracy in the municipality, asking for individuals who had transferred into the administration to return to the shop floor and stop their "free ride on the money that the blue-collar workers make."[15]

According to the reports from the assemblies held during the strike, workers were now "extending full support to the new General Director [Strahinja Kostić] and other leading comrades" and showed an understanding that the results were not dependent on the enterprise, but broader self-management compacts and government agencies.[16] Milan Adžović, a senior worker activist who came of age in the late 1960s, took part in the strike and tried to connect with the prevalent mood of blaming institutions outside of the factory. He joined the condemnation of the municipal bureaucracy but remained skeptical toward calls to change the Associated Labor Act, as he claimed that in reality it had never been implemented properly. The majority of the workers, however, seemed less ready to construct excuses and defend the existing organizational scheme of self-management.

For their part, the management and the factory sociopolitical organizations backed the strike this time around. The IMR party conference went against its municipal leadership. It stated that the communists were not surprised by the strike action, as the workers could not make a living from their wages. The management not only agreed to raise wages, but also approved additional short-term bonus payments to protect living standards amidst the rampaging inflation. Of course, the management's assistance did not come without any strings attached. The management made an effort to connect the mobilization firmly with demands for the lifting of the taxation burden and changes in the political system. In its first issue after the strike, the factory paper published a reader's letter offering an indicative analysis of the strike action. The author was an employee of the Maintenance BOAL. Generally supportive of the strike, the letter complained that those workers who tried to impose themselves as leaders were usually individuals with poor work results and whose contribution to the factory was minimal.

The author attempted to isolate the rabble-rousers still clinging to old slogans, instead uniting the work collective and lower-level administration at the municipal level by presenting a common adversary at the republican and federal levels. He blamed unnamed striking workers for trying to present the strike as a clash between the production line and *režija*. According to the author, this interpretation was false and blurred the main dividing line between hard-working people and "slackers," both of which allegedly existed in all departments among both white and blue-collar workers. Furthermore, the author believed

15 D.J., "Od obećanja se ne živi," *IMR*, September 15, 1987, 1.

16 D.J., "Zahtevi opravdani," *IMR*, September 15, 1987, 1.

that the workers had chosen the wrong targets. The local government, he noted, was filled with "our people": former factory workers whose powers were in any case limited. The letter went on to explain that, apart from internal enterprise issues, the strike debates neglected problems that were more fundamental. The main causes for the insolvency of industrial enterprises, as well as the poverty of the working class, were allegedly the excessive state and the expensive self-management mechanism. Municipal politics was not in this instance capable of offering solutions to this problem. Things should be changed at the top, the letter concluded, more or less openly calling for united action against political powers in both the republic and the federation.[17]

As noted at the beginning, labor strikes were not the only social struggles at the time. In Kosovo, mobilizations based on ethnic identity had already surpassed local politics. The peak of austerity measures there was followed by new popular mobilizations. This time around, it was Kosovo's Serbian population which was expressing anger over the conditions inside the autonomous province. In the course of 1986 and early 1987, various initiatives by Serb activists, fed up with the treatment they received from the local authorities and purported daily harassment by the Albanian majority, evolved into a unified, persistent, and relatively well-organized social movement, which maintained contacts with the Belgrade-based dissident intelligentsia and parts of the Serbian party apparatus. Using the Citizens' Assembly (*zbor građana*), a meeting form introduced as an application of the self-management organizational principle in residential communities, the Serbian activists launched a series of protests in Belgrade with the aim of attracting attention to what they considered the plight of national minority rights in their municipalities.

In February 1986, ninety-five people in peasant garments appeared in front of the Federal Assembly building in downtown Belgrade. They claimed to be informally-selected representatives of forty-two towns and villages in Kosovo and demanded that they be allowed to address the federal leadership. In April that year, some 550 Kosovo Serbs arrived at Belgrade train station and marched through the city streets, joined by Kosovo migrants from the city itself and other parts of Serbia. The protest caused traffic jams in the capital and the newspapers reported that the demonstrators left a powerful impression on bystanders.[18] The presence of protesters in the streets caused fear and paranoia inside the ruling circles of the LCY. Reflecting on the politically turbulent months of the summer and fall of 1987, Ivan Stambolić, at that time the president of Serbia, recalled the heated atmosphere surrounding the parallel meetings of the Collective Presidency of Yugoslavia and the LCY Central Committee in June of that year.

---

17 It should be noted that the letter was published five days after the Eighth Plenary Session of the Serbian LC Central Committee, in which Slobodan Milošević toppled his former mentor Ivan Stambolić, signaling a more radical break with both Associated Labor inside Serbia and the cautious handling of national tensions in Kosovo. As we will see in the next section, its insistence on unity beyond occupational cleavages, against those political leaderships still clinging to traditional slogans, clearly reflects the new orientation of the Serbian party. Šćepan Krsmanović, "Šta se htelo, a šta može?," *IMR*, September 29, 1987, 6.

18 Nebojša Vladisavljević, *Serbia's Anti-bureaucratic Revolution: Milošević, the Fall of Communism and Nationalist Mobilization* (New York: Palgrave Macmillan, 2008), 91–92.

On that occasion, the Kosovo Serb activists had gathered outside the Federal Parliament once again, in order to make sure their grievances would be heard. In his memoirs, Stambolić writes:

> The Presidency of Yugoslavia reaches no decisions, it just warns me of the gravity of the situation, of the real danger of the escalation of mass and broader movements in Belgrade and Serbia, and correspondingly of my responsibility. They are in possession of information that new trains are arriving from Kosovo, that Rakovica is rising up, that Smederevo [a steel plant city close to Belgrade] is on its way, that citizens are joining the protesters in the streets, that "leaders from Francuska 7" [the address of the Serbian Writers' Association] are inserting themselves at the helm of the protests . . . the local police confute the alarming information about Rakovica, the students, Smederevo, the arriving trains. Belgrade remains calm and worried. Confusion is widespread, dramatizations ever greater.[19]

Stambolić later realized that parts of the federal leadership were intentionally exaggerating the threat of protests in order to apply pressure on the Serbian leadership. It seems that the leaders of the other republics were convinced that the mobilizations of Kosovars inside Serbia were an orchestrated affair used by Stambolić to blackmail the federacy into granting more influence to his republic.[20] By spreading panic, they wanted to teach the Serbian president a lesson on how such moves might easily backfire. However, the mere fact that a scare tactic almost succeeded reveals the restlessness and insecurity building up within the leadership. For the ruling bureaucracy of all the republics, the worst-case scenario was the unification of different movements from below and the articulation of an alternative political program, with the nationalist and liberal intelligentsia potentially playing a leadership role.

A few months later, the exaggerated scenario the federal politicians projected onto Serbia turned into a self-fulfilling prophecy inside Slovenia. In late 1987, the leadership of a workers' strike in Ljubljana attempted to establish contact with the Slovene dissident intelligentsia. On December 9, after receiving news that wages had not been raised in accordance with inflation, workers in Ljubljana's heavy machinery manufacturer Litostroj abandoned their workplaces and marched to Slovenia's parliament building in the city center. France Tomšič, the union representative of the engineering department, led the strike. Tomšič had worked as an engineer in West Germany in the 1970s and became politicized upon his

---

19 Stambolić's memoirs on the key events that year can be found in Lekić and Pavić, *VIII Sednica CK SK Srbije*, 269.

20 Stambolić's right-hand man Slobodan Milošević did in fact establish contact with the leaders of the Kosovo Serbs, but he was still by no means in control. The recent historiography shows that, in this particular case, the Serbian party tried to stick to the rules and prevent the Kosovo Serbs from rallying outside the Federal Parliament. The leading activists inside Kosovo, who tried to abort the mobilization in agreement with Belgrade, were temporarily sidelined amid strong pressure from below and the protest went on as planned. See Vladisavljević, *Serbia's Anti-bureaucratic Revolution*, 103.

return to Yugoslavia, through a local initiative against the nationalization of privately-held strips of land in his hometown in northern Slovenia. The fight against the municipal party structures in his hometown gave him much-needed experience in organizational matters and the articulation of demands. Tomšič was also inspired by the writings of the Slovene nationalist opposition and had become convinced that socialist self-management was a mere disguise for single-party dictatorship and an inherently inefficient system, unable to compete with Western market economies. Under his leadership, Litostroj workers formed an independent strike committee, which entered into a prolonged confrontation with the management and the factory party branch, as well as with the local trade union.

At one of the strike's general assemblies, Tomšič proposed the foundation of an independent political party headed by a *Nova revija* contributor, France Bučar. The idea of a political party was never publicly discussed among the striking Litostroj workers, not even inside the strike committee. From the very beginning, the founding of a political party was Tomšič's own idea. He envisioned a social democratic party with a national Slovene program, headed by the intelligentsia and grounded in the industrial proletariat, which could offer an alternative to the LC. According to his memoirs, he mulled this thought over for weeks and finally decided to launch the proposal in front of all the workers, at the pinnacle of a strike assembly focused on economic demands limited to internal factory issues.

To the astonishment of the enterprise management and the factory party leadership, the proposal was accepted by a majority vote. In the heat of the moment, the Litostroj workforce voted in favor of the motion, but the initiative never materialized in this framework. The management and the local party apparatus managed to isolate Tomšič, accusing him of exploiting workers' justified grievances for selfish political aims. The initiative thus failed, but the apparent ease with which the strike assembly adopted a political demand was a clear warning for the authorities. Just one year before, a proposal of that type would have probably been met with jeers; now the workers were ready to vote on it and consider it a viable option.[21]

The politicization of the shop floors corresponded to the more open debates and aggressive style of politics at the top. In Serbia, a new party leadership was about to come to the fore by ousting the opposing faction in a Central Committee session broadcast on public TV. This new leadership readily adopted the nationalist themes formerly limited to dissident cultural circles. In Slovenia, the new liberal-minded leadership started to open the party forums toward grassroots oppositional initiatives and negating the legacy of workers' self-management. The following two sections in this chapter describe these political changes in Serbia and Slovenia respectively, showing how this new breed of politics resonated on the shop floors. The final section will shed light on the

---

[21] For two opposing accounts of the Litostroj strike, see the autobiography of its leader: France Tomšič, *Od stavke do stranke* (Ljubljana: Nova obzorja, 2010); and the management controlled factory press: "Ko postane nevzdržno," *Litostroj: glasilo delavcev Titovih zavodov Litostroj*, December 1987, 2–5.

growing appeals for economic protectionism from the republican leaderships in both republics and how, in the case of Serbia, they overlapped with growing chauvinist sentiments toward other nationalities inside Yugoslavia.

A "Firm Hand" Inside Serbia

By 1987, when the social mobilizations were gaining momentum, the Serbian party found itself stuck between the increasingly radical demands from below and the federal responsibilities at the top. The leader of the Serbian LC, Ivan Stambolić, either had to address the burning issues of national and class inequalities, positioning himself at the head of mounting popular discontent, or remain loyal to official party discourse and its internal procedures. For years, it seemed that the Serbian leadership had managed to do both. In 1984, the party opened up to industrial grievances in order to gain support in negotiations over the exact course of reforms inside the federacy, but decided to end grassroots discussions soon after. Under Stambolić, the Serbian LC also flirted with the nationalist opposition by incorporating elements of its ideology into official discourse, in order to back up the Serbian agenda.[22] However, once the political platform of the Serbian Academy of Sciences and Arts (the Memorandum) was disclosed in 1986, the party launched a fierce campaign against its authors. In the late summer of 1987, Stambolić was about to pay the price for his politics of vacillation. His close collaborator, Slobodan Milošević, used the Eighth Session of the Serbian LC Central Committee to launch a coup inside the Serbian party. In his campaign to defeat Stambolić's wing, Milošević leaned on the rising influence of the nationalist intelligentsia, the social movement of the Kosovo Serbs, and the grievances of the party cadres stemming from Associated Labor.

The new leadership presented itself as openly standing against the status quo in the federacy and being in touch with popular discontent. It immediately put an end to the inherited political culture of drawn-out meetings and informal consultations between the different unofficial factions within the Serbian party. Instead, the high-ranking functionaries closed ranks and adopted a more antagonistic stance in the federal bodies. The abstract notion of unity, whether of different ethnic groups or the working class, was a constant theme among the Yugoslav communists. The Serbian party under Milošević, however, inserted fresh meanings into the slogan by contrasting it with what was portrayed as growing anarchy and the evolution of divergent regional interests over the previous two decades. The main line of reasoning was borrowed from the pages of the Memorandum. Allegedly, Yugoslavia could only gain from a stronger Serbia, as this would accelerate economic reforms, democratize the political system, and call a halt to centrifugal tendencies.

---

22 For an insight into Stambolić's efforts to stand up, more resolutely, for Serbia's economic interests inside the federal party forums, see Prinčič and Borak, *Iz reforme v reformo*, 530; and Neven Borak, *Ekonomski vidiki delovanja in razpada Jugoslavije* (Ljubljana, Znanstveno in publicistično središče, 2002), 130–31. For an overview of the accusations of Stambolić's soft stand on nationalism in his own words, see Lekić and Pavić, *VIII Sednica CK SK Srbije*, 274.

Unlike the nationalist intellectuals, Milošević presented this program not only as Serbia's narrow cry for equality, but also as an integral part of the Yugoslav revolutionary heritage. The political slogan launched was "United Yugoslavia," interpreted as the overcoming of borders everywhere, whether inside the factories, or on regional, republican, or federal levels. The Constitution of 1974 was depicted as a betrayal of the state's original revolutionary aspirations. Serbia was now reviving the discourse of integral Yugoslavism, a theme very much present in the early postwar years, which subsequently lost its appeal when faced with the growing recognition of decentralization as an essential element of democratization and self-management. However, the Yugoslav identity was now fused with desire for a more determined Serbia, as Serbs were allegedly the nation most interested in keeping the country together.

Slobodan Milošević associated the removal of the previous Serbian leadership with liberation from the deeply-entrenched complexes of Serbian society. The first and most burdensome, according to him, was certainly the national complex: the widespread belief that any struggle for the interests of the Serbian people amounted to nationalism. The second complex was ideological: it referred to the view that every form of order and organization in state and society necessarily implied Stalinism. This notion was an implicit criticism of the self-management structures at the municipal and republican levels which stood parallel to the state. It served to free the Serbian leadership from the stigma of centralizers and statists when confronting Associated Labor. Finally, there were also economic complexes; above all, the idea that socialism does not go together with the market, and that the market inevitably implies a return to capitalism.[23]

In November 1988, Milošević dedicated much of his address to the Conference of the Serbian LC to explaining the exact meaning of the ongoing economic reforms. The chance for personal and collective prosperity through differentiation was counterposed to the alleged equality in poverty. The speech noted that workers in Rakovica were forced to steal bread from the factory canteens. Milošević invoked the humiliating character of this assumed practice,[24] using it to promote his vision of a new system in which each member of the working class would be able to capitalize on hard work:

> There is no more space for an increase in poverty. . . . The reform therefore means a break with the illusion that political actors in society can successfully guide economic processes. . . . Economic decision-making should be placed in the hands of the direct producers and their enterprises, their motives and interests, their initiative, their capacity to grapple with risk, with competition, with all foreseeable and unforeseeable challenges carried by the market or-

---

23 Slobodan Milošević, *Godine raspleta* (Belgrade: BIGZ, 1989), 218.

24 During this period, Rakovica's union leaders were projecting the image of workers being forced to steal bread from the factory canteens to feed their families at home, in order to draw attention to social plight in the municipality. Many workers certainly depended greatly on the factory canteen and its subsidized prices for their daily nutrition, and some might indeed have brought food back home. However, the image of "bread stealing" was an exaggerated depiction that aimed to steer emotions and arouse pity.

> ganization of the world economy of which we are part. . . . This is the first and foremost task of economic and social reform . . . to remove the blockades, ideological and others, for an individual and society to be able to *enrich themselves through their labor.*[25]

As one can see, the dismantling of the self-management structures was presented as a fight for the rights of direct producers, interpreted as the freedom to act entrepreneurially and generate income without interference from political bureaucracy. Unlike the more aggressive neoliberal economic experts, hostile to social property and the symbolic status of the working class, Milošević embedded his program in the familiar themes of 1960s market socialism. Socially-owned companies were to remain the foundation of the system. The workers would continue to enjoy their special connection to the ruling party, but the factories should be freed from their bureaucratic burden in order to become profitable once again. In accordance with the traditional liberal interpretation, self-management constituted the workers' right to control the income generated by their enterprises. According to this line of reasoning, the 1970s therefore placed the cart before the horse. If there was no business success, then there was no workers' self-management worth discussing.

The internal strife between manual workers and professionals was to be overcome with the help of new growth opportunities. Increasing market and technocratic influence was related to the wage increases of ordinary workers. As the quotation above emphasizes, the notion of enrichment through one's own labor was key. The liberalization of Yugoslav industry was supposed to punish those who earned their money through monopolies and bureaucratic maneuvers, not ordinary, hard-working people. For the plan to work, Serbian workers had to stand behind the new leadership together with their managers, as their unity would increase the chances of Serbia pushing through reforms at the federal level.

The reform proposals worked on two levels: the micro level, with reforms inside the enterprise, and the macro level, with changes in the constitutional architecture of the federal state. The first set of measures aimed to strengthen the managerial structures inside the factories in order to break the deadlock of the self-management bodies and reinstitute the profitability criteria at the center of enterprise business decisions. Consequently, the latter group of proposals followed the same logic within the federal political frame. The application of liberal economic reforms demanded a partial recentralization of the state, with corresponding internal laws and effective institutions, which could implement this ambitious program. In order to create a unified internal market, the Serbian leadership argued, the Yugoslav state would have to streamline the executive branch and facilitate the decision-making processes at the federal level. Once these institutional prerequisites were achieved, the economic liberalization and steady democratization of political life would help turn Yugoslavia into a coherent and functional state.

---

25 Milošević, *Godine raspleta*, 278–80, emphasis added.

For many workers, the existence of an authoritative figure at the top who could unite the party behind a common program of action, protect workers from the alienated bureaucracies, regulate the market, and bring the system into line with changing times was the preferred way to resolve the crisis. Since the death of Tito, the party-state had no powerful and charismatic individuals capable of elevating popular demands into high politics. As a female IMR worker stated in an interview in 1986:

> Nobody is in control here. Not only inside the factory, but also in the state as a whole . . . nobody has the power to stand up in front of the masses and convince them. The masses do not listen to anyone any longer and they do not trust anyone . . . who could show us the real way . . . if someone could tell us "do it like this" we would do it, but we can't trust anyone.[26]

After years of melancholy inside the party ranks, the appearance of Slobodan Milošević raised hopes that mounting social conflicts could be resolved once again with traditional Titoist methods. The lack of a clear authority and dissatisfaction with loose discipline inside the factory turned into open support for a "firm hand" approach. Inside Rakovica, the factional purge of the local socioeconomic bodies was carried out under the banner of "internal differentiation." It was advertised as a turn toward the greater political and managerial responsibility that the productive base had always demanded. The struggle against Associated Labor bureaucracy would supposedly allow the best, most visionary communist cadres to come to the fore. Local party officials argued that the times of "endless discussions" were over.

The political shift also had clear generational undertones. The managers and party officials, who climbed to their positions during the 1960s and 1970s, had to step down and make way for younger, better-educated, unwavering cadres. The deep-rooted faith in the historical mission of the new generation came to the fore. As one worker claimed, "we need a refreshment, new trends, some new kids around, new scientific disciplines such as the organization of information systems."[27] In IMR, the younger activists saw the political change as an opportunity to strike a blow against the old functionaries. As outlined earlier, the Yugoslav factories contained two different sets of socially active workers, the self-managing activists and the sociopolitical activists. The shop floor perceived both groups as privileged workers, yet, at different periods, one of these structures could be seen as standing closer to direct production or a particular section of the workforce. The older IMR worker activists were more inclined to group inside the self-managing structures. They criticized the sociopolitical organizations, and the party in particular, as springboards for young ambitious workers. On the subject of privileges, an IMR Motor worker who spent fifteen years in the factory stated:

---

26 Milošević, *Žulj*.

27 Vasilj Cvijanović, "Sami sebi cilj," *IMR*, January 26, 1988, 7.

> With little work experience and little invested sweat the young workers switch to *režija*. The work there is easier; there is no accountability, no norm. As soon as they receive some sociopolitical function, young workers migrate into office work or they get a leading position. Why, when we have so many older, more exhausted and more deserving older workers who could take these places? It turns out that sociopolitical work is a privilege.[28]

The fact that the older workers targeted the sociopolitical functionaries as the main beneficiaries of political favors reveals that the generation gap found expression in the two parallel factory structures. For many young workers, entering into sociopolitical work was the only way to advance in the factory, as all the key positions in the governing and administrative organs were held by the older workers.[29] As noted, the most active young IMR workers usually joined the party and, in the course of the 1980s, the factory LC branches changed from being the main supporters of Associated Labor to its fiercest critics. This meant that the IMR party was refreshed with younger cadres and new oppositional language in the late 1980s, despite the wider discrediting of communists.

The breakthrough of oppositional themes into the mainstream did not arouse open debates like those organized by the party in earlier years. In a way, the victory of Milošević's faction depoliticized the factories. The answers finally seemed clear. The new leadership brought with it a rounded program of reforms and the sole question was how to implement it in the fastest way. These two quotations chosen from the factory press reflect this urge to leave quarrels behind and move ahead:

> I would not go into the left and right factions. That is a battle of ideas. What is important is that the party offers the people something concrete.[30]

> I stand for more work and less talk . . . so when it comes to reforms, let us not philosophize, but roll up our sleeves.[31]

Over the years of constant obstructions in self-management bodies, the shop floor developed an animosity toward collective decision-making and the merging of political discussions with professional business conclusions. The new party line encouraged this sentiment. The vision of a worker with a socialist consciousness, who controls not only his enterprise, but also society as a whole, was brushed aside. Self-management was labelled utopian, a system not fit for the local conditions or mentality, as IMR's factory paper stated: "I do not think that social property is not efficient, but the problem is the way we approach it with our Balkan consciousness. We do not see it as ours. As soon as we hear social property, we see it as someone else's property."[32]

---

28 D. Žujović, "Za bolje sutra," *IMR*, April 28, 1986, 6.

29 A 1986 interview with a worker Zdravko Petrović mentions this tendency. See Mića Milošević, "Radnici neće žedni preko vode," *IMR*, July 29, 1986, 6.

30 Milica Lučić-Čavić, "Paraliza a ne kriza," *IMR*, July 28, 1987, 6.

31 "Vreme za promene," *IMR*, June 6, 1989, 2.

32 D. Dikić, "Prošlost zapouku," *IMR*, December 6, 1988, 5.

What ensued by the end of the 1980s was a conservative shift toward more traditional authorities like the professional management, calls for a direct chain of responsibility, and an insistence that each member of the collective should focus on a single task. In order to be successful, the factory allegedly had to steer clear of radical experiments and adopt a conventional division of work and management responsibilities, showcased by single households and private entrepreneurs:

> In each household it is clear who the boss is, who is responsible and who determines how much should be spent and where . . . but, in our social sector, everybody is responsible for everything and nobody for nothing . . . that is why the private entrepreneur performs better . . . everything belongs to him and he keeps it and manages it the best way he knows how. We waste so much material and accumulate stock. A private owner would never allow this. That is why I support the extension of the powers of the executives, but they should also suffer sanctions if they fail.[33]

> I am convinced that without a *firm hand* there is no recovery. Without discipline, there is no progress in society. Take a private businessperson for example . . . how is it possible that he organizes his work in an exemplary fashion? It all depends on the organizer of work . . . if the director is good, the workers are also good . . .in our factory one can stay in a responsible post for thirty years with no results . . . it is because we think that everybody can manage that we have such a situation in the country and in the factory.[34]

References to private business also reveal workers' growing distrust toward non-market criteria for the allocation of goods and wages. The contractual economy was now openly associated with the privileged position of the political elite, clientelism, and misuse. The market, on the other hand, was connected to efficiency, reward of hard work, and clear principles, equal for all:

> Market relations will gain ground only once work is valued and rewarded, instead of wages being given out according to monopolies, party cards, and familiarities.[35]

> I support the housing reform. Let everyone buy his or her own house or apartment. Where in the world have you seen the practice of handing out apartments as gifts? Nowhere! One sees this only here and we are poor [the interviewee was a migrant worker, living in a precarious, self-built house on the outskirts of Belgrade]. Socially-owned housing should be abolished! For the price of a single apartment, the enterprise could make a credit down payment for ten workers to build their own houses.[36]

---

33 "Vreme za promene," *IMR*, June 6, 1989, 5.
34 "Birokratija je uzela maha," *IMR*, May 23, 1989, 2, emphasis added.
35 D. Žujović, "Samostalnost samo na papiru," *IMR*, October 17, 1989, 5.
36 "Ruke za dva takta," *IMR*, June 6, 1989, 6.

Thanks to the new spirit of expedience, by January 1988, the amendments to the old Constitution and the Associated Labor Act—which aimed to empower the directors and increase work discipline on the shop floor—were already in the Federal Parliament procedure. The planned reform of the Associated Labor Act, and the subsequent changes to the Enterprise Law, gave general directors a free hand to hire and fire lower-level executives and ended the right of the factory sociopolitical bodies to have a say in the appointment of directors. They introduced a simple majority vote inside the workers' councils, instead of the previous requirement for unanimity, and limited the number of issues that had to be decided by factory referendums. The new legislature also clearly stipulated the criteria for layoffs, making a measure that had been extremely hard to execute under the old Associated Labor Act much more applicable. A worker could now be fired for various disciplinary offenses, including: unannounced absence from work for more than three days; unjustified sick leaves; failure to abide to fire safety and national defense procedures; or any other "irresponsible behavior, which contributes to the economic troubles of a company."[37]

Belgrade's industrial enterprises seized the political moment to present the new leadership with further demands. In February 1988, IMR, IMT, and their main component manufacturers adjourned a "protest meeting" attended by self-management delegates from the respective factories and an array of municipal and city-level functionaries. The speakers complained about the unequal market position between manufacturers from different republics, especially Serbia and Slovenia. Whereas Slovene companies were allegedly able to raise the prices of their final products, Belgrade factories were acting as the "sole break on inflation."[38] Indeed, the grievances and methods of political pressure were very similar to those practiced by TAM during the early years of stabilization. The freely-operating market and the widest possible autonomy of firms in relation to the state remained the ideal. However, since the new Serbian leadership displayed a greater concern for the interests of its own republic in the federal bodies, producers were tempted to push for protectionism as an intermediary measure.

The calls for protectionism did not contradict the general orientation toward laissez-faire socialism. Following the logic of IMR's reform-oriented professionals, the strengthening of the central state was just a short-term measure needed in order to create the equal conditions for a functioning market, not a return to the redistribution policies of the past. As one IMR foundry worker explained:

> For the market economy in Yugoslavia to function, we must have the same starting positions. At one point, IMR handed over its complete production line to Maribor's TAM. After this, it had to go into debt in order to acquire new product licenses from abroad and had no money to set aside for further development. Hence, the economic crisis caught us at point zero. Nobody can

[37] D.J., "Strogo radno zakonodavstvo," *IMR*, March 15, 1988, 2.
[38] D. Žujović, "Tako se više ne može," *IMR*, March 1, 1988, 3.

convince me that you can make a market economy from zero, without investments. For this, we need the capacities of at least a mid-European level of competitiveness. We already have cadres and we have the yearning.[39]

During the previous years, Slovenia's reforms were cited as a positive example by the IMR management to encourage the Serbian LC to allow similar policies. However, the feeling of lagging behind and a growing market rivalry also produced negative depictions of Yugoslavia's most northern republic and its enterprises. Allegedly, by pursuing asymmetrical reforms, Slovenia was causing an unequal distribution of the burden of the federal anti-crisis measures. IMR was now sending a clear request to the Serbian political leadership to take a more proactive stand in defense of Serbian manufacturers' interests, the same policy that Slovenia had allegedly been pursuing all along behind the backs of the federal leadership. In the eyes of IMR workers and executives, TAM had taken the place of the city rival IMT as the embodiment of the "unfair competitor." Transferred to the field of federal politics, the image of Slovenia inside Rakovica was starting to be similar to that of Kosovo: the northern republic became the symbol of selfish, local interests. This sentiment was in tune with the general trend in the Serbian party. With Slovenia acting as the most persistent opponent of Serbia's reform pushes, the republic was singled out as the main saboteur of a united Yugoslav reform effort.

Bypassing the Working Class in Slovenia

In 1986, the Slovene party elected a new leader at its Tenth Congress. As historian Božo Repe noted, Milan Kučan triumphed with the support of the "self-confident managers and technocrats of a younger generation, who looked at the world through the prism of information technology and computers."[40] Faith in the power of technological innovation and the knowledge economy was widespread among young professionals in Slovenia at the time and strongly associated with market liberalization. The Tenth Congress opened the floor to critical voices stemming from Associated Labor, mostly those of managerial staff and worker-functionaries from higher self-managing bodies. TAM's communists insisted on revision of the decision-making system inside the enterprises. They believed that the excesses of the shop floor self-management institutions, such as workers' assemblies and referendums, reduced the role of central self-management organs and professional management to "collecting and putting a stamp of approval on decisions already made." The second main concern was the organizational division into BOALs, which, according to TAM's communists, blocked the functioning of the enterprise as a cohesive business entity and limited the role of professional managers. Furthermore, TAM delegates at the congress asked

39 D. Dikić, "Prošlost za pouku," *IMR*, December 6, 1988, 5.

40 Repe, *Slovenci v osemdesetih leti*, 25.

for the factory delegations in municipal assemblies to incorporate managers and technical experts, since the present delegations comprising ordinary workers were not competent to reach decisions over complex technical matters.[41]

In April 1987, the Belgrade-based liberal economic journal *Ekonomska politika* praised Milan Kučan for his determination. The article stated that after the initial statements made during the Tenth Congress, many observers—accustomed to the traditional zigzags of party functionaries—expected Kučan to even out the forces inside the apparatus by clamping down on the market advocates. Not only did this not happen, in the months to come the new leadership extended the ideological support for liberal reforms even further. Like Milošević, Kučan relied heavily on traditional liberal interpretations of workers' self-management to justify moving further down the path of reform. In a speech delivered to the Slovene LC session that year, he stated:

> It is impossible to consider reorganization of Associated Labor outside of the market logic . . . without opening up our economy to the world, and without overcoming conflicts with statist economics, which still has a dominant influence on our consciousness. The maintenance of the statist economy reduces a worker to a pure owner of his labor power and a manager to a state bureaucrat . . . in these roles, the director is in need of hierarchical, linear methods of managing, which treat workers solely as holders of labor power and not as managers, carriers of the function of the ownership of social capital. The struggle for the reinstatement of the professional managerial function inside the factories is the struggle against etatism, voluntarism and for the position of worker as the carrier of management functions. . . .[42]

Once again, much like Milošević's efforts inside Serbia, the greater influence of the market was officially conducted in the interest of the self-managing workers and the fight against wage labor. Still, upon closer examination it was clear that professionals, rather than the blue-collar workers, were seen as the proper managers of social property. Among TAM's professionals, the increasing technological gap between Slovenia and Western Europe became one of the prime matters of concern. A party activist from Research and Development, Jože Kadivnik, stressed this issue in the Maribor daily *Večer*: "The experts should be the first and the foremost source of decision-making instead of politicians. Otherwise, if we continue down this road, we will end up as a lonely and undeveloped island in the middle of Europe."[43]

The spread of computers in the production process had a big impact on popular understandings of management inside the factory and gave the white-collar workers an advantage in internal relations of power with the shop floor. In 1986, TAM's youth activist Igor Gračner boasted in the republican congress of the League of Socialist Youth of Slovenia (LSYS) that the factory planned to install eight fully computerized workstations by 1990, and called for the liberalization

41 "Kongres velikih nalog in pričakovanj," *Skozi TAM*, April 11, 1986, 2.
42 "Organizovanje privrede: fleksibilno a ne uniformisano," *Ekonomska politika*, April 6, 1987.
43 "Težko je dobiti ljudi, ko bi delalo z voljo," *Skozi TAM*, January 1986, 5.

of procedures for technological imports.[44] The above-quoted article from *Večer* also carried the thoughts of party cadre Ciril Navinec, from TAM's Financial Accounting. Navinec observed that communists have no more influence over the preparation of final accounts and business reports presented to the self-management meetings, since computers did all the work beforehand. Instead of pictures showing workers in meeting halls, factory paper articles announcing new income distribution schemes started displaying spreadsheets and images of trained personnel sitting behind computers. The distribution criteria were formerly shaped through negotiation and presented in densely-written self-management agreements. The language of these documents was indeed opaque, but they were open to dispute by all sides able to express their interests in the accepted political jargon. The idea of new objectivity and expertise brought by the market and modern technologies made it hard for activists within governing and sociopolitical bodies to question management decisions.

With the arrival of the new leadership, Slovenia's rhetoric in federal-level political debates also gained a new intensity. Frustrated with the slow but steady advance of Serbia's centralizing reform plans at the macro level, Slovenia was gradually pulling back from collective anti-crisis efforts and started "shooting at Belgrade from the cannons of the Slovene fortress."[45] The heating up of debates at the federal level finally encouraged Tezno's functionaries to engage more openly with political topics. The immediate reason was the bankruptcy of the food processing giant *Agrokomerc*, located in Bosnia and Herzegovina. The enterprise tried to go around the federal government's restrictive monetary policy by issuing a large amount of money certificates with no backup, and eventually declared insolvency once the scheme was exposed. The media claimed the company management enjoyed political protection inside the federal organs of the party-state.

In December 1987, Tezno's delegates launched an initiative inside the Chamber of Associated Labor of the Slovenian parliament for public prosecution of all the federal functionaries who knew of Agrokomerc's misdeeds but remained silent. The fact that top politicians were able to emerge from the affair without serious consequences was rendered "insulting" for the workers, since "inside the factories people are punished severely for much smaller offenses," the statement concluded.[46] In the era of a strong federal center and the prominence of the Associated Labor Act, the scandal would most likely have been interpreted as another case of technical experts and local politicians misusing the workers' self-management system against the interests of its all-Yugoslav blue-collar base. However, by late 1987 the blue-collar delegates from Tezno chose to join their republican party in criticism of the federal organs, accusing them of corruption and standing above the law. The basic anti-bureaucratic sentiment was similar to that launched from Rakovica, yet the political personification of this hated

---

44 "Naša vizija reševanja perečih vprašanj družbe," *Skozi TAM*, April 1986, 3.

45 According to Božo Repe, this was Kučan's own definition of Slovenia's tactic inside the federacy. See Repe, *Slovenci v osemdesetih leti*, 26.

46 Danilo Vincetič, "Je to samoupravljanje, če mora delegat umaknuti kočljivo vprašanje?," *Skozi TAM*, December 1987, 8–9.

layer were the centralizing federal structures dominated by communists from less developed republics, not the polycentric amalgam of self-serving party-states envisioned inside Serbia.

Political liberalization was also pursued. After two years of accelerated economic reforms in Slovenia, Milan Kučan concluded that the Yugoslav socialist political heritage did not offer sufficient room for further systematic changes. The Slovene reforms had advanced as far as possible within the frame of workers' self-management and single-party rule. In April 1988, during the Slovene LC conference keynote speech, Milan Kučan proclaimed that socialism could not stagnate without a perspective and present itself as the mere negation of capitalism any longer. Instead, Kučan called for a "developed socialism fit to human needs," a new type of socialist system which was not an isolated ideology, but "an integral part of those processes in the world that contribute to a more humane existence."[47] Apart from a stronger orientation toward personal incentives and a condemnation of egalitarian economic principles, this new type of socialism also abandoned claims to the vanguard role of the working class, the revolutionary party, or the uniqueness of socialism as the only genuine emancipatory project in the world. As the quote above shows, socialism was now seen as just one part of a multifaceted process leading to a better future for humanity.

It remained unclear what global developments Kučan was referring to. Inside Slovenia, however, the concept implied opening the party up to new social movements and a greater freedom of public speech. The Slovene party-state now directly encouraged different political grassroots initiatives to form inside its mass organizations. LSYS had already become an umbrella organization for various new social movements dealing with gay and lesbian rights, ecology, and pacifism. In May 1988, the independent Union of Slovene Peasants and Farmers was founded under the auspices of the main mass organization in the Yugoslav political system, the Socialist Alliance of Working People.[48] This new independent body called for an increase in the permitted size of land ownership and the return of nationalized land to private farmers. By the end of the year, it had gathered 30,000 members. Around the same time, a presidential election was held with an open media campaign and a choice of seven candidates. The unexpected winner was the economics professor Janez Stanovnik, a contender calling for more decisive market reforms and a liberal democratic political system, who ran against the party-endorsed candidate.[49]

In practice, therefore, the political opening inside Slovenia during the first half of 1988 went much further than the 1970s concept of a pluralism of interests

---

47 Dragiša Drašković, "Istina nije u jednini: Konferencija SK Slovenije," *Rad*, April 26, 1988.

48 The Socialist Alliance of Working People was responsible for integrating wider layers of the population into political life, work in local communities, and nominating delegates for the Chambers of Citizens in the municipal and republican assemblies. The organization played a negligible role within factories which were focused on political representation through the other two chambers in lawmaking bodies, namely the Chamber of Associated Labor and the Socio-Political Chamber.

49 Jan Lundin, "Slovenia in 1988: Pluralism and Reaction" (working paper, Department of Soviet and East European Studies, Uppsala University, 1989), 21–22.

under self-management, still officially endorsed in Serbia. Kučan's new type of socialism seemed to be taking its cue from the ongoing reforms in the Western European communist parties, summed up under the key term *Eurocommunism*,[50] rather than the domestic political legacy of a worker-based democracy under one-party rule. This development was certainly the result of political pressures from other republics as much as the mimicry of processes in Western European communist parties. The Slovene LC held a minority position inside the LCY, and it was therefore forced to defend the principles of free speech and oppositional organizing. As Dejan Jović points out, the more Belgrade pressed for democratic centralism and unity inside the federal party, the more Slovene communists advocated minority rights, which they then also had to enact on their home terrain. In any case, the bulk of criticisms inside the local media and the new social movements were directed against the Yugoslav People's Army and central government, and thus came in handy to back up the Slovene stand inside the federal bodies.[51]

In Tezno, the youth organization was the first to reflect the broader trends of political liberalization and adopt a more independent line in relation to the local party. In November 1987, the Coordinating Committee of TAM's LSYS announced that it no longer intended to direct its activists toward the League of Communists.[52] The first words of the factory press report from the LSYS Youth Festival in Celje that year stated: "We refuse paternal care, let us choose the path which recognizes new knowledge, let us prove that 'internal truths' are a thing of the past."[53] Remarkably, LSYS's TAM chapter—on paper, one of the more blue-collar in Slovenia—endorsed the removal of corporatist institutional solutions which established the working class as the privileged pillar of political decision-making in society. In accordance with the idea of a pluralistic civil society standing opposed to the state, TAM's youth activists were now suggesting opening the Chambers of Associated Labor in law-making bodies at municipal and republican levels to the entire constituency, together with the abolition of sociopolitical chambers dominated by the LCY, a system akin to bourgeois parliamentarism.[54]

The local LSYS branches largely abandoned Marxism and began to circulate translations from Western human rights and ecological groups, such as Amnesty International and Greenpeace. Pacifism and ecology became their main topics of concern, the latter being advanced with relative success among the workforce. By 1987, Maribor became one of the most ecologically endangered cities in Slovenia, with air pollution rising above critical limits.[55] TAM's youth activists

[50] In an interview, France Pivec, the head of the Maribor party branch at the time and a close collaborator of Kučan, told me that the Slovene party leadership was increasingly orienting itself toward the reformist course of the Italian Communist Party (PCI). The key text of Eurocommunism, Santiago Carrillo's *Eurocommunism and the State*, was translated into Serbo-Croatian in 1980 and subsequently circulated widely.

[51] Jović, *Yugoslavia: A State that Withered Away*, 322–25.

[52] "Kritično o prenovi Zveze komunistov," *Skozi TAM*, November 13, 1987, 6.

[53] Drago Gajzer, "Spremembe so nujne," October 1987, 4.

[54] Ibid.

[55] M.S., "Zrak naš vsakadnji ni več, kar je bil," *Skozi TAM*, March 1987, 5.

started encouraging the cause of protecting green spaces inside the factory complex. Its 1987 annual report mentioned that the youth had managed to collect 2,400 TAM workers' signatures supporting the closure of Slovenia's nuclear plant.[56] However, the issue of pacifism was not received with the same enthusiasm. In TAM, where a significant chunk of production was oriented toward the Yugoslav People's Army, this kind of message was not well received. In an interview, the former factory youth activist Drago Gajzer testified that TAM's youth organization "did not want to press the workers with this issue."[57]

Slovene civil society was increasingly connecting its criticism of the central state with the theme of demilitarization and the reorientation of the Slovene defense industry toward civilian production. In May 1988, the Slovene youth press published a leaked army plan for state-of-emergency measures inside Slovenia. The document revealed that the army had a list of journalists and dissidents targeted for arrest and planned to replace the local leadership in Ljubljana with a more conservative one. The army reacted by arresting an LSYS activist, a Slovene army lieutenant, and two journalists. Since the affair involved the leaking of military secrets, the whole trial fell under the jurisdiction of a military court, beyond the influence of the Slovene government. The trial inflamed the latent anti-federal feelings among the local population.

The new Slovene leadership benefited from the spread of anti-federal and nationalist messages at home, as it was the sole actor representing the republic in the central bodies of the party-state. To the Slovene public, Kučan could simultaneously position himself as both government and opposition. Inside Slovenia, his role was allegedly to maintain stability by curbing radical oppositional voices, which might provoke political or military intervention from Belgrade. When it came to Kučan's political work inside the central bodies of the Yugoslav party-state, however, the media portrayed him as a principled fighter for Slovene national interests. This duality brought him great popularity in the course of 1988, similar to that enjoyed by Slobodan Milošević inside Serbia. Public support for Kučan jumped from 26.9 percent in April to 65 percent in October.[58]

These figures can lead one to conclude that Slovenes were becoming increasingly homogenized politically. Nevertheless, one should be careful when delivering sweeping judgments of this type. Without a doubt, the citizens were overlooking internal differences and coming closer together when placed under external pressure, but many contradictory tendencies remained. A public opinion poll cited by Dejan Jović shows that Slovenia was the Yugoslav republic most prone to accepting political pluralism, but at the same time, it was also home to the largest percentage of people ready to support the policies of a "firm hand."[59] Despite efforts to promote workers' self-management as the ideology of

56 "Poročilo o delu conference osnovnih organizacij ZSMS DO TAM in njihovih organov v letu 1987," *Skozi TAM*, March 1988, 6.

57 Interview with Drago Gajzer, April 2013.

58 Jović, *Yugoslavia: A State that Withered Away*, 328–29.

59 In Slovenia, 61.1 percent of surveyed citizens were in support of a "firm hand which knows what it wants," instead of "empty talk about self-management." In Serbia 53.4 percent of correspondents agreed with this statement. See Jović, *Yugoslavia: A State that Withered Away*, 322.

maximizing individual incomes, many Slovenes were still connecting socialism primarily with the concept of "equality" and a "classless society."[60]

The new party leader might have been gaining recognition, but more broadly, the Slovene League of Communists was in a state of disarray. In 1988, it was recorded that the total membership had decreased from 126,000, the figure immediately after Tito's death, to a little under 110,000.[61] In TAM, the 1987 Action Conference of the local party chapters revealed that the communists felt "powerless, wavering, and without perspective."[62] The following year, TAM's communists concluded that 137 people, or 18 percent of the membership, had left the organization in the previous period. Of the remaining communists inside the factory, only one-third were active.[63] The 1988 Maribor city conference showed that regular members were not sure how to position themselves in the growing divide between local social movements and the federal party. It described the Slovene youth press as brave for exploring controversial issues and criticizing the Yugoslav People's Army. At the same time, the conference participants did not renounce Yugoslav patriotism, adding that one should not focus only on the negative aspects of life in a common state.[64]

The leadership's abandonment of Yugoslavism, working-class solidarity, and egalitarian visions as the main themes attracted the interest of voters outside of the traditional party milieus. On the other hand, it left the longstanding loyal members in a state of confusion. The party officials were well aware that detachment from the federacy and the egalitarian values of workers' self-management also carried the potential to alienate a significant section of Slovene society beyond the party ranks. In the 1988 Slovene LC conference, functionary Jože Župančić noted regrettably that "50 percent of Slovenes have a low-skilled worker's mentality." These were allegedly individuals "who would like things to remain in place as they are . . . who wish to wait for retirement in their workplaces without stress and requalification."[65] Župančić's use of statistical data was sloppy and likely not based on any concrete study, but used symbolically to prove his point about the alleged resistance to reforms. The notion that 50 percent of Slovenes opposed changes was an exaggeration used to invite sympathy for the predicaments confronted by the reform-oriented leadership. Nevertheless, the approaching explosion of discontent in Maribor would prove that the potential for resistance to the new course was indeed present, particularly in industrial communities such as Tezno.

In contrast to Serbia, by the late 1980s, there was no political force ready to take on those sections of the Slovene population still clinging to the interpretations

[60] In the 1984 survey, 31 percent of the Slovene population continued to identify socialism with "unequivocal social equality," even though this was not an official interpretation. See Sharon Zukin, "Self-Management and Socialization," in Pedro Ramet, ed., *Yugoslavia in the 1980s* (Boulder, CO: Westview Press, 1985), 93.

[61] Repe, *Slovenci v osemdesetih leti*, 5.

[62] "Ta časke težko biti komunist," *Skozi TAM*, June 1987, 6.

[63] Danilo Vincetič, "Začnimo pometati pred svojim pragom," *Skozi TAM*, March 1988, 12.

[64] Danilo Vincetič, "V gospodarstvu so potrebni novi prijemi," *Skozi TAM*, March 1988, 8.

[65] Dragiša Drašković, "Istina nije u jednini: Konferencija SK Slovenije," *Rad*, April 26, 1988.

and ideals of the Yugoslav socialist revolution. Unlike Milošević, whose language still paid tribute to the economic heritage of market socialism, preserved the working class as the privileged political constituency, and propagated the idea of democratizing the existing political institutions, Kučan's reforms suggested a clearer break with the past. The nationalist intelligentsia, for its part, was customarily skeptical regarding class as the category dividing the Slovene nation. In line with the growing influence of the ideas of civil society, the new social movements were not willing to recognize the potential for independent organizing within state socialism. Under communism, there was allegedly no free society. As a result, most forms of existing and institutionalized social organization were ignored. Labor and workers' self-management in particular were identified strongly with the ruling party and this was not the heritage the activists wanted to rely upon when advocating further democratization.[66] Slovene blue-collar workers were left to their own devices, bypassed by all major actors in Slovene politics.

Beggar Thy Neighbor

Organized labor in self-managing socialism frequently related the expansion of its political rights and improvement in their standard of living with demands to curb the real or assumed privileges of other occupational groups. Whether referring to white-collar employees, who allegedly did not produce surplus value, or peasant workers, ranked below "pure proletarians" by official ideology, divisions inside the factory were encouraged by the party, with the intention of imposing itself as the external arbiter between opposing interests. Such divisions were also stressed by the skilled manual workers, in order to demand special treatment as the sole producers of value. In times of crisis, the total income was seen as a fixed sum, and the increase of wages for one occupational group automatically meant loss of income for others.

The Marxist postulate of the exploitation of labor was easily evoked in the years of rising social polarization. Since the inception of self-management, the party insisted the project was potentially threatened by the dual forces of bureaucratic centralism and economic particularism. The chief embodiment of the former harmful tendency was the alienated state bureaucracy, whereas the latter was represented by market-inclined managers. The victory of market-oriented politicians in Serbia and Slovenia in the late 1980s meant that the state bureaucracy was placed under the spotlight. The reform of the Associated Labor Act was portrayed as part of the fight against privileged statist forces, which stifled the flourishing of self-management and modern forms of production. But who was the main representative of the state bureaucracy in these years?

[66] Tonči Kuzmanič, "Strikes, Trade Unions and Slovene Independence," in *Independent Slovenia: Origins, Movements, Prospects*, ed. Jill Benderly and Evan Kraft (New York: St. Martin's Press, 1994), 161.

Ever since the 1960s, when markets and political decentralization became the backbone of Yugoslav socialist ideology, the stress was placed on the apparatus of the central state as the embodiment of bureaucracy. The 1970s brought political condemnation of the uncontrolled market and technocracy. However, the decision was taken not to confront the managerial layer with a return to political centralism, but to conduct an even more radical decentralization under the new Constitution and Associated Labor Act. During the 1980s, in smaller republics—especially the relatively well-off Slovenia—the public still perceived statist forces in traditional terms. The federal bodies were seen as falling under the increasing influence of Serbia and the less developed republics, which supported their empowerment. Yet inside Serbia, new interpretations were rapidly gaining ground, which equated social forces hostile to self-management with complacent regional party apparatuses whose influence rested on the atomization of state functions and the blocking of reforms. In both cases, the focal point of confrontation was displaced from the class antagonism inside the industry and projected along the national lines of individual republics.

By portraying Serbia as the exploited victim of ever-increasing pushes for decentralization, the new dominant discourse in Belgrade assigned the Serbian nation as a whole with attributes once reserved for the proletariat. Slobodan Milošević started to use the term "working class" interchangeably with the term "Serbian people" (*srpski narod*).[67] Workers in other republics were also increasingly being perceived more as members of nationally-defined groups with opposing interests than a unified Yugoslav proletariat. In the eyes of workers in Rakovica, the dividing line between Slovene workers and their elites was fading, as they allegedly all benefited from the unequal constitutional setup. The difference in economic development between the regions seemed to support such interpretations. As already noted, in the second half of the 1980s, the average wage of a production worker in Tezno was almost two times higher than in Rakovica. The following statement by an IMR worker shows how discrepancies in wages created the impression of separate interests, especially at the height of the crisis, when each negotiation of income redistribution between the republics was seen as a zero-sum game:

> I was never able to understand why as we were building Drmno [a power plant in Serbia] the Slovene workers were paid forty, Serbs twenty, and Macedonians twelve million old dinars. Opposing interests among workers can only appear due to different material conditions. No one is crazy to give up what he already has. That is why equal conditions for work and pay should be created for all of us. The Yugoslav working class can have only one interest.[68]

A united labor movement with a common platform was therefore hard to envision from this standpoint, as the only conceivable way for workers in Serbia

[67] Olivera Milosavljević, "Antibirokratska revolucija, 1987.-1989.," in *Dijalog povjesničara-istoričara* 8, ed. H. G. Fleck and I. Graovac (Zagreb: Zaklada Friedrich Naumann, 2005), 319–36.

[68] D.Ž., "Naši radnici govore: Da vidimo šta će biti," *IMR*, November 1, 1988, 6.

or Macedonia to receive higher incomes would involve lowering wages in Slovenia. However, as the worker quoted above noticed, nobody was ready to renounce part of their earnings. The logical conclusion stemming from such understandings was that the new "people's leadership" of Serbia should press the federal government to intervene more decisively and redistribute wealth from northwestern regions in favor of lower-paid workers in the southeast of the country. A truly unified Yugoslavia was viewed as a place where all self-managed enterprises would enter into exchange via the market from the same starting position. Under those circumstances, the income would allegedly be distributed according to "work," instead of the better "work results" made possible by inherited advantages and political protection.

In Slovenia, the problem was seen from the opposite point of view. For workers' representatives in Tezno, the free operation of the market and self-management were not obstructed by unequal exchange, but rather by the existing wealth redistribution mechanisms, primarily the Federal Fund for Accelerated Development of Underdeveloped Republics and Kosovo. Alluding to the loss-making factories outside of Slovenia, TAM's party activist Jože Čuješ complained on the pages of the factory paper about the presence of "petty-bourgeois attitudes, a lumpen way of thinking and consumer habits, creating the false idea that one can live well without work and without respect for the basic value of our society."[69] By attributing non-proletarian traits to the workers in the southeast, Čuješ was portraying them as unworthy of solidarity. In April 1988, TAM's factory paper reprinted an article from the Slovene daily press on the solidarity funding of underdeveloped regions in Yugoslavia. The article started with the usual grievances over technological stagnation and centrally-imposed wage limits, only to end with the topic of low birth rates inside Slovenia. Linking the issue of birth rates to economic relations inside the federation, the text was clearly reflecting the growing influence of nationalist ideology and the fear that the crisis of Yugoslav socialism was putting the very existence of the Slovene nation at stake.[70]

The examples above show that the use of nationalist narratives for self-victimization and denial of rights to workers in other parts of the country was indeed present in Tezno. Still, one can find this type of language only occasionally. As explained, superior production performance and a more favorable market position allowed the Slovene manufacturer to relate its grievances to business freedoms and the urge to continue with modernization, instead of past injustices and ethnic oppression. In Serbia, on the other hand, the media and the party imposed the national question as the prime concern to which all other issues had to be subordinated. The presence of ethnic strife in Kosovo introduced a sense of urgency and anxiety in Serbian society. Few workers in Rakovica could remain indifferent to the images of their fellow nationals' plight. As Milošević pointed out to the members of the LCY Central Committee in October 1988:

[69] Jože Čuješ, "Brez ustrezne spodbude ni rezultatov," *Skozi TAM*, April 1986, 9.
[70] "Kam vse to pelje? (Povzeto iz več člankov *Dela*)," *Skozi TAM*, April 8, 1988, 12.

> Kosovo is not the cause, but the consequence of the crisis of Yugoslav society. However, the fact that it is a consequence does not mean that it should be resolved last. Harassment, rape, and humiliation of the people cannot wait until we get inflation under control, reduce unemployment, increase exports, raise living standards, implement democratic centralism, and discuss the relationship between class and the nation.[71]

In the initial years of the crisis, the discussions about Kosovo in Rakovica's factories were heated, but the language stayed within perimeters set by the politics of "brotherhood and unity," and insisted on the Marxist concept of class divisions within each nation. As a rule, criticism launched in the direction of Kosovo focused on the local power holders, individuals presented as standing in contrast to the ethnically-mixed population. The large numbers of Albanian protesters in the streets, backing greater autonomy for Kosovo, were portrayed as ill-informed or manipulated youth, whose true interests were different from those of nationalist ideologues. This nuanced approach and its careful distinctions largely disappeared with the political rise of Slobodan Milošević and the incorporation of ethnic grievances into the official discourse. Chauvinist themes, formerly limited to the pages of the yellow press, now started appearing in IMR's self-management meetings and the factory press.

Rakovica's delegate in the Serbian Parliament, IMR worker Milorad Despotović, was particularly engaged in the efforts to push formerly censored political topics into official discussions. In March 1987, he accused the party leadership of avoiding connecting the issue of high birth rates in Kosovo with unemployment. Despotović advised the authorities in the autonomous province to "rethink if each family should have ten children."[72] The growth of Kosovo's Albanian inhabitants in relation to its Serbian population was one of the main nationalist concerns in Serbia. Aside from high birth rates, the ethnic structure of the province had also allegedly changed due to illegal migration from Albania. In December of that year, IMR's highest delegate also raised this question. Despotović insisted on knowing Yugoslavia's exact number of refugees from neighboring countries and how many of them had been deported. Despotović also demanded to know how these individuals earned their living, since, as he stated, "we all know the situation concerning the living standards and unemployment of our workers."[73]

Kosovo was being connected ever more directly with IMR's business difficulties. The yellow press reports about vacation houses built by Kosovo functionaries were picked up quickly inside Rakovica. The factory press recorded Despotović conveying the message from his base to the delegates in the Serbian Parliament:

> The workers presented me with the task of sending out a warning through the legal institutions for the last time. The situation in Kosovo is causing unease

71 Milošević, *Godine raspleta*, 270.
72 "O izbeglicama," *IMR*, December 25, 1987, 9.
73 Ibid.

> and insecurity among our workers. We are frustrated in particular with the fact that the funds for underdeveloped regions are used for separatist causes. Rakovica workers give out twice as much for this fund as for our own accumulation. We are especially angry about the fact that land is taken away from the Serbian residents in order to build vacation houses for the functionaries, . . . in Kosovo the taxes, rents, and bills are not paid to the state, . . . where does the province get its money from then?[74]

The fall in the standard of living in Rakovica was directly associated with the supposed cultural backwardness, high birth rates, unlawfulness, and political privileges of Albanians in Kosovo. In September 1988, the Serbian party intensified its campaign to centralize the Serbian and Yugoslav political systems through constitutional amendments. The IMR youth organization leadership distinguished themselves as particularly passionate speakers on this topic, not hesitating to underpin their demands with chauvinist undertones:

> It is shameful that at the end of the twentieth century we have *genocide* in Serbia. The Serbian people lost their statehood in peacetime and the amendments are a chance to regain it. . . . Are we living in an occupied land? We have seminars in Albanian if there are five Albanian students present, . . . so many Albanians have crossed the border since World War Two and we are doing nothing about that. . . . We naively believed in some theoretical constructions that Marxism had on the national question and now we are paying the price for it.[75]

The usage of notions such as "genocide" and "occupied land" reveal the level of anxiety and fear present in Rakovica. The stories of refuge, terror, rape, the infiltration of immigrants from Albania, and the unaccountability of the provincial authorities created an atmosphere of hysteria and inspired some of the workers to start viewing the inherited ideology of "brotherhood and unity" as a "theoretical construct" while adopting nationalist ideas which seemed to correspond to reality. It seems the new concepts were especially well received among the younger workers, who had no personal experience of cross-national solidarity, and a new generation of activists, who viewed the political turn as an opportunity to advance in the sociopolitical bodies by toppling discredited senior cadres.

For most citizens of Rakovica, the question of how any proposed program to achieve Yugoslav unity through a stronger Serbia would resonate with workers in other parts of the country was never an issue. Any hint at nationalism was perceived as rubbing salt in the wound and furiously rejected. Referring to accusations of rising nationalism in Belgrade by the local communist leadership

---

[74] D.J., "Upozorenje poslednji put!," *IMR*, November 1, 1988, 4.

[75] D. Dikić, "Jednoglasno za amandmane," *IMR*, October 4, 1988, 4. Emphasis added. When speaking of genocide, the speaker is referring to the situation in Kosovo, often described in terms of "genocide" by the media. The idea of lost Serbian statehood relates to a popular phrase often repeated in the media, originating from the dissident novelist Dobrica Ćosić's self-victimizing claim that Serbs are always winners in war and losers in peacetime.

in Serbia's northern Autonomous Province of Vojvodina, a speaker at an open meeting called by Rakovica's party to debate the coming political reforms stated:

> Nobody can tell us here in workers' Rakovica, the place where the workers' bread is shared in brotherly fashion between people of all Yugoslav nationalities, that we support "Greater Serbia."... We are convinced that the working class and all the nationalities living in Vojvodina also want unity of Serbia and Yugoslavia, the strengthening of brotherhood and unity, further advancement of self-management, equality between the republics, a faster solution to the accumulated problems, and a peaceful life for everyone in Kosovo.[76]

In Tezno, the younger factory activists also seemed to be those most eager to break with cross-national solidarity. The youth organization perceived the calls for greater unity in Yugoslavia as a mere smokescreen for the bloated administration of the central state, technological backwardness, solidary cover of losses, favor based on political privileges, and the rule of mediocrity.[77] The nationalist grievances under communism were recognized as legitimate, but there was a conscious effort not to bring them to the fore of political discourse. On the 1988 Day of the Republic, the central state celebration of socialist Yugoslavia, TAM hosted the Slovene president of the League of Socialist Youth of Yugoslavia, Branko Greganovič. Greganovič was a student with little connection to the industry. Dressed in a stylish sweater and with the fringe of his hair covering his eyes, the federal youth functionary stood out in a room full of work overalls, business suits, and the traditional peasant costumes worn by the performing folk orchestra.[78] Greganovič's speech was just as offbeat as his appearance. He avoided praising the communist heritage and defiantly focused on the supposedly distorted presentations of the past:

> Too long have we feared every song, every national symbol, and respect of traditional customs. It is no wonder that we live in an atmosphere characterized by distrust and national intolerance, fear of our own past, which we sadly got to know only by means of Potemkin tales of good and evil characters. Historical facts remain unknown, the archives still remain closed. That is why at this very moment an orientation toward the future is most necessary in Yugoslavia, not oratory engagements about good and evil characters and searching for the culprits of the past.[79]

Greganovič therefore showed an understanding, if not outright sympathy, for reawakened nationalism and historical revisionism, but appealed for restraint in a heated moment and focus on the more tangible reforms ahead. The future,

76 "Ustavne promene—jedini put," *IMR*, July 26, 1988, 4.

77 "Poročilo o delu konference osnovnih organizacij ZSMS DO TAM in njihovih organov v letu 1987," *Skozi TAM*, March 1988, 6.

78 See the cover page of *Skozi TAM*, December 9, 1988.

79 Danilo Vincetič, "Jugoslaviji je ta čas najpotrebnejša zavestna usmerjenost v prihodnost," *Skozi TAM*, December 9, 1988, 3.

according to him, entailed business freedoms, separation of the economy and politics, and the autonomy of labor from the party tutelage.[80] The policy of TAM's youth organization toward its comrades from other republics could be best described as politely reserved and increasingly isolationist. In the course of 1987, TAM's LSYS began to boycott youth events on the federal level.[81] In the summer of that year, TAM's factory paper published an interview with Tone Andrelič, the president of the Slovene youth organization. Andrelič praised the youth as harbingers of new technologies and progressive ideas, but made a conscious effort to differentiate between the younger generations in Slovenia and the less economically prosperous regions:

> The surveys say that young people comprehend the crisis differently in the less developed parts of Yugoslavia. For them, the solutions seem to be a strong state and centralization of all functions. They think that the state has to take care of all their problems. We strongly disagree on these issues.[82]

This type of reasoning justified the cessation of communications between the Slovene LSY and the youth organizations in other republics. The smearing of the youth outside Slovenia was similar to the actions of the TAM factory elites to discourage solidarity with workers in the southern republics, by attributing to the latter a lumpen and petty-bourgeois consciousness. The image of youth in less developed republics was deliberately oversimplified. As we have seen in the case of IMR, the new political trends in Serbia also carried strong anti-statist messages. The reliance on the local party-state and strengthening of the federal bodies were viewed as temporary measures required to level the playing field. Otherwise, the newly-found economic wisdom inside Rakovica favored the market and praised private initiatives. Similarities between the anti-statist attitudes spread by the reformists in Tezno and Rakovica can be best observed in relation to the economic policies in Kosovo. The younger activists and professionals in Rakovica were hostile to the solidarity fund, aiming to take control of the local transfers to Kosovo and use them as profit-seeking investments. This was exactly the rationale the Slovene pro-market reformers were applying to all underdeveloped regions.

In April 1987, TAM's youth organization declined an invitation to the annual Yugoslav young metalworkers' competition. The factory paper claimed that there were no political reasons involved, arguing instead that the technical content of the event was not satisfactory.[83] The tradition of youth work brigades

---

80 Danilo Vincetič, "Za ekonomsko varnost ljudi mora skrbeti država," *Skozi TAM*, December 9, 1988, 3.

81 The boycott decision was related to a controversy surrounding the preparations for the Youth Day celebrations that year. LSYS decided to introduce an element of subversion into the event by contracting a local post-punk artistic collective to design a Slovene proposal for the event poster. After the poster had won the competition, it was revealed that the image it featured was an appropriation of a painting made by Nazi-allied artist Richard Klein in 1936. The scandal sparked furious reactions among the Yugoslav public and political condemnation of LSYS.

82 Simona Trčko, "Večina slovenske mladine ve, kaj hoče!," *Skozi TAM*, June 19, 1987, 8–9.

83 Danilo Vincetič, "Dokončen NE za Srečanje mladih kovinarjev Jugoslavije," *Skozi TAM*, April 1987, 8.

was also partly abandoned, with Slovene youth activists choosing to travel to neighboring western countries to take part in smaller events with pacifist and ecological themes, organized by the International Voluntary Service. The 1987 Youth Day celebration in Belgrade caused much criticism among Tezno's youth activists. One of the main songs performed at the event played with negative stereotypes, portraying the Yugoslavs as bad-tempered Balkan people quick to jump into trouble. The tongue-in-cheek performance was supposed to trigger feelings of unity in the face of a common predicament. The factory youth organization had a different view of the event. It insisted that Slovene people did not fit into the stereotypes displayed, and the song was denounced as fatalistic. It was allegedly an acceptance of the current situation, a "laugh at our own incompetence."[84] The message put forward was that, unlike the other republics, Slovenia had a clear idea of how to overcome the crisis and it would not allow itself to waste time by participating in collective celebrations of hopelessness.

The more assertive the working-class milieus in Serbia were in trying to spread their leadership's call for a united Yugoslavia and to present it as an extension of the traditional slogan of working-class unity, the more compelled the Slovene workers were to rally behind their leadership and withdraw from discussions over common concerns. The discussions over the Serbian-led proposals for the reform of the Yugoslav constitution inside TAM's sociopolitical organizations in the course of 1987 and 1988 show this. Those amendments dealing with the reorganization of Associated Labor along clearer market lines were not met with total rejection. Still, the commentators warned that Serbia's strong focus on legal aspects could easily prove to be an empty frame with no real content. Instead of a reliance on the state to introduce market economics, TAM expected a pro-business orientation, adding that exaggerated normativism revealed suspicion toward the autonomy of self-management.[85]

When it came to Serbian proposals for reform of the sociopolitical system and relations inside the federation, the speakers adopted much tougher positions. For instance, the creation of a more uniform taxation system, reintroduction of central economic planning mechanisms, or a common educational curriculum were all discarded as overly centralist and insensitive to differences in regional development and local needs. The reduction of quotas and abandonment of consensus-seeking were not seen as a path toward the democratization of the political system. On the contrary, amid the rise of politics based on national identity, there was a fear that the "one man, one vote" principle would lead to Slovenia being outvoted by the more populous and less developed republics. The idea of introducing the Chamber of Associated Labor into the Federal Parliament was one of the most prominent demands inside Rakovica. TAM's political activists condemned it as an integral part of the efforts to outvote Slovenia. For their part, the Slovene communists placed emphasis on individual civil liberties, abolition of the death penalty, and the legalization of strikes.[86]

84 "Kaj se plete v mladih glavah južno od Slovenije," *Skozi TAM*, April 17, 1987, 8.

85 Jože Čuješ, "Razpravo usmeriti v žarišče," *Skozi TAM*, June 1987, 8.

86 Albert Veler, "Stališča in predlogi k osnutku amandmajev k ustavi SFRJ," *Skozi TAM*, May 13, 1988, 3.

Unlike IMR, where one can spot the workers becoming increasingly responsive to the new political and economic initiatives of their factory elites, it is much harder to detect the reactions of TAM's ordinary workers to the Slovene debates. TAM's discussions of the proposed constitutional amendments were routine events, attracting a closed circle of factory functionaries echoing the official reasoning of the higher party organs. The grievances remained connected to internal factory issues and workers still saw the factory primarily as the place where they earned an income, without depicting the enterprise or themselves in overt political tones. The factory party branches and the union lacked the internal vigor needed to inspire the workers. The sociopolitical activists had no interest in steering discussions inside the industrial base as the managers had established internal, pro-reformist hegemony earlier in the decade. The new messages launched by the Slovene party and the trade union were already a mainstay inside the factory as they were used extensively by TAM's elites during the course of the decade to spur wage differentiation and strengthen the central management.

If there was one organization potentially interested in rallying the workers behind its program, it was undoubtedly the factory youth organization. The local LSYS identified itself with the emerging Slovene civil society much more than with the official reformist policies. Nevertheless, the reach of the youth organization was limited. Despite its growing activism, it remains an open question how much influence TAM's youth organization truly had among the workers in direct production. The 1987 organizational annual report mentions poor dissemination of information among the members and the low participation of BOAL chapters in the work of the standing factory leadership. It seems that TAM's LSY did not overly engage with mobilizations inside the factory. Instead, its activism was most likely initiated and carried out by the full-time staff and reflected broader impulses coming from the university and the more middle-class chapters in the city center. Inside the factory, it is conceivable that youth activists oriented their activities toward the more educated enterprise staff. As Gajzer remembered: "We managed to satisfy only one part of the youth. We were not true proletarians, and attracted individuals from urban Maribor."[87]

The arrest of Slovene civil society activists by the military police in May 1988 triggered public protests in Ljubljana that summer, joined by numerous single-issue groups, cultural institutions, single LC Slovenia party branches, and enterprises. On June 21, a protest in downtown Ljubljana attracted over 20,000 people under the slogan "Freedom, Democracy, Legal Protection." As we have seen, a few months earlier a trade unionist from Ljubljana's Litostroj factory had organized an independent strike committee and sought contacts with oppositional figures. It is thus conceivable that the politicization levels within some plants in the Slovene capital matched the one described in Rakovica. In Tezno, however, one sees no traces of solidarity meetings or mobilizations along these lines. The workers residing in Tezno and its broader countryside did not share the feeling of urgency and national revival present in Rakovica.

---

[87] Interview with Drago Gajzer, April 2013.

Tucked away on the outskirts of the regional center, they were relatively isolated from the burgeoning political activism and fear of potential repression by the central state, spread by activists in Ljubljana or downtown Maribor.

Even if workers in Tezno saw few concrete themes to which they could connect their dissatisfaction in the local political discourse, the general spirit of social liberalization and the trend of expressing blue-collar demands through strikes, which had already entered IMR, would not bypass them. In the course of 1988, strike actions spread to an unprecedented level with individual work collectives starting to stage protests in front of the Federal Parliament building in Belgrade. Workers from both Rakovica and Tezno would join this trend, organizing protest marches outside of their factories and seeking recognition from the party-state. The final chapter will show the different tactics that the Serbian and Slovene leaderships applied to deal with workers' mobilizations and how the blue-collar protests in downtown Belgrade and Maribor corresponded to the broader social mobilizations taking place at the time.

CHAPTER SEVEN

Workers in the Streets

Two Outlets in Rakovica

In the summer of 1988, the Serbian party under Milošević opened up to the grassroots movement of Kosovo Serbs and started not only tolerating, but also actively endorsing, street rallies across the republic. As a result, these mobilizations from below now blended with the communists' official political campaign to reconstruct the constitutional architecture of the country and turn Serbia into a coherent political entity by curbing the autonomy of Vojvodina and Kosovo. Kosovo activists moved from city to city, organizing public gatherings with the help of local supporters. During the month of July, it is estimated that tens of thousands of citizens participated in seven such rallies. In the Serbian media, these demonstrations were heralded as people's democracy in action. In August, the rallies were organized in ten cities with some 80,000 participants. By the end of September, the mobilizations branded by the media as the "anti-bureaucratic revolution" expanded significantly, involving over 400,000 people in thirty-nine cities across Serbia, the two autonomous provinces, and Montenegro.[1]

In Rakovica, the discussions were also starting to move out of the meeting halls into the streets. The municipal party organized the first public gathering that summer with its own forces, independent of the ongoing protest for solidarity with Kosovo Serbs. In July 1988, a Citizens' Assembly, at the plateau in front of the "21. maj" factory, rounded off the campaign for reform of the Yugoslav Constitution inside Rakovica. Some 5,000 residents attended the rally. In the buildup to the gathering, the party activists insisted that Yugoslavia's constitutional model, and Serbia's allegedly weakened position in relation to the other republics, was the main obstacle to economic recovery and political democratization. The gathered workers strongly supported the constitutional reform and agreed with the proclaimed need for recentralization on all levels. The ways in which they envisioned that the centralization of political and economic life would be achieved, as well as the end goals toward which this new unity would be utilized, was another matter altogether.

In their comments, IMR workers usually dismissed the official program of political reforms as too soft and insufficient. Among all the ideas the workers

---

1 Milosavljević, "Antibirokratska revolucija 1987–1989. godine," 324–25.

had, the one heard most often was the demand to introduce the Chamber of Associated Labor into the Federal Parliament.[2] Remarkably, while supporting the push for the eradication of Associated Labor bodies inside the factories, the workers simultaneously adopted the idea of a federal institution for blue-collar representation as one of their highest priorities. Calls were also extended for the dismantling of the Collective Presidency and its substitution with a single-person mandate. Just as in the case of the factory management structure—where a resolute general director in constant communication with the shop floor was preferred—IMR workers envisioned a strong figure, directly responsible to the working class, standing at the top of the party-state as the best solution for the Yugoslav political system. Furthermore, the workers demanded direct elections for representatives in all federal legislative bodies, as well as the introduction of legal prerequisites for the organization of national referendums. Rakovica therefore put forward a much more radical approach to the restructuring of the state than the party leadership. Calls for a clear personal authority at the top and the extension of corporatist agreement between the president and the working class were coupled with far-reaching democratizing impulses, such as direct elections and the institution of national referendums.

Rakovica's communists saw the campaign of solidarity with the new Serbian leadership, conducted in the spring and summer of that year, as only a partial success. The closing rally did manage to gather 5,000 citizens and win over many workers to the new leadership. Nevertheless, skepticism was still widespread. As the president of IMR's LC Conference explained at a roundtable that spring, the workers were still reserved after the negative experience they had with the campaign in preparation for the Thirteenth Session of the LCY Central Committee in 1984.[3] Next to the customary lethargy, the more radicalized layer of workers and the younger party cadres inside the factories found the content of the constitutional amendment proposals too mild.

As we have seen, if it were up to the party base, the federal restructuring would have been conducted in a more radical way and in closer communication with the working class. The conviction that the reform program was insufficiently forceful was also related to the lack of calls for a more just distribution of income and traditional appeals for the struggle against social privileges. The nationalist narrative successfully connected workers' concrete dissatisfaction with the quarrels in the highest federal bodies. However, the fact that many workers accepted the nationalist vision of ethnic relations and the federal state architecture as the most pressing topic does not mean that class tensions inside the factories and wider communities ceased to be important. As we have seen, the accelerated legal reforms under Milošević paved the way for the management to apply stronger pressure on the shop floors. Workers' everyday life and experiences inside the factory kept bringing the issue back to work conditions, occupational differentiations, and homegrown inequalities.

The workers of the Zmaj combine factory in Zemun municipality reflected the heritage of the 1968 student left opposition movement when they poured

[2] D.J., "Neophodne promene," *IMR*, March 29, 1988, 1–4.

[3] "Zašto se ne sprovodi ono što je zaključeno," *IMR*, May 24, 1988, 6.

into the Belgrade streets in June 1988, carrying the slogans "Long Live the Working Class, Down with the Bourgeoisie" and "You Betrayed Tito." By deciding to march onto the Federal Assembly building, these workers followed the example of Bosnian miners earlier that year,[4] as well as a tactic of the Kosovo Serb movement. In front of the Parliament, the city and municipal officials mixed with the factory trade unionists and ordinary workers to address the crowd. The workers failed to present the authorities with a common list of demands. It is interesting to note that none of the speakers in the gathering mentioned any national grievances. The Zmaj factory newspaper recorded the speech of an anonymous worker, which captured the general mood of the protest quite well:

> Everyone receives their wages because of the fact that workers toil. How big has the administration become, how many secretaries and automobiles are there, . . . *where do we see this in the proposed constitutional changes?* We want responsibility in front of the workers; we want to be able to remove those who perform badly. We have the right to demand the lowering of wages for those who do not produce. We have the right to demand expropriations of summer houses![5]

The most indicative part of the cited speech was the clear indignation over the fact that the constitutional changes pursued by the Serbian party leadership did not contain any of the traditional egalitarian messages of Yugoslav socialism. Throughout the intense campaign for constitutional changes in the spring and summer of 1988, Milošević's references to the working class as the cornerstone of socialism were largely a routine inherited from the traditional party language, with no direct connection to concrete movements and demands on the ground. As already mentioned, between May and October, several Work Organizations from all parts of the country rallied in front of the Federal Assembly building in downtown Belgrade. Workers from the Croatian rubber factory Borovo even stormed the parliament in July, but the factory's former director, rather than the political leadership, played the role of the negotiator.[6]

Milošević principally ignored these events. One could say that he stuck to the rules of federalism and refused to intervene in non-Serbian strikes. Even if that was the case, Zmaj, as a Belgrade-based factory, certainly fell under his jurisdiction. The fact is that Milošević already had a political battering ram at his disposal, in the form of the movement of Kosovo Serbs. Under the increasing guidance from the new leadership, the anti-bureaucratic rallies were spreading across Serbia, with experienced activists from Kosovo acting as the organizing

---

4 In May, some 400 miners from a Đurđevik mine in northeast Bosnia decided to organize a march to Belgrade. After reaching the Serbian border, having taken a seventy-kilometer-long walk, the authorities organized buses and transported the protesters to the capital, where they rallied in front of the Parliament.

5 "Protestni marš hiljade Zmajevaca," *Zmaj*, June 30, 1988, 8–9, emphasis added.

6 Miro Crnjaković, "Stari Kalup Žulja," *Danas*, September 13, 1988, 24–25. For a comprehensive analysis of Borovo factory during these years, see Sven Cvek, Snježana Ivčić, and Jasna Račić, *Borovo u štrajku: Rad u tranziciji 1987.-1991.* (Zagreb: Baza za radničku inicijativu i demokratizaciju, 2019).

nucleus. As shown by recent historiography, the Serbian party did not have total control over this movement and there was a fear that political opponents from other republics might use any incident to compromise the Serbian party.[7] The rise of another social movement, based on class identity, with great potential to spread on its own through industrial cities, was the last thing the Serbian leadership wished for at that moment.[8]

The testimonies of Kosovo Serb leaders reveal how Milošević did not greet the news of workers' mobilizations with sympathy and avoided connecting them with the anti-bureaucratic movement. Recalling one of their meetings with the Serbian leader in Belgrade, Milić Maslovarić and Milorad (Migo) Samardžić, members of the protest organizing committee from Kosovo, stated:

> When we were at Milošević's office, you remember when that woman [the secretary] brought him that telex and said "comrade President, they are on their way," and then Milošević started screaming "get out, get out!" That is how mad she made him! Migo winked at me, but I was puzzled, not realizing what was happening. Later I found out how that same day, when we had our meeting with Milošević, the workers from Zemun's Zmaj factory walked out into the streets and gathered in front of the Federal Parliament.[9]

The strike in Zmaj showed that egalitarian values connected to self-management did not disappear from the popular consciousness of Belgrade blue-collar residents in the decade of market reforms. Instead, they continued to circulate away from the public eye, and found their clearest expression inside the trade unions. The wider public associated labor unions solely with social welfare functions, but workers seem to have retained the idea of "real trade unions" as something the system should have strived toward. The growing disillusionment with the party over the course of the 1980s seems to have resulted in workers turning to trade unions, which were among the few organizations still capable of providing some room for expression of their class grievances. In March 1986, the IMR press caught a glimpse of this mood. An assembly line worker was quoted as saying: "Since we have come to a situation where the party has weakened so much, why doesn't the union do something? Under these circumstances, it should engage for the interests of the workers, instead of distributing foodstuffs and organizing excursions."[10]

The bold posture of individual union activists gave workers a reason to project their desires in this direction. During the political opening that occurred around the Thirteenth Session of the LCY Central Committee, the trade union activists often attracted attention in discussions. At a November 1984 meeting

---

7 Vladisavljević, *Serbia's Anti-bureaucratic Revolution*.

8 For a deeper understanding of the political mechanisms of Slobodan Milošević's rule and his mobilization tactics inside Serbia, see Marko Grdešić, *The Shape of Populism: Serbia before the Dissolution of Yugoslavia* (Ann Arbor: University of Michigan Press, 2019).

9 Sava Kerčov, Jovo Radoš and Aleksandar Raiš, *Mitinzi u Vojvodini 1988. godine: Rađanje političkog pluralizma* (Novi Sad: Dnevnik, 1990), 235.

10 D. Žujović, "Dosta je bilo priče," *IMR*, March 19, 1986, 4.

organized by Rakovica's municipal party, where social scientists and politicians put forward their thoughts on the topic of growing social inequality, the "21. maj" factory trade unionists Milan Nikolić and Slobodanka Branković stood out from the rest of the sociopolitical activists. They led vocal attacks against the perceived privileges of the communist elite. Pointing to the unequal distribution of apartments in the city, Nikolić questioned the legitimacy of "people who resolved all their problems" in top party positions. He argued that "in order to understand the problems of the proletariat, the leaders have to be proletarians themselves." The debate continued heating up, to the point where an unnamed worker called for the confiscation of all wealth gained through the "exploitation or appropriation of social property."[11]

In 1986, Milan Nikolić was elected as one of Rakovica's two delegates for the Tenth Congress of the Yugoslav Trade Union Confederation. He also became a municipal delegate in the Belgrade Trade Union Council. At the new City Council inauguration meeting, the rank and file expressed the desire for a more combative organization. The delegates criticized the "strengthening of techno-bureaucratic management" as well as the "growing influence of structures standing outside of Associated Labor."[12] The latter trope was the customary punch against the state bureaucracy, but declaring technocracy as among the main problems facing self-management was a rare feature among sociopolitical activists at the time. It was the language of the previous decade, which obviously had survived inside the lower-level trade union forums and was now looking for renewed recognition. On the federal level, at the Tenth Congress of the Yugoslav Trade Union Confederation, Nikolić took the floor, endorsing the idea of the Chamber of Associated Labor in the Federal Parliament. As in 1968, Rakovica's delegates tried to launch a semi-independent, all-Yugoslav, blue-collar initiative inside the federal trade union. However, the union leadership refused to include Nikolić's proposal in the official protocol of the congress and put it to a vote.[13]

In January 1988, the IMR trade union held its first regular election since the removal of the rabble-rouser Đorđe Golubović in 1986. Surprisingly, the presidency did not pass to any of the veteran union cadres who had controlled the organization after Golubović's fall. Instead, the post was occupied by thirty-year-old Milan Kljajić, a young foreman known for unorthodox management methods and a rebellious attitude toward his executives.[14] At the inauguration ceremony of the new union delegates, Milan Adžović, another critically-minded IMR unionist from the old guard, made it very clear that this election marked a radical break with the old understanding of trade unionism:

> Changing times demand that the trade union reconsiders its work as a sociopolitical organization, . . . what is it that made the trade union become alienated

---

[11] Sl. Avramović, "Hitni potezi umesto teoretisanja," *IMR*, November 13, 1984, 4.

[12] "Predložen Miodrag Lazarević," *IMR*, February 4, 1986, 2.

[13] Popov, *Radno mesto pod suncem*, 24.

[14] In his own words, Kljajić tried to increase productivity in his unit by building up team spirit. He would organize football matches during work breaks, as well as various social events and activities, which often put him at odds with the older BOAL directors.

> from the social and political events and hence from class itself . . . "we sent two members to a seminar, we held eighty meetings," these phrases tell us about the poverty of action . . . I suggest that those who intend to work in the old ways do not accept the function at all.[15]

The trade union was using the limits of the party reformist program to spread its own influence in the municipality. In March of that year, disgruntled by the rigidity inside the higher trade union forums, Milan Nikolić decided to focus his activity on Rakovica and became president of the municipal trade union organization. His inaugural speech further revealed the changing mood inside the local factories:

> It is a sad truth that we ourselves denounced self-management too easily. Incapable of mobilization, we failed to keep and develop it. In addition, lately there are calls for some kind of *strong hand*, which will resolve the problems. To a great extent, it is our own fault. If we had resisted, they would not have been able to take it away. If we had fought, we would have won! Therefore, we must start a new struggle for self-management, that inalienable right of the workers.[16]

With Milan Nikolić at the helm of the municipal union, joined by Slobodanka Branković, the outspoken female president of "21. maj's" union, and Milan Kljajić, the serving president of IMR's union organization, Rakovica's blue-collar workers now gained a commune-level organization responsive to shop floor grievances that was fairly independent of the party-state. Nikolić was the undisputed leader of the group, a figure with authority. A few years older than the others, he had already built up a reputation among the workers as a strong critic of social polarization in the debates around the Thirteenth Session of the LCY Central Committee.

Nikolić was a member of the Serbian LC but, like many of his comrades, he never turned toward nationalism and remained reserved toward the rise of Milošević and the rhetoric based on ethnicity.[17] Using his inaugural speech to make reference to the "strong hand," which would allegedly solve all problems from above, shows Nikolić was aware that the local union was about to enter into competition with the new Serbian leadership for the support of Rakovica's workers. The way he talked about workers' self-management also reveals a certain attachment to the ideal of blue-collar democracy, far removed from the everyday political use of the term, in which self-management rhetoric was used to cover for each twist and turn in party policy. Nikolić thus held the steady dismantling of self-management structures to be a mistake, a rare opinion among functionaries of the sociopolitical organizations, most of whom believed that some kind of downgrade of the Associated Labor system was necessary and inevitable. Nevertheless, the above-quoted depiction of self-management as

15 D. Dikić, "Novi zadaci i obaveze," *IMR*, January 26, 1988, 4.

16 "Milan Nikolić predsednik," *IMR*, March 15, 1988, 4, emphasis added.

17 Nikolić's staunch anti-nationalism was mentioned to me in an interview by his associate Milan Kljajić.

something "taken away" indicates that, even for Nikolić, the battle was largely already lost. The struggle ahead was not for the defense of self-management as it once stood, but for it as a universal right, which should be respected as part of any new solutions.

It did not take long for the municipal trade union activists to put their words into practice. Furious over the latest affair about the misuse of social apartments involving top Serbian trade union functionaries, Rakovica stopped paying some 20,000 subscriptions to the Serbian Trade Union Confederation. When the president of the Yugoslav Trade Union Confederation visited Rakovica to mediate between the municipal and republican unions, he was greeted with a barrage of provocative questions. The trade union activists asked him if he would be willing to lead a strike of starving workers, in what ways he had contributed to the introduction of the Chamber of Associated Labor in the Federal Assembly, and if he thought that the revolution lost steam in the 1960s.

In mid-September 1988, Rakovica's unionists took advantage of the increasingly permissive government stance toward street mobilizations to organize their own protest gathering. The event was largely ignored by the media. However, this protest, held at the same site as the party-sponsored rally in July, was a unique event in many ways. As mentioned beforehand, the Citizens' Assembly (*zbor građana*) institution was initially relied upon by the movement of Kosovo Serbs to organize street protests. The municipal authorities also utilized this instrument of local community self-management to rally Rakovica's workers behind the government reform campaign. The September gathering, in contrast, was organized as a municipal Workers' Assembly, the most basic legislative institution inside each Work Organization. In other words, it was not the application of the existing form, but the creation of a new one through the extension of a factory-based, broad self-management institution to a territorial unit. The rally did not aim to attract all of Rakovica's residents regardless of occupation, but instead was aimed explicitly at the working class.

The local union managed to overcome the isolation of the factory-centered system of workers' self-management. This was the first time that workers from different factories had established mutual contacts outside of the party-state's official channels, and one could detect a measure of self-confidence and blue-collar pride in the public addresses delivered at this occasion. The empowering language heard at the event stood in opposition to the self-victimizing tone often used by workers' delegates in official institutions. The speakers presented workers as the ruling class in socialism; consequently, they did not need to ask for a helping hand from above, but simply reinstate their given rights. In the keynote speech, Milan Nikolić stated:

> We will not stand on the sidelines accusing each other any longer. We will no longer be ashamed for waiting in line for cheap bread, no longer ashamed for sleeping in narrow basements forty years after the introduction of self-management, which allegedly placed us as the ruling class of this country.[18]

[18] D.J., "Ko nas deli?," *IMR*, October 4, 1988, 4.

Encouraged by the newfound solidarity, the main theme of the gathering was working-class unity beyond national and territorial borders. Whereas most of the anti-bureaucratic protests during the summer focused on Serbia and its two autonomous provinces, this gathering tried to address Yugoslavia as a whole and find universal solutions. The rally demanded the removal of all "imposed barriers and artificial borders" that allegedly blocked the "true, united interest: the interest of the working class." There was no clear statement on what this presupposed common interest of all Yugoslav workers was. Nevertheless, the protest did propose the path to realizing it. The official demand launched at the gathering was that the constitutional changes at the federal level must introduce the Chamber of Associated Labor into the Federal Parliament. Instead of, or parallel to, an empowered Serbia, the protest promoted a new federal body which could potentially provide a counterbalance to the disintegrative trends and release direct producers from the political tutelage of politicians in the republics and provinces. In this scheme, the shortest and simplest way to achieve a common market and federal cohesion was the political emancipation of the working class. Petar Savić, a skilled worker from IMR, differentiated Rakovica's blue-collar platform from the official party campaign in the following words:

> The constitutional changes dragged workers' and citizens' attention away from other problems that are of vital importance for society. Today it is hard to distinguish what is more important than the other, but the mass media are so obsessed with constitutional changes inside Serbia that the people also started to think only about this. That is why we organized this rally, . . . less than one quarter of what we suggested found its way into negotiations over the new Constitution. The basic problem is that we still do not feel things are developing toward the true integration of workers into the running of society. This idea is now formulated in the proposal for the introduction of the Chamber of Associated Labor.[19]

The leaderships of the federal sociopolitical organizations rejected the idea of a new federal chamber with majority vote rule, arguing that this would break the balance of influence between the different nationalities, paving the way to centralization and consequently Serbia's domination as the largest republic. The Serbian party toyed with the idea in the campaign period but could never include it in its official demands, since it went against efforts to obliterate the Associated Labor Act—in its view, the main obstacle in the way of a functioning, integrated market. Instead, it offered to open the door to more Associated Labor delegates in the existing chambers of the Federal Parliament.

By the fall of 1988, Rakovica's workers had thus gained two channels through which they could express their frustration with the conditions inside their factories and the general malaise in society. The first one was the party campaign for the withdrawal of state-like rights that had been given to Serbia's two autonomous provinces by the 1974 Constitution. The second one, with more

[19] "Doba buđenja," *IMR*, October 18, 1988, 6.

immediate significance to the workers' everyday routine, was the rejuvenated municipal trade union and its struggle against workers' falling standard of living. Both initiatives managed to attract the attention of Rakovica's citizens primarily by adopting oppositional political undertones, as well as repertoires of action which stepped outside of the conventional institutional procedures.

Milan Nikolić and his colleagues distinguished their cause from the ongoing party campaign by focusing on factory issues and claiming to reflect the ambitions of Yugoslav workers across ethnic lines. They also came up with a couple of unique proposals, from the vantage point of the Serbian industrial proletariat, for tackling the country's broader problems, such as an insistence on the introduction of the Chamber of Associated Labor into the Federal Parliament. However, it remains unclear how many of Rakovica's blue-collar workers were able to detect subtle differences between the discourse of the local union leadership and the republican political line at such an early stage.

It is plausible to assume that for a large part of the 5,000 workers gathered at the Municipal Workers' Assembly, the messages coming from trade union speakers seemed to complement the slogans launched at the party-organized rally earlier that summer, or those at the rallies of solidarity with Kosovo Serbs. The often-abstract themes of working-class unity and the overcoming of dividing lines blended easily with the official discourse of the ongoing party campaign. The following section will show how the trade union leadership's inability to differentiate itself more clearly from the official political line paved the way for a direct intervention from the very top of the party, which once again brought Rakovica into the national headlines and played an important role in the consolidation of Serbia's new leadership.

Deus Ex Machina

During the summer of 1988, a movement that began as a plea for respect for Serbian national rights in Kosovo grew into broader indignation against the privileged layers of society: the "armchair hoggers" (*foteljaši*), as the hated elites were dubbed by the protest crowds. The anti-bureaucratic protesters increasingly connected the national oppression of Serbs with complacent local political bureaucracies in Kosovo and Vojvodina, allegedly able to retain power and enrich themselves thanks to the legal prerogatives granted to the autonomous provinces by the 1974 Constitution. The party-states in other republics which defended the old constitutional order were also recognized as the alienated political caste opposed to the "people." The main enemy was thus the omnipresent exploitative "bureaucracy," from the municipal to the federal level.

The rallies directed their demands less to the LCY and more to the man standing at the helm of its Serbian branch. Slobodan Milošević's ability to communicate with popular mobilizations in a spontaneous fashion and to integrate their grievances into official party politics gave him the aura of an anti-systemic figure: a champion of the people, at war with the alienated apparatuses of the party and the state.[20] Class identity and factory allegiance did not feature prominently at these rallies. The issue of social inequalities was an underlying theme of the movement, but explicit social demands were subordinated to the allegedly more urgent topic of national oppression and legislative reforms. Even if they came to the protest from the local factories, the participants presented themselves as citizens of Yugoslavia, Serbia, and local communes, demanding the curtailing of the autonomous provinces' constitutional prerogatives or even their outright abolition as the political solution to the ongoing ethnic strife in Kosovo and the stalling of economic reforms.

The anti-bureaucratic rallies took place mostly in mid-sized provincial cities, largely bypassing Belgrade. The party-organized rally in Rakovica that summer was an attempt to step outside of the factory meeting halls and conduct a more broad-based politics; nevertheless, the municipal party, not the grassroots anti-bureaucratic activists, organized the event. The speakers were careful not to slip into more radical, oppositional, nationalist rhetoric and their demands were directed toward the official institutional procedures of the common Yugoslav state. It is conceivable that some of the migrant workers from Rakovica had a chance to participate in anti-bureaucratic manifestations in smaller towns close to their home villages during the summer holidays. A larger number had probably heard firsthand impressions about the gatherings from their family and colleagues back home, or, at least, found out about these happenings through the media. Fed up with the drawn-out practices of workers' self-management and the short reach of the factory organs, the blue-collar workers' imagination must have been sparked by visions of mass rallies in which it seemed the protesters were able to communicate their grievances in a popular language directly to the party apex and the Yugoslav public.

By late August, faced with the increasing efforts of Vojvodina's regional authorities to prevent the further spread of anti-bureaucratic protests, the movement started relying on rebellious party branches inside the province's factories, as well as the sympathetic managers of local enterprises, to provide infrastructure for the rallies. These were early signs of the organized entry of labor into the anti-bureaucratic movement. Although such tendencies could

[20] In Kosovo Polje in April 1987, Milošević's intervention in front of the protesting Serbs facing the local police was the event which separated him from the sea of apparatchiks without a public face in the Serbian party. The video footage from Kosovo Polje, a town close to Prishtina in the center of the Autonomous Province of Kosovo, where Milošević arrived as a mediator to help ease ethnic tensions, had a profound effect on the Serbian public. The delegation from Belgrade suddenly found itself stuck in an emergency. Crowds of protesting Serbs surrounded the town hall, where a meeting with the local party leadership was taking place. The police started clubbing the crowd and there was a danger that the conflict between the protesters and the predominantly Albanian police force might escalate. Milošević managed to calm the situation by exiting the meeting and engaging in a spontaneous conversation with the crowd in the street. The camera happened to catch the dramatic moment in which Milošević made way for an elderly Serbian protester to enter the town hall through a crowd of reporters and security men. Behind the Serbian protest delegates entering the building under Milošević's escort, a voice from the crowd asked: "Why are they beating us?" Milošević turned toward the crowd and answered in a firm tone: "No one should dare to beat you!" This moment caught on camera became mythical in the following years.

be spotted in Vojvodina in late summer, the main precedent for the broader overlap of workers' actions and nationalist mobilizations was set on October 4 in downtown Belgrade, by workers from Rakovica factories. This protest proved to be a milestone event for Rakovica's blue-collar cause and the broader anti-bureaucratic movement. Two important things happened on that day. First, Rakovica's workers decided to follow the example of other striking work collectives and display their dissatisfaction in front of the Federal Parliament. Second, Slobodan Milošević broke the reserved stance that Serbian party leaderships had previously kept toward industrial mobilizations, and decided to address the crowd.

The October 4 march to the Federal Parliament was, by all accounts, a spontaneous event. Unsatisfied with the delay in their monthly paycheck, the "21. maj" workers walked out of their factory in the early morning, calling on their fellow workers from neighboring enterprises to join them in front of the Municipal Assembly. Guards and factory officials could be seen at IMR's front entrance, scuffling with individual workers trying to climb over the factory gates and join the protest. The management's resistance was ultimately broken, and the gates were wide open.[21] IMR workers poured out into the street as well. Only in Rekord tire factory did the officials succeed in blocking all the exits, thus preventing its workforce from participating. Nevertheless, even without the workers from one of the crucial factories, in a matter of minutes the protest crowd rose to over 7,000 people.

The municipal party was caught unprepared. From the windows of the municipal administration building that morning, officials could see the river of people approaching them. Struck by this scene, the municipal party secretary, Dušan Đaković, fell to the floor with a burst stomach ulcer. The municipal party apparatus had been becoming more involved in the constitutional reform campaign during the previous months, but it was clueless on how to handle an unplanned protest of this magnitude. Milan Nikolić and the local trade union officials were thus left to face the crowd on their own. The union representatives did not greet this development with open arms either. They were close enough to the shop floor to know that workers' dissatisfaction could explode at any moment; indeed, this was the reason why they started the local trade union initiative in the first place. Still, according to Nikolić, they had hoped that an all-out strike would come at a later date, once the union structures were better organized and the workforce more familiar with the union platform. Upon seeing the crowd, Nikolić concluded that there was no use in trying to disband the protest. All union representatives could do was try to catch up with the marching column or end up left behind.[22]

The Yugoslav flag and Tito's portrait were positioned in the first row of the protest. In his hands, Nikolić held a paper with the demands drafted for the aforementioned Municipal Workers' Assembly held a few weeks earlier. Once

[21] As mentioned earlier, IMR's outspoken General Director Strahinja Kostić resigned over the summer, leaving the company management without influence among the workers once again.

[22] Interview with Milan Nikolić, March 2011.

the crowd had arrived at Rakovica's central square, the workers realized that there was nobody left in the local party-state to negotiate with. A voice from the crowd suggested they march to the Federal Parliament, located some ten kilometers away. The idea was accepted enthusiastically and over 7,000 workers from different companies started to chant "To Belgrade!" The column was on the move again with a new target in sight, its tempo so ferocious that anyone who stopped would be trampled on. Shoes could be seen left behind on the street as the column advanced. The march soon gained a police escort while citizens on the sidewalks and in the windows greeted the marchers. The slogans chanted by the workers included "We want wages," "We want bread," and "Down with bureaucracy." An hour and a half later, the angry crowd was in the city center.[23]

In front of Parliament, the workers made an attempt to storm the building, but were pushed back by police reinforcements and promised that representatives of the federal government and the Yugoslav Trade Union Confederation would address their demands. In the meantime, Milan Nikolić seized the opportunity to speak from the Parliament stairs. He started his speech by presenting the protest as a reaction to the lack of response from state officials to the demands presented in mid-September at the Municipal Workers' Assembly. By drawing this line of continuity, Nikolić was trying to obtain some kind of legitimacy for the spontaneous walkout. Moreover, he was trying to use the conclusions of the municipal assembly as a frame in which to fit the various grievances heard from the gathered masses.

Figure 27. Rakovica workers attempting to storm the Federal Parliament.
Tanjug News Agency Photo Archive, Archives of Yugoslavia, AJ, 112-L-11807-4

[23] D.J., "Poslednje upozorenje," *IMR*, October 18, 1988, 4.

The spontaneous slogans heard from the crowd reveal a variety of complaints. On the one hand, there were the classic slogans used to protest the falling standard of living, such as the aforementioned cries for bread and higher wages. However, slogans such as "We want Sloba" or "Let's go to Novi Sad" could also be heard coming from parts of the crowd.[24] As the police pushed the column away from the Parliament entrance, many workers confronted the uniformed men with cries of "Go to Kosovo." This second group of chants reveals that workers were indeed eager to use the opportunity to raise some of the popular—by then semi-oppositional—political demands. The link between the workers' economic grievances and broader political demands was certainly the increasingly anti-elitist tone of the nationalist rallies, embodied in the idea of the struggle against "bureaucracy."

As explained earlier, the Kosovo Serb activists and their allies used the notion of "armchair bureaucrats" to smear all political opponents of the Serbian initiative for constitutional reform. In the blue-collar milieu the same image could be associated with the factory elites: desk workers, professionals, managers, and self-managing and sociopolitical functionaries. Many workers were certainly eager to embed their local grievances into this broader popular platform. The constitutional reform inevitably raised the issue of Associated Labor and vice versa. The struggle against bureaucracy nestling in the cracks of the fractured party-states of Serbia and Yugoslavia was simultaneously a fight against the factory elites supported by boalization. Milan Nikolić strived for an independent blue-collar platform, but faced with the popular desire for national unity, he was careful to fine-tune the protest language so that it did not contradict the official interpretation of the crisis offered by the Serbian LC and the anti-bureaucratic activists.

Five demands were formulated on the spot. They were a snapshot of different economic grievances and political themes circulating inside the industrial basin. The first demand was an immediate 60 percent increase in wages, so that workers' standard of living could be preserved throughout the rampant inflation. Second, Rakovica asked for a 20 percent easing of tax burdens on its industry. Third, the protest demanded the resignation of the federal government as well as the Presidium of the Council of the Yugoslav Trade Union Confederation. The fourth demand was for a firmer stand against the "counterrevolution in Kosovo and further disintegration of the country." Finally, the introduction of the Chamber of Associated Labor into the Federal Parliament was presented as an underlying demand, which would make all other demands possible by giving the Yugoslav industry a direct voice in the running of the country.[25]

Rakovica's audacity was based on the growing wave of strikes all over the country and the heritage of workers' rights under socialism. There was a feeling that workers everywhere were mobilizing and that their common interest would inevitably come to the fore. As with the speeches in the Municipal Workers'

[24] "Sloba" is short for Slobodan. The second slogan referred to a rally scheduled by Vojvodina's anti-bureaucratic movement activists for October 5, in the provincial capital of Novi Sad, where they intended to bring down the local government.

[25] D.J., "Poslednje upozorenje," *IMR*, October 18, 1988, 4; Zoran Rakić, "Nećemo da čekamo," *NIN*, October 9, 1988, 11–13.

Assembly, notions of blue-collar pride and entitlement were strongly evoked. Nikolić addressed the crowd from the steps of the Federal Parliament with the following words:

> We believed that blue-collar demands would be incorporated into the constitutional amendment proposals. We believed that the time was ripe for reason to rule over the Yugoslav lands and our mutual relations. We based our optimism on the fact that the entire Yugoslav working class shares our views. Now we see that bureaucratic and separatist forces are evading our demands. We will not tolerate this type of disrespect. We will no longer allow various commissions and presidencies to do as they please. It has become clear to us that the bureaucracy is scared of working-class unity.[26]

The main theme running throughout the speech was a firm conviction that the entire Yugoslav working class reasoned in the same way that Rakovica did. The faith in the unity of workers' struggles in different parts of the country was so strong that Nikolić referred to it as a "fact." Indeed, in the previous months workers from Bosnia and Herzegovina and Croatia were skipping their regional authorities and marching directly to the Yugoslav Parliament,[27] but these were all isolated protests with particularistic concerns, rarely daring to address political themes, not to mention tackling the question of an all-Yugoslav workers' platform. Despite the unprecedented strike activity taking place in all corners of the country, the actual political content of the assumed working-class unity was defined by the media and the federal party-state in largely moribund and abstract notions.

The only visible contender offering a fresh interpretation of working-class unity was the new Serbian leadership, but its nationalist orientation made it open to accusations of narrow interests and using the notion of Yugoslav unity as a smokescreen for a dominant Serbia. Wage increases and taxation relief were certainly potentially common demands raised in most of the strikes. The workers in other republics were also equally fed up with the austerity-focused federal government and the corrupt federal trade union apparatus. Yet, one question remained unavoidable: who would profit from the purges in federal bodies? If they were truly to position themselves as the vanguard of the Yugoslav working class, Rakovica's rabble-rousers had to come up with a clear position on the national question.

The difficulty of articulating a united, federal blue-collar platform was best mirrored in the crucial demand for the introduction of the Yugoslav Chamber of Associated Labor. As we have already seen, this was often interpreted as a cover for Serbian-led centralization by workers' representatives in Slovenia. The demand was not included in the official LCY proposals for constitutional changes

---

26 D.J., "Poslednje upozorenje," *IMR*, October 18, 1988, 4.

27 The following work collectives from other republics rallied in front of the Federal Parliament between May and October 1988: Đurđevik mines (Bosnia and Herzegovina), Borovo rubber factory (Croatia), and Agrokomerc food processing (Bosnia and Herzegovina).

and it is instructive to see who Nikolić blamed for this. His speech identified "bureaucratic and separatist forces" as the main reason why the ostensibly all-embracing working-class interests were not placed on the reform agenda. This was a clear allusion to the leaderships in Kosovo, Vojvodina, Slovenia, and all the politicians in the federal structures perceived as adversaries of Serbia's new platform. The question of whether the Serbian leadership should also be held responsible for failing to push through the demands of its proletarian base in the constitutional reform proposals, and insist on them in negotiations with other republics, was conveniently avoided. For Rakovica's trade unionists, the Serbian leadership was exempt from being openly labeled as "bureaucratic."

Despite their bold appearance and readiness to initiate independent mobilizations, the municipal trade union leadership was uncertain about their exact goals and how they would be reached. As Milan Nikolić explained in an interview, many felt they were caught in a situation that demanded skills, ambition, and knowledge beyond their personal potential. Nikolić appeared to be the most capable and outspoken among them, but even he saw himself as an "illiterate" when it came to politics.[28] By daring to undertake autonomous initiatives, the union activists suddenly stood directly in front of the highest levels of power, which made them insecure. Yet, the restlessness of blue-collar workers in their factories forced them to adopt a militant posture and continue moving forward. In reality, the local union leaders improvised, attempting to stay one step ahead of the workers and, at the same time, trying not to clash with the new party leadership.

Taking a stand in the political arena, where the communist party held a monopoly on debate formation, carried substantial risks. Fear of how the party would label grassroots movements was always present. After each strike, Rakovica's union leadership waited for the media reports with great anxiety. They were relieved whenever workers' grievances were vaguely interpreted as a popular push in the direction of the ongoing reforms, as this was a clear sign that no repression would ensue. More importantly, Rakovica's trade unionists were divided when it came to tactics. Nikolić was strongly in favor of independent organizing, breaking with the old political mechanisms and higher trade union structures while remaining skeptical toward the intentions of the new Serbian leadership. On the other hand, many lower and mid-level trade unionists in Rakovica were more dependent on the old organizing patterns and party structures, or identified strongly with the stated aims of the anti-bureaucratic movement.

In front of Parliament, the wait for someone from the institutions under fire to come out and address the crowd lasted for two hours. Once it became clear that the protest would not disband on its own, an improvised podium was set up on the staircase in front of the building. Not accustomed to mass politics, the speakers appeared very uneasy. They were in no position to give in to the demands but were also reluctant to go against the workers. The president of the Federal Parliament, Dušan Popovski, excused himself for not having anything concrete

28 Interview with Milan Nikolić, March 2011.

to say. "I did not expect your arrival today, I do not have a prepared speech," he stated. Instead of a separate chamber for workers' delegates in the highest Yugoslav legislative body, Popovski tried to give assurances that a fixed number of future delegates in the existing chambers would come from the industry and offered his resignation. "Not enough!" and "How big is your wage?!" the crowd shouted back. The speaker stepped down followed by loud jeering.[29]

The presidium secretary of the Council of the Yugoslav Trade Union Confederation received identical treatment. He tried to explain that the federal Trade Union Council was unable to reach a consensus for the introduction of an additional chamber to the Federal Parliament and, therefore, this body could not stand behind Rakovica's proposal. The speaker was dismissed with cries of "You betrayed the workers!" and "Enough of the lies!" The crowd refused to disperse until their demands were accepted. By this time, a few dozen functionaries had gathered in front of the parliament, but none dared to come to the central staircase and address the protesters. The central street in front of the Parliament was blocked for traffic, everyday routine in the Yugoslav capital was disrupted, and media reporters swarmed in to follow the protest.

A rumor started to circulate among the crowd that Slobodan Milošević was about to appear in front of the workers. The chant "We want Sloba!" became louder and more frequent. Even so, the standstill and uncertainty went on for another hour, with no assurances that anyone else would appear on the staircase of the Parliament. Once the tension had reached its peak, Milošević suddenly arrived in front of the Parliament. He chose to approach the main staircase by walking through the crowd, a dramatic appearance in contrast to the other functionaries hiding backstage. As he approached the improvised stage, applauding workers were opening up their rows to make way for the long-awaited speaker. Milan Nikolić rushed to greet the party leader and regain momentum by handing him a list of demands. It was in vain. Unlike the previous speakers, Milošević avoided operating inside the thematic framework already set by the trade union. Instead, the narrative of his speech was carefully built up to bring the crowd into his own realm. He started the address with flattery, repeating the much-cherished leitmotif of the protest: the working class was the key to much-needed unity and Rakovica was not fighting for its own selfish interests, but those of the entire Yugoslavia.

Milošević went on to say that workers and citizens in every corner of the country shared the demands of the protest. The common cause between the workers' strikes, the movement of the Kosovo Serbs, and the populist Serbian leadership was the struggle against disunity and self-serving bureaucracies. The bureaucrats were responsible for blunting the ordinary Yugoslavs' instinct for national and class unity. Milošević described them as the forces separating the "people" [*narod*] between the republics and provinces for the sake of "status and positions." The reforms were important as they would "integrate the country and create a situation where nobody can exploit one another," where "everybody lives from their own work."[30] The notion of exploitation was thus detached from relations between different occupational groups inside the factories and

[29] Zoran Rakić, "Nećemo da čekamo," *NIN*, October 9, 1988, 11–13.

[30] "Govor Slobodana Miloševića radnicima Rakovice: nećemo izneveriti zahteve," *IMR*, October

connected firmly with Yugoslav decentralization and national inequalities.

Rakovica's economic demands were attached more firmly to Serbia's political struggle for the centralization of Yugoslavia's economic and political system, as well as the fight against the "counterrevolution" in Kosovo. Milošević was careful not to name the protest demands one by one. The concrete calls for wage increases, a decreased tax burden, the resignation of high functionaries, and the introduction of Associated Labor into the Parliament were all buried beneath the broader theme of economic and political reform. The closing sentences of the speech implied the closing of an unwritten contract between Milošević and the workers:

> In these hard times, the hardest since the war, rest assured that we all have our tasks, our workplaces, and our responsibilities. Therefore, I suggest that you go back to your work duties and give maximum effort for the stabilization of our economy and the general conditions inside our country.[31]

The contract was two-sided. The new leadership had acknowledged the working class would remain the cornerstone of a reformed Yugoslavia. In return, the workers were expected to cease strike activities, tighten their belts, and increase their work efforts. For most workers, these assurances from the top must have provided much-needed relief. As we have seen, there was a strong sentiment present inside the factories that each group in society should focus on its own tasks, that this work should be clearly enumerated, and that the working class should remain the final judge of these collective efforts. Milošević's speech targeted this thirst for stability and accountability. The crowd greeted his address with loud applause and the chant: "The workers are with you!" Even so, one part of the protesters did not give in yet. The speaker avoided mentioning their specific demands, which did not pass unnoticed despite the euphoria. After the speech was finished, the chant "We want wages!" started building up again. Milošević was forced to repeat his assurances, stating: "You can trust that we will immediately discuss all the questions you have raised here today. Therefore, nobody should wait any longer to fulfill his or her part of the job. Now everyone back to their own work tasks!"[32]

After hearing this second proclamation of readiness to "discuss all the questions raised," the workers began to disperse. The closing sentence of the speech would become iconic in the years to come. The fact that the strike ended after the statement "Everyone back to their own work tasks" was often used in academic and popular discourses to depict workers' alleged will to submit to a strong leader and succumb to nationalist euphoria. Ever since the death of Tito, Rakovica's workers had been unsuccessfully seeking a renewed channel of direct communication with the party leadership. In a moment of open social conflict, Milošević proved capable of lifting himself above both the party and the masses as an arbitrator, an authoritative figure able to judge the legitimacy of popular discontent on the spot.

18, 1988, 4.

31 Ibid.

32 Ibid.

The new rising star was the only high-caliber politician able to give political weight to the grievances from below by filtering them through officially-sanctioned language and giving them a place in the ongoing reform program. His appeal therefore rested on his apparent power to mediate over social conflicts, but also his talent for inserting popular demands of all kinds into debates taking place at the top of the party-state. The first social movement to establish communication with him was that of the Kosovo Serbs. The methods used by the activists from Kosovo seemed to be producing results and workers were tempted to follow their example. There was hope that Milošević would be ready to take the cause of the industrial proletariat under his wing and start endorsing it in public, just as he did with the national grievances of the Serbian minority in Kosovo.

Maribor's Blue-Collar Wrath

As the strike wave began to rise in Slovenia during 1987 and the first half of 1988, very few eyes were focused on TAM as a potential site of industrial action. The company managed to finish the 1987 business year without losses, thanks to the support of local banks. TAM's continuing internal restructuring, the good public standing of its general manager, Vitja Rode, and the effective prevention of in-house dissents made the Slovene functionaries and the media look positively upon the plant. Yet, as we have seen, dissatisfaction with the detachment of decision-making from the shop floor and growing disparities in incomes made the internal atmosphere very tense. In January 1988, after his visit to TAM, the president of the Slovene trade unions, Miha Ravnik, admitted that he was surprised by the reports he heard in the factory. TAM's trade unionists complained that, after numerous instances of concessions given by the authorities to loss-making factories in Slovenia and other republics, the workers were no longer prepared to accept their argument about the impossibility of distributing income before market validation of the final product. Ravnik advised the local trade unionists to resist the pressure from below at any price, meaning to keep a firm stand against the calls for *uravnilovka* and insist that wages could be raised exclusively through further improvements in productivity.[33]

In April of 1988, the president of TAM's unions, Albert Veler, mentioned the clear restructuring plans and the friendly relationship between union functionaries and management as the key reasons why, unlike many other factories, TAM was able to avoid strikes.[34] Indeed, for years TAM's internal corporatist culture had contributed to the diffusion of shop floor dissatisfaction. However, *tamovci* were seeing other workers in Slovenia and Yugoslavia displaying different kinds of confrontational tactics when dealing with their management. In the summer of that year, the subdued blue-collar anger suddenly burst out into the

[33] Danilo Vincetič, "Naloga sindikata je ustavljanje padanja življenskega standarda," *Skozi TAM*, January 1988, 3.

[34] Danilo Vincetič, "Še vedno velja: Nič mimo sindikata!," *Skozi TAM*, April 1988, 4.

open, as Maribor became the first large city in Yugoslavia to experience a four-day long, citywide industrial action. Between June 21 and 24, all the major plants in the city joined in a united protest and occupied Maribor's central square. The workers from TAM stood at the epicenter of this unprecedented movement.

On June 20, news of difficulties paying wages spread through the TAM plant. Many workers could not cash their paychecks at the bank and those who did found the amount much lower than expected. The following morning, workers grouped together on the shop floors in all blue-collar BOALs, exchanging information about the missing wages. A larger group of workers from Motor decided to march through all the factory workshops and call upon their coworkers to join them in a protest action. The action had no structured leadership with individual agitators spontaneously leading the groups. Trade unionists, communists, and self-management functionaries stood aside. As female worker Slavica Strnad later recalled in her account of the event, "some invisible force led us to the factory gate."[35] Around 2,500 workers exited the factory and headed toward the municipal assembly. In front of the local government, a group of the most militant workers started shouting insults at the municipal functionaries and called on the crowd to continue the protest in the city center. The gathering supported this spontaneous suggestion. Participant Franc Pajtler explained what made him follow the radical calls: "What attracted me into this crowd of people? The moment I joined the striking column I recalled how many times I wanted to warn the functionaries about the irregularities around us. We presented the problems at the trade union meetings. Nobody listened to us."[36]

After the professional management managed to detach the self-management bodies and the trade unions from any shop floor influence, many blue-collar workers felt they had no other way to make their voices heard apart from pouring into the street. Unlike Rakovica, where the local trade union and the party managed to impose themselves as points of reference in the workers' struggle, *tamovci* had no institution or authority they could rely on. Franc Pajtler recalled this feeling of seclusion:

> I want to see someone from my union at the podium, someone from my BOAL party organization, but there is no one! I learned from history that in the past the working class fought for its aims and rights under the leadership of the trade union and the communist party. Neither of them was present at this strike.[37]

The crowd refused to form a strike committee or outline a list of demands. The white-collar workers' domination over the factory self-management structures made the manual workers very suspicious toward any kind of representation or structure. Instead of discussing their grievances through the elected strike leaderships, workers insisted that the factory management, together with city

---

[35] Slavica Strnad, "Hočemo konkretne odgovore na konkretna vprašanja," *Skozi TAM*, June 1988, 3–4.

[36] Franc Pajtler, "Sem storil prav?," *Skozi TAM*, July 1988, 3.

[37] Ibid.

and republican authorities, must appear on the spot and provide answers in front of the entire gathering. Only one concrete demand was adopted by the gathering as a whole: an immediate 50 percent increase to all wages. Once the procession had stopped at Maribor's central square, an improvised speaking platform was set up and individual workers took to the stage to vent their accumulated frustrations and share their feeling of powerlessness. Experiences of humiliation under the tight shop floor discipline were recounted. The speakers and the crowd entered into verbal exchanges, feeding off of each other, while publicly shaming the factory managers and political functionaries. The LSYS-related magazine *Mladina* managed to document parts of the speeches from the podium. The example below offers a glimpse of the tones prevalent in the gathering at this point:

> Speaker: How many times have we gathered and then easily given up? When one of us would raise a criticism, who supported us, I ask you? I also criticized, but then I was forced to apologize. To whom?
> Crowd: The Director!
> Speaker: To whom was I forced to apologize, I ask you again?
> Crowd: Thieves, Thieves, Thieves!

The spontaneous gathering in the city center was far from a focused strike; it was more of a collective therapeutic session where workers were finally free to talk publicly about their superiors and share grievances. The insufficient wages and threat of poverty were the most prominent themes. Workers portrayed themselves as breadwinners unable to provide for their families. Their inability to earn the money expected of them caused feelings of shame and insecurity. One worker openly admitted that he was afraid of ending up as a "social case."[38]

The internal coalition between the workers and the factory elites was abandoned. The workers turned against their management and demanded outside mediation. Despite the breakup of the internal corporatist agreement, workers maintained a strong enterprise identity. They saw themselves as *tamovci*, people who manufacture high-quality vehicles. A worker addressing the crowd was recorded stating:

> Comrades, we all saw how they promised us everything and yet they broke all of their promises. They degraded our symbol, our TAM logo. Twenty, thirty years ago, we received nothing but praise. Since we lost Perhavc [the celebrated general director], everything started going downhill. A vehicle cannot move without gas; you cannot make a worker move without food and drink.[39]

Mentioning the degradation of the TAM symbol shows that the crisis was seen as damaging one of the central aspects of the workers' identity, namely pride in their product. Metalworker Franc Pajtler expressed similar concern in a factory paper opinion piece after the strike:

---

38 Slavica Strnad, "Hočemo konkretne odgovore na konkretna vprašanja," *Skozi TAM*, June 1988, 3–4.

39 Igor Mekina, "Tito in lopovi," *Mladina*, July 1, 1988, 36–39.

> Did we go out into the streets only because of the wages or for something more than that? For me it was something else. . . . Pressed with deadlines, we often work during the weekends. After a few months, the buyers are returning these vehicles as defective. The vehicles are constantly sent for additional repairs. Who is responsible for this? It is those who accept unsatisfactory parts from our contractors.[40]

For years, TAM's management tried to place the blame for bad work results on the financially troubled business partners from other republics. However, the protest clearly revealed that workers were more inclined to hold their own *režija* ("those who accept unsatisfactory parts") most responsible for production difficulties. Most of the demands voiced by individual workers went in the direction of greater shop floor control over the professionals and a lowering of the income gap. Speakers proposed increased monitoring of early exits from the factory circle, stricter criteria for business trips, closer measurement of work performance in desk jobs, and a new income-distribution agreement drafted with greater participation from the shop floor. In other words, the protesters wished to make the administration more accountable to direct producers. Demands for greater participation in decision-making were also present. Workers believed that no significant conclusions should be made without blue-collar input and against their will. They also required that the factory press report openly about the strike. "All these things are understood, or should be common sense," they concluded, indicating that the idea of workers' control over factory matters was deeply ingrained even among the workers at market-oriented producers such as TAM.[41]

The factory elites were obviously the main targets of the criticism. However, the power-holders in the broader community, the republic, and the federation were not exempt from blue-collar wrath. An unnamed young worker received a big round of applause when he asked why the government was buying new cars and planes while workers barely made ends meet.[42] The workers' sense of entitlement, as producers of social wealth, also featured prominently. In the words of the metalworker Franc Drešek: "We are not asking for their money, but ours, . . . they act as if they earned it and then hand us crumbs from the table."[43] Individuals insisted that local authorities disclose the sums on their wage checks. For the protesters, it was unacceptable that the administration received wages five times higher than those in industry. According to them, the highest administration wages should not be more than three times the average workers' wage.[44]

In line with the crude division between productive and unproductive work, the speakers did not target solely professional politicians and experts in government administrative bodies, but also lower-paid staff and service personnel. Workers outside of TAM were often identified not according to their occupation, but their

40 Franc Pajtler, "Sem storil prav?," *Skozi TAM*, July 1988, 3.
41 Slavica Strnad, "Hočemo konkretne odgovore na konkretna vprašanja," *Skozi TAM*, June 1988, 3.
42 Ibid.
43 Svetislav Spasojević, "Maribor dani posle," Nin, July 3, 1988, 21–23.
44 Ibid.

enterprise allegiance. The main dividing line remained one between industry, on the one hand, and administration or services on the other. As a worker from BOAL Tools noted: "My wage is enough for bare survival, the cleaning woman in administration often has a higher personal income than me."[45] The fact that the unskilled female laborer, employed in a "non-productive" service sector or government job, received a higher wage than the skilled metalworker in industry was seen as emblematic of how twisted the reward system had become. Workers employed in loss-making companies from basic industries did not receive much solidarity either. Unprofitable companies continuing to produce and distribute wages were seen as allies of the political bureaucracy. Speakers complained that Impol, a Slovene aluminum producer under bankruptcy management, allegedly had higher wages than they did. Additional objections were raised at the fact that the Serbian truck producer FAP was allegedly receiving export grants, while TAM could not pay out wages.[46]

The fact that the Slovene loss-making company was mentioned next to the Serbian truck-producing rival as beneficiaries of state subsidies indicates that the extension of differentiation between administrations and workers along national lines was less developed in Tezno than it was in Rakovica. The notion of bureaucracy was still unspecified and criticism flew in all directions: from one's own white-collar staff, to the loss-making and subsidy-receiving companies in Slovenia and Serbia, to government administration at the local, republican, and federal levels. Moreover, no political leadership was seen standing closer to the average workers from Tezno, not least that in Ljubljana. As one worker stated from the stage: "In Slovenia we have political cowardice. Our politicians cannot do anything and are incompetent."[47]

It seems that, despite the nationalistic arguments made by factory functionaries, the national question debates had yet to reach the shop floors of Maribor in the summer of 1988. As reporters from the Belgrade-based weekly *NIN* noted, a popular movement against the trial of four Slovene citizens, accused of revealing a military secret, was in full swing during the summer of 1988. Maribor was covered with posters of Janez Janša (an LSYS activist and one of the four defendants), but no protest speaker was recorded even hinting at the case. Eager to hear more about the divisions between the Slovene workers and the "southerners" in Maribor, a *NIN* journalist posed the question of national inequalities to one of the migrant workers a few days after the strike. The interviewed worker insisted this was not a topic within the protest: "I am not a Slovene, but I am a worker. This was not a Slovene but a workers' strike. It was the action of my colleagues and me. I am glad I participated."[48]

The fact that discussions about the national question did not gain ground among the workers does not necessarily mean that they were not informed about the political processes taking place. Still, the themes and figures that proliferated during the Slovene political liberalization wave were not seen as having great

45 Slavica Strnad, "Hočemo konkretne odgovore na konkretna vprašanja," *Skozi TAM*, June 1988, 3.
46 Ibid., and "Glas delavcev," *Skozi TAM*, June 1988, 3.
47 Igor Mekina, "Tito in lopovi," *Mladina*, July 1, 1988, 36–39.
48 Svetislav Spasojević, "Maribor dani posle," *NIN*, July 3, 1988, 21–23.

significance for the blue-collar cause. Interestingly, there are clear traces of consciousness about the need to build independent workers' organizations. In contrast to Rakovica, where the local trade union was standing in opposition to the higher union structures but never went as far as suggesting the possibility of organizing outside of the party-state, the workers in Maribor openly connected their fortunes with independent trade unions. The flourishing of grassroots civic society in Slovenia probably inspired them to think in this way. As Tone Osojnik, a foundry worker, noted a few days after the strike:

> There are associations of intellectuals and students. Recently an independent peasant alliance was formed. Why shouldn't we have an association of workers? Why is there so much fear of us workers, even though we are supposedly the ruling class in this country? We do not want a multiparty system, but we do want an independent trade union that can protect my colleagues and me inside of TAM, but also in other factories, cities and republics. I do not want a trade union whose main task is to hand out food stamps.[49]

Were the reform-oriented Slovene authorities afraid of workers' mobilizations in particular, as the worker seems to be suggesting in the statement above? Following the recollection of Franci Pivec, who had just come to the head of Maribor's party that summer, one can conclude there was some truth to this. At the time, the Slovene LC was faced with a burgeoning civil society standing in opposition to communist rule. Nevertheless, the party-state did maintain some kind of contact with most of these initiatives through its front organizations, such as the LSYS. The civil society and the reformist communist leadership tended to close ranks when faced by attacks from Belgrade. On the other hand, the new Slovene leadership had little influence among the blue-collar workers, as it showcased consistent support of the market reforms led by the factory elites. According to Pivec, there was fear that a layer of anti-market managers in uncompetitive factories might support the workers' unrest and block further liberalization. Furthermore, the prospect of a new populist political figure emerging at the federal level raised concerns that strikes in uncompetitive industries oriented toward the Yugoslav market might provide the centralizing, conservative forces with a foothold inside Slovenia.[50]

In the case of TAM, the fear that the factory management might support the strike proved unfounded. Even with its financial difficulties, TAM's KPO seems to have been convinced that the enterprise had a good chance of becoming a highly productive, export-oriented factory beyond the Yugoslav market. For years, the management was trying to shed its image as a "political factory," dependent on the federal defense budget and the low-competition markets of the southern republics. Vitja Rode, the man who started the pro-market restructuring process, retired in 1987. Maksimilijan Senica, a reform-oriented executive from the Engineering BOAL, replaced Rode in the position of general

[49] Ibid.
[50] Interview with Franci Pivec, April 2013.

manager. During the outbreak of the strike, Senica was away on a business trip to the Soviet Union and therefore unable to address the crowd in the central square. Instead of him, the general management board member, Mihael Gole, spoke in front of the professional management. Even if it wanted to tap into the workers' dissatisfaction TAM's management was in no position to make such a maneuver, since the executives maintained a united front against the critical blue-collar voices for years. Gole was jeered off the stage.

The prospect of workers connecting to the populist messages of Slobodan Milošević was also a highly unlikely development. During the summer months of 1988 Milošević was still associated primarily with the Serbian national agenda.[51] Certainly, there were a number of Serbian migrant workers in Maribor, and the more anti-elitist and pro-Yugoslav messages might have potentially resonated beyond the workers of Serbian origin.[52] But there were no federal media which could challenge the agenda of the Slovene party-state, and Maribor was cut off from the debates taking place inside of Serbia. The interviews conducted by the Serbian trade union press in Ljubljana's Litostroj factory shortly after the anti-bureaucratic protests toppled Vojvodina's regional leadership in October clearly show that the dominant mood among the local workers toward the alleged popular movement, celebrated by the Serbian media, was unsurprisingly one of restraint and confusion over its true intentions. As the metalworker Miloš Vilar stated, "it is hard to keep pace with these events, to see what is objective and what not."[53]

The final speaker to address the gathered TAM workers in Maribor's central square was Ivan Čuk, the president of Maribor's Executive Council (the city mayor). Čuk seemed ready to confront the workers head-on and take the crowd's anger upon himself. He explicitly stated that a 50 percent wage rise was unrealistic and, therefore, any kind of negotiation of this demand was not possible. Disregarding the workers' loud protests, he remained on the stage and called on the gathering to elect a strike committee and outline their demands. In his own words:

> If you want to be your own masters and decide about your personal income, if you want to stand up to continuous government interference into your business, then draft your demands accordingly and pass them on to the higher authorities. . . . We need a system in which everyone can control their own work and income.[54]

---

51 Inside Serbia, this image was somehow altered after the fusion of workers' strikes and the movement of Kosovo Serbs in early October 1988 under Milošević's patronage. In the north- western republics, the vision of Milošević as a proponent of Greater Serbia only grew stronger over time.

52 For the similarities of anti-elitist tropes in Serbian and Croatian industrial plants in this period, see: Rory Archer, "'Antibureaucratism' as a Yugoslav Phenomenon: The View from Northwest Croatia," *Nationalities Papers* 47, no. 4 (2019): 562–80. For the appeal of the anti-bureaucratic revolution for non-Serbian workers in Serbia, see Goran Musić, "Provincial, Proletarian, and Multinational: The Anti-bureaucratic Revolution in Late 1980s Priboj, Serbia," *Nationalities Papers* 47, no. 4 (2019): 581–96.

53 "Samoupravljanje mora pobediti," *Rad*, November 1988.

54 "Tamovci stavkali na Trgu svobode," *Skozi TAM*, June 24, 1988, 4.

This was a clear hint that the workers should embed their demands within the dominant liberal discourse and orient the strike toward the official channels of the Slovene reformist party-state. The workers refused this offer. They maintained their conviction that all matters should be discussed publicly in front of the entire gathering, regardless of how long this process might take. In the afternoon, the *tamovci* dispersed with an agreement to continue the protest in the city center the next day. The factory management and sociopolitical organizations used this brief lull to organize and try to regain the initiative. Emergency meetings at the factory and city levels were called for that afternoon. The activity continued through the night. Without any authorization from the protest gathering, the factory trade union leadership formed a strike committee consisting of three striking workers, selected members of the Central Workers' Council, and a couple of union activists. Albert Veler, the president of TAM's trade union, was placed at the head of the strike committee, even though he refused to participate in the walkout a couple of hours earlier.

The factory union leadership was careful not to extend any legitimacy to a non-institutional mobilization. During the protest, the trade unionists stayed inside the factory and organized assemblies, providing an orientation point for those workers who did not join the march. The union took advantage of workers' refusal to draw up a clear list of demands and put forward their own set of demands. The trade union platform was a mixture of factory-centered demands, heard most often in the city center, and a broader agenda for the further dismantlement of the surrounding Associated Labor structures. It called for a 50 percent wage increase, a revision of the internal income distribution system, and a general reduction in wage disparities. On the other hand, the trade union demands insisted that the administration undergo wage cuts equal to that of industry. The list included a 10 percent cut in industry taxation, a 20 percent cut in the budgets of the republic and the federacy, as well as the streamlining of Maribor's city government.[55]

In the evening, the strike committee met with the Central Workers' Council, factory sociopolitical organizations, professional management, as well as the municipal and city functionaries. The meeting encouraged the latter set of demands, noting that the more decisive political reforms were long overdue and that state budgets were bound to shrink anyway, due to the overall economic crisis. The factory-related demands were strongly condemned, especially the linear increase in wages. The city mayor stood out in the attacks. Čuk started his intervention by saying this was not the first time he had addressed such crisis meetings. Workers in Maribor's other industries, such as textiles and food processing, were receiving even lower wages and in comparison to them, Čuk found the workers protesting in the city center to be relatively carefree. He maintained that TAM would thus receive no solidarity from other factories in Maribor, the republic, or the federation. Supposedly, the rival Yugoslav factories had vehicles in storage ready for sale and, if TAM prolonged its strike, they would immediately fill the gap in the market. The mayor insisted that production must continue. In return, he offered to take a couple of factory representatives with

[55] "Tamovci ostanite trezni," *Skozi TAM*, June 24, 1988, 2.

him to Ljubljana so they could explain the crisis to the authorities and appeal for more favorable treatment from the government.[56]

The TAM Workers' Council met separately and issued a list of decisions aiming to reverse the direction of the factory-centered demands. Instead of an antagonistic stance toward the white-collar workers, the self-management delegates tried to channel popular dissatisfaction and use the strike as a push for more radical enterprise reform. The first decision was to end the strike and return to work. Second, the council granted additional payments to workers with the lowest earnings, thus raising the factory minimum wage. Third, the professional management was asked to accelerate TAM's restructuring program. Fourth, the delegates outside of the factory were instructed to press for a 20 percent cut in the budgets of the sociopolitical organizations at all levels. Fifth, the delegates in city bodies were asked to demand a rationalization of SIZ structures and the abolition of Maribor's six separate municipalities introduced at the peak of Associated Labor. Sixth, an appeal was sent to the banks to assist in the development of new projects and factory restructuring.[57]

The morning after the walkout, the strike committee and the management handed out the printed decisions of the Workers' Council to the first shift of workers arriving at the factory gate. The resolutions did not impress the arriving workers, but the initiative produced results as it managed to divide the strike into three groups. One part of the workers decided to return to their jobs. The second group refused to work and remained engaged in discussions with factory officials in front of the plant. Around 1,000 workers decided to repeat the protest in the city center. The trade union had minimal authority among the workforce, yet the habit of resolving grievances inside the factory and not with the help of outside brokers probably kept many workers from marching downtown once again.

The number of protesters from TAM arriving at Maribor's central square had dwindled in comparison to the day before. However, contrary to Ivan Čuk's predictions, workers from other plants in the city now joined the protest as well. Inspired by TAM's walkout, new strikes took place in almost all the major industrial enterprises (Metalna, TVT Boris Kidrič, Zlatororg, Mariborska tekstilna tovarna, and others). It is estimated that some 6,000 workers took part in marches that day. Rare camera footage of the event shows groups of people in blue work coats descending on Maribor from its industrial suburbs, thus creating the impression of workers encircling the city center. The head of Maribor's communists, Franci Pivec, remembers the buildings vibrating from the street marches as if an earthquake had hit them.

The main protagonists of these events remain nameless. Weeks later, in an attempt to discredit the strike action, TAM's paper described one of the main leaders of the march as an "underage worker who had not finished primary education."[58] Indeed, there are many indications that the bulk of the protesters were young and unskilled workers from Maribor's hinterland. Franci Pivec

[56] Danilo Vincetič, "Vse hujša kriza pripravila tamovce do stavke," *Skozi TAM*, July 1, 1988, 9.

[57] "Tamovci ostanite trezni," *Skozi TAM*, June 24, 1988, 2.

[58] Tomislav Perlič, "Vprašanja, mnenja in predlogi z zborov delavcev," *Skozi TAM*, August 1988, 7.

described the event as an "uprising of the hungry."[59] Apart from TAM, the largest single enterprise on strike was Mariborska tekstilna tovarna, a textile factory. This meant that a large number of protesters on the second day were women. One TAM worker saw them in the following way:

> Next to me, there are women who cry because deep inside they feel bitter. Their only thought is how to continue with life. How to survive with their family, how to raise the kids. It is clear to them that there is no future, that our beautiful green Slovenia is becoming darker and gloomier, that the bureaucracy is cutting off our bread.[60]

Each of the workers' columns arriving in the city center usually had party flags and pictures of Tito displayed at the front. The main chants were the classic party-state slogans: "Tito-Party" (*Tito-partija*), alongside "We are Tito's and Tito is ours" (*Mi smo Titovi-Tito je naš*). These affirmative slogans were then coupled with derogatory exclamations, such as "Thieves" (*lopovi*). A clear line was being drawn between the idealized past—Tito, former general manager Perhavc, and the extension of self-management rights—on the one hand, and the economic crisis and production difficulties brought by their successors on the other. In comparison to the chants heard in downtown Belgrade, many of which referred to the ongoing political debates and Milošević, or the strike of Ljubljana's Litostroj workers, who discussed independent trade unionism and an oppositional political party, the language in Maribor seemed frozen in time with nostalgia as the only political reference point.

Rakovica's walkouts were spontaneous and chaotic, but the workers did accept the nominal leadership of Milan Nikolić and the municipal trade union, and merged into one column accordingly. In Maribor, the second day of protest attracted workers from various enterprises, yet there are no signs of attempts to draft common demands or coordinate actions. The central square was used as a shared public space, where grievances were launched from the podium and the political authorities were called to address the crowd and extend their support without any mediators. But apart from the demand for higher wages, the workers had no common organization or shared understanding of their predicament. Separate groups of workers from different factories spread out across the city center, undertaking different actions. One section of the protesters blocked traffic at the main intersections. A large group occupied the central train station, with the idea of traveling and expanding the protest to Ljubljana. The majority demanded that representatives of the republic came to address them at the central square. Maribor's industry was in an undeclared general strike and the city center was under a spontaneous blockade, but without a clear agenda or leadership this show of power was largely futile.

In the case of TAM, the weight of its top management prevented any individual rabble-rouser from making a greater impact inside the self-management

59 Interview with Franci Pivec, April 2013.

60 Franc Pajtler, "Sem storil prav?," *Skozi TAM*, July 1988, 3.

or sociopolitical structures and thus gaining factory-wide recognition. The grassroots leaders who appeared during the strike remained faceless and their influence was probably limited to a particular BOAL or group of fellow coworkers. The forging of a cross-factory identity was also highly unlikely. As explained earlier, the system of self-management discouraged the forming of broader class alliances or a class consciousness, apart from the increasingly sterile official projections of Yugoslav unity based on working-class solidarity. IMR workers developed two tangible identities above their economistic factory allegiance and below the abstract ideology of Yugoslav unity. The first was the municipal identity encouraged by the local trade union. The second was a feeling of belonging to a broader movement for national equality connected to the party leadership. In Maribor, groups of workers carried Yugoslav flags and pictures of Tito, yet there was no coherent, up-to-date, overarching explanatory pattern to connect these timeless symbols to concrete grievances.

After a long delay, a delegation from Ljubljana arrived in Maribor. It consisted of the vice president of Slovenia's Executive Council, Janez Bohorič, and the president of the Slovene trade unions, Miha Ravnik. A rumor started circulating among the workers gathered on the main square that the delegates would first go to the hotel to rest before addressing the gathering. Once the two functionaries finally took to the stage, they were greeted with loud verbal abuse. Their speeches did not contribute to calming the situation down. Unlike in downtown Belgrade, there was no sweet talk. Bohorič and Ravnik stated that wage hikes were unrealistic and suggested that higher wages would have to be won through restructuring and faster market modernization, not alleged political privileges. The press recorded that the speakers repeated phrases such as "nobody else but yourselves can secure a higher income," "if you are not satisfied with your factory leadership, change it," "you create your own income, you elected the people with functions," and "we did not arrive here with a suitcase full of money."[61] The liberal interpretation of self-management, once used to rally the blue-collar workers behind the idea of collective entrepreneurialism and market reforms, was now turned into a cynical tool of dismissal.

The magazine *Mladina* reported how Bohorič, a former general director of the Sava Kranj tire factory, stood on the stage wearing an expensive three-piece suit, in sharp contrast to the mass of blue overalls he addressed. Ljubljana functionaries were joined on stage by Ivan Čuk, Maribor's mayor, who had taken a tough stand against the TAM workers the day before. Clearly, the three men did not come to negotiate. The internal document of Maribor's LC City Committee clearly instructed the communists against "any form of verbal flirtation with striking workers," warning that extending support without "serious side switching" would be a "damaging manipulation with grave negative consequences for self-management."[62] The aim was to reject the blue-collar

[61] Dejan Kovač, "Mine na reformo," *Dnevnik*, June 24, 1988, 3.

[62] Franci Pivec, "Analiza okolnosti Mariborskog štrajka od 21. do 24.VI 1988. I zadaci SK," in *Obustave rada—štrajkovi u Jugoslaviji*, Centar za društvena istraživanja, sveska 79 (Belgrade: Centar za društvena istraživanja CK SKJ, 1988), 279.

demands at any price and terminate any hope that the government would communicate with the workers outside of the official channels. After delivering their speeches, the officials declined to answer any further questions or engage in discussions with the protesters. Instead, they tried to leave the gathering in a truck parked backstage. The first rows of protesters raised the alarm: it appeared that the functionaries were trying to escape. The crowd ran in front of the vehicle. Protesters climbed on top of the truck and opened the back doors. A scuffle ensued between the workers and the police, with Maribor's mayor almost attacked by the angry crowd.

This incident symbolized the beginning of the strike movement's decline. If there had ever been optimism that the authorities might acknowledge the working class as the carrier of social progress in a reformed Slovenia—as the previous communist leaderships did—it was now lost. On the third and fourth days, the protest became increasingly splintered, anarchic, and violent. Seeing that protests downtown brought no results, many workers decided to continue with gatherings inside their factories. The most persistent groups, which continued to gather in the city center, found themselves isolated with no negotiation partners. The Slovene Assembly issued a report, stating that labor conflicts could not be resolved overnight and in the streets. Instead, the industry should seek new solutions in the official bodies of the party-state through market-oriented policies.[63] A group of workers tried to break into the local parliament and confront Ivan Čuk, but could not find a single functionary inside the building.[64]

The atmosphere in the city remained tense, with groups of blue-collar workers from various plants roaming the streets looking for targets at which to vent their anger. The managers, political functionaries, and even ordinary employees felt threatened and reported occasional attacks by the dispersed crowds. Božidar Ipavic, an economist from TAM's trade department, recalled feeling unsafe when passing groups of striking workers on the way to work, since they could recognize him as a white-collar employee.[65] Drago Gajzer remembered an incident where a company car containing LSYS activists was trapped in a blocked street. The protesters surrounded the vehicle and shook it from both sides, petrifying the travelers on their way to a meeting with the city authorities.[66]

On the fourth day of the TAM strike, the management officially recorded 190 unexcused absences from work, concluding that only the "staunchest nucleus" remained on strike.[67] That same day, general manager Maksimilijan Senica returned from a business trip abroad. Upon his arrival, he tried to underscore the basic political conclusions reached by the city authorities and the management board in his absence, and strike another blow to the populist voices:

63 "Na ulici ni rešitev," *Dnevnik*, June 24, 1988, 1.
64 "Anarhija ne dopušča dogovarjanja," *Dnevnik*, June 24, 1988, 7.
65 Interview with Božidar Ipavic, April 2013.
66 Interview with Drago Gajzer, April 2013.
67 "Pregled najpomembnejših dogodkov med stavko v TAM-u," *Skozi TAM*, July 1, 1988, 10.

> There were attempts lately to ascribe the current crisis to the introduction of the market, market laws, and realistic pricing of the factors of production. We have to put an end to this type of speculation. We entered into a crisis precisely because we did not respect market laws and now we are introducing them late, in the deepest crisis, . . . we have to be persistent in our policies because otherwise, the crisis will become even worse.[68]

The Maribor workers' revolt exploded without warning, shook the entire city for a few days, and then disappeared again, seemingly leaving behind no tangible repercussions. After the initial days of media coverage, the Maribor events were soon forgotten in public debates. The Ljubljana-based daily *Dnevnik* was of the opinion that the functionaries' tough stance toward the workers was counterproductive, fearing that industrial actions might become even more ferocious in the near future and give rise to a populist slowdown of reforms.[69] The magazine that stood closest to the new social movements, *Mladina*, found it sad that workers went on strike under the communist symbols. "It is not funny that workers answer the authorities with symbols of the ideology which is responsible for their hopeless situation," the magazine argued.[70] Neither the ruling party nor the opposition was willing to embrace the strike, and TAM workers were forced to reorient toward their factory management.

Three weeks after the walkouts, TAM's political functionaries felt confident enough to conduct a round of discussions on the strike inside the factory, at all levels. Predictably, the sociopolitical organizations concluded that the strike was not an acceptable way to express dissatisfaction. Nevertheless, they claimed it ultimately had positive consequences for the enterprise. Blue-collar dissatisfaction was used as proof that the ongoing economic and political reforms must not be abandoned, but rather accelerated. Furthermore, the authorities were allegedly forced to recognize problems that the management had been pointing out for years. The bank consortium decided to support another proposed reorganization scheme and new product development. The city and municipal governments freed the enterprises from a significant number of their duties to finance common consumption and self-management bodies.[71]

Post festum

On October 5, one day after the dramatic events in Belgrade city center, workers from Rekord—the only Rakovica factory whose workforce remained locked behind the factory gates during the protest—staged their own march to the city center. They managed to break into the Federal Parliament, occupied the main meeting hall, and demanded Milošević speak to them and make the same

---

68 Maksimilijan Senica, "Delavsko potrpljenje ni brezmejno," *Skozi TAM*, July 1, 1988, 8.
69 Dejan Kovač, "Mine na reformo," *Dnevnik*, June 24, 1988, 3.
70 Igor Mekina, "Tito in lopovi," *Mladina*, July 1, 1988, 36–39.
71 "Stavka je dosegla svoj namen," *Skozi TAM*, July 21, 1988, 4–5.

guarantees he gave to their peers the day before. Again, Milan Nikolić was among the first speakers to address them. However, this time he was booed off the stage. Rekord held him responsible for not helping to break the factory lockout the previous day. The workers started launching threats against the delegates present in the hall and Nikolić took the floor, trying to assuage their anger. The Zagreb-based weekly *Danas* recorded their exchange:

> Nikolić: We did not come to Belgrade to jeer. We should resolve our problems inside Rakovica primarily.
>
> The crowd (protesting loudly): No, we will not! We cannot do this on our own!
>
> Nikolić: Please, I am responsible for maintaining order here as the union president, until you revoke me!
>
> The crowd: Step down [from the podium] to the [workers'] base!! We want Sloba!
>
> Nikolić: I was also a worker once. I schooled you . . .
>
> The crowd: Sit down! We want Sloba!
>
> Nikolić: All right, here it is. Comrade Milošević, we address you through the media present among us, through radio. We are waiting for you.[72]

Figure 28. Rekord workers inside the Federal Parliament.
Tanjug News Agency Photo Archive, Archives of Yugoslavia, AJ, 112-L-11807-45

[72] Momčilo Đorgović, "Oktobar u Rakovici," *Danas*, November 10, 1988, 22–23.

Milošević appeared in front of the Rekord workers, repeating his performance from the previous day. The event marked a clear reorientation of the protesters from the local trade union leadership toward the Serbian party apex. Nikolić had tried to steer the strike back toward the local trade union, but after the breakthrough that had taken place the day before, the workers refused this, anxious to confirm that they had gained a much more powerful ally ("no, we cannot do this on our own"). The workers hoped that there would be no further need to take risks and look for new organizational patterns and political platforms that could give expression to the working class. The vehicle for activism was already present in the form of the anti-bureaucratic movement and the leader of the Serbian party.

The Rekord protest exposed once again the generational clash between the younger striking workers and the older trade union leadership. Nikolić's desperate attempt to regain respect in front of the dismissive workers ("I was also a worker once," "I schooled you") simply revealed how far removed he was from the striking workers as a relatively privileged sociopolitical functionary and a member of an older generation bound by different values. The traditional workerist themes promoted by the older activists and the trade union were abandoned in favor of the new politics of exclusion and national unity.

Once Rakovica stopped picketing the Federal Parliament, the media began to frame Milošević as Serbia's strongman. In the northern republics, Milošević was presented as a dangerous populist, persuasive enough to manipulate the striking workers and send them back to their factories.[73] Inside Serbia, the conclusions about Milošević's power were not especially dissimilar; the difference was that he was portrayed as the people's leader. He was now depicted not only as a reformist and the protector of the Serbs, but more generally as the defender of all working people against the alienated bureaucracies. No matter how they approached it, both sides contributed to the cult of personality increasingly building up around the leader of the Serbian party. In late October 1988, Milošević visited the three largest factories in Rakovica. Escorted by the city and municipal officials, he toured the shop floors and was greeted with ovations by the workers behind the machines.[74]

After months of exposure to increasing pressures inside the federacy and accusations of tolerating nationalism, the Serbian leadership was reinvigorated by the increased attention given to class identity. Among the Serbian public, the accusations of mounting Serbian nationalism were, to a large degree, dissipated by images of the alleged blue-collar support for the new Serbian leadership. Rakovica was hailed as the ultimate proof of the Serbian leadership's progressive character, contrasted to the criticisms previously coming from Vojvodina, Kosovo and other republics. If Milošević was indeed a nationalist, why did the social class that was the main carrier of socialist values stand behind him? It suddenly became difficult to attack Milošević without simultaneously discrediting the idea of the working class as the vanguard of social development.

---

73 Ibid.

74 D.J., "Promene tek počinju," *IMR*, November 1, 1988, 1.

The dividing lines between the workers' strikes and the protests of the Kosovo Serbs became thinner, as entire enterprises started joining the anti-bureaucratic revolution in Central Serbia, Vojvodina, Kosovo, and Montenegro. The movement evolved into a series of ambitious, government-organized rallies focused on constitutional issues, the national rights of Serbs, and the unity of Yugoslavia. The factory managements no longer tried to prevent such mobilizations, since they were now part of the officially-endorsed political folklore. The Jugoalat tool factory played the main role in the organization of a rally comprising close to 80,000 people in Vojvodina's capital Novi Sad on October 5. This rally managed to unite Kosovo Serb activists, workers from different regional enterprises, and ordinary citizens, forcing the resignations of the regional party leadership. In Montenegro, workers at a machine construction factory on the edge of bankruptcy, Radoje Dakić, formed the backbone of a popular movement directed against the local party leadership. Montenegro's top politicians would eventually resign in the early days of January 1989.

The anti-bureaucratic revolution reached its pinnacle in the first half of 1989. Backed by their newly-acquired fame, the workers from Rakovica played an important symbolic role in each of these events, with factory flags featured prominently in the front rows of the rallies and workers' representatives sometimes being included into the list of speakers.[75] Their presence was supposed to underline the progressive character of the movement and guarantee Yugoslav unity across the borders of single republics. In February 1989, "21. maj" workers appeared at one of the rallies carrying a ten-meter long banner stating "Workers of Yugoslavia, Topple Your Own Bureaucrats from the Factory to the Federation," a clear call to workers in other republics to join their cause.[76] However, to the non-Serbian workers, this concoction of traditional workerism and national awakening came across either as a naïve surrender to Milošević's populism or a calculated, cynical move to mask the movement's true aims.

In late 1988, the Serbian media started a campaign of slander over supposed Slovene protectionism against Serbian-produced trucks and Slovene producers' unfair competition in export markets. The story of the relocation of truck production from Rakovica to Maribor entered the headlines as a crucial proof of Serbia's systematic deindustrialization after World War Two. TAM became the target of protest letters from appalled work collectives, individual workers, and pensioners in Serbia demanding apology, repentance, and public recognition of Serbia's martyrdom. One of the letters stated that the Slovene workers remained duped by their own bureaucracy and thus contributed to the protracted exploitation of the Yugoslav working class.[77] The IMR Central Workers' Council drafted an open letter to its Slovene business partners asking for support:

[75] This period was marked by three massive rallies: the November 1988 "Brotherhood and Unity" rally in Belgrade, the protests against Slovenia's solidarity meeting with Kosovo in late February 1989, also in Belgrade, and the celebration of the six-hundredth anniversary of the Battle of Kosovo, which took place on Kosovo Polje in June 1989.

[76] Dragan Belić and Đuro Bilbija, *Srbija i Slovenija: Od Cankarjevog doma do "Jugoalata" i Gazimestana, Dokumenti* (Belgrade: Tera, 1989), 46.

[77] Danilo Vincetič, "Zaboga, pustite nas delati!," *Skozi TAM*, March 31, 1989, 2.

> [T]he equality of Serbia is a precondition for the unity of Yugoslavia, . . . we appealed to the leadership of your republic . . . , instead of support, we were met with accusations of homogenization and unitarism . . . we are convinced that the Slovene people are aware that these are fraudulent allegations . . . dear fellow workers and business associates, . . . join us to stop the attacks on Yugoslavia as a guarantee of our shared freedom.[78]

TAM's leading cadres tended to ignore all accusations, labeling them as distractions aimed at sabotaging its reform plans by dragging the factory into political quarrels. Under the headline "For Heaven's Sake, Let Us Work!," TAM's factory paper addressed the IMR appeal by stating: "Brotherhood and unity: those are wonderful ideals, but is it fair to demand equality in poverty for all?"[79] The "zero-sum" logic, according to which extending support to any kind of workers' mobilizations in southeastern republics would automatically mean rubber-stamping a decrease in one's own living standard, thus served as an effective censorship mechanism. It discouraged any politicization and condemned all critical organizing inside of TAM as potentially devastating in such an unstable environment. One of the few Maribor factories which formally answered IMR's letter of appeal was a smaller metal factory, Jeklotehna:

> It was with great satisfaction that we received your appeal . . . , we are convinced that the Yugoslav working class is united in belief that only a healthy economy can put an end to our divisions and our separation from developed Europe . . . in order to solve the present problems we need a culture of dialogue and plurality of opinions, . . . only such an approach brings rational judgment and a further development of our federation. . . . Dear brothers! We do not want to waste our words on politics since we have focused all of our work efforts on the growth of our enterprise, . . we are convinced that this is the best way to contribute to the development of our country.[80]

Jeklotehna's management repeated TAM's reserved attitude and focus on business matters, but it also gave more insight into the different prevailing political outlooks in the two republics. Unlike Serbia, the discourse inside Slovenia recognized "Europe" as a concrete entity, which embodied the desired modernization efforts much more than a strongly centralized Yugoslavia. The "culture of dialogue" and "plurality of opinions" are the stressed values, which stand in contrast to the calls for centralization and the rise of an authoritarian leader. The "rational" is counterposed with "emotional" calls for unity and an obsession with the past. It is worth noting that the communication between the factories in Maribor and Rakovica was conducted by the management, sociopolitical organizations, and the press. The independent mobilizations never came into direct contact and it is hard to estimate the number of workers who shared the visions of their factory elites.

[78] "Poziv na saradnju," *IMR*, March 21, 1989, 5.

[79] Danilo Vincetič, "Zaboga, pustite nas delati!," *Skozi TAM*, March 31, 1989, 2.

[80] "Odgovor iz Maribora," *IMR*, March 21, 1989, 5.

Not all work collectives in Yugoslavia were in a position to ignore the events in Vojvodina and Montenegro and claim to be apolitical. The advance of the anti-bureaucratic revolution forced the Albanians in Kosovo to stand up against Belgrade's centralization pushes. In November 1988, the Albanian population organized street demonstrations, and on February 20, 1989, the Albanian workers staged a general strike in the autonomous province. This strike culminated with some 1,000 miners closing themselves up in the pits of the Trepča mines in Stari Trg and declaring a hunger strike in an attempt to block the constitutional reforms in Serbia. In response to the strike, the Federal Presidency declared a state of emergency in Kosovo and deployed the Yugoslav People's Army in the streets. The majority of the miners exited the pits seeing no further political perspective for their demands in a state of emergency, whereas the most persistent ones were removed by force.[81]

In Belgrade, speculation and gossip about the supposedly faked hunger strike and political manipulation in Stari Trg flooded the media and the workplaces. Rakovica's anti-bureaucratic activists openly called for repression against the movement of Kosovo Albanians.[82] In their eyes, the Albanian workers had exempted themselves from the ranks of the Yugoslav working class by siding with the political leadership of the province. The deployment of police forces against the workers' strike was a major precedent: this was the first public use of force against the working class, the symbol of united Yugoslavia and self-management. The occupations of mines in Kosovo, clashes between the Albanian population and the police forces in the streets, the political support extended by the Slovenian leadership to the Albanian demonstrators,[83] and the unresponsiveness of Slovene factories to solidarity appeals all contributed to the creation of a siege mentality inside Rakovica. It seemed that one after another, the working classes of other nationalities were joining the "counterrevolution," and the only way to counteract this development and "save Yugoslavia" was to abandon the premises of class unity and stand behind the Serbian leadership. In the summer of 1991, the Wars of Yugoslav Secession would officially begin and the IMR factory paper began to publish final farewells to workers killed on the battlefield.

In May 1990, one TAM worker compared himself and his work colleagues to "lambs getting ready for slaughter."[84] Interestingly, he was not talking about the threat of war, but the management's plans for mass layoffs and the sale of the factory to a foreign owner without any consultation with the workforce. The breakup of brotherhood and unity also signaled the end of socialist Yugoslavia's second ideological pillar: workers' self-management. After the short bursts of independent organizing faded in the last months of 1988, the workforces of TAM and IMR returned to dependency on two traditional allies for the conservation

[81] Viktor Meier, *Yugoslavia: A History of its Demise* (London: Routledge, 1999), 88.

[82] "Ni pedalj pred neprijateljem," *IMR*, March 7, 1989, 4.

[83] On February 27, the leadership of the Slovene party-state joined the civil society organizations in Ljubljana for a publicly-broadcast meeting of solidarity with miners in Stari Trg. There are no signs of any solidarity actions organized in Tezno.

[84] Danči, "Čigav je TAM," *Skozi TAM*, May 18, 1990, 11.

of their status, the factory management and the party leadership respectively. However, the rapidly-changing economic and political landscape during 1989 effectively disbanded all inherited mechanisms of industrial corporatism.

TAM's shop floor hopes of being rewarded for passing the initiative to the professional management and accepting the burden of restructuring had failed. As the self-management laws began to be loosened or abolished altogether, the professional management no longer felt any obligation to accommodate workers' voices. As the 1980s came to an end, the management was openly talking about massive layoffs ahead. A TAM worker identifying himself by the nickname "Danči" expressed the letdown felt inside the factory and tried to draw some conclusions with the following words:

> After ten, twenty, or even longer years of work in the company, they can send us to the unemployment line. Why? Did we not do what we were supposed to? Were we not self-managerially taking decisions and confirming many measures that the [professional] management suggested? Did we not support our management when needed? I think the answers can only be affirmative. Maybe this blind faith in loyalty is to blame for us being in this state? Maybe we did not know how to stand up for ourselves? As manufacturers we did our jobs well, but as self-managers we did very poorly.[85]

The ritualized political recognition of the working class was erased as well. By 1990, the communist parties in both Slovenia and Serbia allowed the formation of oppositional parties and attempted to transform themselves into parties of a social-democratic type, thus abandoning any claim to be the vanguard of a proletariat-based revolution. Even in Serbia, where Milošević kept publicly acclaiming the working class and self-management, his actual reform policies were not far from Kučan's path of economic liberalization. The news about the introduction of industry-wide collective agreements, for instance, sparked fury among Rakovica's trade unionists, who seemed to be caught off guard by this development. Slobodanka Branković was outraged: "It turns out the workers, as the owners of the means of production, would sign agreements with themselves! In reality this is a break with the past, a break with social property and workers' self-management."[86] Her colleague Milan Kljajić summed up the feeling of being cheated:

> For a long time we talked about the reforms, but not in the right way, . . . up until recently it was unclear who would carry their weight. In reality we could have guessed that, as always, it would be the workers. . . . High interest rates and inflation are sucking the capital out of our factories. These funds went into individual pockets and the state treasury. This was the largest postwar robbery of workers' property through legal institutions of the system. . . . With these policies the state led us to the so-called "new socialism." We in Rakovica

---

[85] Ibid.

[86] Lj. Vesković, "Raskid sa dosadašnjom praksom," *IMR*, February 13, 1990, 6.

> say we have no socialism any longer. What we do have is an open capitalist enrichment.... We became aware of this two years ago when we tried to organize resistance and inform other workers in Yugoslavia. We can now say that we have lost. They used all means to keep us divided. They were successful and all we can do now is regret the lost opportunity.[87]

A wave of demoralization swept over Rakovica and Tezno. This does not mean that workers ceased standing up to the management and the state in both communities; the 1990s would bring new strikes, gatherings, and attempts to form independent trade unions. However, these were defensive actions undertaken to salvage minimum production and prevent layoffs, a far cry from aspirations to become the ruling class in society. The working class in all former Yugoslav republics was about to enter the rough years of war and deindustrialization, a period during which the workers developed romanticized memories about the crisis-ridden 1980s as a decade of relative prosperity and public awareness of labor's ability to create wealth, run industry, and shape history.

[87] Milan Kljajić, "Pogled iz Rakovice," *IMR*, February 13, 1990, 2.

Conclusion

The Unsettled Working Class

As labor historians of nineteenth-century England and France have shown, the residents of working-class communities in early industrial capitalism can best be described as a scattered, pauper underclass with little sense of common predicament and belonging. The key elements contributing to the formation of an enduring proletariat with class consciousness were predictable occupational practices and routinized temporal patterns. It took decades of closed social mobility, with new generations accepting their belonging to a common group of manual workers as a permanent condition, for stable working-class formations to take shape in these countries.[1] By introducing workers' self-management, the Yugoslav communists hoped to put an end to voluntarist mass mobilizations of peasants into the industry of the early postwar years and allow for a smaller, but more settled, core of urban proletariat to appear.

The installment of self-managed factories with their surrounding infrastructure encouraged the creation of skilled, politically-integrated workforces who identified with their enterprises and the broader notions of the Yugoslav socialist working class. The factory elites in IMR and TAM did their best to spread hegemonic understandings of the world on their shop floors. Workers internalized the official ideology through steady participation in self-managing and sociopolitical bodies, as well as by taking part in the numerous factory manifestations. Perhaps more importantly, self-managing worldviews were adopted through daily contacts, social practices, and joint production efforts on the shop floor. However, not all workers were in an equal position to identify fully with the factory values. The homogenization process like that which took place in early industrial capitalism was offset by high social mobility in the case of Yugoslav modernization, the atomizing nature of workers' self-management, as well as the existence of parallel, informal economic and housing solutions.

Workers of a single self-managed enterprise were far from a consistent group with equal attachments to the shop floor, the factory product, and the enterprise. A layer of the workforce in IMR and TAM achieved significant social mobility inside the industry by sticking to their occupations and internalizing the blue-collar ideology in the process. These were usually male, senior workers with a vocational education or rare work skills acquired during the years spent

[1] See Mike Savage, "Class and Labour History," in *Class and other Identities: Gender, Religion and Ethnicity in the Writing of European Labour History*, ed. Lex Heerma van Voss and Marcel van der Linden (New York: Berghahn, 2002), 61–64; and Michael P. Hangan, *Nascent Proletarians: Class Formation in Post-Revolutionary France* (Oxford: Basil Blackwell, 1989).

on the shop floor. Over the years, most of them managed to settle down in the local communities close to the factory and integrate with the help of decent wages and supported housing. They attended after-work events and leisure activities organized by the factory. As a rule, they were also active in various self-management organs and in the party.

At the other end, we find the young, newly-arrived workers with peasant backgrounds, anxious to acquire all the comforts of socialist modernity. Their prospects of settling in a large city as industrial workers were shattered by the harsh realities of factory work, an inability to advance to better-paid positions, belittling by their middle-class peers in the wider city, and the exploitative practices of their landlords. The older, unskilled workers, earning low wages and residing in distant, semi-rural settlements, were also partly cut off from the merits of urban life and the socialized economy. Many of them were women whose work at gender-specific jobs was inadequately valued, or migrants from other republics who faced marginalization due to their ethnicity and poor language skills. These workers rarely participated in self-managing decision-making and the systematic favoring of more settled workers made them skeptical toward the concept of common enterprise interests.

Place of origin and place of residence played a great role in determining an individual's chances of internalizing the vision of oneself as a shop floor worker who participates equally with his or her peers in the production process. TAM was the largest industrial employer for adjacent agricultural regions, with well-developed transport for its workers. Large sections of its unskilled workers were peasants who made daily trips to the factory. The village and work on the field remained a big part of their life's focus, and as such, they were often absent from the factory during agricultural work seasons. Moreover, a long daily commute prevented them from forming closer ties with their shop floor peers. As noted, the crowds would rush to the factory gates as soon as the end of the work shift was in sight, impatient to start their journey back home or to do other business in the city.

In the case of IMR, peasant workers from the surrounding villages were also present, but the migrant workers usually left their home villages for good, with the intention of making a home in the Yugoslav capital. They lived scattered all over the city and used public transportation to get to work. A large number of them would find housing in the semi-official settlements surrounding Belgrade, with gardens or smaller plots of land attached to them. Workers used the job opportunities offered by the big city to make additional money through moonlighting. Some brought their private business into the factory, using company machines to work on smuggled objects, or they made use of their work collective colleagues as potential customers for their goods. The low-skilled workers living far away from the factory or holding second jobs had no time to attend self-management and sociopolitical meetings. They were rarely politicized, unfamiliar with self-management jargon, and felt they could not contribute to discussions about the progress of production or technological tasks due to their low education.

The precarious conditions were present from the very beginning of Yugoslav socialist industrialization, yet as long as the factories and their surrounding infrastructure were expanding, it seemed the gradual integration of more peripheral parts of the workforce was assured. With the first signs of serious economic slowdown in the second half of the 1960s, the disintegrating tendencies threatened to become more dominant and tear apart the feeble urban industrial core of skilled workers. The migration of trained workers to Western Europe, flight from industry toward the service sector and administration, as well as the halting assimilation of newly-arrived peasant workers into the existing industrial work discipline and political cultures, were clear signs that the socialist modernization project was in deep crisis.

Associated Labor and the abandonment of intensive economic growth managed to reverse the decomposing trends briefly during the 1970s. The outward-reaching factories were supposed to grow into an all-encompassing moderator of social activity, returning the working class and their values to the center of public attention. However, the emergence of new economic crisis in 1979 meant that all the disintegrating processes would return ever stronger. For workers with peasant backgrounds entering the factories in the late 1970s and early 1980s, the industrial plants of the big cities became mere transit gates for other jobs in the city or a place they traveled to daily from their home villages in search of additional income. Even those workers who managed to settle down in industrial neighborhoods in previous decades, and who saw the factory as the center of their life activities, were tempted to abandon the production halls by becoming full-time functionaries in sociopolitical organizations, switching to the more profitable service sector, or starting private businesses. As noted, the communists were aware that the prolonged crisis and the lure of side jobs might break apart even the core layer of skilled workers immersed in the industrial culture.

For a large part of the workforce in both localities, the officially-promoted proletarian worldview could no longer serve as a holistic explanatory pattern which corresponded with their multifaceted daily experiences and embraced all aspects of life in the suburbs of big cities in late socialism. The making of a stable, urban socialist working class in Yugoslavia was a discontinuous process and took place over four-and-a-half decades, a relatively short time span when compared to the nineteenth-century industrialization in Western Europe. When workers were confronted with more severe attacks on labor and social rights in the late 1980s, the search for individual solutions took precedence over the prospect of collective organizing. Beyond a relatively thin layer of highly-skilled workers embedded in the factory milieu, the short periods of rapid industrialization under self-managing socialism failed to create an established, self-reproducing working class with deep-rooted traditions.

Liberal and Collectivist Self-Management

The ideology of self-management never consisted of a fixed set of compatible values. The party federal apex was the absolute political authority, which approached the idea of workers' empowerment in a pragmatic manner. Its ambiguous character was intentional and used by the party to achieve a modus vivendi between the interests of different occupational groups inside the enterprises. The communist leadership did not have complete control over the popular interpretation of its main ideological tenet. Apart from the official party documents, the shifting understandings of workers' self-management were the outcome of interaction between different layers of workers, professional managers, and various self-managing and sociopolitical institutions inside the industry, as well as broader social forums, such as the media and the cultural sphere.

The clear-cut cleavage often encountered in other socialist countries, between the factory management and local party elites as unified representatives of the centralized party-state on the one hand, and labor mobilizations on the other, was not likely to arise in the Yugoslav case. The chain of authority in the industry, which extended from the top planning bodies of the federal government to the factory shop floors in the early postwar years, was broken at company level with the introduction of an elected management and autonomous business decisions in the market. The professional management and the workers' councils were in a position to build a base of support among their workers' constituencies and frame popular grievances as a struggle for more business freedoms against the bureaucratic centralism of the party-state.

The tendency of the Yugoslav state toward ever-increasing decentralization and political rights for the republics, autonomous regions, and municipalities created yet another potential cleavage. Factory elites could use the gaps in the central state's political authority to enter into alliances with the regional party leaderships ready to support particularistic economic interests. Demands for the recognition of local economic needs were often accompanied by nationalist rhetoric, coupled with liberal demands for more autonomy in the market or calls for economic protectionism. What kept these pleas for narrow interests under control was the presence of a strong leadership at the very top of the party-state. The old guard of former partisan revolutionaries, personified in Josip Broz Tito, kept direct contact with the industrial base and presented the unified party as the sole guarantor of working-class political rights and a fair distribution of income. The party apex was apparently the only force powerful and virtuous enough to mediate between the conflicting interests of different occupational groups inside the factories as well as the national grievances inside the federation, thus guaranteeing social stability and progress.

The fully-integrated, politicized working-class layer could therefore pursue its interests by shifting allegiances between the above-mentioned institutional actors. IMR and TAM embodied the two prime strategies within the Yugoslav labor movement. IMR tended to project its future through a grand coalition with the top federal leadership of the party-state. Numerous factors conditioned this orientation. Based in the Yugoslav capital, the enterprise benefited from its proximity to the highest institutional powers. Rakovica's industrial facilities were situated directly beneath Tito's residential palace, and the local managers used this advantage to make direct pleas for political arbitration in business affairs. Moreover, IMR's location as a producer of engines and components at the bottom of the production chain made it dependent on government support in its dealings with final producers that had a stronger market position.

Over the years, IMR evolved from a pioneering developer of imported truck and tractor technology into a supplier of heavy-duty parts for diesel engines, as well as the producer of a smaller series of tractors exported to Third World markets with the help of the state. The factory took pride in serving as a backbone of development for Yugoslav industry. Many politically-active, skilled metalworkers were attracted to this factory, which stood as a connector between a network of smaller suppliers and larger final producers. The enterprise had a history of communist activity among its workforce going back to prewar times. The local communists could rely on the support of the Belgrade party apparatus, the country's largest LCY chapter and among its best organized. Reliance on political mediation and the existence of two parallel manufacturing programs (engines and tractors) turned IMR into a highly decentralized enterprise with weak management. Its lower-level self-management bodies were proactive and gave expression to shop floor grievances. The decision-making model tended toward consensus agreements.

TAM was located in Maribor, the center of an economically healthy region, positioned along Yugoslavia's border with Austria. The factory was a final producer that kept in touch with the latest technologies and marketing techniques from the most developed market economies. It produced mostly for the domestic market, yet its contact with Western partners kept the management hoping for more intensive cooperation agreements and a reorientation toward exports. Founded by the occupying German army during the war, TAM was cut off from the partisan movement. Maribor's party branch also never established solid roots among the industrial workers in the socialist period. The factory employed a great number of low-skilled and peasant workers who faced a strong engineering department and authoritative management.

TAM's micro-corporatist agreement between workers and management relied on the latter's ability to achieve business results by lobbying the political authorities for the recognition of local specificities and commercial autonomy. Accordingly, the liberal interpretation of self-management was the dominant one, with the enterprise introducing and extending support to political initiatives for further decentralization and market freedoms. The orientation of TAM's workforce toward an internal alliance with the management created a centralized and high-handed managerial culture in which particular grievances were strongly condemned and buried beneath appeals for enterprise unity.

Most workers in both factories never used self-management bodies to further independent organizing, not least when going on strike. Instead, they relied on spontaneous, mass gatherings to express demands, often avoiding any official representation, as if wary of bad experiences with the delegate system in their factories and local communities. From the very beginning, workers' self-management was a top-down initiative kept alive by the constant underpinning of the party-state, not an organic demand raised by the working class.[2] This is not to say that factory self-management bodies were not used by the workforce to endorse their interests, but these were mostly defensive actions in the form of boycotts, vetoes, or simple releases of pressure by launching individual grievances. The main function of workers' self-management always remained the integration of skilled blue-collar workers into business decision-making and spreading the spirit of cost-saving, efficient production on the shop floor.

Workers' sway inside the factories was not necessarily connected to the institutionalized representation offered by workers' self-management. As was often the case in socialist societies, in order to achieve their goals, workers utilized management's dependence on their scarce work skills, informal alliances with powerful individuals, and the favorable political climate created by the officially-sanctioned workerist ideology.[3] The irregular supply of inputs and fluctuating work rhythms made the management heavily dependent on a nucleus of skilled and experienced workers who knew how to improvise and organize the production process under tough conditions. Workers' self-management was a way to coopt this crucial layer of workers and win them over to the entrepreneurial vision.

Faced with a high turnover rate and a shop floor filled with unstable peasant workers, the skilled, entrenched layer of workers turned toward the factory and party elites for political support, rather than the blue-collar base. Material concessions were rarely obtained through open negotiation in factory bodies, but through paternal networks and alliances with highly-skilled workers who climbed to important positions in self-management bodies and sociopolitical organizations or advanced to lower-level executive positions. Moreover, the influential activist workers were torn between the collectivist and liberal interpretations of self-management, making it hard for the workers' movement to adopt an unambiguous identity and political orientation.

In IMR, the weak management and productivist ethos made the shop floor orient more toward workerist notions of labor and seek political mediation. In TAM, the workers' representatives were cut off from the blue-collar base and allied with the top professional management, which opened the door for occasional concessions from the top. The emphasis was placed on decision-making rather than production, and the dominant vision of a self-managing worker was that of a collective entrepreneur. In order to regain influence in factories such as TAM, the party pushed for constant atomization of

2 See, Goran Musić, "Yugoslavia: Workers' Self-Management as State Paradigm," in *Ours to Master and to Own: Workers Control from the Commune to the Present*, ed. Immanuel Ness and Dario Azzellini (Chicago: Haymarket Books, 2011), 172–91.

3 See, for instance, Biljana Raeva and Ulf Brunnbauer, "Fabrikarbeiter, Gewerkschaften und Funktionäre im 'entwickelten' Sozialismus: Die Aushandlung von Arbeiterinteressen am Beispiel des Bulgarischen Stahlwerks 'Kremikovci'," *Südost-Forschungen* 72 (2013): 308–12; and Michael Burawoy, *The Politics of Production: Factory Regimes under Capitalism and Socialism* (London: Verso, 1985), 163.

industrial architecture. These attempts to limit the influence of the professional management and raise working-class cadres inside ever-smaller enterprise units handicapped the working class further. Isolated inside BOALs, departments, and groups, the workers developed parochial attitudes and became even more dependent on the dispersed bureaucracy and mid-level executives.

Radical decentralization and the existence of a great number of potential mediators greatly hindered the possibilities for a united working-class movement. As we have seen, workers even had a hard time creating common platforms between different BOALs under a single roof, not to mention coordinated action between different enterprises. Rakovica and Maribor were indeed unique examples in Yugoslavia of workers from various companies marching jointly to the institutions of political power. Yet, even here the apparent unity proved shallow. In the case of Maribor, the collective walkout at the central city square did not result in any structured attempt at collective organizing. Rakovica did acquire a unified leadership and a provisional program in the shape of the municipal trade union, but this leadership was discarded by the local working class at the first sign of political opening at the top of the party.

The multiple cleavages in the decentralized party-state allowed for the formation of fluid alliances and flexible tactics in workers' struggles. These features allowed the Yugoslav proletariat relatively high political freedoms and standards of living, but paradoxically these same factors hindered any potential for a lasting organized workers' movement on a broader scale.

In Search of Allies and Enemies

If workers were faced with structural obstacles when trying to develop a joint identity and create enduring common platforms, envisioning a shared political enemy was an even greater challenge. As already explained, the main axis of class differentiation in the mental conceptions of industrial workers was that between the manual workers in direct production, who created new value, and all other sections of society, who lived off this wealth. Of course, workers rarely took this division to the extreme, to conclude that they were standing alone against the entire population without direct connections to material production. In different periods, a specific "non-productive" social group could be singled out as having little of value to contribute to the rest of society, or as behaving exploitatively in relation to the working class.

The market laws had a great influence on the persisting disparities in Yugoslav industry. Yet, in contrast to Western market economies, where the capitalist could be seen as the personification of abstract market forces, social property made it extremely difficult to point to the individuals and institutions responsible for unequal exchange and distribution. Throughout the 1970s, the official ideology recognized managers and professionals as the main agents of market relations and potential opponents of self-management. The institutional symbols of this social layer beyond industry were "non-productive," white-collar enterprises such as banks or trading companies. However, in periods when liberal interpretations of self-management were on the rise, the market could be seen as a neutral mediator and the state apparatus could have just as easily taken the place of the banks as the embodiment of the exploitative, non-productive sector.

The label "techno-bureaucracy," attached to the perceived foes of workers' self-management, reflects this ambiguity quite well. Emphasis could be placed on the first word in the idiom, indicating technocracy—the managerial layer and technical staff—thus following the more class-based and anti-market understandings of workers' self-management. On the other hand, the term was usually associated more closely with its second component: the state bureaucracy. Workers' self-management was traditionally defined as the struggle against the alienated state, and the Soviet-type command economy system was routinely equated with capitalist societies in terms of its exploitative features and the alleged survival of wage labor. If engineers, accountants, bankers, and traders could be related to production in the mind of the average worker—even if only in vague terms—the political bureaucracy allegedly played absolutely no useful role in a self-managed society.

The pejorative term "bureaucracy" was therefore quite elusive and could be applied indiscriminately not only to economic and political elites, but to all those perceived as "privileged" in comparison with the industrial workers. The class hatred toward banks and trading monopolies or governmental administration could spill over to ordinary workers employed in these institutions. The notion of a female "floor sweeper" (*čistačica*) in a non-productive enterprise or government agency, who allegedly had her housing status resolved more quickly than a skilled male industrial worker, was a commonly repeated theme in both factories. The term could also be applied to colleagues, either from one's own enterprise or surrounding companies, active as delegates in political bodies or self-managed providers of social services (SIZ). Various administrative and managerial positions located between the shop floor and the top professional management inside the factories (*režija*) could also be associated with non-economic reasoning and thus positioned closer to bureaucracy than technocracy.

With the image of the main opponent remaining so elastic on the shop floor, the political elites were in a good position to direct popular anger in accordance with their interests. Even industrial workers in loss-making companies or citizens of underdeveloped regions, objectively faring worse than the average industrial worker, could be brought into connection with the bureaucracy as indirect beneficiaries of political wealth redistribution. During the strike at TAM, workers pointed the finger at the bankrupt Slovene aluminum producer for allegedly handing out wages higher than the ones they received. The same logic could be applied to workers in the less productive industries of the southern republics. In IMR, the workers came to be suspicious of an entire ethnic group in Kosovo (the Albanians) as backers of the bureaucracy, since it refused to support the curbing of regional autonomy and its institutions.

As the 1980s came to a close, the notion of an exploitative bureaucracy was increasingly gaining national connotations. Understanding how the notions of "productive work" and "bureaucratization" were connected to sections of the working class in different regions and used to explain inequalities among the Yugoslav workers is vital for understanding the spread of nationalism inside the working-class milieus. However, the two case studies have shown that the nationalization of everyday life was by no means an automatic process and varied widely depending on the local conditions.

In TAM, local executives had used protectionist notions and particularistic demands with nationalist undertones since at least the early 1980s in order to advance reforms within Slovenia. By the end of the 1980s, this rhetoric was increasingly falling on deaf ears among the TAM workers, who were disappointed by the concrete results of the market restructuring. In late 1980s Rakovica, the language of national entitlement and the demand to put local interests first was something novel and exciting; an ideology which still had the potential to connect to anti-elitist blue-collar sentiments.

The shared ethnic identity made sure the appeals of Kosovo Serbs resonated strongly inside the Belgrade municipality. The Slovene nationalist opposition used the image of the Serb-dominated central state to suggest that the Slovene nation was under threat. Yet, apart from the arrest of four civil society activists by the military police in 1988, there was no pressing source of national insecurity comparable to the case of Kosovo within Serbia. The role played by migrant workers in both localities was crucial in awakening national differentiation. In Rakovica, there was a sizable community of Kosovo Serbs. They were well integrated, spoke the same language as other workers, and did not hesitate to raise political grievances. In Tezno, the migrant workers from other republics were still newcomers and faced a language barrier. Apart from recognizing themselves as different in relation to Slovenes, the migrant workers were of different origins, still nurturing allegiances to the different Yugoslav republics and regions from which they arrived. It was therefore far harder for the "southerners" to organize politically and trigger a potential reaction from the Slovene workers, thus creating ethnic polarization.

The presence of a large number of peasant workers and migrants, as well as the importance of kinship and birthplace connections to the organization of life in an urban setting, made the workers very responsive to regional identity. Next to class solidarity, the official ideology was very attentive to national equality and the political rights of ethnic minorities. By maintaining multiple, particularistic loyalties and identities, the Yugoslav workers increased their chances of being heard and recognized as noteworthy socialist citizens. In times when the media and political discourse started attributing less value to workers' supposedly primary function, as creators of social wealth and self-managers, they were likely to emphasize some of their other social roles and identities in order to gain attention, such as mothers, the youth, or members of oppressed nationalities.

Unanticipated Changes

The ideological shaping of the shop floor struggles traditionally went hand in hand with openings in the political sphere. The persistent economic crisis of the 1980s and the political weakening of the federal center drastically altered the nature of the Yugoslav party-state. The global crisis of planned and protectionist economies gave an advantage to the opponents of workers' self-management. After Yugoslavia had abandoned "market socialism" in the early 1970s, both China under Deng Xiaoping and the Soviet Union under Mikhail Gorbachev turned to economic liberalization as a pathway to further development. Western Europe was heading toward an economic union, making Yugoslavia more aware of its dependence on economic exchange with this core of highly-developed capitalist countries. After years of economic stagnation and the first signs of the end of the bipolar world order, any ambition to maintain the "Yugoslav road to socialism," as a social project unique in the global context, was largely lost among a generation of political pragmatists and technocrats.

The economic crisis deepened social inequalities between different groups of workers inside the factories and exposed the clientelistic practices in the distribution of common social goods. The self-management elites, made up of former blue-collar workers, were discredited through corruption and their privileged status in relation to ordinary workers. By wrongly assuming that self-management would neutralize class differences and unify all employees behind the interests of collectively-owned firms, Yugoslav socialism was creating an alienated and angry working class, which saw an increasing divide between the promises of self-management and the realities of everyday factory life. The economic crisis and the lack of democratic control over factory decision-making bodies opened the door for liberal interpretations of self-management to position themselves once again as valid oppositional discourses, identifying political interference and the reluctance to conduct more radical reforms as the root causes of industrial malaise and skewed distribution.

Without the existence of the strong federal center and figures with revolutionary prestige to maintain ideological rigor, the republican leaderships gained a chance to further their distinct agendas and embrace the ideas of market liberalism and nationalism more openly. There was a need to replace the worn-out concepts of the "contractual economy" and "workers' self-management" with a new language of optimism and more up-to-date perspectives of development, based on the latest technologies, leaner enterprise bureaucracy, increased government accountability, rejuvenation of party cadres, opening up to the world market, and a stronger defense of particular, local interests. The Serbian and Slovene parties seemed to be adapting most successfully to these new themes.

The communist leadership in Slovenia became convinced that this was probably the last chance for a radical reform of its economy, if the system were to survive at all. The local party-state was rapidly advancing a sovereign program of liberal restructuring inside its enterprises, based on input from market-oriented enterprise managers and integration into the Western European market.

The Slovene leadership revived the traditional liberal interpretations of self-management, contrasting them with the highly unpopular austerity measures introduced by the federal government. The factory elites discouraged egalitarian sentiments and tied manual workers to the ongoing reform campaign by pointing to the income gap and the difference in overall development between Slovenia and the rest of Yugoslavia. Any step in the direction of solidarity with the less-developed regions was presented as the path to "equality in poverty."

On the other hand, reformist forces in Serbia were stuck in an impasse by insisting on a new, common federal institutional frame as a prerequisite for economic and political changes. The growing radicalism of the Serbian leadership was the result of a sense of urgency and its lagging behind Slovenia. By 1988, the popular pressure for reforms became so strong that the Serbian party decided to break the taboo surrounding the use of street mobilizations as instruments of political struggle and actively rally citizens behind its plan of action. During the summer of 1988, politics was extended beyond the stale meeting halls. Public rallies in the streets were increasingly becoming the officially-endorsed new instrument of mass politics. By connecting factory grievances to broader political themes of constitutional order and lack of unity inside the federal party-state, Milošević aimed to rally some of the blue-collar activists behind the nationalist agenda and, in the process, blurred the borders between class and national inequalities.

Despite the rapid changes in the nature of Yugoslav socialism, workers in both localities continued to rely on micro-corporatist agreements and grand political coalitions to defend their interests. In TAM, the 1980s marked a reorientation toward internal alliances with the professional management. However, as the expected business results were not fulfilled, the workers broke the corporatist bond in the summer of 1988 by walking out of the factory and searching for political mediation. Receiving no recognition from the Slovene leadership, the majority of workers returned to their factories, while those who continued to protest soon found themselves isolated and without a clear aim. In IMR, the construction of factory unity was on the horizon in the second half of the decade, but the dynamic was undercut by the political inclusion of the workers' cause offered by Slobodan Milošević.

In the late 1980s, elements of some kind of self-managed socialism were thus still firmly extant inside both of the working-class communities. Workers voted in favor of reforms to Associated Labor, but they did not expect that legislative changes would lead to a major shift in the overall development paradigm, expecting that the ruling party would still safeguard their interests. As it turned out, the period between 1986 and 1991 would prove to be radically different from all previous examples of self-management reforms. In an atmosphere of prolonged social turmoil and open criticism of the socialist legacy, workers' self-management as an alternative socialist system was all but abandoned, with the political and enterprise elites no longer willing to support its institutions. The Yugoslav state started to dissolve and the working class found itself in a desolate position, having to invent new organizational patterns and traditions amidst rampant nationalism, war, and economic breakdown.

Bibliography

Archives

Industrija motora Rakovica, Factory Archive, Zbora radnika OOUR Vozilo, 1979–1989.

Kamra: Digitalized Cultural Heritage of Slovenian Regions, www.kamra.si.

Museum of National Liberation, Maribor, Oral History Project, http://www.muzejno-mb.si/spomini/home.html. Las accessed February 2015.

Open Society Archives, Budapest: Records of Radio Free Europe/Radio Liberty Research Institute; Publications Department; Background Reports (HU OSA 300-8-3), www.osaarchivum.org.

Pokrajinski arhiv Maribor (Regional Archive Maribor), Fond: Tovarna avtomobilov Maribor; Zapisniki delavskega sveta, 1976–1989 (SI PAM/0990).

Interviews

Drago Gajzer (TAM League of Socialist Youth activist), Maribor, April 2013.

Branko Gerlič (TAM journalist), Maribor, April 2013.

Bender Gorast (TAM LCY activist), Maribor, April 2013.

Božidar Ipavic (TAM employee), Maribor, April 2013.

Radoš Karaklajić (President of the IMR Socialist Youth), Belgrade March 2011.

Milan Kljajić (IMR trade unionist), Belgrade, March 2011.

Cveta Matjašić (TAM worker), Maribor, April 2013.

Mića Milanović (IMR Socialist Youth activist), March 2011.

Milan Nikolić (President of Rakovica Municipal Trade Union), Belgrade, March 2011.

Franci Pivec (President of LC Maribor City Committee), April 2013.

Momčilo Plećaš (IMR LCY activist), Belgrade, March 2011.

Workplace Periodicals

IMR: List Radne organizacije Industrije motora Rakovica, 1975–1990.

Litostroj: *Glasilo delavcev Titovih zavodov Litostroj*, December 1987.

Motor: List kolektiva Industrije motora Rakovica, 1965–1970.

Skozi TAM: *Glasilo Delovne skupnosti Tovarne avtomobilov i motorjev Maribor*, 1965–1971.

Skozi TAM: Izdanje na Srpsko-hrvatskom jeziku (Serbo-Croatian edition), 1975–1986.

Skozi ZIV TAM: Glasilo delavcev delovnih organizacij združenih v ZIV TAM, 1975–1990.

Zmaj: Industrija privrednih mašina, June 1988.

Literature

Adizes, Ichak. *Industrial Democracy: Yugoslav Style; The Effects of Decentralization on Organizational Behavior*. New York: The Free Press, 1971.

Allcock, John B. *Explaining Yugoslavia*. New York: Columbia University Press, 2000.

Anić, Tomislav. "Radništvo i propaganda: 'socijalističko takmičenje' u Hrvatskoj 1945.–1952." PhD diss., University of Zagreb, 2010.

Arandarenko, Mihail. "Waiting for the Workers: Explaining Labor Quiescence in Serbia." In *Workers after Workers' States: Labor and Politics in Postcommunist Eastern Europe*, edited by Stephen Crowley and David Ost. Lanham, MD: Rowman and Littlefield, 2001.

Archer, Rory. "'Antibureaucratism' as a Yugoslav Phenomenon: The View from Northwest Croatia." *Nationalities Papers* 47, no. 4 (2019): 562–80.

——. "*Imaš kuću—vrati stan*. Housing Inequalities, Socialist Morality and Discontent in 1980s Yugoslavia." *Godišnjak za društvenu istoriju* 3 (2013): 119–39.

Archer, Rory, and Goran Musić. "Approaching the Socialist Factory and its Workforce: Considerations from Fieldwork in (Former) Yugoslavia." *Labor History* 57, no. 5 (2016): 44–66.

——. "'Not all Canteens Are Created Equal': Food Provision for Yugoslav Blue-Collar Workers in Late Socialism." In *Brotherhood and Unity at the Kitchen Table: Food in Socialist Yugoslavia*, edited by Ruža Fotiadis, Vladimir Ivanović, and Radina Vučetić, 73–97. Zagreb: Srednja Europa, 2020.

——. "The Belgrade Working Class between Tito and Milošević: New Geographies of Poverty and Evolving Expressions of Grievances in an Era of Crisis, 1979–1986." *Revue d'études comparatives Est-Ouest* 50, no. 5 (2019): 53–79.

——. "When Workers' Self-Management Met Neoliberalism: Positive Perceptions of Market Reforms among Blue-Collar Workers in late Yugoslav Socialism." In *Labor in State Socialist Europe, 1945–1989: Contributions to a History of Work*, edited by Marsha Siefert, 395–418. Budapest–New York: Central European University Press, 2020.

Archer, Rory, Igor Duda, and Paul Stubbs. "Bringing Class Back In: An Introduction." In *Social Inequalities and Discontent in Yugoslav Socialism*, edited by Rory Archer, Igor Duda, and Paul Stubbs, 1–20. Farnham: Ashgate, 2016.

Arsić, Mirko, and Dragan R. Marković. *68: Studentski bunt i društvo*. Belgrade: Prosvetni Pregled, 1984.

Bartha, Eszter. *Alienating Labour: Workers on the Road from Socialism to Capitalism in East Germany and Hungary*. New York: Berghahn Books, 2013.

Belić, Dragan, and Đuro Bilbija. *Srbija i Slovenija: Od Cankarjevog doma do "Jugoalata" i Gazimestana; Dokumenti*. Belgrade: Tera, 1989.

Bennett, Christopher. *Yugoslavia's Bloody Collapse: Causes, Course and Consequences*. New York: New York University Press, 1995.

Bernard, Sara. *Deutsch Marks in the Head, Shovel in the Hands and Yugoslavia in the Heart: The Gastarbeiter Return to Yugoslavia (1965–1991)*. Wiesbaden: Harrassowitz Verlag, 2019.

Bićanić, Rudolf. *Economic Policy in Socialist Yugoslavia*. Cambridge: Cambridge University Press, 1973.

Bilandžić, Dušan. *Historija Socijalističke Federativne Republike Jugoslavije: glavni procesi*. Zagreb: Školska knjiga, 1985.

Bockman, Johanna. *Markets in the Name of Socialism: The Left-Wing Origins of Neoliberalism*. Stanford, CA: Stanford University Press, 2011.

Bokovoy, Melissa K. *Peasants and Communists: Politics and Ideology in the Yugoslav Countryside, 1941–1953*. Pittsburgh: University of Pittsburgh Press, 1998.

Bokovoy, Melissa K., Jill A. Irvine, and Carol S. Lilly. *State-Society Relations in Yugoslavia, 1945–1992*. New York: St. Martin's Press, 1997.

Bonfiglioli, Chiara. *Women and Industry in the Balkans: The Rise and Fall of the Yugoslav Textile Sector*. London: I.B. Tauris, 2019.

Borak, Neven. *Ekonomski vidiki delovanja in razpada Jugoslavije*. Ljubljana: Znanstveno in publicistično središče, 2002.

Bošković, Blagoje, and David Dašić, eds. *Socialist Self-Management in Yugoslavia, 1950–1980: Documents*. Belgrade: Socialist Thought and Practice, 1980.

Breže, Borivoj. "Tovarne v Mariboru." Museum of National Liberation, Maribor, Oral History Project, http://www.muzejno-mb.si/spomini/home.html. Accessed February 2015.

Broz, Josip Tito. "Treba preduzjeti mere koje će omogućiti normalniji razvoj naše zemlje (Govor u Splitu, 6. maja 1962)." In *Jugoslavenska revolucija i socijalizam*. Vol. 2, edited by Josip B. Tito and Miloš Nikolić, 112–24. Zagreb: Globus, 1982.

Brunnbauer, Ulf, ed. *(Re)Writing History: Historiography in Southeast Europe after Socialism*. Münster: Lit Verlag, 2004.

——. "Compartmentalized Pasts: Workers' History in Socialist Yugoslavia." Paper presented at the 2016 European Social Science History Conference, Valencia, March 30–April 2, 2016. https://ostblog.hypotheses.org/751.

Burawoy, Michael. *The Politics of Production: Factory Regimes under Capitalism and Socialism*. London: Verso, 1985.

Calic, Marie-Janine. *Socijalna istorija Srbije, 1815–1941: Usporeni napredak u industrijalizaciju*. Translated by Ranka Gašić. Belgrade: Clio, 2004.

Calori, Anna, and Kathrin Jurkat, "'I'm Both a Worker and a Shareholder.' Workers' Narratives and Property Transformations in Postsocialist Bosnia-Herzegovina and Serbia." *Südosteuropa: Journal of Politics and Society* 65, no. 4 (2018): 654–78.

Carter, April. *Democratic Reform in Yugoslavia: The Changing Role of the Party*. Princeton, NJ: Princeton University Press, 1982.

Carter, F. W, and H. T. Norris. *The Changing Shape of the Balkans*. London: UCL Press, 1996.

Cox, John K. *Slovenia: Evolving Loyalties*. London: Routledge, 2005.

Crampton, R. J. *The Balkans Since the Second World War*. London: Longman, 2002.

Cvek, Sven. "Class and Culture in Yugoslav Factory Newspapers." In *The Cultural Life of Capitalism in Yugoslavia: (Post)Socialism and Its Other*, edited by Dijana Jelača, Maša Kovanović, and Danijela Lugarić, 101–21. Cham: Palgrave Macmillan, 2017.

Cvek, Sven, Snježana Ivčić, and Jasna Račić, *Borovo u štrajku: Rad u tranziciji 1987.-1991.* Zagreb: Baza za radničku inicijativu i demokratizaciju, 2019.

Cvetković, Srđan. "'Kradljivci tuđih leđa,' Obračun sa anarholiberalističkim grupama u SFRJ posle 1968." *Istorija 20. veka* 3 (2011): 39–56.

Deutscher, Isaac. "Socialist Competition." *Foreign Affairs* 30, no. 3 (1952): 376–90.

Dimitrijević, Bojan B. "Monopolističke ambicije i 'kašnjenje' u proizvodnji vazduhoplovne industrije u Kraljevini jugoslaviji." *Istorija 20. veka* 3 (2012): 19–38.

Djordjevich, Dušan J. "Clio amid the Ruins: Yugoslavia and Its Predecessors in Recent Historiography." In *Yugoslavia and Its Historians: Understanding the Balkan Wars of the 1990s*, edited by Norman M. Naimark and Holly Case, 3–22. Stanford, CA: Stanford University Press, 2003.

Dobrivojević, Ivana. "'Svi u fabrike!' Instant industrijalizacija u Jugoslaviji, 1945–1955." *Istorija 20. veka* 2 (2009): 103–14.

Dolenec, Danijela. "Preispitivanje 'egalitarnog sindroma' Josipa Županova." *Politička misao* 51, no. 4 (2014): 41–64.

Dragović-Soso, Jasna. *"Saviours of the Nation": Serbia's Intellectual Opposition and the Revival of Nationalism*. Montreal: McGill-Queen's University Press, 2002.

——. *"Spasioci nacije": Intelektualna opozicija Srbije i oživljavanje nacionalizma*. Translated by Ljiljana Nikolić. Belgrade: Fabrika knjiga, 2004.

Drašković, Dragiša. "Istina nije u jednini: Konferencija SK Slovenije." *Rad*, April 26, 1988.

Duda, Igor. *U potrazi za blagostanjem: O povijesti dokolice i potrošakog društva u Hrvatskoj 1950-ih i 1960-ih*. Zagreb: Srednja Europa, 2005.

Đukić, Slavoljub. *Kako se dogodio vođa: borbe za vlast u Srbiji posle Josipa Broza*. Belgrade: Filip Višnjić, 1992.

Dyker, David A. *Yugoslavia: Socialism, Development and Debt*. London: Routledge, 1990.

Estrin, Saul. *Self-Management: Economic Theory and Yugoslav Practice*. Cambridge: Cambridge University Press, 1983.

Flakierski, Henryk. *The Economic System and Income Distribution in Yugoslavia*. New York: M.E. Sharpe, Inc., 1989.

Fočo, Salih. *Štrajk između iluzije i zbilje*. Belgrade: Radnička štampa, 1989.

Gagnon, V. P. *The Myth of Ethnic Conflict: Serbia and Croatia in the 1990s*. Ithaca, NY: Cornell University Press, 2004.

Goati, Vladimir. *Politička anatomija jugoslovenskog društva*. Zagreb: Naprijed, 1989.

Gow, James, and Cathie Carmichael. *Slovenia and the Slovenes: A Small State and the New Europe*. London: Hurst & Company, 2000.

Grabeljšek, Dragana, et al. *National Structure of Population in SFR Yugoslavia, Vol 1: Data on Localities and Communes*. Belgrade: Savezni zavod za statistiku, 1991.

Grandits, Hannes, and Karin Taylor, eds. *Yugoslavia's Sunny Side: A History of Tourism in Socialism (1950s–1980s)*. Budapest–New York: Central European University Press, 2010.

Grdešić, Marko. "Exceptionalism and Its Limits: The Legacy of Self-Management in the Former Yugoslavia." In *Working Through the Past: Labor and Authoritarian Legacies in Comparative Perspective*, edited by Teri L. Caraway, Maria Lorena Cook, and Stephen Crowley, 103–21. Ithaca, NY: Cornell University Press, 2015.

——. "Mapping the Paths of the Yugoslav Model: Labor Strength and Weakness in Slovenia, Croatia and Serbia." *European Journal of Industrial Relations* 14, no. 2 (2008): 133–51.

——. *The Shape of Populism: Serbia before the Dissolution of Yugoslavia*. Ann Arbor: University of Michigan Press, 2019.

Halpern, Joel M., and David A. Kideckel, eds. *Neighbors at War: Anthropological Perspectives on Yugoslav Ethnicity, Culture and History*. University Park, PA: The Pennsylvania State University Press, 2000.

Hanagan, Michael P. *Nascent Proletarians: Class Formation in Post-Revolutionary France*. Oxford: Blackwell, 1989.

Hayden, Robert M. *Social Courts in Theory and Practice: Yugoslav Workers' Courts in Comparative Perspective*. Philadelphia: University of Pennsylvania Press, 1990.

Hetemi, Atdhe. *Student Movements for the Republic of Kosovo: 1968, 1981 and 1997*. London: Palgrave Macmillan, 2020.

Höpken, Wolfgang. "Party Monopoly and Political Change: The League of Communists Since Tito's Death." In *Yugoslavia in the 1980s*, edited by Pedro Ramet, 29–56. Boulder, CO: Westview Press, 1985.

Horvat, Branko. *Privredni ciklusi u Jugoslaviji*. Belgrade: Institut ekonomsih nauka, 1969.

Hudson, Kate. *Breaking the South Slav Dream: The Rise and Fall of Yugoslavia*. London: Pluto Press, 2003.

Iršič, Milena, ed. *Tovarna avtomobilov in motorjev Maribor, 1947–1987*. Maribor: ČGP Večer, 1987.

Isaković, Zlatko. *Identity and Security in Former Yugoslavia*. Aldershot: Ashgate, 2000.

Jajčinović, Milan. "Doći ćemo opet: Protiv koga se bune radnici u radničkoj državi." *Danas*, June 26, 1988.

Jovanov, Neca. *Radnički štrajkovi u Radnički štrajkovi u SFRJ od 1958. do 1969. godine*. Belgrade: Zapis, 1979.

Jović, Dejan. *Jugoslavija—država koja je odumirala: Uspon, kriza i pad Četvrte Jugoslavije 1974–1990*. Zagreb: Prometej, 2003.

——. *Yugoslavia: A State that Withered Away*. West Lafayette, IN: Purdue University Press, 2009.

Katznelson, Ira. "Working-Class Formation: Constructing Cases and Comparisons." In *Working-Class Formation: Nineteenth-Century Patterns in Western Europe and the United States*, edited by Ira Katznelson and Aristide R. Zolberg, 3–41. Princeton, NJ: Princeton University Press, 1986.

Kenney, Padraic. "Framing, Political Opportunities and Eastern European Mobilization." In *Frames of Protest: Social Movements and the Framing Perspective*, edited by Hank Johnston & John A. Noakes, 143–62. Lanham, MD: Rowman & Littlefield, 2005.

Kerčov, Sava, Jovo Radoš, and Aleksandar Raiš. *Mitinzi u Vojvodini 1988. godine: Rađanje političkog pluralizma*. Novi Sad: Dnevnik, 1990.

Kidrič, Boris. *Sabrana dela, I–V*. Belgrade: Izdavački centar Komunist, 1985.

Kostić, Cvetko. *Bor i okolina: sociološka ispitivanja*. Belgrade: Savremena škola, 1962.

Kovač, Miha. "The Slovene Spring: Interview with Miha Kovač." *New Left Review* I, no. 171 (September–October 1988): 115–28.

Kovač, Oskar. "Foreign Economic Relations." In *Beyond Yugoslavia: Politics, Economics and Culture in a Shattered Community*, edited by Ljubiša S. Adamović and Sabrina P. Ramet, 281–300. Boulder, CO: Westview Press, 1995.

Kresal, France. "Mariborska tekstilna industrija 1922–1992—vzpon in zaton." In *Mesto in gospodarstvo: Mariborsko gospodarstvo v 20. stoletju*, edited by Željko Oset, Aleksandra Berberih Slana and Žarko Lazarević, 257–89. Maribor: Inštitut za novejšo zgodovino in Muzej narodne osvoboditve Maribor, 2010.

Kuzmanić, Tonči. "Strikes, Trade Unions, and Slovene Independence." In *Independent Slovenia: Origins, Movements, Prospects*, edited by Jill Benderly and Evan Kraft, 159–79. New York: St. Martin's Press, 1994.

Labović, Bojan, dir. *Umrli gigant: Tovarna avtomobilov in motorjev Maribor*. Ljubljana: Studio Legen, 2002. DVD.

Lakićević, Mijat, ed. *Ispred vremena, 1963–1973, sudbonosna decenija, uspon i pad srpskih liberala, uzroci i posledice od tada do naših dana, kroz prizmu Ekonomske politike, novine kakvih više nema*. Belgrade: Fond za otvoreno društvo, 2011.

Latifić, Ibrahim. *Jugoslavija 1945–1990: Razvoj privrede i društvenih delatnosti*. Belgrade: Društvo za istinu o antifašističkoj narodno oslobodilačkoj borbi u Jugoslaviji 1941–1945, 1997.

Lekić, Slaviša, and Zoran Pavić. *VIII Sednica CK SK Srbije: nulta tačka "narodnog pokreta."* Belgrade: Službeni glasnik, 2007.

Lorber, Lučka. "Functional Changes in Tezno, The Industrial Zone in Maribor." *Revija za geografijo* 2, no. 1 (2006), 95–108.

Lundin, Jan. "Slovenia in 1988: Pluralism and Reaction." Working paper, Department of Soviet and East European Studies, Uppsala University, 1989.

Luthar, Breda, and Marusa Pušnik, eds. *Remembering Utopia. The Culture of Everyday Life in Socialist Yugoslavia*. Washington, DC: New Academia Publishing, 2010.

Maček, Jure. "Tovarna avtomobilov in motorjev Maribor v obdobju prve petletke." In *Tovarna avtomobilov Maribor: Sledovi mariborskega gospodarstva v arhivskem gradivu Pokrajinskega arhiva Maribor 60 let—spominski zbornik*, edited by Slavica Tovšak, 48–77. Maribor: Pokrajinski arhiv Maribor, 2007.

Magaš, Branka. *The Destruction of Yugoslavia: Tracing the Break-up 1980–1989*. London: Verso, 1993.

Mann, Michael. *Consciousness and Action Among the Western Working Class.* London: Macmillan Press, 1973.

Marinković, Darko. "Štrajk u Industriji motora Rakovica." In *Obustave rada (štrajkovi) u Beogradu,* edited by Vukašin Pavlović, Ivan Radosavljević, and Zoran Stojiljković, 99–130. Belgrade: Veće Saveza sindikata Beograda, 1987.

——. *Štrajkovi i društvena kriza*. Belgrade: Institut za političke studije, 1995.

Marković, Predrag. *Trajnost i premena: Društvena istorija socijalističke i postsocijalističke svakodnevice*. Belgrade: Službeni glasnik, 2012.

McFarlane, Bruce. *Yugoslavia: Politics, Economics and Society*. London: Printer Publishers, 1988.

Meier, Viktor. *Yugoslavia: A History of its Demise*. London: Routledge, 1999.

Mežnarić, Silva. *Bosanci: A kuda idu Slovenci nedeljom?* Belgrade: Filip Višnjić, 1986.

Miljković, Marko. "Western Technology in a Socialist Factory: The Formative Phase of the Yugoslav Automobile Industry, 1955–1962." Master's thesis, Central European University, 2013.

Miller, Nicholas J. "Reconstituting Serbia, 1945–1991." In *State-Society Relations in Yugoslavia 1945–1992*, edited by Melissa K. Bokovoy, Jill A. Irvine, and Carol S. Lilly, 291–314. New York: St. Martin's Press, 1997.

Miller, Nick. *The Nonconformists: Culture, Politics, and Nationalism in a Serbian Intellectual Circle, 1944–1991*. Budapest–New York: Central European University Press, 2007.

Milosavljević, Olivera. "Antibirokratska revolucija, 1987.–1989." In *Dijalog povjesničara-istoričara* 8, edited by H. G. Fleck and I. Graovac, 319–36. Zagreb: Friedrich Naumann, 2005.

——. "Država i samoupravljanje: 1949–1956." PhD diss., University of Belgrade, 1987.

Milošević, Mića, dir. *Žulj*. Belgrade: Centar Film, 1987. VHS.

Milošević, Slobodan. *Godine raspleta*. Belgrade: BIGZ, 1989.

Motes, Mary. *Kosova–Kosovo: Prelude to War, 1966–1999*. Homestead, FL: Redland Press, 1998.

Musić, Goran. "Provincial, Proletarian, and Multinational: The Anti-bureaucratic Revolution in Late 1980s Priboj, Serbia." *Nationalities Papers* 47, no. 4 (2019): 581–96.

——. "'They Came as Workers and Returned as Serbs': The Role of Rakovica's Blue-Collar Workers in Serbian Social Mobilizations of the late 1980s." In *Social Inequalities and Discontent in Yugoslavia*, edited by Rory Archer, Igor Duda, and Paul Stubbs, 132–55. Abingdon: Routledge, 2016.

———. "Yugoslavia: Workers' Self-Management as State Paradigm." In *Ours to Master and to Own: Workers Control from the Commune to the Present*, edited by Immanuel Ness and Dario Azzellini, 172–91. Chicago: Haymarket Books, 2011.

Nikolić, Kosta, Srđan Cvetković, and Đoko Tripković. *Bela knjiga—1984: Obračun sa "kulturnom kontrarevolucijom" u SFRJ*. Belgrade: Službeni glasnik, 2010.

Olujić Oluja, Dragomir, and Krunoslav Stojaković. *Praxis, Društvena kritika i humanistički socijalizam: Zbornik radova sa međunarodne konferencije o jugoslavenskoj ljevici; Praxis-Filozofija i Korčulanska ljetna škola (1963–1974)*. Belgrade: Rosa Luxemburg Stiftung, 2012.

Ost, David. "Class after Communism." *East European Politics and Societies and Cultures* special issue, 29, no. 3 (2015): 543–64.

Pavković, Aleksandar. *The Fragmentation of Yugoslavia: Nationalism and War in the Balkans*, 2nd edition. London: Macmillan Press Ltd, 2000.

Pavlović, Momčilo, and Predrag J. Marković. *Od radničkog saveza do Saveza samostalnih sindikata Srbije*. Belgrade: Institut za savremenu istoriju, 2013.

Pavlović, Vojislav G. "Stalinism without Stalin: The Soviet Origins of Tito's Yugoslavia 1937–1948." In *The Balkans in the Cold War: Balkan Federations, Cominform, Yugoslav-Soviet Conflict*, edited by Vojislav G. Pavlović, 11–42. Belgrade: Institute for Balkan Studies, 2011.

Pavlović, Vukašin, Ivan Radosavljević, and Zoran Stojiljković, eds. *Obustave rada (štrajkovi) u Beogradu*. Belgrade: Veće Saveza sindikata Beograda, 1987.

Petrović, Dragan. *Istorija industrije: Razvoj i razmeštaj industrije Beograda u XIX i XX veku*. Belgrade: Srpsko geografsko društvo, 2006.

Pittaway, Mark. "Introduction: Workers and Socialist States in Postwar Central and Eastern Europe." *International Labor and Working-Class History* 68 (2005): 1–8.

Pivec, Franci. "Analiza okolnosti Mariborskog štrajka od 21. do 24.VI 1988. I zadaci SK." In *Obustave rada—štrajkovi u Jugoslaviji*, Centar za društvena istraživanja, volume 79, 271–89. Belgrade: Centar za društvena istraživanja CK SKJ, 1988.

Popov, Nebojša. *Društveni Sukobi-Izazov Sociologiji: 'Beogradski jun' 1968*, 2nd edition. Belgrade: Službeni Glasnik, 2008.

———. *Radno mesto pod suncem: Radničke borbe u Srbiji*. Belgrade: Službeni glasnik, 2011.

Prašnički, Martin. "Oris glavnih razvojnih mejnikov in proizvodov TAM." In *Tovarna avtomobilov Maribor: Sledovi mariborskega gospodarstva v arhivskem gradivu Pokrajinskega arhiva Maribor 60 let—spominski zbornik*, edited by Slavica Tovšak, 9–33. Maribor: Pokrajinski arhiv Maribor, 2007.

Prinčič, Jože. "Direktorska funkcija v jugoslovanskem socialističnem gospodarskem sistemu." In *Biti director v času socijalizma: med idejami i praksami*, edited by Jurij Fikfak and Jože Prinčič, 57–103. Ljubljana: Založba ZRC, 2008.

———. "Mariborsko gospodarstvo v času prilagajanja socialistični ureditivi in miselnosti (1945–1953)." In *Mesto in gospodarstvo: Mariborsko gospodarstvo v 20. stoletju*, edited by Željko Oset, Aleksandra Berberih Slana, and Žarko Lazarević, 159–203. Maribor: Inštitut za novejšo zgodovino in Muzej narodne osvoboditve Maribor, 2010.

———. *Slovenska industrija v jugoslavenskem primežu, 1945–1956*. Novo Mesto: Tiskarna Novo Mesto, 1992.

Prinčić, Jože, and Neven Borak. *Iz reforme v reformo: slovensko gospodarstvo 1970–1991.* Ljubljana: Fakulteta za družbene vede, 2006.
Prout, Christopher. *Market Socialism in Yugoslavia.* Oxford: Oxford University Press, 1985.
Raci, Faton. *Demonstrations in Kosovo in 1981: The Short History that Preceded Demonstrations, The Reasons Behind, Media Coverage and Possible Organizers.* Pristina: Kosovo Institute of Journalism and Communication, 2009.
Radeljić, Zdenko. *Savez sindikata Jugoslavije i Hrvatske: Kronologija (1945–1985).* Zagreb: Radničke novine, 1986.
Radošević, Slavo. "The Collapse of Yugoslavia: Between Chance and Necessity." In *Yugoslavia and After: A Study in Fragmentation, Despair and Rebirth,* edited by David A. Dyker and Ivan Vejvoda, 65–80. New York: Routhledge, 1996.
Raeva, Biljana, and Ulf Brunnbauer. "Fabrikarbeiter, Gewerkschaften und Funktionäre im 'entwickelten' Sozialismus: Die Aushandlung von Arbeiterinteressen am Beispiel des bulgarischen Stahlwerks Kremikovci." *Südost-Forschungen* 72 (2013): 287–318.
Ramet, Pedro. "Apocalypse Culture and Social Change in Yugoslavia." In *Yugoslavia in the 1980s,* edited by Pedro Ramet, 3–26. Boulder, CO: Westview Press, 1985.
Ramet, Sabrina P. *Balkan Babel: The Disintegration of Yugoslavia from the Death of Tito to the Fall of Milosevic.* Boulder, CO: Westview Press, 2002.
——. *The Three Yugoslavias: State-Building and Legitimation, 1918–2005.* Washington, DC: Woodrow Wilson Center Press, 2006.
Reiquam, Steve. "Is Slovenian Nationalism on the Rise?" Radio Free Europe Research, RAD Background Report, no. 190 (Yugoslavia), August 9, 1983.
Rendla, Marta. "Mariborski gospodarski gigant TAM v skrbi za izboljšanje življenjske ravni zaposlenih." In *Mesto in gospodarstvo: Mariborsko gospodarstvo v 20. stoletju,* edited by Željko Oset, Aleksandra Berberih Slana and Žarko Lazarević, 553–77. Maribor: Inštitut za novejšo zgodovina, 2010.
Repe, Božo. *Slovenci v osemdesetih leti.* Zbirka zgodovinskega časopisa 23. Ljubljana: Zveza zgodovinskih društev Slovenije, 2001.
Rizman, Rudolf M. *Uncertain Path: Democratic Transition and Consolidation in Slovenia.* College Station: Texas A&M University Press, 2006.
Rusinow, Dennison. *The Yugoslav Experiment 1948–1974.* Berkeley: University of California Press, 1978.
Rutar, Sabine. "Towards a Southeast European History of Labour: Examples from Yugoslavia." In *Beyond the Balkans: Towards an Inclusive History of Southeastern Europe,* edited by Sabine Rutar, 323–57. Berlin: Lit, 2014.
Savage, Mike. "Class and Labour History." In *Class and other Identities: Gender, Religion and Ethnicity in the Writing of European Labor History,* edited by Lex Heerma van Voss and Marcel van der Linden. New York: Berghahn, 2002.
Schierup, Carl-Ulrik. "Quasi-Proletarians and a Patriarchal Bureaucracy: Aspects of Yugoslavia's Re-peripherialization." *Soviet Studies* 44, no. 1 (1992): 79–99.
Schult, Ulrike. *Zwischen Stechuhr und Selbstverwaltung: Eine Mikrogeschichte sozialer Konflikte in der jugoslawischen Fahrzeugindustrie 1965–1985.* Münster: Lit Verlag, 2017.
Seroka, Jim, and Radoš Smiljković. *Political Organizations in Socialist Yugoslavia.* Durham, NC: Duke University Press, 1986.
Sever, Bela. "Rode Vitja." In *Enciklopedija Slovenije,* vol. 10, 250. Ljubljana: Mladinska knjiga, 1996.

Siegelbaum, Lewis. "The Late Romance of the Soviet Worker in Western Historiography." *International Review of Social History* 51, no. 3 (2006): 463–81.

Silber, Laura, and Allan Little. *The Death of Yugoslavia*, revised edition. New York: Penguin Books, 1996.

Sokolov, Andrei. "The Drama of the Russian Working Class and New Perspectives for Labour History in Russia." In *Global Labour History: A State of the Art*, edited by Jan Lucassen, 397–452. Bern: Peter Lang AG, 2006.

Sörensen, Jens Stilhoff. *State Collapse and Reconstruction in the Periphery: Political Economy, Ethnicity and Development in Yugoslavia, Serbia and Kosovo*. New York: Berghahn Books, 2009.

Spasojević, Živojin, ed. *Monografija 50 godina IMR-a*. Belgrade: Industrija motora Rakovica, 1977.

Stanković, Slobodan. *Slovenian leader against draconian prison sentences in Kosovo*. Radio Free Europe Research, RAD Background Report, no. 278 (Yugoslavia), September 28, 1981.

Stanojević, Miroslav. "Workers' Power in Transition Economies: The Cases of Serbia and Slovenia." *European Journal of Industrial Relations* 9, no. 3 (2003): 283–301.

Statistički godišnjak Beograda. Belgrade: Gradski zavod za statistiku i informatiku, 1989.

Statistički godišnjak Jugoslavije 37. Belgrade: Savezni zavod za statistiku, 1990.

Štih, Peter, Vasko Simoniti, and Peter Vodopivec. *A Slovene History: Society, Politics, Culture*. Ljubljana: Inštitut za novejšo zgodovino, 2008.

Stokes, Gale, John Lampe, Dennison Rusinow, and Julie Mostov. "Instant History: Understanding the Wars of Yugoslav Succession." *Slavic Review* 55, no. 1 (1996): 136–60.

Suvin, Darko. "The Economico-Political Prospects of Boris Kidrič: A Betrayed Disalienation." Last modified May 20, 2015, accessed July 14, 2019. https://darkosuvin.com/2015/05/20/the-economico-political-prospects-of-boris-kidric-a-betrayed-disalienation.

Thompson, E. P. *The Making of the English Working Class*. New York: Pantheon, 1964.

Tomc, Gregor. "Classes, Party Elites and Ethnic Groups." In *Yugoslavia: A Fractured Federalism*, edited by Dennison Rusinow, 58–77. Washington, DC: The Wilson Center Press, 1988.

Tomšič, France. *Od stavke do stranke*. Ljubljana: Nova obzorja, 2010.

Tovšak, Slavica. "Šest desetletij od začetkov Tovarne avtomobilov Maribor." In *Tovarna avtomobilov Maribor: Sledovi mariborskega gospodarstva v arhivskem gradivu Pokrajinskega arhiva Maribor 60 let—spominski zbornik*, edited by Slavica Tovšak, 3–8. Maribor: Pokrajinski arhiv Maribor, 2007.

Turkish Comisso, Ellen. *Workers' Control under Plan and Market: Implications of Yugoslav Self-Management*. New Haven, CT: Yale University Press, 1979.

Udovički, Jasmina, and Ivan Torov. "The Interlude 1980–1990." In *Burn This House: The Making and Unmaking of Yugoslavia*, edited by Jasmina Udovički & James Ridgeway, 80–109. Durham, NC: Duke University Press, 2000.

Unkovski-Korica, Vladimir. *The Economic Struggle for Power in Tito's Yugoslavia: From World War II to Non-Alignment*. London: I.B. Tauris, 2016.

——. "Workers' Self-Management in the 'Yugoslav Road to Socialism': Market, Mobilisation and Political Conflict 1948–1962." PhD diss., London School of Economics, 2011.

Vagner, Anton. "Kooperanti Tovarne avtomobilov Maribor." In *Tovarna avtomobilov Maribor: Sledovi mariborskega gospodarstva v arhivskem gradivu Pokrajinskega arhiva Maribor 60 let—spominski zbornik*, edited by Slavica Tovšak, 43–47. Maribor: Pokrajinski arhiv Maribor, 2007.

Van der Linden, Marcel, ed. *Workers of the World: Essays Toward a Global Labor History*. Leiden: Brill, 2008.

Van Voss, Lex Heerma, and Marcel van der Linden, eds. *Class and Other Identities: Gender, Religion and Ethnicity in the Writing of European Labor History*. New York: Berghahn, 2002.

Velimirović, Tiosav, et al. *Zakon o udruženom radu*. Belgrade: Privredna štampa, 1976.

Vladisavljević, Nebojša. *Serbia's Anti-bureaucratic Revolution: Milošević, the Fall of Communism and Nationalist Mobilization*. New York: Palgrave Macmillan, 2008.

Vukliš, Vladan. "Writing Social History of Socialist Yugoslavia: The Archival Perspective." *Archival Science* 17, no. 1 (2016): 55–77.

Woodward, Susan L. *Balkan Tragedy: Chaos and Dissolution after the Cold War*. Washington, DC: Brookings Institution Press, 1995.

——. *Socialist Unemployment: The Political Economy of Yugoslavia 1945–1990*. Princeton, NJ: Princeton University Press, 1995.

Zorko, Franjo. *Kronologija delavskega gibanja in družbenega razvoja Maribora in njegove okolice, 1885–1983*. Maribor: Založba obzorja, 1989.

Zukin, Sharon. "The Representation of Working-Class Interest in Socialist Society: Yugoslav Labor Unions." *Politics & Society* 10, no. 3 (1981): 281–316.

——. "Self-Management and Socialization." In *Yugoslavia in the 1980s*, edited by Pedro Ramet. Boulder, CO: Westview Press, 1985.

Županov, Josip. "Znanje, društveni sistem i 'klasni' interes." *Naše teme* 7, no. 8 (1983): 1048–54.

——. *Samoupravljanje i društvena moć*. Zagreb: Naše teme, 1969

Index

CEU Press Book Series

Work and Labor: Transdisciplinary Studies for the 21st Century

The peer-reviewed Book Series *Work and Labor: Transdisciplinary Studies for the 21st Century* contributes to an emerging field of inquiry drawing from the insights of transnational history, geography, anthropology, and sociology. The Series seeks fresh perspectives on: structures, cultures, and habitats of working lives; regimes of value in capitalist, state-socialist, and developmental contexts; structures and practices of power and inequality that undergird them; situated biographies, constructed within and against such structures and practices; and transnational inequalities and geographies of labor and capital. *Work and Labor* also publishes local and regional case studies of work, whether within or outside Central and Eastern Europe, that specialize in any relevant empirical field or combination of fields, including migration, urbanism, family and community, gender and other categories of difference, state policies, social movements, union politics and labor activism, and past and present crises of labor and hegemony.

Inquiries and submission of manuscripts
Please contact Susan Zimmermann, zimmera@ceu.edu

For Product Safety Concerns and Information please contact our EU representative GPSR@taylorandfrancis.com Taylor & Francis Verlag GmbH, Kaufingerstraße 24, 80331 München, Germany

Printed and bound by CPI Group (UK) Ltd, Croydon, CR0 4YY
11/09/2026
02215133-0002